D0024911

DEVIANCE AND PSYCHOPATHOLOGY:

The Sociology and Psychology of Outsiders

by

ROBERT ENDLEMAN, Ph.D.

ROBERT E. KRIEGER PUBLISHING COMPANY
MALABAR, FLORIDA
1990

Original Edition 1990

Printed and Published by
ROBERT E. KRIEGER PUBLISHING COMPANY, INC.
KRIEGER DRIVE
MALABAR, FLORIDA 32950

Library of Congress Cataloging-in-Publication Data
Endleman, Robert.
Deviance and psychopathology / by Robert Endleman.
p. cm.
Bibliography: p.
Includes index.
ISBN 0-89464-344-4
1. Deviant behavior. 2. Mental illness. I. Title.
HM291.E63 1990
302.5'42--dc19 88-13949
CIP

10 9 8 7 6 5 4 3 2

CONTENTS

PREFACE

The field of "deviance"—study of outsiders, people in one way or another at odds with conventional society—has been staked out by sociologists as *their* domain. But alongside all the sociological work in this area, a lot of other work has been written asking *psychological* questions about many of these same people. That work has come from psychologists and psychoanalysts. Rarely have the sociological and the psychological works been brought together in any systematic way. And typically—though not invariably—sociologists have steered away from psychological questions, and especially from anything psychoanalytic. Many are actively hostile. The result has been a loss for productive work and thinking in this area. My view is this: if we are really going to understand crime, delinquency, drug use, sexual deviations and the other topics of "deviance," we need both sociological and psychological approaches and materials.

So for each topic covered in this book, I deal with the sociological studies *and* the relevant psychological and psychoanalytic ones, and try to show, where possible, how these should be integrated. As both sociologist and practicing psychoanalyst I have the tools to do this.

Some prospective readers or teachers may be wondering why "Deviance" and "Psychopathology" are linked together in the title of this work. They may wonder, "Is he saying that all deviants are psychopathological (psychologically 'sick')?" The answer is definitely NO: some are, some are not. Unlike some other sociologists, I am NOT saying that the deviants are definitely NOT sick. I am saying that this thought must be kept open as an empirical question. For each case, there are four possible answers: not deviant and not sick; sick and not deviant; deviant and not sick; and deviant and sick. (A classic fourfold table.) For each kind of deviance, and subtypes within it, I try to unravel which of these is the correct answer.

I urge other sociologists, here specifically those dealing with deviance, not to close themselves off from the enriching possibilities of this combined approach. Don't let a "received wisdom" of sociology with its prevalent anti-psychoanalytic bias, prevent you from exploring these possibilities.

To psychologists and to fellow psychoanalysts in my audience, I urge you too, not to neglect what another field, in this case sociology, has to contribute: psychological study of sexual variants, for example, needs to be enhanced by understanding of the sociological context of these orientations, including cross-cultural studies showing how variably different societies deal with this phenomenon.

Social workers and faculty in Schools of Social Work should find much of value in this work, for they have typically drawn on both sociological and psychoanalytic work to formulate basic orientations for their practitioners. Here both of these orientations are applied specifically in the analysis of what we can call "psycho-social pathologies."

I want to thank all who have helped me, in many ways, to complete this book. I salute all the students, patients, forbearing family and friends, and colleagues, mentors and predecessors in these several fields. Specific intellectual indebtedness will be evident in the body of the work and in the bibliography.

I especially want to thank Robert Krieger who has demonstrated once again his confidence in the viability of psychoanalytic sociology by undertaking publication of this work. And a special word of appreciation for my tireless and endlessly meticulous editor Elaine Rudd, whose attentions made this a much better book.

Of course, as usual, the product as a whole, with whatever remaining deficiencies, is my own responsibility.

CHAPTER 1
INTRODUCTION

What This Book is About

This is a book about outsiders of society, people who don't fit into conventional molds. These are the *eccentrics and weirdos, the kooks and crooks, the nuts, sluts and perverts, the mad, the bad and the sinfully cheerful. They are hookers and boosters, cons and other criminals, amateur and pro, juvenile and grown. Also junkies, winos, alkies, sniffers, potheads, cokeheads, crackheads, acid freaks and other chemical adventurers. They are bohemians, beatniks, hippies, and latter-day descendants; they are radicals and revolutionaries. And there are people who commit rape or incest, taboo breakers on the who and the how of sexual kinks, crazies, psychopaths and the mentally odd, seekers of taboo modes of ecstasy and of oblivion, and any and all at war somehow with organized society.*

Such oddballs have been of perennial interest to writers, journalists, dramatists and creators in film and electronic media. The psychological and sociocultural sciences have also taken a look. Psychologists and psychoanalysts have dealt with some of these. Among the social sciences, the sociologists have been those primarily involved in the serious and systematic study of such persons, under the rubric of "the sociology of deviance." The sociologists tend to consider such outsiders as *their territory.*

The sociologists' interest has had a variety of motives and modalities. In some cases it is journalistic, even sensationalist. It may be reformistic: let us clean up these horrors. In a variation, let us clean up the horrors of the law and conventional society in their treatment of these poor outsiders. Alternatively, it is human interest drama; violation is what points up the dramatic and critical in human life. The interest may be soberly "scientific." Let us understand, neither condone nor condemn. Occasionally it is concerned with "causes," the question why is this happening? In the study of deviance that attempts to be scientific, sociologists have over the years developed the prevailing sociological viewpoint on deviance which considers it a *social* matter, seeing it as a social product, to be explained by *sociological* principles. This perspective sees the individual "deviants"—those considered to be out of line with society—as themselves products of social forces. Correspondingly, the question of why any individual "chooses" or turns to, a life that embraces some deviation from society, is considered by such sociologists, to be irrelevant. Many sociologists of deviance have explicitly steered away from any psychological approaches to the deviant, on the ground that such study amounts to reductionism, reducing a sociological phenomenon to a psychological one. In another version, there are sociologists who object to a psychological view, thinking that must always imply a judgment of sickness. In answer, such sociologists claim the deviant is definitely *not* sick.

Others say the question is irrelevant. For them, "deviance" does not consist of particular deviant acts by "deviant" persons, but rather of the *attribution* of the quality of deviation to those acts, and to the persons committing them. That attribution (they say) has nothing to do with the nature of the acts or of the persons involved, nor of their psychological state. Rather it is the application of a normative judgment by others, of the act or the actor involved. And the same kind of act or the same kind of person as actor, in other contexts, strata, lands, or times, may not be counted as deviant at all. This is the kernel of the "labeling" perspective sociologists apply to deviance. It is radically relativistic, saying any act or person may be counted as deviant or out of line in some circumstances or contexts and not in others.

By contrast, another whole line of approach asks the question, what is it about this person that leads him to engage in this nonconforming behavior? This question may *seem* to imply that there must be something psychologically wrong with a person to do this. But of course it need not. All it says is that we want to explore *what* is going on psychologically inside the person(s) involved, regardless of whether or not that something is to be counted as pathological by standards of mental health. However some sociologists of deviance seem to want, almost desperately, to deny any possible linkage of deviance with psychological sickness, and therefore to rule out psychological questions completely.

Needless to say, I strongly disagree.

In opposition to such psychological attention, some sociologists shift the focus of concern from the typical layman's question, "What makes those people act in that strange or outrageous way?" to this: "What makes certain people in the society make the judgments they do, that *regard* this behavior as deviant? How are these judgments connected with other aspects of social structure, of culture? How do relevant officials come to select *these* persons as the deviants?" For example, where other investigators have asked, "why is juvenile delinquency so heavily concentrated in the lower class?" the labeling theorist sociologists ask, "Why are those in official positions, such as police, more likely to identify and label *as* delinquent, youngsters who are lower class?" What goes on in such processes of identifying, labeling, and stigmatizing? Who are the labelers and who the labeled, in terms of their respective positions in the social structure?

What has developed, therefore, is a huge gulf between two kinds of study, one sociological, the other psychological. In many ways this is a squabble over disciplinary territory, exacerbated by the extreme compartmentalization and departmental specialization that marks modern academe.

My position is that this gulf is deplorable, leading to less rather than more understanding. While we do need to be clear which type of question we are asking at a particular point, I argue that it is essential to ask both to get a full picture. Scholars of both types seem to assume that *either* everything must be explained by psychology, or everything must be explained by social processes, meaning for the labeling sociologists, the interaction between "deviants" and "labelers." My approach rejects both alternatives.

Sociologists of deviance who take the view of "sociology as science," continue to maintain a posture of sociological value-neutrality: the sociologist as social scientist should not be in the business of making value judgments on the persons he is studying, or of trying to take practical action to deal with, or change, or perpetuate, any given social situation. Rather, in this view, the sociologist's job is to be as objective as possible, to give a true picture of what is going on, to distinguish empirically observed reality from the values and ideals that animate people generally in the society. This sounds meritorious, an advance over the penchant of earlier generations of social scientists for excessive moralizing and reformism in relation to "social problems" (Compare C. Wright Mills 1943).

However, look closer. The shift in emphasis in type of question asked, from questions implicitly accusatory toward the deviant, to questions more recently being raised about the social process of stigmatization, now implies (sometimes even states) a judgmental view negative not toward the deviants, but toward the accusers, the official labelers, the powerful stigmatizers. Here scientific value neutrality is absent, or if professed at all, is spurious. Now the "deviants" are seen primarily as victims, while the officials are oppressors. They are the police, courts, social workers, teachers, psychotherapists, and all connected with any system dealing with the deviants.

In typical labeling sociological literature on deviance, even the pretense of value-neutrality is dropped. These theorists are openly aligned with a value position that favors their version of "liberation." They mean freeing labeled delinquents, addicts, sexual deviants and madmen, from punishments imposed on them by officials such as police, court personnel, mental hospital staff, and generally by busybodies who won't let people be "different." Conservatives emphasize "law and order" and the danger to the public of violent crime in the streets, and want to "get tough" with such offenders. By contrast, labeling theory sociologists are more apt to see the offender himself as victim, police as brutal and arbitrary in their exercise of discretion, and prisons as continuing and intensifying victimization. In a person with severe psychological problems that psychiatrists consider psychotic, labeling sociologists tend to discount or deny sickness, to see the person as victim arbitrarily labeled and stigmatized, and the hospital as a system of control and punishment. Here the antipsychological, particularly antipsychoanalytic, stance of such sociologists is most blatant.

Such sociologists are likely, in respect to certain kinds of deviance, e.g. sexual variation and mental illness, to regard the very raising of questions about the psychological status of the persons identified as deviants, as itself part of the process of stigmatization and, in effect, punishment, of the individuals involved. (One reviewer of my book *Psyche and Society,* objecting to a particular passage, comments: "This will only confirm the already poor reputation of psychoanalyis among feminists, gays and others, who already see psychoanalysts as the thought police of a repressive social order" [Robert Paul 1982: 335]). That lurid Orwellian imagery suggests the degree of ideological embattlement of not only the gender-role and sexual-orientation rebels, but also of their social scientific supporters such as (evidently) the author of that review, and most of the labeling theory sociologists. Evidently psychoanalytic probing is disturbing.

Many sociologists take a viewpoint such as the one just mentioned—the "labeling" theory—in reference to deviance. Those sociologists can be described as seeing deviance as existing entirely in the eyes of the beholder. For them, deviance consists of the *attribution* of the quality of deviation to certain acts or persons. They include such scholars as Howard Becker 1963; Kai Erikson 1962, 1966; Erich Goode 1978; John Kitsuse 1962; Robert Perrucci 1974; Thomas Scheff 1966; Edwin Schur 1971.

By contrast, another cadre of sociologists interested in deviance regard it as something that really exists, that there are real people committing genuinely deviant acts, acts that deviate from, violate or otherwise depart from definite norms of the society (or subgroup to which the actor belongs). They see such behavior as deviant whether or not it is detected, or identified by onlookers, officials, etc., and whether or not the act or the person is so labeled.

Sociologists who take this view include Marshall Clinard 1963, Richard

Cloward and Lloyd Ohlin 1961; Albert Cohen 1955; Walter Gove 1975; Travis Hirschi 1969; Robert Merton 1938; Walter Reckless 1962, 1973; Edwin Sutherland 1949. On this question (the reality of deviance) my own view concurs with this group. Generally, they are not as likely to be counted among those sociologists most hostile to psychoanalysis.

Neither a psychological view, including the psychoanalytic one, which probes inner psychodynamics of the persons involved, nor a sociological one either of the labeling orientation which focuses on social interactional processes, nor a sociological one that emphasizes social structure, provides all the answers to all of the important questions about deviance.

My view is that we need both sociological and psychological (preferably psychoanalytic) approaches.

They can be seen rather, as different but complementary approaches. We are all individual personalities with intrapsychic processes. We also all play social roles, live in interaction with others, pay attention to, ignore, or violate social norms. We all also participate in, sometimes creatively expanding or modifying, an ongoing culture, or parts or segments of several different ongoing cultures and subcultures. No one part of these analytically distinguishable processes excludes the others. We need to know what on the individual psychological level makes the persons who are considered "deviant" act the way they do, think and feel as they do, be the kind of persons they are. We also need to ask, if the stigmatizers subject the deviant to stereotyping, discrimination, or any kind of victimization, how do they, the stigmatizers, come to be acting that way? What are *their* intrapsychic processes, their projections, displacements, reaction-formations? How are their reactions influenced by their prior intrapsychic experiences with important people in their lives? What important people?

A psychoanalytic-sociological approach such as mine maintains that the psychodynamics—of the deviants, *and of the onlookers, accusers and stigmatizers* too—are an essential part of the total picture. Our understanding of what is going on is defective, incomplete, without inclusion of this element and its correct designation and analysis.

Why is this so difficult?

First, certain basic misunderstandings prevalent among the sociologists (and among psychoanalysts) need to be cleared up. Let me address these.

Basic Orientation: Why Understanding Deviance Needs a Psychoanalytic-Sociological Perspective

Three main points need to be made:

1) Psychological orientation is necessary, alongside of and integrated with, sociological approaches, for adequate understanding.

2) Concern with psychological factors does *not* presuppose psychopathology; and

3) Deviance does not equal psychopathology.

Let me elaborate on each of these themes.

A Psychological Orientation Is Not Only Relevant for Understanding Deviance; It Is Necessary

Far from being antagonistic to adequate sociological understanding of deviance and of reactions to deviance, a psychoanalytic-sociological exploration of the subjective reactions of all of the participants in the deviance and deviance-defining process, is essential. More generally, all social science needs an underlying psychology of human nature and of human reactions, and for my purposes, the best such psychology, imperfect as it may be, is psychoanalysis.

Interestingly, sociological studies have all along included, usually implicitly, and often in opposition to their manifest messages, an assumed psychology of human responses. What I want to do here is to bring such psychology in, explicitly, into the analysis of particular human phenomena. For example, consider the following sociological works, often cited as nonpsychological or antipsychological.

Case 1. Emile Durkheim on Suicide

Durkheim's most famous and most influential argument for a distinctively *sociological* approach, eschewing psychology, therefore psychological reductionism, is itself, on close inspection, built upon an unacknowledged but necessary set of psychological assumptions and presuppositions. His theory of *anomie,* ostensibly a preeminently sociological conception, in fact rests on the assumption of inner subjective processes, without which there is no sense at all in positing a "lack of integrative ties," or a "lack of bondedness toward the norms of the society." His celebrated formulation of the relationship between suicide and anomie (*Suicide* 1897), to be plausible, today should be reformulated as follows: "Suicide results from unrelieved conflicts, stresses and anxieties in individuals. Social cohesion would provide psychological support for people subjected to such stresses. In the situation of *anomie,* i.e. normlessness, such supports are lacking." To be sure, that was not Durkheim's own phrasing, but it is implied in his analysis. It clearly refers to internal subjective states. So while Durkheim the theoretician and methodologist (*Rules of the Sociological Method* 1895) rejected using any psychology, there it is. In effect, it is smuggled back in. Psychoanalytic sociology says, in answer, that it is better to include the psychology in the first place. And the best psychology is psychoanalysis. Some deviance sociologists do in fact use a psychology, explicitly or implicitly, not necessarily formulated in terms of a particular psychological theory such as psychoanalysis.

Case 2. Nondelinquents in a High Delinquency Area

Walter Reckless and his colleagues (1956), asking why some youngsters in a high delinquency area nevertheless did *not* turn to delinquency, find it is a difference in *self-concept* that distinguishes them (Reckless *et al.* 1956; Scarpitti *et al.* 1960). The nondelinquent boys saw themselves as lawabiding, as having a good relation with each of the parents; saw the parents as interested in the sons' welfare. Though this is not psychological at any depth-dynamic level such as used in psychoanalysis, it does refer to the internal subjective state of the persons involved. (See further discussion of this study in Chapter 2.)

Case 3. Delinquent Subculture

Albert Cohen in *Delinquent Boys* (1955) posed the sociological question: how to account for the existence and features of the juvenile delinquent subculture? His answer is in effect collective-*psychological:* working class juvenile males face similar problems of "adjustment," for which the gang subculture provides a kind of "solution." They fail to come up to the "middle class measuring rod," and therefore suffer affronts to their self-esteem and masculinity. Here we see something closer to what might be done by psychoanalytic sociology, since the psychology implied, though not explicitly psychoanalytic, seems indirectly derived from it. For now I am not focusing on the specific psychological propositions put forth by Cohen (see later discussion, in Chapter 2), rather that it does take seriously in some sense, the psychology of the deviants, and sees that as connected to the sociological question. No Durkheimian separation here.

What a psychoanalytic sociology of deviance proposes to do is to take the kind of analysis done by Cohen or Reckless *et al.* further, into the intrapsychic dimension of the subjects, by an explicit application of psychoanalytic psychology.

Concern with Psychological Factors does Not Presuppose Psychopathology

One of the prominent sources of resistance by many social scientists to psychoanalysis, or applying it to social questions, is the assumption: "are you asking what makes a person do that (something deviant)? you must be figuring that the person is sick (crazy)." The assumption is, of course, unjustified. To quote an old irreverent song, "that ain't necessarily so."

Where did that misconception come from? Possibly, in part, because psychoanalyis, as a *practice* is a clinical psychology attempting to heal psychological malfunctioning, psychopathology. Not too surprisingly, the clinician on first encounter with a prospective client or patient, tends to be *looking for* the indicators of illness, and to be less attuned to the indicators of psychic health. But psychoanalysis as a *theory* wants to understand, psychologically, *all* aspects of human behavior, regardless of pathology. That in turn is what makes psychoanalysis amenable to integration with sociology and anthropology and any other social sciences. All of these need to take into account the relationship between *subjective* personal experience and objective or suprapersonal (social structural or interactional) aspects of people's lives in society, economy and polity. (See Endleman 1981, Part I, for fuller development.)

Does Deviance Equal Psychopathology?

The answer to that question is clearly, NO. Are the deviants always psychologically sick? Are psychologically sick people necessarily deviant? Answer in all cases NO, not invariably. Are all crooks psychologically odd in some way? all prostitutes psychopathological? Are homosexuals all psychologically sick? All bohemians, all radicals? What of drug abusers? But surely the mentally ill in hospitals are really crazy, and not simply the victims of labeling as some labeling type sociologists claim? And are all the psychologically sick people necessarily deviant?

My answers to all of these are, in some cases yes, in some cases no. The deviant *may* be psychologically sick, or may not; the psychologically sick *may* be deviant, or may not.

First we have to clarify once again that the concepts of deviance and of psychopathology come from two different realms of discourse. *Deviant* is a concept in the sociology of normative order, meaning simply varying from or violating the *norms* of the society, i.e. those rules, regulations and understandings which tell the people of the society how they *should* behave, feel, and think, as well as how they *should not.* Acts or stances toward the world that depart from such norms can be described (objectively, by the outside social science observer, value-neutrally) by the adjective "deviant." A person who acts, feels or believes in such a manner, by the noun "deviant." The whole analysis is full of problematics which do not concern us here for the moment.[1]

By contrast, *psychopathology* is a concept in the psychology of *intrapsychic* processes, referring to processes (or a total personality orientation) that are disordered in some important and identifiable manner. The standard referred to is a standard of psychological health or adequacy of functioning. To be sure, this is not a value-neutral concept. Rather it is one referring to the value of mental health, the idea that it is better to be healthy than to be sick, and to the belief that one can specify the basis of the standards of psychological health being referred to, which are missed in the situation we are calling "psychopathology." A whole literature in psychoanalysis and clinical psychology addresses itself to these questions. It is not the same as society's norms for correct or conforming conduct that are the point of reference for the concept of "deviance," since fulfillment of those norms may or may not lead to or constitute psychological health.

I am fully aware that there are enormous problematics, even within one theoretical tradition such as classical psychoanalysis, about exactly how to formulate "standards of psychic health," and have dealt with those questions at length elsewhere—Endleman 1981, Part V. Here I am concerned only to state that *theoretically* it can be done.

The deviant may or may not be psychologically sick. The psychologically sick may or may not be deviant. A tabulation of the combinations produces the following classic fourfold table:

		Sick?	
		Yes	No
Deviant?	Yes	(1)	(2)
	No	(3)	(4)

Occupants of cell (1) and cell (4) are easy to identify:

Cell (4): *Not Sick* and *Not Deviant,* or *Healthy* and *Conforming.* Here we find the psychologically healthy conformist. This is a theoretical construct, of course; there may be few or no such persons in reality. Or we could phrase "healthy" to mean not clearly neurotic or psychotic or otherwise psychologically impaired. By conforming we mean people going about their business and not breaking any important rules of the folkways, mores, or laws.

Cell (1): *Sick* and *Deviant.* For example, an extreme paranoid schizophrenic, who commits some illegal offense. The schizophrenia is clearly a psychopathological disorder. And committing an illegal act, like attacking and robbing someone on the street, certainly qualifies as deviant. In fact such a person would probably qualify as deviant on the basis of the schizophrenia alone, if its manifestations include florid delusions and gross distortions of reality testing. Here this person is deviant if people around him define him as out of line with the norms of expectable behavior—"right people don't think and act that way," and "his beliefs are crazy." "Crazy" as used by laymen is as much a reference to deviance as it is to psychic ailment.

It is cells (2) and (3) that give difficulty. Can a person be deviant and not sick? Answer: YES. Can one be sick and not deviant? Answer: YES. Examples:

Cell (2): *Deviant* and *Not Sick. A Non-neurotic Criminal.* Many a criminal does not seem to be suffering from any identifiable psychopathology. He organizes his life activities, including his lawbreaking, in a reasonably rational manner; he has an intact reality orientation (in some cases superior knowledge about how the law actually does function in society). He has very little if any inner conflict about his criminal activities. He may be adept at using various rationalizations. For example, he may say, "no one really gets hurt by this, I steal only from companies that can afford it, they're insured anyway." But these beliefs are hardly delusional. One could say about him that he has a weakly developed superego, but except in the extreme case of the psychopath, it is problematical to count that as psychopathology. And he is clearly deviant in that he violates laws of the society.

This view of a person may be too superficial. For a variant psychoanalytic-sociological view of such cases, arguing that there really is psychopathology here, see Devereux 1980, chapters 3, 7.

Cell (3): *Sick but Not Deviant.* This is very likely the most problematical combination. Probably nearly all of the *seriously* mentally ill, the psychotic, are sociologically deviant as well, in the manner suggested in the example for (4) above. However, in some less flagrant forms of psychopathology, the individual may be seen by others in society around him as not out of line in any obvious way. He may be presumed to be basically conforming and "adjusted."

Example: *The Compulsive Accountant.* Here is someone who performs punctiliously his highly routinized duties in an occupation demanding attention to detail, such as accounting, librarianship, and the like. Psychologically this person can be found to be expressing an obsessive-compulsive character disorder. In psychoanalytic terms, this kind of person deals with anxiety by extreme routinization of behavior, ego-syntonic rigidity in responsiveness, constrictiveness of life activities (not experienced as conflictful). These characteristics would be seen as constituting a kind of psychopathology. The keynote is rigidity in responsiveness, disabling the individual from making, when needed, new adaptations by changed behavior. Clinically, as long as the social and occupational setting continues, supporting the "adjusted" behavior patterns, the person has little or no inner sense of anything amiss. The good performance of work duties (within limits), and the lack of deviation from folkways, mores and laws, would qualify this individual as non-deviant, or conforming and "adjusted" in sociological terms.

Example: *The Good Citizens of a Totalitarian Society.* These individuals would be more extreme examples of Cell (3), Sick but Not Deviant. These "good citizens" submit without struggle to the sadistic controls of a totalitarian regime. These people would be "adjusted" and "conforming," but it would take a collectively sanctioned psychological sickness to maintain this behavior.[2]

Needless to say, most actual persons in any modern society do not fit neatly into any one of these categories, being only partially sick, or partially (or only in some special way) deviant. Or they are hard to classify in either dimension. All we want to indicate, at this point, is that we should not prejudge on the basis of a demonstrated deviance, that the person is psychically sick, or the other way around. Rather we look at available evidence from whatever disciplines, and try to answer.

Conceptions of Normality

The analytical independence of the categories of deviance and psychopathology rests on our recognition of the existence of different standards of judgment on the question of "normality." In earlier publications (Endleman 1967, ch. 7, and 1981, ch. 15) I distinguished three *kinds* of conception of "normality" and "abnormality": the statistical, the cultural, and the transcultural. These are:

Statistical. In this conception, "normal" is the average (mean, median or mode), the general run of what actually appears, while "abnormal" refers to unusual or rarely appearing. The person of average intelligence is normal; the genius and the idiot both abnormal. So too "abnormal" in this sense applies to people of unusual or rare appearance, of rarely encountered skill or virtuosity, and people who have rarely encountered psychic experiences, such as (in our society) visions. This is the simplest conception of "normality," not to be confused with either of the others.

Cultural. Here, "normal" equals conforming to the norms of one's own culture, or "adjusted" to the expectations of living in that society, playing one's expected roles; feeling "in line with" the people and standards around you; and "abnormal" means nonconforming or deviant, or maladjusted, out of line with expectations, "marching to a different drummer." One could be statistically abnormal while culturally normal, and culturally abnormal while statistically normal. The average person cheating on income tax, where this is widely prevalent, would fit the last category.

Transcultural. Most significantly to be distinguished from the other two conceptions, is the *transcultural* standard or *mental-health* standard of normality. Here "normal" means psychologically healthy, functioning well, maintaining strong ego capacities, adaptable, maintaining resilience, capable of withstanding stress, and the like. "Abnormal" here means psychopathological or psychologically sick, in any of a number of dimensions. This person is beset by unresolved inner conflicts which impede everyday functioning. Or he suffers from severe impulse inhibition or inability appropriately to restrain impulse gratification. Or he cannot clearly assess reality. He may have subtle or gross distortions of cognition, affect and/or volition. Or he is delusional or neurotically or psychotically depressed. He may be any other version of neurotic or psychotic, or psychopathic, or borderline or narcissistic or suffering any other kind of character disorder.

The standard in this last kind of "normality" conception is that of a dynamic psychology of human functioning that is, theoretically at least, independent of any particular culture. It is not a relativistic standard (whereas the cultural is.) "Health" is not synonymous with "adjustment" (the latter a cultural conception), nor is "sickness" synonymous with "maladjustment." Rather adjustment may be either healthy or sick, and maladjustment may be either healthy or sick, or anywhere in between. Neither is health to be equated with prevalent or average, with *statistical* normality. The healthy may be prevalent and average, or unusual and rare; and so may the statistically average be psychopathological.[3]

Thus "deviance" is a category referring to *cultural* abnormality; "psychopathology" a category referring to *transcultural* abnormality. The criteria for judgment, as well as the mode of assessment, in each case, are different. The distinction is essential for clarity of analysis.

The stance of psychoanalytic sociology is in opposition both to those who automatically look for psychopathology in each individual who is sociologically deviant, and to those who make a blanket denial that there is ever any psychopathology in the deviant.

Is a Psychoanalytic Sociology of Deviance Feasible?

Clearly my answer is YES. It would be not only a psychoanalytic study of the psychology of the particular deviants, alongside a study of the societal reaction to such deviance. It would include both of these, but more. It would integrate these two kinds of study. It would also include a psychoanalytic study of the reactors, the stigmatizers, the official providers of treatment or punishment and the rest of the societal reactions. It would look for the indications of the kinds of collective fantasy involved in the interaction between the intrapsychic processes (not only the behavior) of the designated deviants, and the intrapsychic processes of the reactors, the putatively (culturally) normal. It would ask also why the culturally normal "need" the deviant, and how the two combine in an interactive process to play out a collective unconscious drama.

Variety of Motivations

The motivations of any particular individual to commit particular deviant acts, or to commit himself to a whole deviant career, can be quite variable, from one person to another. In some cases these may qualify as a kind of psychopathology or psychological sickness. However the burden of proof is on the social or psychological scientist to demonstrate that the sickness is there, and how so, and not to use the deviance itself as the "evidence" for psychic disorder. In other cases the motivation may be connected with psychological processes that are basically healthy, or at least not demonstrably sick. It is possible, perhaps probable, that there will be some psychological similarities in all the individuals attracted to a particular kind of deviance, and, where it exists, to a particular deviant subculture. But at the same time the appeal may be different for different individuals. (Compare my discussion of three types of student radicals of the 1960s—the Apocalyptic, the Proto-Commissar and the Humanistic Worker—see Endleman 1972 and 1981: 357–367, and Chapter 8 in this volume.) True, psychological clinicians or clinically-trained social scientists may be more likely to *look for* indications of psychopathology in the deviants under consideration, but that is no good reason to foreclose the whole question, rather than to leave it open for investigation.

Universalities of Human Nature

To deal with the psychological questions here, we need an explicit underlying psychology of "human nature." Relativists have long been telling us that there is no such thing as a universal "human nature," and want to rule that term entirely out of modern discourse. For them, all cultures are so different that human beings in various cultures are simply not comparable with each other. Clearly I dissent from that extreme view. True, cultures can be unlike each other, can dissimilarly organize people's lives, their perceptions of reality, their emotional responses. But these differences are grafted upon common universal qualities that all human beings share. These qualities are rooted in their biopsychic evolution, their commonality as members of one and only one species throughout the roughly two to four million years of the existence of this species. They are rooted also in the universality of certain problems that every society, every culture, has to deal with in the nature of the human condition. These are problems of subsistence, of order, of security, of reproduction, of answering basic common human needs (food, sex, shelter, health care, attachment, and relation to ultimate existential questions and systems of values. (See Endleman 1981, Part II, for the evolutionary picture; and Parts I and V for analysis of implications of the universalities.) There is a groundwork pattern, dictated by biology and phylogenetic development, and by commonalities of psychosexual development, that sets basic developmental problems in a definite sequence and chronological frame. That pattern applies to all human beings. These universalities far transcend the differences in culture. Mothers caring for infants are far more alike the world over and throughout history, than they are dissimilar. The experience of parenting and of being parented has certain universal human qualities, demands and dilemmas. These are distinctively dealt with, true, in different cultures, but those variations are within a finite range—otherwise the species would not have survived. This evolutionary process gave us as a species not only with upright posture and bipedal locomotion, but an extraordinarily vulnerable neonate, absolutely dependent, for survival, on physical and psychological care. It also gave us the peculiar human sexuality that is lifelong, nonseasonal, extremely peremptory, prodigious, precocious, prolific, displaceable, malleable, potentially liable in aim, modality and object, very variably connected to the anatomical distinctions of the two sexes, and very complexly connected with that other primary drive, namely aggression. That sexuality also involves the paradox of the strong physical distinction between the sexes and psychological bisexuality. (For a fuller presentation of this evolutionary history and its implications, see Endleman 1981, Part II.)

The basic inner forces that psychoanalysis calls instinctual drives, sex and aggression, are problematical for human beings in any society: there are costs in the possibility of gratification or in lack of gratification, in relation to a general and universal problem of *equilibrium* in the personality. This common human nature means that each of us has potentialities for conforming to social rules and for violating them.

It does not mean, as some observers have distorted Freud, that every small human child is a natural criminal and would if left to his own devices, violate all kinds of social rules. In any case, the child is never "left to his own devices." He is always from earliest infancy living in a social world. That is all the more significant because in infancy and early childhood he is extremely vulnerable and dependent on the important people around him. Thus it is as much a part of "human nature" to want to win the approval of these important others, and to want an internal system of moral rules, as it is to want gratification of rampant biologically-based impulses. We need to consider the consequences of this infantile helplessness, the patterning of the developmental stages, the significance of infancy and early childhood patterns carrying over (transmuted, to be sure) into later stages of personality development. This "human nature" also involves the basic psychological mechanisms of defense and adaptation, operating, largely, on an unconscious level—repression, identification, projection, introjection, reaction-formation and the rest—that have been explored by psychoanalysis. These are universal to humankind. (Anthropological studies confirm that universality.) It is these elements of universal human nature that enable us to construct the transcultural standard of normality.

The developing child has not only biologically given drives, but also the capacity, and the motivation, to develop ways of controlling his own behavior. He can learn to assess the reality of the world around him in all its complexity, and to delay gratification of momentary impulse in the service of a future goal of higher value. He can acquire the capacity to evaluate and choose from among alternative modes of action, or alternative means to a particular goal. These capacities, collectively called in psychoanalyis the *ego,* clearly connect the child with the social world. Their development is problematical, especially in childhood, but at all stages in life. They may be firm and rigid, firm and flexible, or shaky and uncertain, in any of their aspects, with significant consequences for the total functioning of the personality. They are clearly relevant for the question of conforming to or deviating from the rules of society.

Then too, each developing child acquires other functions and capacities, psychologically interior. They involve the internalization of the parents and caretakers, and of the moral rules that those significant other persons impose on the child as a member of society. That internalization too is a complex and difficult process, leading to one or another kind of *conscience.* In its unconscious connections, that is called by psychoanalysis the *superego.* In some version, and with a variable degree of strength, this develops in all human beings. It is problematical, and never a simple matter. It is obviously relevant for adherence to or violation of rules of society.

These three elements, impulsive, executive and reality-testing functions, and conscience, are called in psychoanalysis, id, ego and superego, and are of course part of the universal processes for human functioning, eternally problematical internally and in relation to the external social world.

An important feature of this psychoanalytic psychology of human nature is the recognition of human *internal conflict.* Different parts of the personality can be in conflict with each other. Conflict can exist between conscious and unconscious elements, or between two or more parts of the unconscious, or of the conscious, or of any of these with surrounding reality. Of the mechanisms human beings use to deal with these conflicts, some may involve rule-violating, i.e. deviant, conduct.

Further aspects of this basic psychology of human nature will be taken up when we consider psychological factors in each of the major forms of deviance in the chapters that follow.

Sociological Universals

Alongside the psychological universals of "human nature" are other universals that involve society. Every society has a set of norms of right and wrong conduct. In a lot of details these norms can vary from one society to another—plural marriages are allowed in some societies, taboo in others. But in addition to that variation, there are universals. All societies that we know consider it wrong to commit incest; and to violate exogamy rules (marry someone of a prohibited category). All prohibit ingroup homicide, and certain other forms of ingroup violence. All regard it wrong to carry on sexual activities with taboo objects. None regard exclusive homosexuality as acceptable. All have *some* kind of property rules; some kind of rules indicating who—what age and sex, for example—does what tasks. All have a number of other norms, some specific, some of a general category. All societies negatively sanction rape, and cheating (even though these terms are variously defined in different societies.)

The existence of these universalities contradicts the relativistic viewpoint that pervades much of the usual sociology of deviance.

Commentary: Ideological Presuppositions

There is also a question of ideological presuppositions. In the prevailing sociological literature on the topics to be dealt with here, there are certain assumptions about major matters that are often taken for granted. I think they should be spelled out, since my own approach, that of psychoanalytic sociology, an attempted integration of psychoanalysis and sociology, departs significantly from those of most conventional sociology.

The first presupposition relates to the nature of human beings. Most sociology assumes that human beings are by nature good and pure and made bad or impure only by society—in other words essentially a Rousseauian conception. By contrast, Freudian psychoanalaysis is much closer to a Hobbesian view: human beings have basic instinctual drives—of sex and aggression—which are eternally problematical and require control and channelization; and for those who need a moral vocabulary, these drives are seen as basically "bad." Ever since their first enunciation, Freud's propositions about infantile sexuality, at the core of the psychoanalytic viewpoint, have been greeted by their detractors as claiming human infants are wild bad animals. Such an image contrasted with the Victorian age's romantic mythology of infancy and childhood as a time of innocence and purity. Similarly in reference to aggression, the common sociological outlook seems to assume that aggression is entirely a product of frustrating and thwarting experiences, and therefore, theoretically at least, expungible from the human condition. That view is not, of course, confined to sociologists, since many in the revisionist camps of psychoanalyis also tend to agree as do most cultural anthropologists. The Freudian psychoanalytic view, by contrast, takes it that aggression generally is innate in human beings, arousable to greater or lesser degrees by different kinds of interpersonal experiences, to be sure, but never totally to be avoided or eliminated. This approach argues that the evidence of the behavior of human beings in all societies known to us shows that aggression is always present, and the problems revolve around the ways in which it may be exacerbated by harsh experiences, or channelized into more ego-integrated behavioral patterns, or kept under control by societal functions.

Another set of problems in basic preconceptions refers to cultural determinism and cultural relativism. Most modern social science takes a view derived (largely) from cultural anthropology of the period between the two world wars. At its extreme, this theory says not only that all cultures differ on most matters of custom, but also that all cultures are equal in reference to basic human needs. These needs are all malleable and the products of culture, rather than given in anything like a common "human nature." That view also claims that patterned human reactions are entirely a product of culture, as opposed to nature.

Freudian psychoanalysis and the version of psychoanalytic social science that underlies the present work, reject that relativism. In our opinion, human behavior is a product of the basic instinctual nature of human beings *and* of the impact of culture and society, not exclusively one or the other. It also takes as central, the recognition that where cultures are different, they can be evaluated differentially in terms of satisfaction of basic human needs. This means that cultures are *not* all equal. A society can systematically degrade or deprive portions of its population. It can allow or even promote avoidable suffering in categories of its own people. It may act against available knowledge to the detriment of human members. It can in many other ways act against human rationality. A culture that leads its bearers to act typically against standards of rationality, is clearly to be evaluated as inferior to one where people are led to try to maintain standards of rationality.

This is a crucial question when we consider the matter of mental illness. The culturally relativistic view of that matter turns out to be useless and in some cases nihilistic, arguing as it does that what is considered mentally ill is different in various cultures, without any universal point of reference. By contrast, the *trans*cultural view here propounded, argues that human beings are a singular species with a singular evolutionary history, the main outlines of which we can now fairly confidently trace. Consequently humans have common universal psychological problems and dilemmas, for which we can specify more adaptive or healthy patterns of solution, and others less so, therefore sick patterns. For example, delusions appear in any of the cultures that have been studied on this matter, and are not to be equated with culturally stylized beliefs (see Devereux, and see Chapter 5 in this work for fuller development).

In summary, the understanding of deviance requires both sociological and psychological (in this case psychoanalytic) approaches, and an effort to integrate these two. That I try to do in this work.

We now turn to particular substantive types of deviance. First, crime and delinquency.

Notes

1. There are difficulties, for example, about plural and ambiguous norms, central and peripheral norms, subsocietal differences in norms. The central point for now is that the concept means "departing from the norms." It does *not* have an intrapsychic reference point.

2. Of course, in any such situation, the burden is on the psychoanalytically minded social scientist to *demonstrate* the qualities of psychopathology involved, and not simply presuppose them *a priori* on the basis of the social scientist's ideological disapproval of the totalitarian politics of the society, a difficult feat indeed. Notice also discussion of the other side, the allegedly sick, but probably healthy, dissidents from the regime of such a society, like the U.S.S.R. See Chapter 5.

3. See Endleman 1981: 346–355, for elaboration of the eight possible combinations of normal-abnormal on these three dimensions. See also Devereux 1980, Chapter 1 (originally 1956) for a major antecedent influence on my formulation.

REFERENCES

Becker, Howard S. 1963. *Outsiders.* New York: Free Press.

Clinard, Marshall. 1963. *The Sociology of Deviant Behavior* Rev. Ed. New York: Holt, Rinehart, Winston.

Cloward, Richard, and L. Ohlin. 1961. *Delinquency and Opportunity.* New York: Free Press.

Cohen, Albert. 1955. *Delinquent Boys.* New York: Free Press.

Devereux, George. 1940. "Social Negativism and Criminal Psychopathology." *Journal of Criminal Psychopathology.* 1:325–338. (Reprinted in Devereux 1980, chapter 3.)

__________. 1951. "Neurotic Crime vs. Criminal Behavior." *Psychiatric Quarterly.* 25:73–80. (Reprinted in 1980, chapter 7.)

__________. 1980. *Basic Problems of Ethnopsychiatry.* Chicago and London: University of Chicago Press.

Durkheim, Emile. 1895. *Rules of the Sociological Method.* (English trnsln. New York: Free Press, 1950.)

__________. 1897. *Suicide.* (English trnsln. New York: Free Press, 1951.)

Endleman, Robert. 1967. *Personality and Social Life.* New York: Random House.

__________. 1972. "The Student Revolt: Afterthoughts and Prospects." *Contemporary Sociology.* 1:3–10.

__________. 1981. *Psyche and Society: Explorations in Psychoanalytic Sociology.* New York: Columbia University Press.

Erikson, Kai. 1960. *Wayward Puritans: A Study in the Sociology of Deviance.* New York: Wiley.

__________. 1962. "Notes on the Sociology of Deviance." *Social Problems.* 9:307–314.

Goode, Erich. 1978. *Deviant Behavior: An Interactionist Approach.* Englewood Cliffs, N.J.: Prentice-Hall.

Gove, Walter, ed. 1975. *The Labeling of Deviance: Evaluating a Perspective.* New York: Wiley (Sage).

Hirschi, Travis. 1969. *Causes of Delinquency.* Berkeley: University of California Press.

Kitsuse, J. I. 1962. "Societal Reaction to Deviant Behavior: Problems of Theory and Method." *Social Problems.* 9:247–256.

Mills, C. Wright. 1943. "The Professional Ideology of Social Pathologists." *American Journal of Sociology.* 49:165–180.

Paul, Robert A. 1982. "Review of R. Endleman, PSYCHE AND SOCIETY." *Journal of Psychoanalytic Anthropology.* 5:333–336.

Perrucci, Robert. 1974. *Circle of Madness: On Being Insane and Institutionalized in America.* Englewood Cliffs, N.J.: Prentice-Hall.

Reckless, Walter. 1962. "A Non-Causal Explanation: Containment Theory." *Excerpta Criminologica.* 1:131–134.

__________. 1973. *The Crime Problem* (5th edition). New York: Appleton-Century-Crofts.

Reckless, Walter, S. Dinitz, and E. Murray. 1956. "Self-Concept as an Insulator against Delinquency." *American Sociological Review.* 21:744–746.

Scarpitti, Frank R., Ellen Murray, Simon Dinitz, and Walter Reckless. 1960. "The 'Good Boy' in a High Delinquency Area: Four Years Later." *American Sociological Review.* 25: 555–558.

Scheff, Thomas. 1966. *Being Mentally Ill.* Chicago: Aldine.

Schur, Edwin. 1971. *Labeling Deviant Behavior.* New York: Harper and Row.

Sutherland, Edwin. 1949. *White Collar Crime.* New York: Holt, Rinehart, Winston.

CHAPTER 2
CRIME AND DELINQUENCY

The most obvious type of deviance is violation of the rules of society that are embodied in formal laws. The exact boundaries of such explicit criminal law are variable. We are referring to law as distinct from less formal rules and norms that sociologists call folkways and mores. Folkways are customs of modest normative weight. *Mores* are much more emotionally weighty rules, any violation of which induces a reaction of horror or outrage from others, and believed by the people to be necessary for the welfare of the society. The laws are a distinctive set of norms in that they are formal, and in literate societies written down, and have an enforcement mechanism attached, as well as specific penalties for violation.

Some kind and degree of violation of laws is found in all societies. Dealing with violation is an essential aspect of any normative order, enabling the people of the society to define the boundaries between permissible and disallowed conduct.

Every society has concern to regulate the use of force and fraud in people's pursuit of goals, and in a society with formal law, like our own, these regulations are a major part of the criminal law. There are always violators at any given time. The extent of violation can vary from one period to another, and from one location to another in modern society, or between different modern societies.

All societies that we know abhor, and negatively sanction, murder, theft, robbery and incest (Wilson/Herrnstein 1985: 22).

In all modern societies with systems of private and corporate property, protection of that property from appropriation by unauthorized persons, is a major concern of the criminal law. Misappropriation makes up by far the major portion of the criminal offenses against the law. It can take the form of ordinary larceny, or robbery, (personal confrontation with the victim, often with a threatening weapon), or burglary, or of fraud, including some complicated forms of deception known as confidence games. For as many centuries as there has been property of any kind, there has also been criminal activity to shift the property from legitimate owners to others.

Other offenses include a variety of sexual activities considered wrong in that society. Some of these, like incest in whatever form, violation of exogamy rules, predatory sex with children, and rape [variously defined] are evidently universally disapproved and negatively sanctioned, by custom or law. Many of the perversions are prohibited by law in modern societies.

How many offenses are committed, in each of the numerous categories, and where, in physical and social space, and who commits these offenses, are subjects dealt with in sociological studies. Do numbers of these, and in more sophisticated analyses, *rates* (numbers in relation to a population unit) change over time, and vary from one location to another? What are the trends? What kinds of persons commit what offenses—kinds in terms of age, sex, class, ethnicity, race, urban-rural; and kinds in terms of psychological elements—what kinds of character structures?

Here are some of the main trends: a disproportionately high percentage of known offenders are male (over 90%); are 15–30 years old; are found in urban localities; and are of lower socio-economic class. At the lower end of this 15–30 year age range, we have juvenile delinquency, concentrated heavily in lower-class urban males. All of these trends, with slight variations in detail, have been persistent for decades. They also have close parallels in other modern urban industrial societies.

How do we understand these findings? Do the juvenile offenders of today become the adult criminals of tomorrow? Are there any indications that crime and delinquency could be eliminated from modern society? Are there instructive differences in rates and patterns, among different modern societies?

While the scientific investigators are interested to find out and explain what happens, other concerned parties address themselves to the question of what to do about it, the policy questions.

Sociological Analyses

Though the subject matter of crime inherently demands an interdisciplinary approach, modern criminology has come, since the 1940s, to be largely in the domain of sociology. (Wilson and Herrnstein deplore this fact [1985] noting its policy sources and implications.) If the roots of crime are seen as entirely in *social* conditions, these are seen as changeable, therefore the proper subject of public policy efforts. By contrast, if roots are in part biological, or psychological in ways that connect with biology, the prospects for change are much more discouraging.

Émile Durkheim

Much of modern sociological work on crime starts with Durkheim. In

Rules of the Sociological Method (1895) Durkheim argues that crime is a perfectly "normal" phenomenon. He meant, of course, in the statistical sense. Every society has it; there is no indication that it disappears, or even declines, in more advanced societies. Not only does every society have it. It is a *necessary* feature of society. It is through the reaction to crime that the "collective sentiments" that constitute in effect the social glue of society, are mobilized and reinforced.

Merton

Robert Merton's paper "Social Structure and Anomie" (1938) developed Durkheim's ideas further and gave a special sense to Durkheim's term *anomie.* Deviance generally (including criminality), rather than something pathological, is a feature of any normal social structure. Where a society produces stresses leading to some form of anomie (a state of disjuncture, and at the extreme what Durkheim referred to, i.e. a state of normlessness), there is pressure on persons to depart from the norms of society, that is to commit acts of *deviance.*

A society institutionalizes certain goals that all persons are supposed to pursue, e.g. religious salvation, aesthetic fulfillment, or achievement of personal success. It also institutionalizes certain *means* toward the reaching of the required goal, that are the preferred or the obligatory means, and specifies other means as being improper or illegitimate. So, Merton says, for our society, the institutionalized goal for personal aspiration is "success." "Success" is something very elastic of definition, but supposedly recognizable when it is achieved. It is to be "achieved" by persons as individuals (or at most families) rather than by collective groups. Then there are *legitimate* means for the achievement of success, namely hard work, study, acquisition of skills enabling higher level occupational work, and pursuit of a legal vocation. With a culturally demanded goal of personal "success" which involves a combination of high income, wealth, status recognition and/or power, there are also possible a number of means for its pursuit, that are different from the ordinary. Some of these are not only different, but *illegitimate* according to the norms of society.

If the conditions in the society are such that it is impossible for many to reach the institutionalized goals only by the prescribed and legitimized means, then there is pressure to *deviate* from the norms. The deviation can take the form of continuing to pursue the prescribed *goals,* but departing from the prescribed *means.* Merton calls this "innovation." He picked the most nonpejorative term possible.

Many of the forms of innovation are at the time they are used, illegal or criminal acts. It is possible that some of these, in turn, under changed conditions of society, will come to be regarded as no longer illegitimate, but now permissible. This new definition may be not only informal, but also by law. Such a transformation occurred in reference to a major feature of modern business practice, taking interest on a loan, which had earlier been condemned as "usury" (see Benjamin Nelson 1950).

So criminal, law-violating activities, especially in the property realm, are an expectable form of deviance when a society creates a disjuncture between cultural goals and availability of legitimate means to achieve such goals. Merton calls such a disjuncture "anomie." The legitimate means in this case would be hard honest work, training, and the like.

Merton's theory provides a framework of explanation for many, but certainly not all, forms of crime. It would help explain all those that involve property violation and fraud to attain monetary rewards. It also applies to murder for profit or as part of profit-motivated organized crime. It is applicable to prostitution. It also fits that part of juvenile delinquency that takes the form of utilitarian theft.

It does *not* explain crimes of personal violence unconnected with larceny, as in crimes of passion, assaulting or killing a sexual rival. It is not applicable to mass murder, killing for personal revenge, killing in terrorist attacks for a political cause. It does not fit rape, or other sexual "offenses," which may include sexual activities that part of the population does not consider against the norms, but are prohibited by law. It misses nonutilitarian aspects of juvenile delinquency, such as stealing for kicks, the taking of drugs, vandalism, and sexual offenses.

The rest of Merton's discussion deals with other forms of deviance relating to goals and means. Innovationism, including utilitarian crime, has a "plus" on the goals (acceptance) with a "minus" on the means (rejection). Or one could score minus on both goals and means, "retreatism." This is a withdrawal from normative society, as in forms of vagabondage or bohemianism. A minus on the goals and plus on the means, constitutes "ritualism." Here one downgrades without totally rejecting the goal of success, while emphasizing proper means—respectability, conforming to mores, honesty, hard work. Here we find the "poor but honest folk." Yet another variation consists of partial acceptance and partial rejection of both goals and means, with efforts to replace the rejected ones by others considered morally superior. One may find a drive toward *transformation* of the culture and social structure, as in politico-economic radicalism. This last category Merton calls "rebellion."

Merton's ideas provide a framework for sociological analysis of deviance in terms of the regular functioning of a complex society, not as pathological aberrations. Here only the aspects of it relating to crime and delinquency are considered.

On the question: *who* are the persons committing offenses? Merton's focus is sociological. The question is, where in the social structure, are these people located? This is to be answered in terms of who is blocked from the legitimate means for the pursuit of success. The answer points to people who are deprived by the class structure of modern society. So according to this theory, one would expect higher rates of crime in the lower classes. The findings are that for certain kinds of crime, ordinary predatory property crimes, this tends to be true. However, it does not fit a whole range of property crime such as embezzlement, stock frauds, complex financial lawbreaking—"white collar crime"—committed largely by middle class persons. For them one has to stretch the conception of lack of availability of legitimate means to include *their experience* of deprivation in relation to the height of their aspirations. A small or middle level businessman or middle management white collar worker may aspire to become a millionaire, but have a very low chance of doing so.

Parenthetically, we can note also this: Merton is usually cited as exemplifying a "pure" sociological approach that excludes psychology, which he explicitly states he intends. But here too, as in Durkheim on suicide as discussed in the previous chapter, there is a good deal of implicit psychology necessary to his analysis. For example, in his discussion of the "retreatist" orientation, he notes that this kind of person is "unable to adopt the illegitimate route" (crime) because of "internalized prohibitions," surely a reference to the psychological functioning of the individual. It is a reference derived, evidently, from psychoanalytic thinking. Further, he notes that in a situation of "anomie," the *kind* of deviant adaptation—innovation, ritualism, retreatism or rebellion—a person turns to, is "determined by the particular *personality.*" Elsewhere he writes that "it is unlikely that interiorized norms are completely eliminated." Thus a good deal of psychology is retained, in this paper, in opposition to the explicit theoretical intent to remain rigorously sociological. The psychological elements, present in bits and pieces, are not systematically integrated with the basic sociological positions, or systematically developed in terms of one consistent psychological theory.

Cohen on Delinquent Subculture

Albert Cohen in *Delinquent Boys* (1955), a work already discussed in one connection (see previous chapter), introduced the concept of the delinquent *subculture.* Subculture is a term applicable to many other forms of deviance as well. It means that the deviation, here delinquency, is not simply a set of variously aberrant acts by random individuals. It is rather systematic, involving a collectivity of individuals similarly situated in society. These individuals develop and practice a style of life that has a definite pattern to it. That pattern in turn is related to the situation and problems faced by the deviants in their relationship to respectable and legitimate society. So the sociological question posed by Cohen here is: how do we account for the existence and the features of this subculture, not just for individual delinquents?

His answer to this question is a kind of collective-psychological one. Working and lower class male youngsters, facing middle class norms and demands in the schools and other agencies of respectable society, find themselves unable to come up to these demands, feel a psychological strain, and need to find ways to deal with and resolve that strain, which they find in the *subculture* of delinquency. This is defiant, negativistic, non-utilitarian, hedonistic, in some aspects predatory, malicious, bent on short-run gratifications, and group-oriented. This subculture elaborates a set of norms largely the opposite of those of respectable "middle class" society. It is not primarily oriented to material gain as such. It is much more affective and expressive, rather than conative, instrumental and rationally volitional. Much of it resembles play and youthful not very harmful hijinks. This study can be seen as a latter-day elaboration of the classic work of Thrasher on Chicago youth gangs of the 1920s (1927).

All of these characteristics fit into the *psychological* needs of these boys and youths. This work injected a strong theoretical stimulus into sociological studies of juvenile delinquency. It was followed in turn by the work of Cloward and Ohlin.

Cloward and Ohlin on DELINQUENCY AND OPPORTUNITY (1960)

Richard Cloward and Lloyd Ohlin looked at their own practical experience with a variety of teenage delinquents, and found that Cohen's analysis did not adequately explain all of them. They argued that there was not just one juvenile delinquent subculture, but three different versions of it. Each of these they tried to explain theoretically, in terms developed from Merton's work. First there is the "criminal" subculture, where the boys are devoted to stealing not only for hedonistic kicks (as in Cohen's picture) but for the material value of what is stolen. They are eager to develop skill as thieves, and the more proficient are on their way to becoming professional adult criminals, either as free-entrepreneur professional thieves, as in Sutherland (1937), or as members of adult criminal gangs. In some cases, they can become lower rank members of organized criminal racketeering groups. These are much more likely to emphasize predation as a way of life, carried out in as rational and utilitarian a way as possible.

The second subculture variation is the *violent* one, which the authors call the Conflict Subculture. These youths are engaged in violent attacks on many different targets, and particularly in violent gang fights against other similar gangs. Ostensibly the defense of territory (which they call "turf") is the rationale. They develop a whole ritual of organized group conflict, sometimes along racial or ethnic lines—but often not—which becomes the center of life for the boys involved. The violence can be deadly, sometimes employing modern weapons nearly up to the state of the art in military technology. Alongside of these trappings, the aura is much like that of jousts between medieval knights (compare Endleman 1967, "Play Elements in Delinquency," 434–435). The pattern is not at all related to the rational calculated instrumentality emphasized both in conventional economic society and its occupations, and also in the predatory criminal underworld of professional and organized crime, with their interest in money and advantage.

The third juvenile delinquent subculture is focused on the use of drugs. The drugs range from marijuana to heroin, amphetamines, barbiturates, psychedelics, cocaine, and whatever else is currently "in," singly or in combination, all of them prohibited substances (an important appeal). Cloward and Ohlin call this the Retreatist Subculture, the term obviously from Merton. These youngsters do not engage in stealing, except as an accessory, a way to get money to support the drug habit, but not as a way of life, nor as a step toward an adult criminal career as in the Criminal Subculture. Nor do they regularly engage in violence, with gang warfare as the center of life. Basically, if any of these individuals had been so involved, they have dropped out of that kind of activity.

Cloward and Ohlin attempt a theoretical explanation of the three types: The criminal fit closely Merton's paradigm of Innovation: they see themselves as blocked from legitimate opportunities to pursue the goal of monetary success, so turn to crime.

The violent are likely to be "double failures," that is have failed in reference both to legitimate means of pursuing goals, and to illegitimate means. As for legitimate means, they have done poorly in school, have developed no skills usable in developing an adult vocation, and have no regular work habits.

They have also failed in terms of the "*illegitimate* opportunity structure," i.e. the opportunity or the personal resources to acquire criminal skills leading to the acquisition of money and some kind of status. This can be simply out of lack of opportunity, because the chance to develop stealing skills exists in some poor neighborhoods but not in others. It could also occur because of personality characteristics in the individual. These may involve an inability to discipline oneself sufficiently to work at acquiring criminal skills, or to control strong impulsive feelings, especially aggressive ones. Such self-discipline would be needed in carrying out any at all sustained "work." Criminal stealing of a more rational kind, even though not time-regimented like legitimate work, has qualities more like work than play. A related study of the same period by Yablonsky (1962) shows the "leaders" of fighting gangs to be psychologically the most disturbed.

The Retreatist—the drug users—are even more failed individuals; they are double failures like the violent, but also, if they have been involved in the violent activities, have dropped them as well. In some cases a whole gang does this together. The authors point to ironic situations where social workers trying to work with gang youth, find themselves relieved that the youngsters have given up fighting and killing each other, but now are all stoned most of the time. Consequently they are also more tractable except when they individually use violence to commit predatory offenses to get money.

This work is a considerable advance on Cohen's single-subculture theory, but has a lot of problems of its own. Other investigators have pointed out that the actual juvenile delinquent world does not so neatly fall into three such distinct life-styles, but in fact many situations show elements of two or all three of these together, in individuals and in groups.

Miller on Lower Class Culture and Delinquency

The anthropologist Walter Miller made a contribution in terms of the concept of culture. Noting that the vast preponderance of juvenile delinquency in modern America, and other Western nations, is concentrated at the lower end of the socio-economic scale, Miller argues that there is a direct relationship. This theory is not presented as being derived from opportunity deficits at that class level, but rather in terms of the surrounding *culture* of the "lower class."[1]

Miller argues that lower class culture embodies a number of "focal concerns" that fit neatly into juvenile delinquent activities and attitudes toward the world. These are concerned with toughness, trouble, excitement, autonomy (of a group as against control by higher-ups), street smarts, and fatalism. All of these, Miller argues, are pervasive in the lower class setting generally, and each in turn fits into the patterns typical of juvenile delinquents, whose "subculture," by the accounts of Cohen, Cloward-Ohlin and many others, emphasize precisely these themes.

Other Sociological Theories

Many other sociologists have propounded particular theoretical perspectives on crime, or on deviance generally. Labeling theory or interactionist theory has been discussed in the previous chapter in reference to deviance generally. These theorists have not focused as much on crime, perhaps because it is more difficult to sustain the notion that this kind of violation does not really exist. A homicide has occurred, but no perpetrator has been apprehended. Can we really say no crime has occurred?

Another series of sociologists can be grouped under the category of *conflict theorists.* These come in three varieties, cultural conflict theory, social conflict, and neo-Marxist ("critical") theory. Cultural conflict theory (Sellin 1938) points to crime as a product of conflict of cultures or subcultures. For instance, a Sicilian immigrant in New Jersey kills his teenage daughter's 16-year-old seducer, is proud of defending the family's honor, and amazed that the police arrive to arrest him for murder. *Social* conflict theory (Vold 1958) argues that a pluralistic complex society produces many opposing interest groups that vie with each other to influence the legislative process that fashions the criminal law, thus determining who is likely to be involved in violation of the law. *Neo-Marxist* conflict theory is represented by Turk 1969; Chambliss and Seidman 1970; Quinney 1970 and other works; Spitzer 1975. These authors are variations on radical or critical theory of Marxist hue. Capitalist industrial society determines the class bias of the whole system of criminal law and how it is administered and enforced, belying the mythology of democratic political process and equal access to the law. Those in power *criminalize* acts antagonistic to their maintaining power, or reflecting common conduct of subordinate populations. This theory connects with aspects of labeling theory; here the ruling class *defines* the nature of criminal acts.

Less vulgar-Marxist versions (Spitzer 1975) ingeniously combine three theoretical traditions. Using functionalism one argues that deviants serve functions for the powerful. With anomie theory, alienated youth are "social dynamite." And through the perspective of labeling theory, one sees state agents defining deviance.

The problems with these conflict theories, especially the last, revolve around whether we can really analyze all crime and criminal law as reflecting the class power battles of the alleged capitalist ruling class. Are laws against homicide simply a weapon against the poor? Are not the rich threatened as much by personal violence and killing as others? Against whom are laws against business fraud directed? Against drug use, sexual deviations?

Summary of Sociological Theories

Sociological perspectives on the causes of crime can be classified into three types (Hirschi 1969, applied to delinquency, but applicable to all crime), as follows:

1) Strain or motivational theories: people have legitimate desires—for

success, money, status—which they find cannot be satisfied by legitimate means. (Merton, Cohen, Cloward/Ohlin, others)
2) Control or bond theory: the person's bonds to conventional society and culture are weak or broken (Hirschi 1969, Reckless 1962, 1973; others).
3) Cultural deviance: the deviant conforms to a set of standards not accepted by the larger society (elements of Cohen's theory; Miller; in a way, Sellin). These emphasize that distinctive deviant subcultures develop standards of their own, often conflicting with conventional ones, and it is to these that the deviant conforms. Or conforming to an ethnic subculture (Sellin) or a class one (Miller) may make one deviant, even criminal, in the wider culture.

In all of these, there is no explanation of why *some* individuals in the situation indicated, do turn to criminal or delinquent activities, while others, similarly situated, do not. Not all persons experiencing a discrepancy between aspirations and available opportunities, turn to deviant means to try to reach their aspirations. In fact, in working- and lower-class neighborhoods, which are alleged to be the breeding ground for delinquency and crime, the vast majority of the population does *not* turn to criminality, except possibly of a very minor and marginal variety, like gambling, not defined by themselves as violating behavior. Conversely, many people growing up in advantaged positions of middle or upper class do turn to delinquency, as in car stealing or drug dealing while still in their teens, or to adult "white collar" crime.

Similarly, not all those whose bonds to conventional society and morality are weak, do in fact turn to criminal means; some simply withdraw into a passive nonaggressive state, accepting the paucity of their lives. Similarly in reference to cultural deviance, the appeal of countercultural modes that may be available, varies a great deal from one individual to another. In reference to a "cultural deviance" kind of theory, again there is no indication of why some individuals are attracted to such a cultural milieu while others of similar background, are not. (Even in Sicily, let alone New Jersey, not all fathers defend the family honor by killing the daughter's seducer.)

In all of these, the difficulty is that the sociological theory does not provide an explanation of the particular individual case. Nor do these viewpoints touch in more than a very superficial way, upon the internal dynamics of either individualized or group-conforming kind of deviance.

Psychological and Psychoanalytic Studies

For any of these questions, we need to turn to *psychological,* including *psychoanalytic* studies.

First, a few of these done by sociologists, with at least implicitly, and sometimes explicitly, concern for psychological elements.

Reckless et al. on Nondelinquents in a High Delinquency Area

In a study now considered classic, these researchers asked the question, if there is a lot of delinquency in a neighborhood, but not *all* of the youngsters there participate in it, which are the ones who do *not?* They did some systematic research on this question. Their answer is that those who do not are different psychologically, from those who do: they are different in "self-concept," i.e. how they viewed themselves and the important people in their lives. They saw themselves in positive terms, as lawabiding citizens, as having good relationships with their parents. They saw their parents as fair-minded and interested in the welfare of the sons. They defined themselves as boys who would not become entangled with the law.

On each of these points they contrasted strikingly with the delinquent boys. And these differences held up in a follow-up study done four years later (Reckless *et al.* 1956; Scarpitti *et al.* 1960).

Reckless on Containment Theory

Walter Reckless in his solo work developed a general theory of deviance, certainly applicable to crime, called "containment theory" (Reckless 1962, 1973). The basic question is *not* why do people deviate from the norms, but rather why do they *conform* to them? Answer: each person has two kinds of controls upon him, one set external, one set internal. These together *contain* his conduct. If they are both strong, he will basically conform to the dictates of his society. If both are weak, he is likely to deviate from the norms. The likelihood of deviation is a *probability,* not an all or nothing matter. That probability will be high if both containments are weak; moderately high if either external or internal control is weak while the other is strong; and very low if both controls are strong. Each individual is subject to pressures and pulls from both inside himself—the pleasure-seeking drives given in the personality, and other internally-generated forces toward optimal gratifications—and from outside himself: lures, enticements, opportunities, encouragements, from the social environment. Containment that restrains an individual from moving with such pulls and pressures, possibly in the direction of deviant behavior, comes from both external and internal sources. The *external* one comes from whatever supportive groups the individual has, mainly family and other primary groups, in times past including the clan, the neighborhood, the village, the caste, the tribe, the religious sect. In modern urban industrialized society, these last are likely to be weaker, but one or more of the following may operate: a roles structure providing scope for the individual; reasonable limits and responsibilities for members; opportunity to attain status; cohesion among members; sense of belonging; identification with one or more persons within the group; provision of alternative means of satisfaction (when a desired means is closed). *Internal* containment consists of "self" components: 1) favorable self-image in relation to other persons, groups, and institutions; 2) awareness of being an internally-directed goal-oriented person; 3) relatively high frustration-tolerance; 4) strong internalized morals and ethics; 5) well-developed ego and superego (Reckless 1962: 132-133).

This promising theory enables integration of sociological with psychological approaches, taking seriously both the structure of society and the inner structure of the personality, succumbing neither to psychological nor sociological determinism.

Cohen's Subculture

Cohen's theory has already been discussed. It is in effect a collective-*psychological* analysis, deriving, evidently from psychoanalytic ideas, though not used at any great depth level, or in terms of any consistent or systematic psychological theory. Cohen's thesis is that these boys come from a "working class" environment, but he does not deal with the question of *which* boys from that milieu are the most likely recruits to that delinquent subculture. Reckless and his colleagues' research provides a partial answer.

Other Researches Providing Psychological Clues: Wilson and Herrnstein

James Q. Wilson and Richard Herrnstein (1985) amass a huge amount of evidence from many studies, to indicate that *alongside* the sociological factors that predispose toward criminality, there are basic differences between persons who turn to crime and those who do not, differences of a psychological and biological nature.

Essentially along lines somewhat similar to what I am doing in this work, they argue that wherever certain sociological conditions exist favorable to crime, still some persons do commit criminal acts, and *others do not.*

These two categories are different *kinds* of people. Here are some of the ways Wilson and Herrnstein indicate. The criminals are more likely to have a mesomorphic body type; to have had fathers who were criminals (even in the case of adopted boys, who could not have known their biological fathers); to be of somewhat lower intelligence; to be more impulsive and extroverted (Wilson & Herrnstein 1985:66, summarizing several chapters of the book).

Significantly, while Herrnstein the psychologist of that team, as a conditioning-reinforcement type behaviorist, is skeptical of psychoanalytic formulations; much of what is presented in that work is not inconsistent with what I am arguing here. The "impulsiveness" and "extroversion" they point to, which can be linked to the biological differences they explore, can also be linked to what is dealt with in psychoanalytic studies of psychopathic personalities and others who have a low level of control over impulses (see below). The mesomorphic body type was demonstrated as being more common in criminals than in non-criminals, in research of years ago that has been neglected or denigrated in recent years, probably because of ideological convictions of criminologists who do not want to consider aspects of the person or his situation that could not be changed. (The same for anything indicating inherited tendencies.) That body type in turn tends to be more action-oriented, more intolerant of delay, and more likely to strike out in situations of frustration and thwarting—exactly where delinquents are likely to demonstrate their impulsive patterns. Impulsiveness, a key psychological factor, probably has deep roots—likely, Wilson and Herrnstein think, biologically rooted—and evident from the time of birth. (Mothers report some babies were "difficult" from the very beginning.) This is one score on which that was so. Self-control is of course not impossible for such babies to learn, with patient and intelligent guidance from caretakers, but more difficult than for other children. I realize that in reference to the constitutional factors Wilson and Herrnstein adduce here, there are massive controversies. However I am not convinced they are wrong. It is likely that those who emphasize sociocultural factors, probably also politico-economically liberal in ideology, are more likely than others to dismiss these questions out of hand.

The Yochelson and Samenow Study

Another significant study, not psychoanalytic in orientation, is that by Samuel Yochelson and Stanton Samenow (1976, 1977, 1986) called *The Criminal Personality.* This study explores, over thousands of hours of contacts with confirmed long-term criminals, how these men, and a few women, function, and how their minds operate very differently from those of normal lawabiding citizens. It deals with their resistance to change by any of the "therapeutic" measures usually tried, and earlier tried by themselves, by depth-psychologically-oriented practitioners. They explain why, at length, and describe their alternative.

As part of their description, they summarize the childhood background of a typical now-adult criminal as follows:

From an early age, he seeks excitement through engaging in forbidden activities. Regardless of family background or parental attitudes, he departs from the expected, does things unacceptable to parents and society. If family members tolerate his conduct, things are alright. If they object, he rebels.

He lies and deceives. He demands that others trust him, but betrays them. He pursues what he wants, regardless of effects on others. He is secretive. In the neighborhood, he shuns responsible peers, and seeks out excitement with those who are defiant and unconventional. He sees conforming people as boring, and school as irrelevant, because it offers no excitement. He continues in school for pragmatic reasons. Dropping out would cause others to be more watchful over him. In school, he asks for exemptions from requirements, uses shortcuts, cheats, and plagiarizes. He may be bright enough to get by with minimum academic effort. Keeping up a respectable academic record avoids suspicion. Only if his behavior becomes entirely intolerable is he expelled.

At home he refuses or evades household chores. Occasionally he does some chores to mollify his parents. He has the same attitude toward work—do as little as possible. He works only when it facilitates some criminal objective. Or he uses work as an arena for crime or sexual exploits, to pilfer, bribe, embezzle, make sexual contacts. Or a job is a cover of respectability.

His sexual activity is enormous, from a very early age. He has no latency period. He has many partners and different kinds of partners, younger and older, of both sexes, He has a great variety of sexual activities, all exploitative in purpose. He has no concept of love, interdependence, trust, or of putting himself in the other's place.

Because he is rarely detected, he becomes increasingly confident that he can get away with his offenses that run the gamut of property, assault, and sex categories. While he is still a child, if he is caught, the penalties are minimal. Only later, in adolescence and only if he amasses a long police record is he likely to face serious punishment.

A major point of Yochelson and Samenow's analysis is that all of this delinquent and later criminal behavior began very early in childhood. The future criminal showed typical patterns as a very young child, which confirm the findings of other studies. Those studies show he is excitement-prone, restless, impulsive, intolerant of ordinary restraints. He lies and deceives. He is contemptuous toward the conforming and lawabiding, who are dismissed as bores, squares, stupid idiots, and the like. Significantly, they also found in all of their cases, that it did not matter what class level the family background. They were all difficult, restless little boys, many of them uncontrollable.

The one difference from the Wilson/Herrnstein generalizations was in reference to intelligence. The Yochelson study men seem to be of at least average, and in some cases, above average intelligence, as indicated by those who could "get by" in school with extremely little effort, and a variety of other indicators. They also point out that after working with these men for a while, they were sure the criminals were *not* mentally sick in any manner familiar to psychiatrists, psychoanalysts, or clinical psychologists.

The portrait of such a man as an adult has these features: He believes himself to be a good person, not a criminal. He claims he gives to charity and helps poor people, ignoring the fact that he constantly injures others by his criminal activities. He commits all the thinking errors common to these criminals. He is very fearful. To commit crimes he cuts off both external deterrents and internal ones (conscience). He is a predator seeking power. He demands to be recognized as number one. He is incapable of interdependence. He uses all kinds of tactics to make fools of others. When he doesn't get his own way, he feels put down and angry. Then he is all the more relentless. He cannot make responsible decisions, and except for criminal exploits, he cannot think long range.

Psychopaths

Much of the description just given fits closely with the classical portrayals of *the psychopath* (Cleckley 1950).

The term psychopath should be retained, rather than the more recently fashionable "sociopath" or "antisocial personality." The reason is that it suggests, correctly enough, an *intrapsychic* emphasis, in contrast to the more externally-behavioristic emphasis of "sociopath." The view implied by "psychopath" is that this personality is not simply the product of social forces. See also Dinitz 1977, and McCord and McCord 1964; and in the earlier literature, Lindner 1944.

There are of course serious difficulties in categorizing this as a distinct type of personality. Some workers with criminals, including Yochelson and Samenow (1976), think "psychopath" has become practically a waste-basket term. It is, they claim, at best descriptive, rather than analytical, and of no use as guidance in direct work trying to change criminals. Of course we have to note that not all criminals are psychopaths, and not all psychopaths are criminals. Specific criminals may be more or less close approximations of the type. Shapiro (1965), discusses psychopathic characteristics that may be more or less apparent in particular individuals.

Recognizing that the following is an ideal-typical portrait, which may be more or less closely approximated in individual cases, here are the main characteristics:

The psychopath is a person evidently without conscience. If he has a functioning superego at all, it is extremely weak and defective. He appears to have no guilt or remorse whatever about his various antisocial activities, no capacity to identify with or take the role of the other, including his victims. He has no obvious indications of anxiety. He may be of high intelligence, with ego functions intact in the area of assessing external reality, including exactly how the law and its enforcers function in areas affecting his interests. He may have a superior capacity to size up other individuals particularly if they are potential victims or potential adversaries. He seems to be without inner conflict about his antisocial actions, and exhibits no external evidence of guilt whatsoever. What is wrong is getting caught.

He is neither neurotic, consumed with inner conflicts, nor psychotic, out of touch with consensual reality. He is resistant to any kind of rehabilitation or re-education. However, he may know how to "con" agents by pretending inner change, while not altering his behavior at all. If he has committed a serious crime and there is a possibility of using the insanity defense, he may do so. Though clearly he is not mentally sick, he may calculate it is to his advantage to be placed in a hospital rather than a prison (Yochelson & Samenow 1976, chapter 2).

An example of the prevalent confusion of deviant and sick, including in the minds of many "experts," is that onlookers, including mental health practitioners, assume that the man "must be mentally sick" to do all these terrible things—rob, steal, assault, rape and the like. But careful psychiatric evaluation indicates no mental illness; he is not neurotic, or psychotic, or borderline, or sick in any of the standard ways identifiable by psychiatrists or psychoanalysts. Deviant he is, but sick he is not.

Techniques of Conscience-Mitigation

Sykes and Matza on Techniques of Neutralization

Two sociologists, Gresham Sykes and David Matza, presented a paper, "Techniques of Neutralization" (1957) billed as "A Theory of Delinquency," which it is not. It is, rather, an exploration of ways delinquent youngsters avoid or fend off the force of conscience, by "neutralizing" it. Contesting Cohen's conception that the delinquents do not subscribe to conventional norms, but develop their own counternorms, almost entirely opposed to the conventional ones, Sykes and Matza argue that the evidence indicates that most delinquent youngsters not only know, but largely accept, the standards of society, against stealing, assaulting, defrauding, hurting others, but find ways to reduce the impact of such norms on their behavior. These authors argue that the boys do in fact internalize these norms, but find ways to justify themselves when they disobey them, or are about to do so. These are the "techniques of neutralization." They deny responsibility: I didn't really do it, it's not my fault, I grew up in a bad environment. They deny injury: I didn't really hurt anyone; I took it from a rich kid, his family can afford it. They deny the victim: he had it coming to him; he asked for it. They condemn the condemners: the police are corrupt themselves; the teachers are always playing favorites. Or they appeal to higher loyalties: I didn't do it for myself, I did it for the gang; I did it for my people.

Sykes and Matza claim that these justifications are not only given after the fact (of delinquent violation) but operate even before, in effect stilling the voice of conscience in advance. They are not more rationalizations.

This is an important paper, not a general theory of delinquency, but an exploration of one aspect, the *psychology* of why the internalization of moral norms of society, while operating, nevertheless does not operate well enough to prevent the delinquent action. Rather, conscience, the voice of such internalization, can be evaded, and here are some of the techniques for doing so. Clearly this is a *psychological* work.

Though the authors nowhere in the paper acknowledge it, the theory seems to come right out of psychoanalytic literature: the psychoanalysis of the "bribing of the superego," (Bergler 1948), and of "superego lacunae" (Adelaide Johnson 1949). Of course the paper lacks psychoanalytic depth in exploring the dynamics of why and how youngsters resort to such "neutralizations." Publishing this work in a leading sociological journal, they hew close to the sociological trend of rejecting anything smacking of psychoanalysis. This approach is similar to what Merton did. He frequently used psychoanalytic ideas without acknowledging their source. For example, see his concepts of manifest and latent functions (1949), the terms borrowed blatantly from Freud's work on manifest and latent aspects of dreams. Of course it is also possible that this—the Sykes/Matza work—is a case of parallel or independent invention, since sociologists are generally so ignorant of psychoanalytic literature. In any case the parallel is obvious.

Redl and Wineman on Dynamics of Gang Delinquency

The work of Fritz Redl and David Wineman describes more explicitly and directly the dynamics of how guilt is evaded by delinquent children (Redl 1945; Redl and Wineman 1951, 1953).

Redl (1945) deals with the psychological dynamics by which delinquent gangs operate. The members are neither solo deviants nor rationally planning criminals. Rather the gang supports them in activities violating norms they do believe in, but are able to violate in the gang situation because of the psychological support mechanisms the gang provides. There is a "process of magical seduction," according to which, whatever delinquency-directed impulses are active in an individual boy, are strengthened within the gang climate by the drive-satisfaction of other gang members, particularly those more fearless ones who furnish the "bad example." Another mechanism is the "exculpation magic of the initiatory act." A gang member or leader does something forbidden first, bringing about unconscious removal of guilt in the others when they do the same thing following him. Gang members provide ego support through the organization of ways and means of delinquent activity. Because a "leader" has supplied ways and means of carrying out delinquent acts, he reduces the possibility of guilt feelings over wrongful acts. What the gang provides is a group code which substitutes for or overrides the individual superego. The group code has a content different from or in some respects contradictory to, the moral codes of conventional society. The gang also makes efforts to inoculate the members against the personal superego that has whatever remaining loyalty to conventional morality. It does this by keeping the gang member alienated from "code-dangerous outgroups," meaning groups other than and antagonistic to the gang, and representing conventional morality. Such outgroups are segregated and hated, vilified, and depersonalized; and the gang makes it taboo to identify with them.

In two works coauthored with David Wineman, *Children Who Hate* (1951) and *Controls from Within* (1953) Redl explores further the depth psychology of delinquents, by an intensive analysis of the disturbed delinquents in a correctional facility.

The boys, engaged in behavior counter to the dominant value system of the society, defend their impulse gratification at all costs. One method is "tax evasion," evasion of the tax of guilt through a host of strategies, corresponding to the neutralization techniques. These include repression of one's own intent. Familiar examples are these: He did it first. Everybody else does it. We were all in on it. Somebody else did the same thing to me, before. He had it coming to him. I had to do it, or lose face. I didn't use the proceeds anyway. But I made it up to him afterward. He's a no-good so-and-so himself. They're all against me.

The youngster seeks out delinquent support, by ferreting out the "wrong" type of friends. He has an affinity for gang formation and mob psychology. He is susceptible to seduction into initiatory acts. He is alert to lures of delinquency. He develops delinquency-prone ideals. He has the delusion of exception: I am exempt from normal demands; laws of cause and effect do not apply to me. Both his ego-functioning and his superego functioning are defective and skewed.

Superego functioning is defective in many ways. It is defective in content. The boy may identify with antisocial qualities in parents or the neighborhood. Identification with positive values may be fragmentary and exist only in "islands" of his personality. He has poor signal function, that is, he is only dimly aware, *in anticipation* that a particular prospective act is wrong. He has poor identification. He readily displaces guilt, as in many of the tax-evasion techniques just cited. Or he uses specific guilt-evasion techniques. Guilt over misdeeds provokes, in him, aggression. Then we see a repetition of the misdeed. This is followed by further evasion techniques, including this one, "just because I'm a crook, you pick on me."

Ego functioning is also defective, and intensifies problems of the poor superego functioning. When flooded with guilt, he is likely to be overwhelmed with anxiety leading to aggression. He has poor resources to deal with fear, anxiety, or insecurity generally, or with impulse flooding. He has extremely low capacity to delay gratification. He *can't wait.* If he has to, he breaks into hostile aggressive acts. He cannot recognize what his own behavior contributes to a situation. Therefore he is always ready to blame someone else or fate or chance. If an adult is nice to him, he then becomes unreasonable in his demands, and when these are not fulfilled, he goes into an explosion of hate. Since he does not know *when* to ask for help from an adult, he gets into situations he cannot handle. He has extreme difficulty in facing failure or mistakes or success. With failure, he goes into torrents of aggression. If he makes a mistake he sees this as caused by machinations of a hostile world. If he has a success, he crows and brags and lords it over other children.

His frustration tolerance is extremely low, as is his capacity to resist temptation; he is very susceptible to group psychological excitement. He has grave defects in being able to use imaging of previous satisfactions and gratifications, as indicators that though the present moment may be barren or frustrating, better moments can come, and he can contribute to them.

These studies indicate that delinquent behavior by youngsters is not *only* the product of social environmental forces, because not all lower class (or any class) youngsters take part in these activities, or get attracted to a delinquent subculture, but rather boys of specific psychological characteristics.

Much of what Redl and Wineman delineate here, is observed also in many adult criminals, as indicated in the Yochelson *et al.* studies, in Cleckley, Lindner and others.

Other Superego Defect Discussions: Johnson on Superego Lacunae

In an incisive paper, "Sanctions for Superego Lacunae of Adolescents," Adelaide Johnson (1949) argues that in some adolescents, we find "superego lacunae," that is, unformed segments of his normative orientation. He may be fully oriented toward acceptance of most social norms, while not entirely so to others. Hence his superego has, in effect, "holes in it." This is a consequence of unconscious permissiveness in the parental figures, who are themselves ambivalent toward the norms prohibiting criminality. For example, they show very mixed reactions toward dishonesty in others, themselves and/or the child. The child may sense that any delinquent acts of his may evoke unconscious gratification in them. The parents have thus encouraged criminal behavior in the child as a means of giving themselves vicarious gratification of their own unconscious antisocial strivings. Or the child may correctly sense that delinquent actions on his part can be used as a weapon in his relations with his family.

One of the implications here, is that criminality may ensue not only from defective internalization of the norms, but also from internalization of defective norms.

Criminal from a Sense of Guilt

One psychoanalytic formulation, deriving from Freud, in an early presentation set forth by Franz Alexander and H. Staub (1931), sees much criminality as expression of a kind of neurosis. The dynamics are that a force of unconscious guilt is operating prior to commission of any crime. Committing a criminal act provides for the person a feeling of relief, in effect, punishment to alleviate the guilt already experienced.

Summary of Psychological Factors

What can we conclude from these various not entirely consistent nor entirely contradictory psychological studies, in relation to the roots of crime and delinquency?

First, whatever the sociological conditions that are likely to predispose some people toward delinquency or crime, in all of those situations, not all individuals so affected do in fact turn to criminally deviant activity—some do, some do not. Those who do can be distinguished by being more likely than others to have certain psychological characteristics, such as poor ego functioning and poor superego functioning, operating in any of the ways indicated here. Some (but assuredly not all) criminals or delinquents fit more or less closely the personality type called the psychopath. Most or all have a history going back to when they were very young children, of antagonistic relationships with parents, other caretakers, and authorities of various kinds. From a very early age, this child was restless, intractable, sought excitement, reacted negatively to ordinary routine and to ordinary external controls. He had a difficult time delaying gratification. Even as a small child, in many cases, he showed an amoral, cynical approach to the world. His relations to others were marked by a predatory using of others, manipulation, lying and deceit, surface conforming to protect oneself, and the like. Significantly, while most of the crime statistics collected sociologically show "ordinary predatory crime" to be heavily concentrated in the lower reaches of the class structure, the studies of the psychological patterns indicate these individuals are found at all class levels in society. Many may have had parents who colluded in the corrupt development of the child by unconscious permissiveness and implicit support for deviating patterns, providing vicarious satisfaction to the parents (the superego lacunae pattern). Psychological patterns here indicated, made many youngsters more likely recruits into juvenile delinquent subcultures, of one or more of the criminal, the conflict or the retreatist pattern (Cloward/Ohlin), and/or later recruitment into any of the subcultures of adult crime, professional or organized. Some of the participants seem to be entirely amoral. Others have value islands of conventional morality, counteracted by the various neutralization techniques readily available to participants in the deviant subcultures. Alternatively, or additionally, for that matter, arguments supporting such techniques can be easily learned from media crime stories, in which characters abound, like those of the delinquent gangs, on both sides of the law.

Violence and Dangerous Offenders

Most troubling of all aspects of crime are the perpetrators of violence, those who commit assault, violent robbery, rape, and homicide. While statistically offenses against property are by far the majority of crimes occurring in modern society, crimes of violence are more salient and frightening. The wish to end the life of a particular human being is a universal human potentiality, though only a miniscule portion of people actually try to carry out homicide. The preoccupation with killing as a possibility and the drama associated with it is attested by the enormous part stories and accounts of homicide or murder, whether from reality or fiction, play in people's attention. Huge industries in the media thrive on the public appetite for this kind of fare at all taste levels. Identification with the killer, the victim, or any of the other accessory characters, is a potent source of fascination: this person could be me, my loved one, my hated enemy, members of my family. This is a conflict I might be in. The killing could be for love, for fame, for loot, for recognition, for status, for success. A few major forms or patterns of conflict provide the plots for all the dramas. The differences among them are in the details of trappings. Great literature, great drama, epic poetry, and a host of other media, all mine these themes, perennially, and play them for tragedy. A host of lesser crafters down to the sleaziest popular press and electronic media, all work these mines as well, playing them for pathos and thrills. No wonder, these are universal appeals.

The violence that occurs in reality gets its share of media publicity, the more lurid or gory the details the better. More serious journalism tries to take a deeper or longer look, or reflect on the significance. Some events result in trials that amount to great real-life morality plays of our time. And some serious scholars try to bring understanding, from philosophical, social scientific, or clinical psychological angles, or from the angle of wise practitioners in any of the policy fields involved in a particular case.

A lot of ideas are propounded, but discouragingly, few answers that educe anything like a consensus from the variety of "experts." Law enforcement practitioners at all levels, many of them wise, conscientious and expert (at least in particular fields) have little to present that they can agree on.

One book exemplifies all these generalizations. It is a collection of "expert" papers coming from a variety of disciplines or fields of practice. John P. Conrad and Simon Dinitz edited the collection, under the title *In Fear of Each Other: Studies of Dangerousness in America* (1977). The difficulty in predicting dangerousness is highlighted by the first article, by Conrad. A pathetic petty criminal named Stephen Nash spent ten years in Soledad prison in California, and seemed to be harmless on release. Within a few weeks he was arrested and charged with seventeen murders of skid row derelicts, mostly by strangling. He cheerfully admitted all of them and had no explanation for his ferocity. A psychiatrist who examined him could find nothing to explain what he did. During all his time in Soledad (1944–1954), nobody saw anything that would predict his affectless murderous rampage.

In reviewing this book (Endleman 1983) I noted "with dismay that neither clinicians nor social scientists have very impressive records in analyzing, providing policy guidelines for, or practically intervening in reference to violent crime" (p. 540).

It is instructive and chilling to cite some of the material from the book.

Though cities have always been dangerous, the authors here tell us that most American cities' violent crime rates, from the early 1960s to the mid-1970s, tripled or quintupled, a rise not conceivably accountable by shifts in reporting systems. Typically, only about 20% of violent crimes reported to the police result in an arrest, and only about 8% in a conviction. "Violent crimes" here mean homicide, robbery, rape and assault.

Reliable prediction of future dangerousness is problematic. No expert can confidently predict that any particular person, regardless of prior record, will commit a violent act. In one careful study, with clinicians' evaluations, one-third of prior felons rated "dangerous" did in fact commit another violent offense within five years. Is this a poor record? or a good one? compared to what?

Due to the dilemmas of the juvenile justice system as now practiced, most juvenile offenders, including the "hard core" who commit the majority of the offenses, many of them violent, are free on the streets most of the time. The resulting failure to protect the public from the really dangerous ones among them has eroded public confidence in the law, and placed the young themselves in a state of anomie, that is, there are no predictable consequences for one's actions. We know of thousands of youngsters growing up in chaotic and disorganized conditions like those of the two young men named George described in Chapter 2 who suffered a succession of foster homes, "training institutions, and "terrible deprivations,—but we cannot predict who or how many will become the kind of killers/rapists they did before getting out of their teens. Nor do we know just what to do with them if they could be identified in advance.

Would incapacitation—keeping the culprits off the streets—reduce crime? Van Dine, Dinitz and Conrad (Chapter 6) calculated how many of the violent crimes that led to arrest in a particular county in 1973 would *not* have been committed had the offenders been safely behind bars on a mandatory five-year sentence for a prior offense he had been convicted of in 1968 or later. Answer: 115, out of 638 "cleared" offenses (18%) involving 68 offenders out of 342 (20%). The authors call this "only a modest effect" on the violent crime rate of that year, a debatable value judgment. (Is one-fifth so little?) A different research, using a different strategy and assumptions (Shinnar, cited by Van Dine *et al.*), comes up with the opposite conclusion: that sterner, stiffer, longer prison terms would indeed substantially reduce the current violent crime rate through incapacitation.

Confusion abounds about how to identify dangerousness. One sociologist (Pfohl) attacks psychiatric evaluation for its emphasis on understanding the *individual* while he wants an emphasis on sociocultural forces in the genesis of crime. If he had his way, what is now only a partially effective means of identifying dangerous trends would be replaced by something worthless in trying to identify *which* of the individuals facing "racial oppression, the oppression of poverty" and the like, are likely candidates for committing brutal violent crime.

Homicide: Sociological Variations

All societies, as already stated, prohibit ingroup homicide. But what *is* that? The definition varies from one society to another. Sociologically, not all killings are alike. Permissible killing includes killing the enemy in war, or killing members of other tribes, in primitive societies, also impersonal killing by the state, like the execution of traitors and of persons convicted of capital offenses. Felonious killing includes impersonal killing for predatory advantage in organized crime. Killing is used as a social control mechanism in organized crime, to get rid of rivals, or to set an example to members of the gang. Leaders may kill, or have killed, members who have violated the gang's group code. (Note police are sympathetic to this kind of homicide; and the feeling is "Nothing personal buddy, but this has to be done.") The victim can even be a kinsman, like the son-in-law of the boss, as in *The Godfather.* Then there is killing in revenge, backed up by a feudal code, or a code of honor supported by public mores. An example is the stoning to death of an adulteress to the present day in Muslim societies and other places, or the killing of the adulteress's paramour by her husband, in modern Western societies, met with sympathy even though prosecutable (and usually prosecuted) by law. All of these are instances where the killing is considered allowable or even obligatory by some or most members of the public. More complex on this issue are political assassinations (see discussion of Clarke below and Chapter 6).

Then there are individual killings that are planned, to get revenge, or to eliminate an obstacle. If premeditated and planned with malice aforethought, these are "murder" in modern law. If without malice aforethought, they are "manslaughter." Then there is *incidental* killing, one that occurs in the context of another crime, such as robbery, rape, other sex offenses, or to silence a victim or a witness.

Psychologically, one can distinguish homicides where the offender is basically sane and rational, from those involving definite psychopathology. On the latter there is endless controversy, with no consensus among psychiatrists, psychologists and other mental health practitioners (besides agreeing that the killer is *not necessarily* sick) about the general trends, or about any particular case. There is also endless (and probably not resolvable) controversy over the moral, social and legal merits of using the insanity plea in homicide cases. (See Chapter 6 for further discussion.) John Hinckley being found "not guilty by reason of insanity" for his attempt to assassinate President Reagan evoked a howl of protest from the public and a barrage of hopelessly contradictory commentary from "experts." Where psychiatrists or psychoanalysts do see psychopathology, how they diagnose the sickness and describe the dynamics varies enormously. Alexander in work already cited, points to a "criminal from the sense of guilt." He also sees other cases as involving a "neurotic character," essentially equivalent to what others have called psychopathic personality, one version of which commits murder. Experiencing what other persons may consider minor injustices is to this individual so enraging, it provokes a breakthrough of violent aggressive urges. Bergler, in work previously cited, identifies a "mechanism of criminosis," as distinguished from a mechanism of neurosis. Here the murderous act represents revenge against the denying and frustrating mother, leading to a "Herostratic act" that in turn leads inevitably to punishment by the authorities, which appeases and gratifies the offender. (Herostratos in 356BC burned down the temple of Artemis at Ephesos to "become renowned"—it worked.)

Wertham on the "Catathymic Crisis"

Fredric Wertham (1950) identifies another syndrome that he calls the catathymic crisis. He studied intensively a number of apprehended killers, including an adolescent who killed his mother. The hero of that story, *Dark Legend,* is a kind of modern real-life Orestes. It is this boy, Gino, who is the basis for the formulation of the catathymic crisis.

Here, injurious life experiences produce an unbearable and seemingly insoluble inner situation leading to persistent and increasing emotional tension. The subject holds an external circumstance entirely responsible for the tension. His thinking becomes more and more self-centered. Apparently suddenly, a crystallization is reached: the idea that some particular violent act is "the only way out." He goes through prolonged inner struggle, with extreme emotional tension. Finally he commits (or attempts) the violent act. Immediately he feels complete removal of tension. He goes through a superficially normal period; the act is still seen in the light of the earlier justification. An inner equilibrium is established which leads to insight. The subject is now aware that the outer situation does not explain his act, and that deeper forces are involved. This person is not psychotic, and in fact, thinks Wertham, the subject was probably prevented from falling into psychosis by this act. Wertham does not claim this concept of catathymic crisis explains all cases of strange murders. Far from it. Others may involve definite indications of psychosis. Still others may be schizoid personalities. Each case has to be investigated in detail by the best psychoanalytic means available.

The lack of agreement among psychiatrists and psychoanalysts about just *what* is going on psychologically in these cases, either generally, or in any particular case, reinforces the skepticism of the public and other social or psychological scientists, about the usefulness or wisdom of the practitioners. This is especially so when in an insanity-defense case of a person accused of murder, each side brings out "expert" witnesses who contradict one another substantially. Whom or what is the court or the public to believe? These are intractable problems. In clinical practice, even the apparently simplest case evokes divergent diagnostic and dynamic interpretations from different clinicians.

The reality in reference to homicide is probably best approximated thus: many different kinds of people commit killing; some are evidently mainly rational and psychologically intact, carrying out the killing with forethought and intent and with reasonable precautions against getting caught. Others are evidently psychologically disturbed in a variety of ways, some of the disturbance indicated by obvious blunders that lead to getting caught. Such blunders suggest, plausibly enough, a need to get caught and be punished.

How different killers are psychologically disturbed can be different from one case to another, and any one case can be so complicated as to come across as entirely mysterious and baffling even to "experts" and much more to the layman public. It is hard for savvy professionals to have to admit "we don't know," but that must be the informed professional statement on this matter today, and perhaps "we will never know." (That is no justification for not trying, of course.) The various well-qualified experts reporting in the Conrad/Dinitz book have to conclude that there is *no* reliable way of predicting who is likely to commit a violent offense, even from among those who have already repeatedly done so. (See above.)

Can we identify particular childhood precursors for such violent offenses? Yes, *after the fact,* we can report that such killers are more likely than others to have had an infancy and childhood of brutality and neglect. But the dilemma is that thousands of others have also had such a childhood, and have not committed a violent offense. (Yet!)

Assassins, Mad and Sane

In *American Assassins: the Darker Side of Politics,* (1982), a political scientist, James W. Clarke, reports his study of sixteen individuals who killed or tried to kill, prominent American political leaders, mostly presidents, over a 140-year period. (I will discuss this study in more detail in Chapter 6. For now, a brief summary.) Clarke claims that the prevailing conception of assassins in America is that they are all crazed individuals, all psychotic, mad killers. By contrast, Clarke finds on close examination of these sixteen persons only three fit closely into that category; another type (five persons plus two others close) were clearly *not* psychotic, but clearly rational *politically-* motivated killers. The others were more mixed, psychologically, but Clarke contends definitely not crazy. (See later detailed discussion in Chapter 6.) Clarke's main point: trying to kill the president does not *prove* a person insane.

Discussion: Relation of Psychological to Sociological Studies

There are myriad unanswered or inadequately answered questions here. There is no *one* criminal personality type, or one criminal personal history, though a number of types and variations can be identified. In none of these cases can a person with the indicated characteristics or history be reliably *predicted* to commit crimes.

The sociological theories are inadequate in important ways. Where crime (or particular kinds) may be more prevalent in certain socio-economic milieux, that does not indicate which persons in that setting do turn to crime or delinquency and which do not. For that question we turn to psychological studies. We can delineate certain of the psychological dynamics operating to get a person starting or continuing to participate in a delinquent or criminal subculture. In the case of homicide, we encounter more mysteries than firm answers, and very little reliable prediction. But clearly such an act connects with deeply rooted personality patterns. Since criminal and delinquent activities are so diverse, and the populations participating so diverse, we must find it improbable that any single formula is going to explain them all. Modern societies produce a host of "criminogenic conditions"—very heterogeneous cultural backgrounds in the population; impersonal mass conditions which may isolate individuals and also provide cover for any offender seeking not to be identified. Persons struggle endlessly to seek the culturally-demanded goals of personal "success" and are faced with limited real legitimate opportunities. Media messages extol reaching for the goals, regardless of the means, and question the moral legitimacy of many of the rules that say certain means are wrong. Many people believe that the political and economic leaders are all themselves corrupt, thus further challenging the moral legitimacy of the laws and the mores. Primary group ties have eroded, that among other things provide the bonds that contain personal conduct, and discourage the kind of cynicism or at least skepticism that pervades the deviant, especially the criminal, worlds. Media presentation commonly glamorizes and sensationalizes criminal activities, and often presents an affectless, amoral picture of violence. Personal murder has a perennial fascination thousands of years old (perhaps as old as humanity, as suggested in *Totem and Taboo*) that is unlikely to be eradicated from the human condition. In myriad ways, society needs crime and delinquency.

The crime world also overlaps with the political world in a variety of ways, not only in reference to politically-motivated assassinations as just discussed. The overlap further complicates analysis. Radical political groups often use criminal means to seek their objectives, for example robbing Brink's trucks (and killing drivers or police in the process) to get money for the "revolution," killing police or enemies or traitors to the movement. A news report as I write tells of a juvenile gang in Chicago that is offering its services as terrorists, to the Libyan government. Political office-holders have the constant temptation to commit or accept corrupt practices, in many cases linked to organized crime. Organized criminal groups have on occasion offered their services to the American government to accomplish objectives impossible to reach by legitimate means.

Notes

1. I'm aware of the problematics of that designation; basically no one has solved the problem of drawing the class boundaries precisely for modern free-market societies, because they are essentially unstable. So any designation, such as this one, is a rough approximation. Some authors distinguish working class—referring to people in manual labor jobs on a fairly steady basis, and emphasizing respectability and work—from "lower class." "Lower class" is called by others "underclass." It is below the level of the working class, lacking regular work and concern for respectability. A classic study is *Tally's Corner* by Elliot Liebow (1965). Miller's terminology seems to include both working and lower class in that sense.

REFERENCES

Alexander, Franz, and Hugo Staub. 1931. *The Criminal, the Judge and the Public.* London: Allen and Unwin.

Bergler, Edmund. 1948. *The Battle of the Conscience.* Washington, DC: Washington Institute of Medicine.

Chambliss, William J., and Robert B. Seidman. 1971. *Law, Order and Power.* Reading, MA: Addison-Wesley.

Clarke, James W. 1982. *American Assassins: the Darker Side of Politics.* Princeton, NJ: Princeton University Press.

Cleckley, Hervey. 1950. *The Mask of Sanity.* St. Louis: Mosby.

Cloward, Richard and Lloyd Ohlin. 1960. *Delinquency and Opportunity.* New York: Free Press.

Cohen, Albert K. 1955. *Delinquent Boys.* New York: Free Press.

Cohen, Albert K., and James Short Jr. 1958. "Research In Delinquent Subcultures." *Journal of Social Issues.* 14: 20–37.

Conrad, John P., and Simon Dinitz, eds. 1977. *In Fear of Each Other: Studies of Dangerousness in America.* Lexington, MA: Lexington Books (D. C. Heath).

Dinitz, Simon. 1977. "Chronically Antisocial Offenders." in Conrad and Dinitz, 1977, pp. 21-42.

Durkheim, Emile. 1895. *Rules of the Sociological Method.* (English translation, New York: Free Press, 1950.)

Endleman, Robert. 1967. "Play Elements in Delinquency." in Endleman, *Personality and Social Life.* New York: Random House. pp. 421–440.

__________. 1983. Review of Conrad & Dinitz, **In Fear of Each Other.** *Journal of Psychohistory.* 10: 539–542.

Freud, Sigmund. 1913. *Totem and Taboo.* in *Standard Edition:* 13, 1955: 1–164.

Hirschi, Travis. 1969. *Causes of Delinquency.* Berkeley, CA: University of California Press.

Johnson, Adelaide M. 1949. "Sanctions for Superego Lacunae of Adolescents." In Kurt Eissler, ed. *Searchlights on Delinquency.* New York: International Universities Press.

Liebow, Elliot. *Tally's Corner.* 1965. Boston: Little Brown.

Lindner, Robert M. 1944. *Rebel Without a Cause: the Hypoanalysis of a Criminal Psychopath.* New York: Grove Press.

McCord, William, and Joan McCord. 1964. *The Psychopath: An Essay on the Criminal Mind.* Princeton: Van Nostrand.

Merton, Robert K. 1938. "Social Structure and Anomie." *American Sociological Review.* 3: 672–682.

__________. 1949. "Manifest and Latent Functions." in Merton, *Social Theory and Social Structure.* New York: Free Press: 21–82.

Miller, Walter. 1958. "Lower Class Culture as a Generating Milieu for Gang Delinquency." *Journal of Social Issues.* 14: 3: 5–19.

Nelson, Benjamin. 1950. *The Idea of Usury.* Princeton, NJ: Princeton University Press.

Pfohl, Stephen. 1977. "A Psychiatric Assessment of Dangerousness: Practical Problems and Political Implications." in Conrad and Dinitz, 1977: 77–102.

Quinney, Richard. 1970. *The Social Reality of Crime.* Boston: Little, Brown.

Reckless, Walter. 1962. "A Non-Causal Explanation: Containment Theory." *Excerpta Criminologica.* 1: 131–134.

__________. 1973. *The Crime Problem.* 5th ed. New York: Appleton-Century-Crofts.

Reckless, Walter, S. Dinitz, and E. Murray. 1956. "Self-Concept as an Insulator against Delinquency." *American Sociological Review.* 21:744–746.

Redl, Fritz. 1945. "The Psychology of Gang Formation and the Treatment of Juvenile Delinquents." *The Psychoanalytic Study of the Child.* 1: 367–376.

Redl, Fritz, and David Wineman. 1951. *Children Who Hate.* New York: Free Press.

__________. 1953. *Controls from Within.* New York: Free Press.

Scarpitti, Frank R., Ellen Murray, Simon Dinitz, and Walter Reckless. 1960. "The 'Good Boy' in a High Delinquency Area: Four Years Later." *American Sociological Review.* 25:555–558.

Sellin, Thorsten. 1938. *Culture Conflict and Crime.* Social Science Research Council. Bull. 41.

Shapiro, David. 1965. "Impulsive Styles: Variants." in Shapiro. *Neurotic Styles.* New York: Basic Books. 157–168.

Spitzer, Stephen. 1975. "Toward a Marxian Theory of Deviance." *Social Problems.* 22:641–651.

Sutherland, Edwin. 1937. *The Professional Thief.* Chicago: University of Chicago Press.

Sykes, Gresham, and David Matza. 1957. "Techniques of Neutralization: A Theory of Delinquency." *American Sociological Review* 22: 664–670.

Thrasher, Fredric. 1927. *The Gang.* Chicago: University of Chicago Press.

Turk, Austin T. 1969. *Criminality and Legal Order.* Chicago: Rand McNally.

Van Dine, Stephan, Simon Dinitz, and John Conrad. 1977. "The Incapacitation of the Dangerous Offender: A Statistical Experiment." in Conrad and Dinitz, 1977: 103–118.

Vold, George B. 1958. *Theoretical Criminology.* New York: Oxford University Press.

Wertham, Fredric. 1950. *Dark Legend.* New York: Doubleday.

Wilson, James Q. 1975. *Thinking About Crime.* New York: Basic Books.

——————, and Richard Herrnstein. 1985. *Crime and Human Nature.* New York: Simon and Schuster.

Yablonsky, Lewis. 1962. *The Violent Gang.* New York: Macmillan.

Yochelson, Samuel, and Stanton Samenow. 1976. *The Criminal Personality: Vol. I. A Profile for Change.* New York: Jason Aronson.

——————. 1977. *The Criminal Personality: Vol. II. The Change Process.* New York: Jason Aronson.

——————. 1986. *The Criminal Personality: Vol. III: The Drug User.* Northvale, NJ: Jason Aronson.

CHAPTER 3
SEXUAL DEVIANTS: HOMOSEXUALITY AND PROSTITUTION

Homosexuality*

Many supporters of "gay liberation" would argue against including discussion of homosexuality at all in a book about deviance, claiming there is nothing deviant or abnormal about homosexuality; homosexuals are rather, in their view, a persecuted and discriminated against *minority group*.

We have to differ. I shall use the term deviant in the standard sociological way, as a descriptive term without negative value-judgment. The description refers to forms of conduct that the society—or a majority of its members, *regards* as going against the norms in some way. The social scientist using this term is not implying agreement with the negative value-judgment, simply reporting it.

Homosexual behavior, consummating sexual behavior with a partner of the same sex, by preference and choice (and not under duress), *is* considered in this society as deviant, going against the norms of proper conduct, by *most* people of this society. It is considered "abnormal" in one sense or another. To the religious (of Judaic and Christian persuasions), it is sinful. It goes against the word of God. To the law it is criminal. Many describe it as "unnatural," going against the demands of nature. Mating of man and woman is necessary for reproduction and therefore survival of the species. Some see it as *statistically* abnormal; it is practiced by only a small minority of the population. Others see it as against the norms and thus sociologically deviant. And many (though not all) mental health practitioners see it as clinically abnormal, as psychologically "sick."

Homophile protesters have challenged each of these views, singly or in combination. They contend that homosexuality need not conflict with certain readings of Christian or Jewish doctrine. They wish to portray it as simply an alternative, equally valuable, form of love. Some gay supporters call it an alternative "life-style."

* This section is adapted, revised, from Endleman 1981, Chs. 11–14, 1984 and 1986.

There are problems with this: not all homosexuals participate in gay subculture(s). Many do not want to be identified with a whole category just on the basis of sexual orientation. And is this just a matter of taste, like preferring strawberries to raspberries?

As for "deviant," some gay activists even question that "most" of the population derogate homosexuality. However, a 1985 Gallup Poll shows that 47% of those polled say that homosexual relations between consenting adults should *not* be legal (as opposed to 44% saying it should be.) The "should not" opinion is even up from 39% in 1982, while the 1977 figure was 43%. The negative opinion is stronger for older age groups (Gallup Poll, 12/12/85.) Helen Hacker finds similar continuing negative views among college students. (Recent research).

Some homophile-supporter sociologists wish to supplant the word "deviant" here by the word "variant." Hopeless word magic.[1]

These recent years have seen a huge upsurge of "gay-liberation" propaganda activity, that has been so strong that anyone intending to be regarded as liberal and enlightened today dares not say anything that might be construed as offensive by that "liberation" force. Witness a large proportion of social scientists, including most sociologists. For example nearly all sociological writers on deviance, in discussing homosexuality, take an almost totally gay liberation line against considering the homosexuals as abnormal on any count. In the world of psychotherapy, whatever they may privately hold as clinical opinions, most psychotherapists will typically refrain from giving any opinion, or at least hesitate to characterize homosexuality as psychopathological. As for psychoanalysts, the picture is more mixed, as will be discussed later in this chapter.

As for the law, the gay liberation forces are most vociferous, and politically active on this issue. They contend that it is unjust for the law to count as criminal, sexual congress of two same-sex adults, and have succeeded, along with the support of a sufficient part of the public, in having 26 of the United States repeal laws criminalizing "private consensual adult homosexual acts." No laws are on the books against such acts for females, so the impact of this change is for males. Most Americans of liberal conscience, whatever their private feelings for homosexuals, agree with this move. That still leaves homosexual rape or sex with minors, as criminal offenses, alongside parallel acts by heterosexuals. Similar changes have occurred recently in Canada, Great Britain and a number of other modern countries. Still that leaves most of the states of the United States with something like "sodomy" laws on the books, enforceable, and actually enforced, as in the recent much publicized case in Georgia where the guilty verdict was upheld by the Supreme Court (see *The New York Times* 7/1/86: p.1).

As for regarding homosexuality as "sick" (psychologically) this is an arena of controversy. The gay liberation forces consider the matter settled; the answer is "no," as decreed by the American Psychiatric Association ruling in 1973. (See discussion later in this chapter.) The relevant professional publics are divided, with classical psychoanalysts continuing to regard it as psychopathological, other mental health practitioners more mixed. (See further discussion below, also Endleman 1981, Chapter 12, and Endleman 1986.)

Regarding statistical abnormality, here the prevailing opinion of most professional observers remains that *probably* only a small minority of the population are exclusively or preferentially homosexual in practice. There are intrinsic problems in counting here: as long as homosexual practice is still, as it is, prevailingly culturally disapproved, it is likely that a substantial—but unknown—percentage of persons actively engaged in homosexual practice, will not openly admit this. Consequently it is impossible to know what the total "homosexual" population is, so estimates are made. The only large-scale study that included a major segment of the total population, the Kinsey reports, estimate 4 to 5% of the males, and probably less than 1% of the females, as exclusively or preferentially homosexual (Kinsey *et al.* 1948, 1953). By contrast, gay liberation spokespeople give various estimates running from about 10% to as high as 20% today—but of course they are an embattled political minority group, expected to inflate their numbers.

The Kinsey studies also indicated that about 35% of the males in the "sample" had had homosexual contact at some point in their lives. Gay activists love to use this figure to suggest that homosexuality is widespread, therefore statistically fairly "normal." But the reference to "some point in their lives" could include (and did commonly include) a single incident, or at most very few, usually in adolescence or early youth, in a predominantly heterosexual sexual history. Most of these could not even be classified as "bisexual," which suggests something like equal resort to heterosexual and homosexual activity.

The Kinsey figures are from the 1940s. Are they all out of date today? Is homosexuality in fact, as often alleged, much more prevalent today? Again we have no way of knowing for sure, but many observers think so. Possibly the "gay-rights revolution" has led many people of ambiguous sexual preference, to turn predominantly to homosexuality, feeling that it is no longer so taboo. They may accept the gay liberation line that "if you're in doubt, then you're gay." (An interesting example of identification with the aggressor, an "oppressed minority group" agreeing with its enemies, the prejudiced heterosexuals, in claiming that you must be entirely one or the other.) Others may now be less likely to *conceal.* They become more open about their homosexuality. Some have been in effect forced to "come out of the closet" by coming down with AIDS, like some famous entertainment stars. (More on AIDS later in the chapter.) Thus we cannot be sure the real numbers have increased.

Some people argue in evolutionary terms, that if this were the prevailing practice in any particular society, the population would soon die out. Therefore homosexuality is "unnatural" and counter-evolutionary. Opponents of this view may ask, what society has ever died out because of this practice? Anthropologists could answer: We do know of some societies that have come dangerously close to extinction because of very low reproductive rates, usually attributed to the demoralizing and disruptive effects of conquest by people of more complex civilizations.[2]

But because of homosexual practices?

Consider: In one of the many tribal societies with institutionalized homosexual relations of all males in the initiation ceremonies, (but with expected adult heterosexuality), Van Baal reports of the Marind-Anim in New Guinea, that the females had an "alarmingly low fertility rate" (Van Baal 1966).[3] (See discussion of this and other Melanesian societies with institutionalized male homosexuality, later in this chapter, and in Endleman 1986.) I don't know of any follow-up studies of the Marind-Anim since that time, and it is possible that they have come close to extinction.

In another society with ritualized initiation homosexuality, that was studied more recently, Herdt (1981) reports: though heterosexual relations with the wife is the norm in adulthood, such relations are hedged with myriad taboos and regulations, which severely restrict the amount of actual coitus. Men and women are regarded as belonging to two categorically different worlds. Heterosexual intercourse is regarded as depleting the man of precious semen. Thus marital sex life is infrequent and experienced as a joyless chore. This attitude seems not to bode well for the survival of the tribe.

An alternative formulation of the evolutionary argument may be, how *much* variation from heterosexual supremacy in a society, can a society allow or even encourage, without threatening its reproductive survival? 20%? 40%? 50%? The answer would have to be a guess, "some, but not too much."

Homophile spokesmen are likely to reply to the evolutionary argument for the "abnormality" of homosexuality, in another fashion. The problem in modern societies is not, they say, a problem of *under*population at all, or anything so preposterous as the extinction of a whole society, but rather just the reverse—*over*population. Therefore modern societies should welcome a greater prevalence of homosexuality. Of course other gay activists argue that homosexual activity does *not* interfere with reproduction anyway, because many even predominantly homosexual men do father children either by heterosexual intercourse, or by donation to sperm banks for artifical insemination. Similarly, in regard to female homosexuals, of those we know now, many have in fact had children by (usually prior) heterosexual marriages, so they have not been taken out of the baby-producing market.

Current Sociological Approaches

As indicated, most sociologists when they deal with homosexuality (in general deviance textbooks, or elsewhere) take a line almost exactly corresponding to gay liberation views. Their view is as follows. Homosexuality is not abnormal. It is not sick. It does no harm to anyone, therefore should not be interdicted by law. Thus all the laws are unfair and unjust, and should be repealed, that criminalize sodomy or other homosexual acts, by consenting adults in private. Homosexuals constitute a persecuted minority group. Members of the public who feel negatively toward homosexuals are themselves suffering from a sickness, namely "homophobia." The view of homosexuality as "unnatural" or as sinful (or both) is seen as a relic of ancient and irrational religious prejudice.

Sociologists generally (though not all) have a prevailing sympathy for the underdog. That feeling is especially evident in the sociology of deviance. Homosexuals surely qualify. If the sociologist in question ever pretended a viewpoint of value-neutrality—make no judgments on either side, try to analyze, not moralize—that stance is readily abandoned in reference to an allegedly persecuted minority underdog group like the homosexuals. And for those sociologists who adhere to the liberal part of the spectrum politically—which probably includes most sociologists—a sympathetic outlook toward such underdogs is practically *de rigueur*. Combine that influence with the prevailing antagonism toward psychoanalysis—seen now as a primary enemy of the homosexuals—and you have the elements of a massive ideological slant on the subject. Thus most sociologists' presentations on this subject include dissenting from psychoanalytic views and counteracting or refuting common opinions which they, the sociologists consider to be unfounded stereotypes about homosexuals. 1) Popular opinion is that they are few in number: no, there are many tens of thousands; 2) That they are all alike: no, they are in fact very diverse; they are of all class backgrounds, all educational levels, all physical types, all occupations, a whole range of political opinions. (These points about diversity *are* borne out by large-scale systematic research, e.g., Bell and Weinberg 1978, of which more below.) 3) That all the male homosexuals are effeminate, all the females masculine: no, not at all, only a small proportion of the male gays are effete, limp-wristed, effeminate; the majority are indisdinguishable from heterosexual males by appearance or manner; and the lesbians indistinguishable from heterosexual females. (This too is confirmed by research); 4) That they're all sick: answer, no, they're not. (Not clearly confirmed by research; subject of current controversy. For details, see discussion below.)

Refocusing the Questions

Another feature of sociologists' concern and research on homosexuality is to refocus the questions. Why keep asking if and how homosexuals are "sick?"—they're not. Why keep asking where this sexual orientation comes from—its etiology? That's an irrelevant question for sociologists anyway, or it's a pernicious question because (so it is argued) it presupposes psychopathology, which is unwarranted, and by implication denies homosexuals full human status in society. Why not ask instead how homosexuals lead their lives? how do they deal with persecution, stigmatization? how do they form a subculture (or subcultures). Subcultures not only give meaning to, and enrich, their daily lives, but also add to the common culture of the society, enriching that intricate mosaic that makes up a complex heterogeneous society and its many different subcultures. Also why not ask how homosexuals (along with sympathetic supporters) have made themselves into a political force in this society, alongside of other persecuted and discriminated-against minority groups like the blacks, other ethnics, and women?

Also, some sociologists argue, why accept the prevalently anti-homosexual biases of this society, when many other societies have considered homosexual practice as normal or at least allowable—why not consider our *culture* as abnormal where it is against homosexuality, rather than the homosexuals?

Homosexual Subculture[s]

One contribution of sociological discussion of homosexuality appears in the description and analysis of homosexual subculture[s]. (See ethnographic section in Bell and Weinberg 1978; and earlier studies by Leznoff and Wesley 1956, Simon and Gagnon 1967, Evelyn Hooker 1967, Martin Hoffman 1968, Cory 1951, Schofield 1965, Weinberg and Williams 1974, and many others, including several papers in the Gagnon and Simon 1967 collection.)

There are whole social worlds in which homosexuals participate, and others do not, the world of informal gay social contacts, in addition to purely sexual contacts, the world of gay parties, bars and baths, beaches, resorts, restaurants, theaters, businesses. Complete industries have been developed addressing a gay clientele, travel agencies, clothing specialty stores. Entire segments of the entertainment industry are reputedly under control of a gay in-group, sometimes luridly portrayed as a "gay mafia."

Participation in the gay subculture varies a great deal. In big cities, it is possible for a gay to carry out his whole life in contact only with other gays. For others, perhaps those largely "in the closet," participation is minimal, perhaps limited to situations purely for sexual contact (bars, baths, and the like).

The functions of a homosexual community, unclear and unstable as its boundaries may be, have been summarized by the sociologist Helen M. Hacker, (1971: 86–87) as follows: It provides: 1) social support for a positive self-image; 2) shared norms and practices, overcoming anomie; 3) a sexual marketplace; 4) other, nonsexual gratifications (friendship, recreation, etc.); 5) a sense of identity; 6) enjoyment of camp behavior; 7) an agency of social control against impulsive acting out; 8) an upward mobility opportunity structure; 9) reduction of anxiety and conflicts, relieving tensions of concealment, enabling more productive performance outside the (homosexual) community; 10) social services to meet individual problems and crises.

However, while the homosexual subculture may provide positive supports for homosexuals, by its nature it may also emphasize the *difference* of the gays from the majority population. Thus the homosexual activists are caught in the contradictions between appeal to special status and special affinity to others of the same persuasion, and the desire to get across to the general population that they are just like everybody else.

Large-Scale Studies: the Bell/Weinberg Study

A number of sociologists have attempted studies of some aspects of homosexuality, with sizable "samples." The outstanding one so far has been that of Alan Bell and Martin Weinberg, assisted in one aspect later by Sue Kiefer Hammersmith. (Bell and Weinberg 1978: *Homosexualities: A Study of Diversity among Men and Women* and Bell, Weinberg and Hammersmith 1981: *Sexual Preference: Its Development in Men and Women.*)

The 1978 book reports on the study of about 1000 homosexual men and women, with a large control group of heterosexuals, using a complex interview schedule intricately coded and analyzed. It tried to cover all aspects of the subjects' lives, not only the sexual. The homosexual persons represent, the authors claim, as wide as range of types of homosexuals as one could find in modern society, not limited to patients in therapy or to showcase examples chosen by an activist organization.

Findings

As their title indicates, the homosexuals are very diverse. They come from many different social origins, work in a variety of occupations, have many distinctive life-styles, cover the whole range of incomes, physical types, mannerisms, sociopolitical views, and degrees and kinds of participation in homosexual subcultures.

On crucial matters relating to sexual orientation, they can be classified into five distinct types:

1) *Close-coupled:* much like "happily married"; monogamously mated to one particular partner, sexually faithful; happy homebodies; well adjusted psychologically; comfortable with their sexual orientation. (More of the lesbians than of the gay males, fit this type: 40% versus 14%.)

2) *Open-coupled:* "married," but less faithfully, by agreement; many other sexual contacts; less self-accepting as homosexual; less well-adjusted. Few of the women are in this category; many of the men. The men have a lot of sex with many partners.

3) *Functionals:* "swinging singles;" as sexually active as possible, the males more so than the females; very promiscuous; much cruising; huge number of different partners. Happy and exuberant about sex and about their sexual orientation; sometimes reckless, leading to problems. Very much in the gay subculture—more so for the men than the women.

4) *Dysfunctionals:* the troubled and tormented; fit most closely to the image of psychologically disturbed, unhappy homosexual; also very promiscuous; much cruising; more distressed about their own sexual orientation. Worst adjusted on the psychological scales used.

5) *Asexuals:* least active sexually; likely to be solitary and lonely; least involved in the gay subculture; psychologically maladjusted; least accepting of own homosexual orientation.

Differences between Females and Males

The authors find many differences between the lesbians and the gay males. Lesbians are more like straight women than like any men. Gay males are more like straight males than like any women. The lesbians are much more likely than the gay males to be seeking love, romance, tenderness, relationship, with sex. They have much less impersonal sex with strangers; do much less, in fact hardly any, cruising. Gay men are more likely to split sex from tenderness, to be very promiscuous. In this they do fit the stereotype. They are more likely to have impersonal sex; much less likely to sustain a close long-term relationship with one partner.

The homosexuals are much more likely than the heterosexuals to have had difficulties with the law on matters *unrelated* to homosexuality. For example, they are more likely to have been arrested on various charges. There is not a high incidence of arrests on charges relating to homosexuality itself. They are also more likely to have attempted suicide.

The authors do not try to be scrupulously value-neutral in their presentation. They clearly sympathize with the ideology of gay liberation, and aim their presentation to combat what they see as unwarranted negative stereotypes. They have two main themes: 1) homosexuals are not all alike; they differ greatly among themselves. This is amply demonstrated by their findings. 2) Homosexuals are not psychologically sick. This they claim, but their findings show otherwise. Their key summary on psychological health is this:

> It would appear that homosexual adults who have come to terms with their homosexuality, who do not regret their sexual orientation, and who can function effectively sexually and socially, are no more distressed psychologically than are heterosexual men and women. (p.216)

It is evident from their findings, however, that people who do in fact fit all these qualifications constitute only a very small minority of the homosexual population studied.

Overall scores of all the homosexuals on the "psychological adjustment" scales are significantly lower than for the heterosexuals. This is true also for specific subscales. For the males, they score lower than the straights on self-acceptance; higher on loneliness, worrisomeness, psychosomatic complaints, depression, and paranoid trends. For the females, they score worse than the heterosexuals on overall happiness, self-acceptance, suicidal ideation, and seeking professional therapeutic help.

The authors try to minimize the significance of these lower overall adjustment scores, by arguing that the poorer showing is concentrated in two types, 4) and 5), but 2) does not do so well either. They compare each of the subtypes of the gays with *all* of the straights. This is a tendentious procedure. Any meaningful comparisons of gay subtypes would have to be with comparable subtypes of the straights, e.g. heterosexually happily married, heterosexual "swinging singles," etc. which the authors do not do. (For more detail on this criticism, see Endleman 1981: 288-291.) Also, they significantly omit from the picture for "psychological adjustment" both the males' evident promiscuity and their troubles with the law. The high degree of promiscuity clearly indicates a driven preoccupation with sexual release, usually by impersonal contact, and inability to sustain a close, loving long-term relationship. The troubles with the law suggest what is found in psychoanalytic case studies, a masochistic taunting of authority, evidently in quest of punishment.

The 1981 book on etiology will be discussed later.

Cross-Cultural Studies

Gay liberation protesters contend that many other societies consider homosexuality normal and therefore it is our *society* that is abnormal in not holding that view, that our whole culture is suffused with that disease they call "homophobia."[4]

What is the evidence on this point from anthropological and historical studies? Here is a summary of findings (for details see Endleman 1986a and Endleman 1981: 295–313).

1) Among the hundreds of societies investigated for this study, *absolutely none* give unequivocal approval to *exclusive* homosexuality in either sex.

2) As for the occurrence of homosexual practices: Are there any societies where it is entirely absent? Answer: evidently yes, probably a small minority. Broude and Green (1976: 417) found 11.9% of codable societies had "no concept of homosexuality." This was true of three societies reported by Whitehead (1981) and one in Africa by the Parin team (1963). *Absence* of any homosexual activity is reported (evidently after attempts to uncover it) for one Polynesian society (Marshall 1971), one in New Guinea (Langness 1967) and two Amerindian tribes. Absence can also be *deduced* for several African tribes, and two in Melanesia. (See discussion of all these in Endleman 1986: 206–207.) Some anthropologists argue, however, that negative statements cannot be confidently made, since any denial of the practice by the tribesmen that includes a word for it, suggests that it does exist, though secret and taboo. This stricture would not apply to cases where they say they never heard of such a thing, and had to have it explained to them. In any case, we can summarize that it is absent or extremely rare, in a small minority of societies.

3) There is an important sex difference. It is much rarer for females than for males. This may be a function of less reporting, because women are considered less important than men in any case, or homosexual practice by women is seen as not automatically disqualifying for childbearing. The institutionalized role (berdache-like) is much rarer for females than for males; and stage-specific institutionalized and ritualized male homosexuality rarely has a female counterpart.

4) Where some homosexual practice does exist, prevalance varies greatly: Berdache-like gender-crossers are limited to a very small proportion of the population. However, in the stagespecific ritualized homosexuality, 100% of the age-appropriate males are included (see below). Otherwise prevalence varies from very low to quite high. A most common pattern is of adult males ordinarily primarily heterosexual, having occasional homosexual contact on the side, with the older adult male being considered the "masculine" partner (and therefore not condemned). This situation appears in many societies.

5) There are two forms of *institutionalized* homosexuality known in tribal societies, each of them fairly widespread:

One is gender-crossing: a male takes on the clothing and occupational tasks of the female, and is recognized and socially designated by a special term, translatable as man-woman. Or a female, similarly, becomes a woman-man. In this role homosexual practice is common. For example, the *berdache* of many Amerindian societies; and similar roles in many other societies in many parts of the world. (For details, see Endleman 1986, and sources, Williams 1986.) The role was always limited to a very small percentage of the population. The incumbent met with at least discomfort and embarrassment, if not disapproval, usually mitigated by the belief that it was supernaturally ordained from birth.[5] In the same tribe, otherwise, homosexual practice is disapproved, ridiculed and stigmatized. The existence of the role did not indicate that the tribe regarded homosexuality as anything like "normal." Most examples have the role for males, a few for males and females, and only two for females but not males.

The other form of institutionalization consists of a life-stage-specific practice of homosexuality for one sex only (the males), as part of initiation ceremonies, to be abandoned later in favor of heterosexual marriage. It is universal for all males of the tribe, supposed to be kept secret from the females, not regarded as anything like "homosexuality" in any Western sense, and not supposed to be exclusive in adulthood. The latter is definitely disapproved and stigmatized, as is even bisexual practice after marriage. These do occur, but are considered normatively wrong. Homosexual practice in the ceremonies is intended to "masculinize" the boy or adolescent by the injection of power- and strength-giving semen by an older male. (See Herdt 1981 for detailed analysis of a recent tribal case, and discussion of it and a number of others with similar patterns, in Endleman 1986; see also Herdt 1982, 1984; and Knauft 1987.)

6) Normative responses to homosexual practice vary widely from one society to another. The only firm generalization is that *nowhere* is *exclusive* homosexuality unambiguously approved. Homosexual practice is allowable in some forms or contexts, in some societies, and disapproved in others, sometimes very strongly, e.g. with the sanction of the death penalty. Broude and Green (1976) found that over two-thirds of codable societies indicated negative or strongly negative normative responses to homosexual behavior. (A figure very different from Ford and Beach's report [1951] of 64% of societies considering it "acceptable and normal"—a figure dear to homophile supporters, but clearly incorrect. See Endleman 1981: 296ff, for critique.) For more complex societies, Endleman 1981: 306–311, attempted an impressionistic overview, with the aid of historical work such as Karlen's (1971.) Karlen concluded that even the historical cases most cited for high incidence and high normative approval (ancient Athens, Renaissance Europe) are far more ambiguous and variegated

than gay liberation propagandists portray. Athenian homosexuality was limited to a small leisured elite (bisexual at that)—see Vanggaard 1972 and his sources—while the general population was negative. Similarly such practices and favorable (tolerating) normative responses in Renaissance Europe were limited to courtly circles. Further both practices and normative responses have waxed and waned over the centuries, with no one long-term trend, either more approving or more disapproving. It seems, homosexual practice and more positive (at least permissive) attitudes are more likely in more elite circles in many different societies. Any complex society may include a range of normative responses, from prevailingly negative in the common population, in rural areas, in the religious and the law, to more accepting in sophisticated secular urban elites.

Psychological and Psychoanalytic Studies

In Chapter 1 I posed a fourfold table about the relation of deviance to psychopathology, crossing one dimension: Deviant? Yes, or No, with the other: (Psychologically) Sick? Yes or No. Where, in what box of these four, would we place homosexuality? Gay liberationists and the sociological (and some psychological) supporters, would place it in cell (2) Deviant? Yes, and Sick? No. The material we have to look it now would place many, perhaps most, cases in cell (1) Deviant? Yes, and Sick? Yes, though for a few other cases, cell (2).

Homosexuality Psychopathological?

The prevailing current view of most *classical* psychoanalysts is that there is clearly psychopathology in most cases of preferential homosexuality. It may be stated that the homosexuality itself *is* the sickness (Socarides 1978); or is commonly *associated with* pathological processes (Bieber *et al.* 1962; Stoller 1975; many others); there is variation around this view (Ovesey and Person 1973; Eisenbud 1982.) Among other kinds of psychoanalysts (mainly "revisionists") there is skepticism that sickness is always involved (Thompson 1947; Mitchell 1978.) Still other clinicians, generally *not* psychoanalytic, are more likely to claim that homosexuals are *not* sick, their view in line with and cited by gay liberationists (Hoffman 1968; George Weinberg 1972; Tripp 1975).

Part of the reluctance of anyone in the healing arts to say there is anything sick about homosexuals derives from the common impression, supported by gay liberation ideologues, that if you say sick, you are also saying immoral, illegal, unnatural, sinful, abominable—the whole litany of "abnormality" attributed to homosexuality by one or another segment of the society. That in turn implies that you support stigmatization and persecution of homosexuals, criminalization of homosexual acts, discrimination against gays in work, housing, the military, and the like. It therefore takes enormous effort—not to mention courage—to try to get across a differentiated view that says you do not agree with any of the latter, but you do think the clinical evidence from careful psychoanalytic studies supports the recognition of psychopathology, in some form.

Psychoanalytic Studies

Psychoanalytic studies start, of course, with Freud (1905). Freud accepted an evolutionary viewpoint. One of his critics, Roy Schafer (1974) regards this opinion as a defect in Freud. Freud obviously did not. Nor do I. I think it is essential in linking psychoanalysis with sociocultural analysis (Endleman 1981, part 2).

With an evolutionary perspective, survival of a species or a society depends on reproduction, which depends on heterosexual relations. That does not mean, of course, that survival of the society requires that absolutely every individual in the society must be exclusively heterosexual, only that most must be. Divergence from this is pathological. Intrapsychically, obligatory divergence from heterosexual genital coitus in quest of mutual orgasm, constitutes technically a *perversion,* in a clinical, not a moralistic judgmental, sense. Such divergence may or may not be associated with other features of psychopathology.

Classical psychoanalytic work of today (e.g. Socarides, Bieber, Stoller), sees in exclusive or strongly preferential homosexuality, a definite psychopathology, either intrinsically or by usual association. Pathological processes exist in the psychosexual development of the individual (see Wiedeman summary 1974, and Endleman 1981, Chapter 12).

Stoller (1975) says that for a phenomenon to constitute a single specific clinical condition, it must show in all instances of it: 1) the same pattern of behavioral and experiential symptoms; 2) the same psychodynamics; and 3) the same etiology. Homosexuality fails to fit on all three counts; 1) there is no common set of symptoms in all cases; 2) the dynamics are different in different cases; and 3) the etiology is different in different cases. Therefore homosexuality is not, correctly, a clinical syndrome. There *is* homosexual behavior and fantasy, yes. And saying it is not a single clinical syndrome does not mean no pathology is present; clearly, in Freudian perspective, there is.

Freud said the neonate is originally "bisexual." He meant *psychologically.* He did not mean that we are all likely to be sexually attracted to and sexually active with partners of both sexes; but rather that same-sex attraction and arousal is among the *potentialities* of all human beings, and is, in fact, in sublimated form, an important element in nonsexual group bonds of all kinds.

Male Homosexuality: Etiology and Dynamics

Both by psychoanalysts and by social scientists, male homosexuality has been much more attended to than female. This probably reflects androcentric bias in the culture at large, including the notion that women are not as important anyway, or a related idea that homosexuality in women is not as much a threat to society as that in men.

Though there is not invariably a single pattern of psychogenetic sources, certain patterns are more prevalent than others. The largest, both intensive and extensive study is that of Irving Bieber and his associates (1962). It found the most frequent pattern was that the family constellation consisted of a "close-binding intimate" mother and a father who was either detached and hostile; or detached and domineering toward the son; or physically or psychologically absent. The mother has an intense possessive relationship to the son—dominating and overprotective—encouraging extreme dependency. She both seductively stimulates him sexually and blocks his development of heterosexual interest and action. She shows intense psychological rapport with the boy, blocks his attempting dangerous activities of a "masculine" kind, thus inhibiting his masculine gender identity.

The mother and father are typically in a bad, sexually unsatisfying marriage. The mother turns to this boy for compensatory gratifications, often setting up an alliance with him against the father. This situation makes resolution of the Oedipus complex particularly difficult. The father may collude with this process, by his unavailability or indifference. Or he gives up the possibility of having any influence on the son's development, by submission to the mother's overwhelming power over the boy. Or he is dominated by the mother himself. Alternatively, he reacts with hostility to the boy, and may express this in brutal ways, which only intensifies the boy's castration fears.

Other formulations of the etiological patterns include these: in reaction to the dangers of engulfment in the mother-son symbiosis, the boy flees to the father as the primary love object, and has not the positive but the reverse-oedipal complex, loving the father and rivaling the mother. Or the incestuous drive toward the mother and linked rivalry toward the father, encountering the incest taboo and particularly the hostility of the father, lead the boy in great anxiety to abandon these wishes, and to try to appease the father in submission, abasing himself homosexually to the father's power. Extreme castration anxiety, more than normally experienced, is a factor here, leading to an intense phobic reaction to the female genitals, and intense need for the sexual partner to have the prized male genital, to reassure the male against castration. Incorporation of the partner's penis (orally or anally) may also signify acquisition of the partner's masculinity. (Compare the "Sambia" tribe—Herdt 1981, discussed above.)

Socarides (1978) discusses a pre-oedipal type, deriving from developmental *arrest* at a very early stage, thus involving *fixation,* from oedipal types where intense oedipal conflict leads to the desparate solution of *regression* to pre-oedipal phases. The pre-oedipal type represents more severe pathology, stereotyped and extremely compulsive (1978: 80). The Bell and Weinberg gay men that would correspond to that type are compulsively driven to an endless succession of promiscuous contacts, battling underlying depression with manic defenses that show up in their (apparently paradoxically) high scores on the "exuberance" scale—"feel frequently 'on top of the world."

Dynamics refer to the forces operating in the personality, many of them unconscious, that bring about the constellation concerned, and how it works. The dynamics here are related to the etiology just discussed. Dynamically, we can find in male homosexuals, in addition to or instead of the foregoing, one or more of the following: dominance-submission games magically reenacting father-son or brother-brother power struggles of childhood. They may involve extreme narcissistic disorder requiring the partner to be a replica of oneself, therefore the same sex. Alternatively, taking care of a younger male partner may work as a "magic gesture" to relieve one's own intense dependency longings. Possibly the dynamics might involve defiance of authority, in masochistic quest for punishment, which also may be enacted socially, as in encounters with law enforcement. As another possibility, in defiance of strongly held taboo, these are acts of destructiveness combined with destructiveness toward the partner. (Compare, today, AIDS-risking behavior.) It may represent assumption of a "negative identity," where being something bad is experienced as superior to nothingness. Any of these constellations may co-exist in the same individual, an effect of over-determination. (See variations depicted in other psychoanalytic works: Bergler 1956; Hatterer 1971; Ovesey 1969; Stoller 1975; various authors presented in Marmor 1965.) Detailed analysis of the individual is required to trace the etiology and the dynamics that specifically apply.

Though it is not inevitable, it seems (at least to classically minded psychoanalysts) most likely that pathogenic processes are involved in the formation of the homosexual preference. Once formed, and consolidated in adulthood, it is *possible* that the variation in sexual preference can be relatively "encapsulated," and not necessarily associated with other pathological features in the personality. However, such an outcome is probably relatively rare. (The few cases of seemingly "healthy" or "well-adjusted" homosexuals noted in the Bell-Weinberg study as well as in other studies, may be such instances.)

More likely, however (as demonstrated in psychoanalystic case studies), the preference variation is associated with a variety of other psychopathological features. As Stoller put it, the person may be relatively free of clinical disorder, or he may be neurotic, or psychotic, or character-disordered, or narcissistic-disordered, or schizoid, or psychopathic, or paranoid. In reference to psychosis—it may be associated with psychosis; it maybe intensified in the psychotic episode; it may appear only in psychotic episodes; or it may *disappear* during the psychotic state (Socarides 1978: 57–61). One form of homosexuality appearing in the context of schizophrenia, Socarides identifies as a distinct type: "schizo-homosexuality" (1978: chs. 17, 20).

Any such associated psychopathology may well be *exacerbated* by external social pressures, in the form of stigma or persecution, or by the person's own internalization of societal norms against homosexuality, producing torments of guilt or shame. However, it is unlikely that *all* of the associated psychopathology is attributable entirely to such outside social oppression, as gay liberation rhetoric likes to proclaim. Stereotyping by outside society, now often accentuated by the gay liberationists, may intensify consolidation of homosexual preference and homosexual identity ("if you're in doubt, you're gay," "gay is good" etc.—when do heterosexuals have to shout "straight is good"?) at the cost of psychologically potentially available alternatives.

Relation to Bell-Weinberg-Hammersmith Study

Bell and Weinberg, joined by Sue Kiefer Hammersmith (1981), analyzed the data of their 1970 study, in reference to the question of *etiology*, where does the homosexuality come from? Taking the answers respondents gave to a whole battery of questions about their family of origin, each of the parents, and other significant family figures, and their early and later childhood experiences, they try to trace connections, by complex statistical analysis.

Findings:

The homosexual adult male had, as a boy, a negative relation with his father, was the favorite of an overprotective mother who dominated the father. He was considered "unmasculine" as a child (low adherence to gender-appropriate play) and had a lot of homosexual arousal and homosexual activity in childhood and adolescence.

All of these patterns of origins the authors dismiss as statistically not significant; or as not indicating anything causal, because, they say, they are simply part and parcel of the same phenomenon, the adult homosexuality. Therefore they conclude that none of the psychoanalytic, psychological, or social-environmental theories adanced by others to account for etiology, are valid, and that we must look instead to something prior to all of these, namely biology. (See Endleman 1984, for my critique of their study and their analysis of their own data.)

In fact, what they do present as elements showing some relationship, are in reality consistent with the main psychoanalytic ideas on this topic. (Again, the blatant discrepancy between their actual findings, as in the Bell-Weinberg 1978 study and what they *claim* their findings indicate, suggests it is their adherence to gay-liberation ideology that blinds them as social scientists.)

Female Homosexuality: Etiology and Dynamics

Female homosexuality has different pathways of development from male. There is no one psychoanalytic theory (agreed to by all psychoanalysts) on the genesis of this sexual orientation in the female, and it is likely that lesbianism is simply not a single diagnostic category, any more than male homosexuality is. Again this does not mean there is no psychopathology associated, only that it can be derived from any of a number of different etiological patterns, and serve any of a number of different kinds of functions in the personality organization.

Current psychoanalytic work on this tends to emphasize *pre*oedipal phases, more than oedipal ones, as crucial factors in this orientation.

The scenario may proceed as follows: in the earliest infancy, the girl baby has an intense symbiotic tie with the mother. Later she must make separation-individuation from the mother. She may be impeded if the mother is psychotic or severly disturbed and will therefore not allow the daughter to do this. Or the mother may, by early rejection, force too early individuation. The threat of symbiosis may turn the little girl toward negative identification with the mother: "I do not want to be that woman, or what that woman wants me to be." In the rapprochement phase of individuation-separation, the girl may have great difficulty making that re-approach, and thus turn to the father. This is an early *pre*-oedipal turn to the father. How he receives the daughter's needs for closeness and/or individuation, will make a crucial difference here. If he gives her the feeling of rejection, abandonment or mistreatment, she may then return to the mother, regressing, in part, to the early symbiosis, but now eroticized. In the adulthood sequel, the partner's body becomes the symbol of the mother's breast that needs to be reciprocally penetrated and incorporated as in the early symbiotic phase (Eisenbud 1982; Socarides 1978).

Castration complex and penis envy, part of all female psychosexual development, here take particular forms. Penis envy may be particularly strong. If the little girl is put by mother, in a double bind of being pushed toward "masculine" assertiveness and then punished for enacting that demand, she may feel: "If I were a boy and had a penis, I would not be punished for being a boy." Also, "If I were a boy and had a penis, I could serve my mother." The oedipal situation is especially complicated for the girl who has had any of the prior events just discussed, with negative identification with the mother, or a paranoid or psychotic mother or stepmother.

Any of these scenarios may result in a reverse-oedipal constellation: "if I may not have my father, I will *be* my father" or "as my father I can regain my lost mother." Tabooed oedipal longing for the father may generalize to all males. But the conditions for this happening are pre-oedipal distortions of one or more of the kinds discussed.

Females with homosexual orientation are more likely to be similar to other females than to any males. Their gender identification is likely to be definitely feminine, though troubled in various ways. Unlike anatomically-female transexuals, they do not think of themselves as "really" males trapped by mistake in a female body. Rather they see themselves as females who love other females. They are more likely than gay males, to place emphasis, in sex, on love, mutuality, relationship, tenderness, etc. rather than primarily on sexual contact and satisfaction. Also unlike gay males, they are not apt to be promiscuous and constantly on the prowl for sex.

There may be a variety of other associated dynamics: powergames, sado-masochistic involvements, narcissistic disorder, need for self-destructive defiance, compulsive search for the "perfect" partner (the lost fantasied good mother), exacerbations of specifically feminine kinds of envy and resentment, rage against all males as "oppressors."

The homosexual variation may be relatively "encapsulated," and not be associated with other pathological formations—though this is probably rare. Or it may in fact be associated with any of a variety of other pathologies, exacerbated by societal rejection and stigma. For some, however, that very rejection and stigma may be an important part of the appeal—membership in a kind of mysterious secret society elite—then serving as a secondary gain sustaining the deviant pattern.

Related Findings from the Bell-Weinberg-Hammersmith Studies

These studies found the female homosexuals *less* "poorly adjusted" than the gay males, and with less difference between themselves and comparison female heterosexuals than gay males have from straight ones. They were also more likely to be classifiable as type 1) "close-coupled"—40% compared to 14% for males. Because psychoanalytic work suggests that the earliest relationship with the mother is, in a way, a homoerotic one, it is possible that the adult homosexual orientation is psychologically closer to psychic "normality" in the clinical sense, than the corresponding orientation in the male.

Regarding etiology, Bell, Weinberg and Hammersmith found these features: the girl had a negative relationship with a hostile rejecting mother and a detached father who did not want her to be like her mother, and was considered "unfeminine" in her childhood. Though BWH are at pains to deny statistical significance to any of these trends, and reject any causal relationship (see above), their striking agreement with psychoanalytic clinical findings is impressive.

The American Psychiatric Association's "De-Pathologizing" of Homosexuality

Some readers may be wondering, what is all this discussion in the late 1980s, about whether homosexuality is psychological illness, or how so, when in 1973 the American Psychiatric Association changed its influential handbook (the Diagnostic and Statistical Manual—DSM) to eliminate homosexuality from its list of disorders. In the new DSM-III, the category "Sexual Orientation Disturbance" no longer includes homosexuality *per se;* rather only "ego-dystonic homosexuality." That means you are sick only if you are dissatisfied with your homosexuality. The decision is documented in Hite 1974a and 1974b, and Kendell 1983. The decision was effected, evidently, as a result of intense political pressure on the APA by gay liberationists. The decision is of course psychodynamically absurd. The psychologically most pathological persons might very well feel comfortable with their disorder, and not seek treatment, and the less sick feel more tormented. Its being hailed by gay-liberationists and their social science supporters as a great victory also supports the recognition of this as a political decision, not as a reasoned scientific or clinical position. Most *psychoanalysts* are likely to dissent from this decision. Many of them decline to be members of the American *Psychiatric* because of manifold disagreements with the psychiatrists on several issues, including, as in this case, sociopolitical ones.

AIDS

The AIDS epidemic has affected the situation of homosexuals in America very intensely. Up to the late 1970s, it appeared that aspects of the "sexual revolution" relating to homosexuality had markedly improved public opinion toward the homosexual minority. Laws against homosexual behavior had been changed in many states, as well as in other modern societies, and challenges to overt discrimination against homosexuals in employment and housing were making progress in many places.

In the early 1980s, with the identification of AIDS as affecting primarily male homosexuals, the public situation became more difficult. The public began to learn about this invariably fatal disease and associated it primarily with homosexuality. Fundamentalist Christians could see it as "God's punishment upon the sinful." Another view was that it was "nature striking back at people carrying on unnatural practices." So long as the publicized victims were mostly gay males, the issue, for much of the general population, could be ignored or put out of awareness. Or it could be given a very low priority of public issues about which "something should be done," on the assumption that the victims brought it on themselves anyway. Then it became known that also at great risk were intravenous (IV) drug users, the source of the contamination being dirty needles shared by several persons. The majority of these are also male. Heterosexuals among them may also contaminate their female sexual partners, and their babies. As some heterosexual women became stricken by the disease, the source of infection was identified as sexual contact with bisexual men, or with IV drug user men. The infection of the woman in turn put in danger her male, presumably heterosexual, partners. It also threatened any children she may subsequently have. Consequently, these facts put AIDS into the category of a public danger, generally affecting any of the population, not only gay and bisexual males and IV drug users.

By the time of this writing, mid-1988, the epidemic has reached great dimensions, and the public health authorities are trying frantically to give the public accurate and rational information and advice on this issue.

In the process, the current AIDS concern has brought into the open, a great deal of anti-homosexual sentiment. This includes blaming the homosexuals for the epidemic, regarding them as having brought divine retribution upon themselves (and whomever else) for their sinful behavior. It involves, commonly, putting all homosexuals into a particular kind of pariah status.

Hard public opinion poll data indicate, however (Gallup Poll, 12/12/85) that 59% of the public polled on this question say that their opinion about homosexuals has *not* changed since the AIDS epidemic; 37% say their opinion has changed for the worse. But note that the "not changed" response has to be seen in the light of the response (same poll) of 47% saying that "homosexual relations between consenting adults should *not* be legal" (as compared with 44% saying they should be legal, and 9% undecided—in other words a slight majority of those responding saying they favor continuing current criminal sanctions against private consensual homosexual behavior. Also the "not legal" response is in 1985 up from 39% in 1982 and 43% in 1977. (Of course the usual caveats have to be made about the validity of data from public opinion polls of this sort, but these are the best we have for sampling a whole population, in this case, the United States, population about 240 million.)

So what do these data tell us? Not that there has been a sweeping and global worsening of attitudes toward homosexuals, but there has been some (over a third), and no significant change in a negative feeling toward homosexuals in at least half the population.

All of this information calls into question the extent to which the society as a whole has moved toward a "live-and-let-live" position about homosexuality. Considering the psychodynamics of response to homosexuality, one would have to expect that any further advances toward "liberalization" would be self-limiting. This would be so, considering that *male* homosexuality at least is in its nature felt to be threatening to the "normal" population. This would be especially so to the males, subject to strong castration anxiety. (Note in the Gallup poll of 1985 just mentioned, men were, and continue to be, more negative than women, toward homosexuals.) Such sense of threat does not easily allow a casual acceptance of the kind counted as desirable by the new "conventional wisdom" of the "liberated."

Add to this, anger on the part of those more conventional people, at being considered bigots and reactionaries for their (in their minds) "natural" revulsion to this perversion, and we have the ingredients for a substantial backlash.

By mid-1988, we have been getting a flood of media messages warning us that the *whole* population is now in danger of contracting AIDS, not only the elements reported as at risk, male homosexuals, IV drug users and hemophiliacs. Now we are told that the general population, meaning heterosexuals of both sexes, is just as much at risk. We are now told that the epidemic has already spread to heterosexuals, who can therefore infect each other and their children.

Evidently the implication, and apparently the intent, is to "democratize" AIDS, especially to destigmatize it from being largely a "gay disease."

As of this date (10/88) what is the evidence about how the disease is contracted, and by whom? Current indications are that in America, 70% of those infected are gay males; about 20% are IV drug users, mostly males. What about heterosexuals, then? All the extant studies now indicate that the only way heterosexuals can be infected is by sexual intercourse with an infected person, most likely a bisexual male, or by sharing a needle with an infected IV drug user. They show that transmission by heterosexual intercourse is much more likely from male to female, only rarely from female to male.

Michael Fumento in a thoroughly researched article in COMMENTARY Magazine (Nov. 1987), shows that all the alarums about AIDS spreading in the heterosexual population are unjustified, full of misinformation and distortions, with misleading or simply false statistics. The probability of getting AIDS from a single heterosexual encounter, so long as neither partner is a bisexual man nor a drug abuser, has been calculated by one expert (Jeffry Harris of MIT) at less than one in a million.

Even if one partner is infected with the HIV virus, the probability of the other partner getting it by one heterosexual contact, is infinitesimally low, and reported cases much more likely to derive from *anal* rather than vaginal intercourse.

Another main point in Fumento's article concerns tertiary transmission. Primary transmission is to a member of a high-risk group—male homosexual, bisexual, IV drug user, hemophiliac. Secondary occurs when a primarily infected person passes it on heterosexually to a member of a non-high-risk group; most secondary recipients are steady female partners of male IV drug users. Tertiary transmission then occurs when a secondary recipient passes it on to another heterosexual.

If this transmission occurred in significant numbers, it would portend an epidemic for heterosexuals. But, significantly, this has *not* been happening. Heterosexual cases, female partners of IV drug users, began showing up in 1981. If tertiary transmission had been occurring, it would long before now have cut a wide swath through the heterosexual population. But that has not occurred.

What has happened here is yet another episode in the politics of homosexuality. Gay activists here are not only defending a persecuted minority, but actively promoting a viewpoint which seriously misleads the majority population. They do this in their effort to destigmatize the plague as the primarily homosexual disease which it is. This effort connects with politicized gays in their various other activities which generally have the function (and purpose) of "normalizing" homosexuality. That effort has not been entirely successful, but has however made substantial inroads into the "conventional wisdom" of the population, particularly that part of it considering themselves "liberal."

One effect of AIDS on homosexual politics comes from the fact that in the earlier stages of public consciousness of this disease, that is late 1970s and early 1980s, gay groups like the Gay Men's Health Crisis were at the forefront of new developments. They particularly worked, with some success, for changing sexual behavior patterns of gay men, to reduce risks. They claim to have caused a very substantial reduction of the more usual venereal diseases, syphilis and gonorhhea, among the gay male population. And they have been at the forefront of the fight against AIDS. One of their concerns has been to promote "safe sex," to try to counter the prevalent, and inevitably very risky, sexual patterns pervasive in the gay male population. These patterns involve promiscuous pursuit of endless sexual encounters with an endless number of partners; high levels of cruising, or casual sexual pickups; and adventurousness in perverse sexual behavior, much of it anal, that is bound to be "riskier sex." The gay activists here were in effect caught in a bind: they want to combat "risky sex." But they do not want to perpetuate public images of male homosexuals as irresponsible promiscuous sexual adventurers. They want instead to present an image of entirely "normal" devoted couples in stable marriages very similar to their heterosexual counterparts. That image in turn was belied, at least as of about 1970, by the Bell-Weinberg research (see earlier in this chapter) which found that only 14% of the gay males were then, *currently* in a "close-coupled" relationship. That study showed that for the majority of the gay male population, promiscuity was rife, with hundreds of different sexual partners per year. At the same time, the Gay Men's Health Crisis wanted to confront the gay population with the dangers of promiscuous sex. That required the GMHC to take a public stand on this issue, even at the very real risk of confirming the "prejudiced" straight world's negative images. These politicized homosexuals claim they have been very successful in changing the sexual behavior of most gay males, although contradictory findings are now appearing about this claim.

In one ethnographic study of a current gay community, the sociologist Martin Levine (1988) reports that since about 1980 there have been substantial changes in gay male sexual patterns, away from risky recreational sex to less risky relational sex. He says that the prevailing patterns of sexual behavior of gay males of the 1970s and earlier have been largely abandoned. He is referring to the multiple partners, the intense cruising for anonymous partners, the quest for ever more perverse variations, including prominently sado-masochistic anal sex. The AIDS danger, Levine claims, has transformed all that behavior. Patronage of gay baths is considered out of bounds. Even that of gay bars is much reduced. The new norm is to establish a long-term monogamous relationship, with emphasis on *relationship,* not on sex.

It is important to note the word "norm," here. These may well be the new norms, as Levine claims, that is the conceptions shared in a particular community about how people *should* behave. But does that correspond to the reality of the actual behavior?

Levine in that paper does not present any statistical data. It is essentially a report on his own participant-observation impressions of that particular gay scene.

By contrast, a quantitatively organized report, by Karolynn Siegel (1987), indicates that of the gay males in a systematically chosen sample, a substantial proportion of them report a preponderance of sexual behavior that is definitely risky, including multiple partners, and anal sex without condoms. (Paper presented to the American Society of Clinical Oncology, May 1987.)

If Siegel's is a more accurate appraisal of current, late 1980s, gay male sexual behavior, than Levine's, then what this amounts to is many gay males in effect playing Russian roulette with sex. Surely by now knowledge about AIDS is readily available, especially in the gay population. Though of course these findings may not be generalizable to the whole male gay population, they do fit with what had been commonly reported earlier, in countless studies by social and psychological scientists of all ideological persuasions. It especially confirms what came out of clinical studies: a suicidal recklessness as one pattern of masochistic and counterphobic behavior. That such promiscuity endangers not only the individual himself, but also all partners, indicates the masochism here is part of a *sado*-masochistic pattern.

There are also some notorious individual cases, not clear how isolated, such as that of a gay male prostitute, infected with the HIV virus, who knowingly and deliberately exposed a whole succession of partners, without their knowledge, to infection from him, and who also donated blood to a blood bank (*Newsday,* 6/30/87, p. 5). Surely an extreme of sadomasochistic defiance.

Summary Consideration of Homosexuality, from Sociological, Anthropological and Psychoanalytic Viewpoints

Discussions of homosexual orientation became enlivened by issues raised by a politico-social movement styling itself gay liberation. That movement set out to challenge and overturn negative conceptions and responses about homosexuality and homosexuals, in social mores, in the law, in religion, in the military, in scholarship of various kinds, in social practice and social policy regarding occupations, housing, law enforcement, and in therapeutic treatment. They want to portray as irrational prejudice the negative views of homosexuality coming from these various sources.

Sociologically we have to recognize this form of sexual orientation as deviant in the sociological sense, that is, as going against the norms of the society. Most of the members of the society regard it as wrong or abnormal in some sense. That sense ranges from unnatural, to immoral, to sinful, to criminal, to psychologically sick. Civil libertarians take it that, whatever one's personal feelings toward homosexuality, no harm is inflicted on others by private consensual adult homosexual acts, therefore agree with rescinding laws criminalizing such acts, as has been done by many of the United States and several other modern Western nations. Law still interdicts homosexual rape or infliction of sex upon minors.

Informally social attitudes toward homosexuals have possibly moved some, though not much, toward a more tolerant live-and-let-live attitude. This may be so at least where people are expected to display an up-to-date emancipated response. Still public opinion polls and polls of particular segments, e.g. college students, continue to show largely negative attitudes. Social scientists, especially sociologists, are mostly with gay liberation, and largely out of line with the public at large.

The gay movement locates its "enemies" in conservative clerics, politicians and judges, and some therapy professionals, especially classical psychoanalysts, who see homosexuality as usually associated with some kind of pathology. Other therapists are more divided on the issue of sickness.

The largest-scale sociological study—Bell-Weinberg-Hammersmith—demonstrates lower "psychological adjustment" in the homosexuals than in the comparison heterosexuals, and life-history antecedents of the homosexuals rather in line with psychoanalytic formulations. On both counts the researchers try to deny the meaning of their own findings.

Anthropological and historical evidence indicates a variety of patterns regarding both the appearance and prevalence of homosexual conduct, and normative attitudes toward it, in different societies. The one firm generalization is that in *none* of the tribal or complex societies studied, is exclusive homosexuality unambiguously approved. Exclusive homosexuality continues to be extremely rare in most of the societies surveyed, though homosexual conduct alongside heterosexual does appear in many societies, while homosexuality appears to be entirely absent in a few.

Two forms of institutionalized homosexuality appear, each in a number of societies (never both in the same society): 1) a gender-crossing role, with associated homosexual practices; 2) a stage-specific ritualized homosexuality for all males in initiation. In 1), commonly called *berdache* in native North America (other terms elsewhere) a male adopts female clothing and occupations, is regarded as a man-woman, is allowed homosexual practice. Others' reactions are embarrassment, discomfort and attribution of supernatural causation. There are very few in any one tribe. A few societies have a corresponding role for a female.

2) The other form of institutionalized homosexuality involves *all* of the adolescent males in the initiations, and is followed by heterosexual marriage, with norms against continuation of homosexual practice in adulthood, and great condemnation of exclusive homosexuality in an adult. (No corresponding institution for females.) It is felt as anti-female, kept secret from females. Arranged heterosexual marriages tend to be loveless and with limited sexual contact. One tribe with such an institution is re-

ported to have "very low female fertility rates," possibly an indication that survival of the society by heterosexual reproduction is jeopardized by the homosexual institution. In these tribes the male becomes a fierce warrior, in no way like the Western "homosexual."

Otherwise, male homosexuality appears in part of the population in many societies at many periods of history, sometimes tolerated in certain elite quarters, but seldom generally approved by the whole population. Extent of and normative attitudes toward homosexuality seem to have waxed and waned over the centuries, with no one consistent trend. Many societies, (e.g., circum-Mediterranean) regard adult males taking the insertor role toward younger passive males, as well as having sex with women, as being masculine men, in no way demeaned by the man-boy contact; while an adult male who is being penetrated is considered homosexual and despised. "Real men fuck women and boys."

Female homosexuality is either much rarer, or simply less noticed and recorded, as being of little importance, and/or as no threat to reproductive conduct, the societies concerned all being male-dominated.

Prostitution

It is appropriate to discuss homosexuality and prostitution side by side. Both are forms of sexual deviance of some prevalence in modern society. Both are seen as immoral, degrading, disgusting, sinful, and variably, against the law. Both have been proscribed in Western culture since Biblical times. The two are curiously linked, linguistically, by the word *gay*. In English, that is now a widely used term for homosexual (more specifically the *male* homosexual—lesbians are not fond of having the term applied to them). "Gay" used to be applied (nineteenth century and probably earlier) to female prostitutes, or promiscuous women generally (see LaBarre 1982).

Prostitution has been called "the oldest profession." This is incorrect. Shamanism is.[6] But prostitution has been so persistent in "civilized" societies all through historical time, that it has been mistakenly thought to be the oldest profession. There is endless and insoluble debate about the line to be drawn between prostitution and easy sexual availability on a basis without commitment or intimacy. The latter characteristics, incidentally, fit a great deal of male homosexuality, as already discussed.

There are sociological studies and analyses, and psychoanalytic and psychological ones regarding prostitution as a form of sexual deviation. These two sets can be put side by side and integrated.

Sociological Studies: Kingsley Davis

Years ago, Kingsley Davis (1937) set forth a distinction among three kinds of question that can be raised about prostitution:
1) How do we account for the *institution* of prostitution?
2) How do we account for variations in the *amount* of prostitution?
3) How do we account for why specific *persons* (or specific *types* of person) enter the profession? (Davis 1937)

Answers to the third question, why particular women become prostitutes, would not provide an answer to the first question, of why the institution of prostitution exists.

Sociological analysis is addressed to the first and second question. Regarding the first, Davis's basic proposition is that the institution of prostitution fulfills certain sociological functions not fulfilled by other institutions, especially not the official institution in which sexual contact is legitimately allowed (in fact, prescribed) i.e. marriage, and the associated institution of the family.

Davis argues that prostitution exists because there is a demand for impersonal sex without commitment and without intimacy, precisely the features of prostitution that make it immoral in the eyes of respectable society. Prostitution is not simply sex used for an ulterior purpose. That would include most wives as well, getting economic support and various other advantages from being married. Rather it is sex used for an ulterior purpose, money, in a context lacking institutional approval such as the purpose of procreation, and lacking the *Gemeinschaft* situation such as provided in marriage and the family. Also, the "ulterior purpose" includes the satisfaction of perverse desires and tastes on the part of the customer, which he thinks he could not ask of his wife; the "craving for variety; for mysterious and provocative surroundings; and for sexual intercourse free from entangling cares and civilized pretense."

Prostitution also provides sexual outlet for men so physically repulsive, old, ugly, or deformed, as to be unable to get sex on a voluntary basis from a willing woman. So long, therefore, as there is a scale of physical attractiveness in the world, so long will the demand continue, for commercial sex. Even in a society with freely available recreational sex, there will still be the dilemma that one sexually desires a particular partner who does not reciprocate that desire. Then the resulting frustration could lead to the recourse to force or fraud, or use of money reward, thus back to prostitution. Though such a situation of universally available recreational sex might reduce the demand for prostitution, it could not eliminate it entirely. "Free sex" would also reduce the scope of marraige and the family institutions. So we can say, sociologically, that prostitution is not the enemy of marriage and the family; rather free recreational sex is the enemy of both the family and of prostitution. But it is unlikely it could ever abolish either.

Note that Davis's paper was published in 1937, a half-century ago. It is still cited in any sociological discussion of prostitution today. Does it still hold up? Certainly the greater freedom of sex purely for pleasure, without entanglements and without commercial contract, has become a reality in the Western world, with the near-universal availability of fairly reliable contraception. Has the predicted resulting decline of prostitution come about? As with other sexual deviations, reliable statistics are hard to come by, and efforts to estimate the number of working prostitutes are just that, guesses. But this much can be said: prostitution is still very much with us. Of course the other conditions Davis stipulates continue to persist, that there are still some unattractive people, and it is impossible that all sexual attractions will be reciprocated. And even "free" sex with a willing partner, can still make either partner (or both) feel there is *some* entanglement, that it is not entirely without a degree of emotional commitment. The need for such emotional involvement is still there in some of the participants, even where they start out with a definition of their relationship as involving no commitment or obligation.

Of course some other societies show how a kind of sexual free-for-all can exist, alongside of marriage, and without prostitution. The Mohave Indians—see Devereux 1939, 1950—have such a system. People have sex with anyone they want who is momentarily willing. If one desired partner is not willing, another will be. With ready availability of *some* desired partner, there is no over-valuation or idealization of any particular person, nor of love itself, and certainly no romantic love. There is no commercial prostitution, but there *is* marriage and family, which coexist with the abundance of recreational sex before and outside of marriage. Lack of prostitution makes the Mohave like nearly all other tribal societies. Prostitution entered such societies only with contact with people of the "higher" civilizations, and conditions of breakdown of ancestral tribal culture.

One of Davis's main points is to reject any *economic* explanation of prostitution. Poor economic conditions may explain why any particular girl enters prostitution, but not the existence of the institution. You might just as well say "economics" explains the existence of business enterprise. Prostitution *is* a business enterprise. In any society with pecuniary relationships—certainly ours qualifies—sexual contact *can* be put into a pecuniary context. We need to specify, then, the conditions under which it does, and Davis does so explain. Where there is a demand of a certain type, and the resources to back up the demand, the supply will be forthcoming.

Psychological Studies: Jackman, O'Toole, Geis

Norman Jackman, Richard O'Toole and Gilbert Geis (1963) wrote on "The Self-Image of the Prostitute." This paper provides answers to question 3), why does a particular woman enter the profession? They find that the prostitutes interviewed had been isolated in the urban environment; the greater such isolation, the more likely they are to define as acceptable, patterns of behavior condemned by general social values. They know their conduct is condemned, but easily find rationalizations. Most were alienated from one or both parents. The rationalizations they employ for their violation of generally accepted social values (which they share) include these: everyone is rotten and corrupt anyway; I am no worse; at least I am not hypocritical about it. Society does not really scorn prostitutes; they only pretend to. We have plenty of customers, don't we? We make plenty of money. I couldn't make this kind of money in any legitimate job I could get—work long hours as a waitress? or a domestic? or in a factory? This way I can support my child (or husband, or other relatives.) Some claim to be good respectable persons, or believe other women envy their luxuries and personal freedom.

They have two main types of reference group: a) The criminal contraculture—they associate with other kinds of lawbreakers and with bohemians, and have a solidarity with those-outside-the law. These women have contempt for the conventional world, whom they see as dull, frightened and hypocritical, while they admire big money, however made, and the trappings of luxury.

b) Dual worlds—this kind of prostitute keeps her professional life segregated from a respectable personal life, of husband and children, whom she claims to be supporting. She sees herself as in, but not of, the world of prostitution, and disidentifies with and holds in contempt the criminal and freewheeling characters that the type A hookers associate with willingly and enthusiastically. She can disidentify with the act of selling her body sexually, depersonalizing the experience: "it's not me who's doing this." Some of these give financial help to parents and other relatives, in addition to husband and children. They think they are good mothers to their children (though aside from weekends, they spend little time with them.)

Still another type identifies with neither the criminal world (though in contact with it) nor with the dual world. Rather they are essentially alienated; they feel normless, apathetic, empty, lacking direction, goals, or meaning in life, or real ties to anyone of either sex, and entirely dissociated from the sexual activity with their clients.

These were generally low-status prostitutes, from low socio-economic backgrounds. Psychologically such a woman shows great underlying anxiety, and poor emotional contact with anyone. She dissociates from and depersonalizes sex. She feels empty and worthless. She elaborately deludes herself; and exonerates herself with rationalizations and neutralizations.

She may come from a background of poverty, but that does not explain her entrance into this profession: most women in poverty do not resort to prostitution, and some from comfortable or even affluent economic circumstances do.

Psychoanalytic Studies: Freud, Glover, Greenwald

Glover (1945) wrote of the *Psychopathology of the Prostitute.* There is also psychoanalytic work from both sides of the relationship between the prostitute and the man who seeks her out. Freud (1910) wrote of "A Special Type of Object Choice by Men," referring to men who can be sexually potent only with a degraded woman; a prostitute will fit that role well. He also explored (1912) a "Universal tendency toward debasement in the sphere of love," which can apply to either sex, where debasement is required. The intrapsychic situation is one where the person cannot fuse tenderness and sex.

Greenwald's Call Girl

The psychoanalyst Harold Greenwald published a study of high-money prostitutes, *The Call Girl* (1958; later edition *The Elegant Prostitute,* 1970). He studied intensively 20 such women, some of whom were in psychoanalytic therapy with him. He found etiological backgrounds such as the following: Commonly the woman came from a "broken home." In some cases the mother had married several times. The children were regarded by the mother as a burden. This girl herself was definitely rejected by the mother, and abandoned by the father. Sometimes she was also seduced at an early age by a stepfather. She was typically early rewarded for sexual favors by an older man or boy, like a stepfather, foster father, grandfather, or stepbrother, and sworn to secrecy about the experience. Now as an adult she shows great hostility toward both parents. She has intense underlying anxiety, covered by a facade of toughness, "cool," suaveness, sophistication.

She is typically confused about her sexual identity. In some instances, she gets her most intense satisfactions from sexual relations with other women. These may be arrests in development, or regressions to preoedipal stages. Frequently, the dynamics and/or the etiology, are similar to those of many female homosexuals. She shows damaged reality-adaptation, in spite of a superficial hard-headedness about the world, marked by a great deal of wishful thinking. Her interpersonal relations are generally inadequate. The strongest relationship she has may be to the pimp. Symbolically, the money she gives him, often a substantial part of her earnings, is "thrown away" at him, in effect a gesture of contempt.

She shows a kind of "pseudoconformity" to the conventional world; she loves conventional status symbols like Cadillacs, minks, a fancy address, being seen at famous nightclubs, dropping hints of famous entertainers as clients. Economic need was not evidently an important predisposing factor; she was most likely to come from a middle or upper middle class childhood home. Many in fact had, currently, other possible sources of income.

An underlying intense feeling of isolation and worthlessness pervades her life. She uses defenses such as: displacement (especially of incestuous wishes); projection ("respectable society is just as bad; they're just a sham"); denial (e.g. of homosexual feelings); and introjection (of "bad objects", as in suicide attempts—frequent among these women.)

Other Studies

A number of other studies have been made by sociologists or social psychologists. (See Winick and Kinsie 1971; and many years ago, a classic study by Reckless called *Vice in Chicago*—1933.) There are some memoirs from prostitutes themselves (e.g. Xaviera Hollander 1972; and a number of different prostitutes, some identified, some anonymous, telling their own stories in a collection of deviants' self-reports, as in McCaghy *et al.* 1968.) Some present ethnographic observations, or these combined with self-reports. Their findings tend to be consistent with those of Jackman *et al.* and Greenwald. Most belie the common assumption that a particular girl goes into prostitution primarily for economic motives or in response to economic deprivation. However the availability of what appears to the girl to be "good money" may well be a prominent rationalization for continuing in such work. They all show self-delusions and rationalizations of the kinds described, signalizing that the women concerned are not unaffected by the prevailing norms on this issue. Many in their "tough" stance rail against the "hypocrisy of conventional people," claiming for themselves greater honesty. Many proclaim that they are offering a much needed "service" to the public, and morality be damned.

Goldman's Psychoanalytic-Sociological Essay

Marion S. Goldman (1988) in a significant recent essay, attempts a combination of sociological and psychodynamic analyses. Goldman deals primarily with the question why particular women become prostitutes, and why particular men become customers. For the prostitute two kinds of precondition must be present, one external, the other internal. The external derives from social structure and culture. Here Goldman basically follows a feminist line, arguing that the conditions are patriarchal control, a system of sexual exchange, and family structure where mothering is carried on almost entirely by women.

On that last point Goldman has a problem. No society exists in the world where it is *not* true that infant and early childhood care is entirely or primarily in the hands of women (compare Chodorow 1978). Many of the societies that do have female mothering do *not* have prostitution, namely most tribal societies. Therefore we simply cannot adduce female mothering as an external condition for prostitution.

Sexual exchange, says Goldman, is built into our system; women must exchange their sexual favors for support as wife, mistress, or ambitious career woman, since males are the gatekeepers. Sexual exchange systems inevitably (to Goldman as to other feminist thinkers) involve male power over females, so that it is always the female who is the provider of the sexual services, the male who is the buyer.

The foremost external condition for a woman becoming a prostitute is poverty. Goldman comes back to that again and again, citing numerous sociological and journalistic accounts. Still she recognizes that poverty alone is not sufficient, that there must be internal, psychological factors. As I have pointed out above, many poor women do not turn to prostitution, and some well-off women do.

The motivational dynamics Goldman adduces are essentially those presented by Greenwald's study. They are rooted mainly in *pre*-oedipal experience: a depriving, non-nurturant mother provokes lifelong rage. The girl does not develop a whole, intact sense of self. Commonly the little girl learns early to exchange her sexual favors for material considerations from a father, stepfather, other male relative. This happens as early as before the age of six. Elements of exchange, male power and secrecy appear in these contacts, repeated in the later prostitution.

For the male customers, Goldman draws on Freud (1910, 1912). The boy in the oedipal period must renounce mother as a sexual object. If that renunciation remains incomplete, he continues in later life idealizing one kind of woman, like his mother, for whom he has affection, but seeks sexual pleasure with another kind, prostitutes and other degraded women. Adding to the attractiveness of the "fast" woman is the implied presence of countless other men who also enjoy her favors. These represent symbolic fathers.

Another factor is that in the narcissistic male, the father was distant, removed, relatively inconsequential, while mother was the main household power, swinging between seduction and anger toward the boy; the boy flees such intimacy, splits maternity from sexuality, good women from bad. This outlook ties in with the wish for perversions in the sexual contact with the prostitute.

Even in a present-day atmosphere of freely available sex with willing partners, many young men prefer going to prostitutes, to avoid "involvement," commitment, and intimacy.

One factor in the customer demand is the alleged or assumed biologically stronger sexual need of males compared to females. Goldman questions any biological basis for this claim. It is, however, asserted as a human universal by such scholars as Donald Symons, *The Evolution of Human Sexuality,* (1979) and from there taken up by anthropologists such as Thomas Gregor (1985). Gregor finds it taken for granted by the tribalists of the Mehinaku, as is reported also for many other societies. Gregor believes that this *is* universally true, and on a biological basis. Goldman points out that what is important here is that in our society, men *believe* that this is so.

Significance of Sociological and Psychological Studies

The import of all of these studies is that while there are general sociological conditions conducive to the existence of prostitution as an institution, what leads particular women into the trade is much more likely to be idiosyncratically psychological, in a variety of ways. And what leads particular men to patronize the prostitutes, is also likely to come from an idiosyncratic misdevelopment of sexuality from the oedipal stage.

For the women, the family histories are diverse, but very commonly include disruption and turmoil, brutality by parents toward this daughter and/or toward each other; early induction into sex by male relatives, with some kind of material reward; early promiscuity, often with pathetic quest for acceptance and "love."

In many cases but not all, there is predatory control by a pimp, to whom the prostitute submits in a craven manner that must appear pathological to outsiders. Something like the dynamics that Greenwald describes of his fancy hookers with their pimps, may be the common psychology of these enslaved relationships.

The social and legal setting has vacillated from one locale or country to another, and from one time to another, with no consistent pattern. Periodically there are efforts at a "humane" transformation by decriminalizing prostitution, trying to put it all under some kind of legitimate control, attempting in the process to reduce the spread of venereal diseases. Then these high-minded changes are abandoned, and an older largely corrupt system returns. Locally in a limited time period, there can be a burst of crackdowns on the "houses," with multiple arrests and crackdown on "corrupt" police and other officials, a widespread closing down of houses, to be followed not much later (perhaps a matter of months), by the re-opening of the houses under different managements and with scrambled personnel. Soon we find "business as usual." (See Reckless 1933 for description and analysis of such a cycle in Chicago in a period of the 1920s; the basic theme is: plus ça change. . .)

Most discussions of prostitution deal with the *female* prostitute. Another topic is *male* prostitutes. Of the heterosexuals of these, the more enterprising find rich women to escort and service—"gigolos"—probably more common in Europe than America. Homosexual male prostitutes range from expensive companions to street boys. These last are probably the most despised of the prostitution world, combining the stigmas of poverty and both homosexuality and prostitution.

Summary Notes on Homosexuality and Prostitution

Both homosexuality and prostitution have their subcultures, combined in the case of homosexual prostitution. The psychological characteristics of the individual participants do not explain the *existence* of the subculture, but may in particular instances provide a particular coloring to the features of the subculture. For example, the psychological characteristics of a certain type of male homosexual may infuse a particular gay subculture. An instance would be a very campy scene, which reflects extreme self-depreciation, in effect self-hatred, as well as hatred of women. This attitude is presented in an ironic manner amusing to the participants. The ambiance and behavior suggest heavy defenses against an underlying despair such as additionally revealed in high rates of both suicide and suicide attempts. The psychological features in turn are not totally explainable in terms of intrapsychic dynamics—though these dynamics are one essential aspect. The psychology has to be looked at also in terms of interactions between the stigmatized outsiders and the conventional society.

There is a modicum of truth to the allegation of homophile supporters that if some of the gays are "sick" it is because of oppression by straight society. The point of the psychoanalytic observers is that they could not be the whole story, considering how tormented many homosexuals are even in the most benign and compassionate immediate environment. The psychoanalysts would also note that studies including data on the early childhood of these individuals show evidence of pathology from very early childhood, long before the influence of stigma from the larger society is likely to have been experienced.

The same for the prostitutes: those who are suffering from a chronic despair and alienation, covered only thinly by a brave and tough veneer, are not in that situation solely by the oppression of conventional society. They were already troubled human beings before they got heavily involved in "the life."

Notes

1. "Deviant," they say sounds too pejorative; it sounds as though the social scientist is agreeing with the negative value judgment made by others in the population. By contrast, "variant" would sound more value-neutral. Making such a change of course would be futile, and a recourse to word-magic. "Deviant" was introduced by sociologists in the first place, in order to *be* value-neutral, in place of referring to the behavior as sinful, immoral, disgusting, abominable, and the like. If the proponents of "variant" get their way, that word too will come to be regarded by the embattled minority as implying a negative value judgment, and will have to be replaced. How about "wonderful dissenters?" Compare the peculiarity of the word "gay" for homosexual. (See Weston LaBarre 1982, under the pseudonym Urson Cawqua.)

2. On the indigenous population of the Americas, pre-European conquest, Julian H. Steward writes:
"The first European contact had devastating effects on the numbers of Indians, bringing a sharp decline everywhere and *rapid extinction* in some areas. [Emphasis mine—RE] During the first two centuries after the Conquest, the total number was at least halved. Many factors were involved in the decline . . . Epidemics . . . [e.g. of small pox] . . . Warfare . . . Lack of fertility . . . seemingly a symptom of cultural disequilibrium . . ." (Steward 1945, p. 191) Similar things happened in other parts of the tribal world overrun by members of large-scale and technologically much more advanced societies. A tragic case is that of the aborigines of Tasmania, a small island south of the main island of Australia, who in the nineteenth century were killed by the British settlers, and became extinct. (See Kroeber 1948: 764) In other areas, for example New Guinea, indigenous intertribal developments, like competition for ecological niches, have led to "the dwindling of population [in particular tribes, which] undoubtedly placed groups in danger of displacement, *extermination* or absorption" (Keesing 1982: 19. My emphasis). Throughout Melanesia contact frequently brought breakdown of indigenous culture patterns, leading to demoralization and drastically lowered fertility; in many cases tribes dwindled in population below the replacement level, and small numbers of survivors became absorbed into other tribes. (Róheim 1950: 242–3). In the same work, Róheim refers to greatly reduced family size to the point of danger of lack of replacement) in the peasantry in a section of Hungary in his youth (*ibid* pp. 370ff).

3. However, note that the Marind-Anim high sterility rate was also attributed to chronic vaginal and secondary pelvic infection, in turn attributed to a custom of *otiv-bombari,* the serial heterosexual intercourse by many men with one or two young women, submission being mandatory for all young women. Van Baal also refers to this process (1966, p. 818). In fact this deficiency was so extreme that reproduction in the Marind-Anim fell to below replacement level, and this was compensated for by capturing children from other tribes. See discussion in Knauft 1987.

4. A barbarous neologism: if translated directly from its Greek roots, it would mean "irrational fear of the same [sex, presumably]" where as they are trying to say, "irrational fear of [and hostility toward] homosexuals" which would have to be "homo-eroto-phobia" probably too difficult for the masses intended to be influenced—one wag suggested, "how about fag-o-phobia?" Along with other elements of gay-liberation mystification, which all good liberals must accept, this barbarism seems to be here to stay, and has already become part of psychological and social science literature. A doctoral candidate in psychology has written a thesis comparing degree of "homophobia" in different Puerto Rican youths—as though this were an established clinical syndrome. It is also by now an established part of "with it" journalism. *Peccato.*

5. Williams's recent study of berdache (1986), (not yet published at the time I completed my Overview Essay [1986]) is written from a gay-liberation viewpoint using the author's open homosexual orientation to advantage in interviewing a great many contemporary Amerindian homosexuals most of whom he seems to consider as berdaches. (I question that designation.) Williams challenges much of conventional anthropological wisdom on berdaches, especially the view that the role as an *institutionalized role* has largely disappeared under the impact of acculturation and domination by whites with a prevalently anti-homosexual view. He denies that there is anything negative in other tribalists' attitudes toward the berdache or toward male homosexual behavior in general. Although he makes no estimate about numbers, his whole discussion implies it is widespread. Much of his account seems heavily vitiated by special interest.

6. Judging by archaeological evidence, the oldest profession is *shamanism,* antedating prostitution by hundreds of millenia, in fact being probably as old as human culture. The shaman is an amalgam of doctor, priest and psychoanalyst: healer of human ills of the body or soul; found in tribal societies of Old Stone Age culture. The shaman is the first of any kind of full-time specialist occupation. (All men hunted, all women gathered.) For the psychology of shamanism, see Chapter 5.

Prostitution appears much much later, essentially at the beginnings of civilization, with an agricultural base, complex division of labor, urban centers, trade and some money economy. Present in most such civilized societies ever since, it got to be called "the oldest profession."

REFERENCES

Bell, Alan P., and Martin Weinberg. 1978. *Homosexualities: A Study of Diversity among Men and Women.* New York: Simon and Schuster

Bell, Alan P., and Sue Kiefer Hammersmith. 1981. *Sexual Preference: Its Development in Men and Women.* Bloomington, IN: Indiana University Press; an Official Publication of the Alfred C. Kinsey Institute for Sex Research. 2 vols.

Bergler, Edmund. 1956. *Homosexuality: Disease or Way of Life?* New York: Hill and Wang

Bieber, Irving *et al.* 1962. *Homosexuality: A Psychoanalytic Study.* New York: Basic Books

Broude, G. J., and S. Greene. 1976. "Cross-Cultural Codes on Twenty Sexual Attitudes and Practices." *Ethnology* 15:409ff

Chodorow, Nancy. 1978. *The Reproduction of Mothering.* Berkeley: University of California Press

Cory, Donald Webster. 1951. *The Homosexual in America.* New York: Greenberg

Davis, Kingsley. 1937. "The Sociology of Prostitution." *American Sociological Review.* 2: 744–755

Devereux, George. 1939. "Mohave Culture and Personality." *Character and Personality.* 8: 91–109

__________. 1950. "Heterosexual Behavior of the Mohave Indians." in G. Róheim, ed. *Psychoanalysis and the Social Sciences.* 2:85–108

Eisenbud, Ruth-Jean. 1969. "Female Homosexuality: A Sweet Enfranchisement." in G. Goldman and D. Milman, eds. *Modern Woman.* Springfield, IL: C. C. Thomas, 247–268

__________. 1982. "Early and Later Determinants of Lesbian Object Choice." *Psychoanalytic Review.* 69:1:85–109

Endleman, Robert. 1981. *Psyche and Society: Explorations in Psychoanalytic Sociology.* New York: Columbia University Press. Chs. 11–14

__________. 1984. "New Light on Deviance and Psychopathology?: The Case of **Homosexualities** and **Sexual Preference.** *Journal of Psychoanalytic Anthropology.* 7:75–100

__________ 1986. "Overview: Homosexuality in Tribal Societies." *Transcultural Psychiatric Research Review.* 23:187–218

__________ 1988. "Psychoanalytic Sociology and the Sociology of Deviance." in J. Rabow *et al. Advances in Psychoanalytic Sociology.* Malabar, FL: Krieger. 163–186

Erikson, Erik H. 1959. "Identity and the Life Cycle." *Psychological Issues.* No. 1.

Ford, Clellan, and Frank Beach. 1951. *Patterns of Sexual Behavior.* New York: Harper

Freud, Sigmund. 1905. "Three Essays on a Theory of Sexuality." *Standard Edition.* Vol.7, 1953. London: Hogarth

__________. 1910. "A Special Type of Object Choice by Men." *Standard Edition* 11: London: Hogarth, 1957: 163–177

__________. 1912. "The Universal Tendency toward Debasement in the Sphere of Love." *Standard Edition* 11: London: Hogarth, 1957: 177–191

Fumento, Michael A. 1987. "AIDS: Are Heterosexuals at Risk?" *Commentary,* 84: 5: 21–27

Gagnon, John, and William Simon, eds. 1967. *Sexual Deviance.* New York: Harper

Gallup Poll. 12/12/85

Glover, Edward G. 1945. *The Psychopathology of Prostitution* London: Institute for the Scientific Treatment of Delinquency

Goldman, Marion S. 1988. "Prostitution, Economic Exchange, and the Unconscious." in Jerome Rabow *et al. Advances in Psychoanalytic Sociology.* Malabar, FL: Krieger. 197–209

Greenwald, Harold. 1958. *The Call Girl.* New York: Ballantine. (Later edition, *The Elegant Prostitute.* New York: Walker, 1970)

Gregor, Thomas. 1985. *Anxious Pleasures: The Sexual Lives of an Amazonian People.* Chicago: University of Chicago Press

Hacker, Helen Mayer. 1971. "Homosexuals: Deviant or Minority Group?" in E. Sagarin, ed. *The Other Minorities.* Waltham, MA: Ginn: 63–92

Hatterer, Lawrence. 1971. *Changing Homosexuality in the Male.* New York: Dell

Henican, Ellis. "AIDS Carrier Who Sold Blood Charged with Attempted Murder." *Newsday,* 6/30/87, p.5

Herdt, Gilbert. 1981. *Guardians of the Flutes.* New York: McGraw-Hill

———, ed. 1982. *Rituals of Manhood: Male Initiation in Papua New Guinea.* Berkeley, CA: University of California Press

———, ed. 1984. *Ritualized Homosexuality in Melanesia.* Berkeley, CA: University of California Press

Hite, C. 1974a. "APA Rules Homosexuality not necessarily a Disorder." *Psychiatric News* 9:1

———. 1974b. "Members Uphold DSM-II Change." *Psychiatric News.* 9:9

Hoffman, Martin. 1968. *The Gay World* New York: Basic Books

Hollander, Xaviera. 1972. *The Happy Hooker* New York: Dell

Hooker, Evelyn. 1957. "The Adjustment of the Male Overt Homosexual." *Journal of Projective Techniques.* 21:18–31.

———. 1967. "The Homosexual Community." in Gagnon and Simon, eds. 1967: 167–184

Jackman, Norman R., Richard O'Toole, and Gilbert Geis. 1963. "The Self-Image of the Prostitute." *Sociological Quarterly.* 4:150–156

Karlen, Arno. 1971. *Sexuality and Homosexuality.* New York: Norton

Keesing, Roger. 1982. "Introduction." G. Herdt, ed. *Rituals of Manhood.* Berkeley, CA: University of California Press. 1–43

Kendell, R.E. 1983. "DSM-III: A Major Advance in Psychiatric Nosology." In: R. L. Spitzer *et al. International Perspectives on DSM-III.* Washington: American Psychiatric Press

Kinsey, Alfred, W. B. Pomeroy, and Clyde Martin. 1948. *Sexual Behavior in the Human Male.* Philadelphia: Saunders

———. 1953. *Sexual Behavior in the Human Female.* Philadelphia: Saunders

Knauft, Bruce M. 1985. *Good Company and Violence: Sorcery and Social Action in a Lowland New Guinea Society.* Berkeley, CA: University of California Press.

———. 1987. "Homosexuality in Melanesia: Review Essay." *Journal of Psychoanalytic Anthropology* 10:2:155–191

Kroeber, Alfred L. 1948. *Anthropology.* New York: Harcourt, Brace

LaBarre, Weston (under pseudonym Urson Cawqua). 1982. "Two Etymons and a Query: Gay, Fairies, Camping." *Maledicta* 6:224–230

Langness, L. L. 1967. "Sexual Antagonism in the New Guinea Highlands: a Bena-Bena Example. *Oceania* 37:161–177

Levine, Martin. 1988. "Restructuring Gay Eroticism: Changing Patterns of Sexuality Among Clones." Paper presented at Meetings of the American Sociological Association, Atlanta. August

Leznoff, Maurice, and William Wesley. 1956. "The Homosexual Community." *Social Problems* 3:257–263

Marmor, Judd, ed. 1965. *Sexual Inversion.* New York: Basic Books

Marshall, Donald S. 1971. "Sexual Behavior on Mangaia (Polynesia)." in: D. S. Marshall, and R. Suggs, eds. *Human Sexual Behavior: Variations in the Ethnographic Spectrum.* New York: Basic Books

McCaghy, Charles *et al.* eds. 1968. *In Their Own Behalf: Voices from the Margin.* New York: Appleton Century Crofts

Mitchell, Stephen A. 1978. "Psychodynamics, Homosexuality and the Question of Pathology." *Psychiatry* 41: 254–263.

Ovesey, Lionel. 1969. *Homosexuality and Pseudohomosexuality.* New York: Science House

Ovsey, Lionel, and Ethel Person. 1973. "Gender Identity and Sexual Psychopathology in Men: A Psychodynamic Analysis of Homosexuality, Transsexualism and Transvestism." *Journal of American Academy of Psychoanalysis.* 1:53–72

Parin, Paul, Fritz Morgenthaler, and Goldy Parin-Matthèy. 1963. *Die Weissen Denken Zuviel: Psychoanalytische Untersuchunger in Westafrika (Dogon)* (The Whites Think Too Much: Psychoanalytic Investigations in West Africa [Dogon].) Zürich: Atlantis; Munich: Kindler. (French Edition: *Les Blancs Pensent Trop.* Paris: Payot. 1966.)

Reckless, Walter. 1933. *Vice in Chicago.* Chicago: University of Chicago Press. Reprinted 1969. Montclair, NJ: Patterson Smith

Róheim, Géza. 1950. *Psychoanalysis and Anthropology.* New York: International Universities Press

Schafer, Roy. 1974. "Problems in Freud's Psychology of Women." *Jl. of the American Psychoanalytic Association.* 22: 459–485

Schofield, Michael. 1965. *Sociological Aspects of Homosexuality: A Comparative Study of Three Types of Homosexual.* Boston: Little Brown

Siegel, Karolynn. 1987. "Sexual Behavior Patterns of New York Gay Men." Paper presented to Americal Society of Clinical Oncology

Simon, William, and John Gagnon. 1967. "Homosexuality: the Formulation of a Sociological Perspective." *Journal of Health and Social Behavior.* 8:177–185

Socarides, Charles W. 1978. *Homosexuality.* New York: Jason Aronson.

Steward, Julian H. 1945. "The Changing American Indian." in Ralph Linton, ed. *The Science of Man in the World Crisis.* New York: Columbia University Press. 282–305

Stoller, Robert. 1975. *Perversion: The Erotic Form of Hatred.* New York: Random House

Stoller, Robert, and Gilbert Herdt. 1985a. "Theories of Origins of Male Homosexuality: A Cross-Cultural Look." in Stoller, *Observing the Erotic Imagination.* New Haven: Yale University Press. pp. 104–134.

__________. 1985b. "The Development of Masculinity: A Cross-Cultural Contribution." in Stoller, *Presentations of Gender.* New Haven: Yale University Press. pp. 181–199.

__________. 1985c. "Theories of Origins of Male Homosexuality: A Cross-Cultural Look." *Archives of General Psychiatry.* 42: 399–404.

Symons, Donald. 1979. *The Evolution of Human Sexuality.* New York: Oxford University Press

Thompson, Clara. 1949. "Changing Conceptions of Homosexuality in Psychoanalysis." in Patrick Mullahy, ed. *A Study of Interpersonal Relations* New York: Hermitage Press. 211–222

Tripp, C. A. 1975. *The Homosexual Matrix* New York: McGraw-Hill

Van Baal, J. 1966. *Dema.* The Hague: Martinus Nijoff

Vanggard, Thorkil. 1972. *Phallos: A Symbol and its History in the Male World.* New York: International Universities Press

Weinberg, George. 1972. *Society and the Healthy Homosexual.* New York: St. Martin's

Weinberg, Martin, and Colin Williams. 1975. *Male Homosexuals: Their Problems and Adaptations.* New York: Oxford

Whitehead, Harriet. 1981. "The Bow and the Burden Strap: A New Look at Institutionalized Homosexuality in Native North America." in S. Ortner and H. Whitehead, eds. *Sexual Meanings: The Cultural Construction of Gender and Sexuality.* Cambridge: Cambridge University Press.

Wiedeman, George. 1974. "Homosexuality: a Survey." *Journal of the American Psychoanalytic Association.* 22: 651–696

Williams, Walter L. 1986. *The Spirit and the Flesh* (The Berdache in American Indian Cultures). Boston: Beacon Press

Winick, Charles, and Paul Kinsie. 1971. *The Lively Commerce.* Chicago: Quadrangle Press

CHAPTER 4
DRUGS

Use—Universal and Ancient

Use of various chemical substances to alter human psychological states, is very ancient, probably as old as humanity. We find it in the technologically most primitive societies, suggesting it may well have been present at the earliest stages of the emergence, in evolution, of the human species. "There appears to be no human culture so simple in material culture as to lack some sort of mood-altering drug as an escape from the workaday world" (LaBarre 1980, p. 62). In societies with any kind of written records, there is evidence of it from the earliest of such writings.

This is an important elementary point to make, since much of the contemporary i.e. late-twentieth century, discussion assumes drug use is a dilemma only of recent times. Whether it is a "dilemma" at all, is variable from one society or period to another, or from one kind of substance to another. For example, both Hindus and Moslems in India taboo alcohol but regard cannabis usage permissively.

Human beings throughout the world have discovered and used one or more substances that intensify awareness, mitigate pain, produce desired drowsiness, or put one in a special extraordinary state. Such substances can also get one into contact with supranatural forces in the universe, keep a person awake longer than usual or through arduous and unusual tasks, alleviate all manner of medical ailments, or simply make one feel happy.

Brewing beer, traced as one of the features of the Neolithic (New Stone Age) Period, at least 10,000 years ago, is now being adduced as a spur for the beginning of domestication of plants and animals (the criteria of the Neolithic) by two anthropological scholars. Solomon Katz and Mary Voigt (1986) hypothesize that ancient hunter-gatherers could have accidentally discovered that wild wheat and barley soaked in water to make gruel, left in the open air, would be converted by natural yeast to a dark bubbling brew that produces a psychoactive euphoric effect on the drinkers. That brew is also an important nutrient, a source of protein. This discovery of the accidentally produced beer would lead the hunters to try to grow these grains deliberately. This introduced agriculture, with revolutionary effects on future culture. An essential part of the Katz and Voigt argument is that "individuals and societies appear to invest enormous amounts of effort and even risk" in the pursuit of mind-altering foods and beverages. That assumption is very much in line with any present-day studies of the quest for and use of psychoactive substances. Quest for beer, not bread was paramount.

Ancient Sumerians of the fifth century B.C. used opium, referring to it as the "joy plant." Ancient Assyrians knew of the hemp plant, source of cannabis drugs, at least eight centuries before Christ. In India, various types of hemp derivatives have been in use for hundreds, perhaps thousands of years, yielding visions, heightened concentration, and other psychedelic effects. Besides holy men, ordinary people in India have used such drugs for escapist purposes. In the Western hemisphere, Inca priests used psychoactive drugs to get in closer touch with the supernatural powers. Mescaline, acquired from the button of the peyote, has been used sacramentally for many centuries in a great number of American Indian societies. "In Mexico, peyote [lophophora williamsii] was used seasonally in an agricultural-hunting religious festival, preceded by a ritual pilgrimage for the plant" (LaBarre 1969, p. 7).

Alcohol or other drugs have been used to induce special abnormal states. The Viking *berserk* is believed by some specialists to be artificially provoked by eating poisonous mushrooms on the eve of battle (Fabring 1956). Modern gangsters take heroin or cocaine before committing especially audacious crimes. The dangerous assassin sect in Persia consumed hashish. The name is the source of the term assassin.

The hemp plant (*cannabis sativa*), source of marijuana, hashish, bhang, gangha and various other drugs, is mentioned at a date calculated to be 2737 B.C. by the Chinese emperor Shen Neng. In Muslim countries where alcohol use is taboo, hashish is widely used, accounting for a high percentage of Arab worker absenteeism in Egypt and other Arab countries (Masters and Houston 1966).

Drugs considered illegal and dangerous here and now, have been treated differently in other societies. For example, regarding cannabis drugs: "To the Hindu, the hemp plant [cannabis] is holy. A guardian lives in bhang [marijuana] . . . Bhang is the joy giver, etc. . . . the students of the scriptures of Benares are given bhang before they sit to study. At holy places, yogis take deep draughts of bhang . . . [with bhang] ascetics pass days without food or drink.". . . (Thio 1983, p.334). Devereux (1980) notes, in many cultures, the reliance on drugs or alcohol to induce special abnormal states.

Three thousand years ago, the West had *nepenthe* (known to Homer) which was probably opium; the East had its legendary *soma*—central in the Indian *Rig Veda* sacred texts—its identify a mystery for three and a half millenia. R. Gordon Wasson (1968) solved that mystery: it is the mushroom, *Amanita muscaria,* the fly-agaric, which has psychedlic effects (see LaBarre 1980, pp. 108–115).

The Aztecs used a sacred mushroom, now identified as *psilocybe mexicana,* the active ingredient of which is psilocybin, a major psychedelic, later synthesized.

Plants of the *solanaceae* family—like thorn apple, belladonna, mandragora and the henbanes, have for centuries been in use, evidently with psychedelic effects, in European witchcraft.

Effects attributed to one drug in one period may be similar to those attributed to an entirely different drug at another period. For example, many mid-nineteenth century writers, e.g. Elizabeth Barrett Browning, Swinburne, and Poe, all spoke glowingly of the effects of the extract of the Oriental poppy capsule—probably opium—in terms similar to those being applied in the 1960s by advocates to LSD (see Cohen 1968).

Is Drug Use "Deviant"? Is It Psychopathological?

The basic answer in each case is: that depends.

In modern America, as in other modern industrialized advanced large-scale societies, drugstores are overflowing with a huge variety of pharmacological agents, for sale over the counter, or by prescription from a physician, for every imaginable kind of malady or discomfort. We take pills to keep us awake; others to help us go to sleep. We take aspirins or other analgesics to fight aches and pains. We drink millions of gallons of coffee and other caffeine-based beverages. We use enormous quantities of analgesic preparations to mitigate a great variety of physical pains. We gulp down huge amounts of tranquilizers to calm us down when we feel jittery or "nervous." We do not consider it abnormal to drink a substantial quantity of alcohol beverages, so long as we don't "overdo" it, i.e. regularly get extremely inebriated. We do all of these on legally available substances and preparations. "I can't decide whether to take an upper and go to the party, or a downer and go to bed and get some sleep for a change," says a young woman character to another in a *New Yorker* cartoon, and we are to understand that she isn't necessarily talking about illegal drugs. "Why be unhappy? depressed?" we have beamed at us from the media. "Take X, Y, Z . . ." Also, "Why be overweight? No excuse for it—take P, Q, R . . ." Other substances are touted to make skinny people fatter.

So, is taking drugs deviant, against the norms? For the vast majority of drugs we consume, for the vast majority of people, definitely not. But for some substances, that the law has declared out of bounds, yes it is—but not for all of the population. Some people regard their purchase and consumption a basic right, or fashionable, appropriate to presenting oneself as a certain kind of person. Controversies rage about whether certain legal restrictions on particular substances, like marijuana, should be overhauled, relaxed, or entirely abolished. And if yes for abolition for one now-illegal drug, what about others? If pot yes, heroin too? Cocaine? LSD?

Psychopathological? Controversy here too. Some think if drug use is deviant, it must also be psychologically sick. Others, including this writer, say not necessarily. The two dimensions are not the same and can be cross-tabulated: deviant-and-sick, deviant-and-not-sick, sick-and-not-deviant and not-sick-and-not-deviant are the possible combinations (see Chapter 1). More generally, we can ask what psychological functions are served, by using a particular drug, or combination of drugs? Is the partaker seeking relief, relaxation, ecstasy, or oblivion, or what? And whatever the answer, is *that* psychopathological, by any transcultural standard? Since not everyone in the society partakes of the "deviant" drugs, what selective principle is at work, that sets which ones do and which do not?

The question about selective factors can be asked in either psychological terms—what kinds of personality, or in sociological terms—persons in what sociological category regarding age, sex, class position, ethnicity, rural or urban, region?

Drugs and Cultural Norms

The prevailing attitudes in a society, toward various drugs, can be classified into four categories.

1) Permissive, even positive: it is considered allowable, even a positive thing to do, to take particular drugs. This applies in modern American society, generally, to all kinds of cola drinks with psychoactive ingredients, to coffee and tea, i.e. the caffeine in the coffee and tea, and to all kinds of medications prescribed by physicians or legally available without prescription.

2) Permissive but with control: these substances are to be regulated and controlled for access, not to be banned outright. This policy applies to alcoholic beverages, and nicotine products. Liquor and tobacco cigarettes can be advertised in print media but not on TV. There is no complete consensus on the control elements here. To some the present regulations are not enough, to others they are too much.

3) Negative: for most of the population, but not all, these substances are considered bad, and laws against them are correct. For subcultures within

the society, however, the substance is regarded positively, and supporters think laws against it should be relaxed or abolished. The laws however are, at the moment, on the books, but their enforcement spotty and uneven. To this category belongs marijuana; the hallucinogenic (psychedelic) drugs (possibly); and probably also cocaine. Controversy abounds about these substances, and about the laws governing them.

4) Very negative, and with strong consensus, these drugs are destructive and definitely should be banned by law. Definite and strong laws on them, and with strong, but not always effective, efforts at enforcement. Included are heroin and other opium derivatives. Possibly, the hallucinogenics and cocaine are currently (late 1980s) moving into this category.

This set of categories emphasizes that how a drug is seen by the prevailing cultural norms, is not static, but potentially or actually, in a state of flux. For example, *some* proponents of legal change for marijuana want to see it moved from category 3) to category 2), arguing, among other things, that making it more like alcohol, would enable regulation of the trade, taking control away from criminals, and providing revenues to the state, while allowing consumers greater freedom of choice. Others want to see it moved to category 4), with repressive laws strengthened and more rigorously enforced.

Bases of the Categorization

That not all substances fall into the extremes of complete permission (category 1) or complete disapprobation (category 4) reflects the pervasive value conflict in this society on the issues drug use raises.

These value conflicts reflect the dissension between what survives of the culture of puritanism and more secular culture. In this society puritanism is still substantial, as in the influence of fundamentalistic religion, possibly growing at present, late 1980s. The other side of the conflict is secular culture, more positive toward hedonism in all forms. An exaggerated version of the latter appears in the "counter-culture" of the 1960s and its survivors and continuations into the present. A basic slogan is: "if it feels good, do it" (see Chapter 7). Significantly, exotic drugs, especially the psychedelics, were a major part of that scene. Anti-puritanism is a major secular trend of modern society. It is also involved in any "Dionysian" activities, activities reaching out for the extremes of experience, as against those of moderation and control. Perhaps "activities" is not the best word here, since one of the components of the anti-puritanical culture is precisely opposed to activism of any kind, embodying an immersing of oneself in passive experience.

Another formulation of the pervasive value conflict in modern society is that of control versus lack of control; one of the perceived threats of drug use is the feeling that the user loses not only control over himself, but also any interest in maintaining such control. He "gives himself up to the influence of the drug . . .", felt by proponents of more puritanical culture to be a despicable abdiction of personal responsibility. This value conflict applies differently to alcohol as compared with other drugs. In the Western world alcohol has been in effect "domesticated" for a long time, and ordinary "social drinking" is not perceived as a threat by conventional people. Threat occurs only when the drinking becomes "excessive." However in popular imagery, such loss of self-control appears almost automatically in reference to any of these other drugs. Mild intoxication is permissible with alcohol. By contrast, the other drugs—"*the* drugs"—are associated with something weird, frighteningly exotic, and any intoxication is seen as threatening.

From the perspective of the dominant culture, the "culture of rationality," partaking of any of these other drugs—marijuana, heroin, cocaine, amphetamines, or psychedelics—is regarded almost entirely negatively. It is seen as immersion in feeling as opposed to thought, and losing contact with time as ordinarily perceived.

One element of the difference is the role of subcultures. Ordinary, nonaddictive, alcohol use, recreational in nature, does not automatically involve the user in a subculture. With marijuana use that is much more likely. Part of the basis of the subculture is the very illegality of pot, and the realization that conventional people, nonsmokers, regard it negatively. With heroin, the association with illegality is even stronger, and the likelihood is also high, of association with a deviant subculture involving a criminal underworld. For LSD and other psychedelics, subculture is an intrinsic feature.

Classification of Drugs

Any classification is of course arbitrary, and relatively helpful or not depending on its use. We just gave one that revolves on how use of that drug is regarded by the mainstream culture and treated by the laws.

Another classification, that seems obvious but actually presents difficulties, is to distinguish by the type of action of the drug upon the user. That kind of action is both pharmacologic and psychological. The pharmacological depends on the chemical nature of the substance, its dosage, and its interaction with human physiology. Psychological refers to how it works on the mind and emotions. It also connects with the sociocultural. Psychological variables include set and setting, that is the "mind-set" of the user, and the setting in which the drug is taken. The setting refers to differences between being with friendly and supportive co-members of a drug subculture, as distinguished from solitary or other use. All psychoactive drugs have in common that each one has some particular believed in and sought after effect upon physical and psychological functioning.

One classification is this: depressants, stimulants, hallucinogenics, and cannabis drugs.

Depressants

These drugs depress (slow down) central nervous system (CNS) functioning; they are analgesics that reduce pain, including narcotic drugs, that is, drugs producing physical dependency. These latter are the opiates, opium and its derivatives morphine, heroin, and codeine. Also here are synthetic analgesics (demerol, methadone, Percodan and others); general depressants (hypnotics and sedatives) such as bromides and barbiturates, and ethyl alcohol (ethanol, or simply, alcohol). Here too belong the "minor" tranquilizers, Valium, Librium, Miltown, Quaalude, Sopor, Parest, and others.

Stimulants

These stimulate CNS, elevate feeling. They produce arousal, alertness, even excitation, and inhibit fatigue and lethargy. They include caffeine, nicotine, amphetamines and cocaine. There are also many other varieties consumed in other parts of the world.

Hallucinogenic(or psychedelic—"mind-manifesting") Drugs

These include mescaline (from peyote or other plants, a natural hallucinogenic), psilocybin ("magic mushrooms"); and the synthetics of the mid-to-later twentieth century, LSD, DMT and others. The psychedelics produce an intensely altered state of consciousness, heightening or making perceptions more exotic, producing "deep insights," religious ecstasy, a mystical experience.

Cannabis drugs

Marijuana, hashish, others. Some researchers (Tart 1969) include marijuana among the psychedelics, but others (Goode 1978) say that is incorrect, because cross-tolerance occurs among all the other psychedelics, but not between any of them and marijuana; therefore classify the cannibis drugs separately. I follow this practice. (The question of "tolerance" raises difficulties however, since tolerance in the sense applied to addictive drugs like heroin, meaning you need increasingly larger doses to get the same effect, is said not to occur with the psychedelics.)

Marijuana: effects

For marijuana, common subjectively reported effects are these: "relaxation; an enhancement of the sensation of pleasure—particularly sex, music, and food; a feeling of lethargy; a sharpening of the appetite; sensing that more time has passed than is measured by the clock; a meandering stream of consciousness; forgetfulness and absent-mindedness; impairment of short-term memory; enhancement of sense of humor, finding many more things funny than usually; an impairment of cognitive functioning; an inability to read or study or to think in a logical rational fashion." Goode also mentions impairment of motor skills, such as driving a car. (Goode 1978, p. 203—note this from a researcher favorably disposed to marijuana smoking.) Some users claim it has a "psychedelic effect." Some claim marijuana "points the way" to deeper awareness, that the user is free to follow or not as he chooses. Again the skeptic may wonder about the illusion involved in such claims.

A major sociological article on marijuana use (Becker 1963) argues that one has to "learn" to have the sought-after effects of pot smoking.

The consensus of most experts is that it is not addictive, producing neither physical dependence, withdrawal symptoms, nor tolerance. However many experts note "psychological dependence." That seems to be variable, depending on prior psychological characteristics of the user (Bruin 1969, p. 325). It is also not associated with release of aggression, and no association of marijuana use with violent crime has been reported.

Its association with criminality is said by sympathizers to be related entirely to the prevalent anti-marijuana laws, which make possession of even small amounts, as well as passing, illegal in most places. But other researchers have argued that its use reduces inner controls the individual may have against committing crimes (other than violation of drug laws.) For many users, smoking marijuana automatically puts them into not only the drug subculture but also into the subculture of at least petty crime. Thus the drug may be a facilitator of criminal acts, at least indirectly.

The classification just used refers to usual pharmacologic action and psychological concomitants.

However, such categorizing needs several cautions. Any drug may have more than one effect, thus overlapping with another category. Effects may not appear consistently from one user or occasion to another. Effects are not invariably what is expected; a user may take a stimulant and get a depressant effect, or take a depressant and feel stimulated (common with alcohol); or get only depressive effects from a hallucinogenic. Hallucinogenics are notoriously unpredictable in effects. Regular users are likely to combine two or more drugs at any time. The user may not know the concentration and identity of the drug being taken. Effects of even common combinations, such as heroin with amphetamine, are only approximately known. There is a folklore among active users. Its content is notoriously unreliable and unstable from one group of users to another, even one individual to another. The very unpredictability of effects may be a major part of the appeal for the user; they are playing a kind of pharmacologic Russian roulette, sometimes in reality with fatal results.

Therefore all studies of the effects of "drug of choice" are to be considered only general indications.

"Dangerousness" of Drugs

There is no consensus on how "dangerous" particular drugs are for users. Sympathizers of the various drug subcultures dismiss reports of such dangers. Sympathizers include many sociologists interested in drug use (for example Goode 1978, chapters on drugs).

The users and the sympathizers tend to argue that all alleged dangerous effects are entirely propaganda of the drug-control agencies. (Unlikely to be generally true.) Or the sympathizers may be selective, strongly positive in reference to one drug but more negative in reference to others. Sympathizers with marijuana may not approve of heroin.

As is true about other kinds of deviants, the underdog status of most users of illicit drugs gives them automatic claim to the sympathies of certain kinds of social scientists, as already discussed in other chapters. Sympathizers will almost reflexively discount any statements from other kinds of authorities, particularly medical specialists, who are thought to represent the drug-control agencies of the government.

Marijuana harmless?

Marijuana is commonly presented by such sociologists as a totally harmless substance. It is, accurately, portrayed as not addicting. But that it can have any of a variety of other harmful effects on users is argued by many researchers. (See Addiction Research Foundation 1983, which documents negative effects of marijuana on intellectual performance, cardiovascular system, the immune system, lung functioning, chromosomes, testosterone levels in males, and the drug's cancer-causing potential. See also Yochelson and Samenow 1986: 75, and Peggy Mann 1980, reporting on a number of recent studies.)

Goode (1978) is among the sociologists writing on drugs who seems determined to prove that marijuana is not dangerous. He cites a number of studies that showed some damaging effects of chronic marijuana use, and then counters each one with another study that "disproves" the first one. One study shows lower testosterone levels in chronic users. Another refutes this finding. One indicating chromosomal damage, is refuted by another showing no chromosomal differences between users and non-users. Another pair says yes and no regarding cerebral atrophy. Another does so regarding diminution of cellular immunity (Goode 1978, 205). Goode does concede, however, that one unrefuted study does demonstrate that heavy chronic use causes impairment of lung functioning.

By contrast, Peggy Mann 1980, presents for a popular public a summary of a whole series of authoritative studies that document a variety of damaging effects of chronic long-term marijuana use. A summary of a major expert's conclusion is that "There is not a single paper on the crude drug marijuana which gives it a clean bill of health, not a single paper to support it as an innocuous drug" (Dr. Carlton Turner, quoted by Peggy Mann). Mann catalogues the widely recognized psychological effects of pot on junior high and high school students: lowered school performance; increased irritability; general apathy; depression; drastic otherwise inexplicable mood changes; feelings of isolation; cutting off of parent-child communication; and a general loss of interest in everything except pot smoking and its subculture.

How does one account for such drastic differences of opinion on the "dangerousness" of pot? Mann, though writing for a mass-media magazine, cites reputable scientific authorities. Her paper is especially concerned with what she sees as an ominous spread of marijuana use to ever-younger cohorts of schoolchildren, including anecdotes of toddlers of two or three being given pot at home. (Though admittedly this may not be a widespread phenomenon, that it happens at all is certainly sobering.) Much of her paper refers to high school and junior high school students. Part of what she describes is youngsters adopting marijuana use from parents who were part of the hippie rebellion of the 1960s, and for many of them, pot was the mildest drug they have used.

Yochelson and Samenow, as indicated, also cite many scientific studies documenting harmful effects of marijuana.

A major part of what is perceived (by opponents) as harmful about marijuana use, has been called the "amotivational syndrome," meaning lack of motivation to do hard, sustained, systematic work. This is evidently culture-bound, since it does not appear in Jamaica, where marijuana is often smoked in preparation for doing a difficult task (Cited in LaBarre 1980, p.104).

It is possible, of course, that the scoffers at danger, like Goode, and the viewers with alarm, like Mann, may be looking primarily at different populations. And all generalizations about "the effects" of pot are suspect, without specification of who is doing the smoking, as well as the setting. The Bruin report's (1969) reference to some cases of psychological dependence according to prior predisposition, and in some instances "personality defect and incipient or preexisting psychic disorder as essential for the habit formation," is a telling remark not followed up in that paper. Just as LSD use may be enormously disorganizing (to the point of psychotic break) for some individuals, while only mildly consciousness-altering for others, the same should be said for marijuana use, rather than wholesale disapproval as in Mann, or approval as in Goode. We need also note the cautions already mentioned about circumstances, and dosages, and whatever else may be mixed with the drug taken, as well as details of individual predispositions and vulnerabilities of different users. In short, pot may be harmless for some, perhaps most users (in moderate, nonchronic usage) but very dangerous for others. For adolescents and especially for young children, it is probably far from an innocuous drug.

Marijuana use has not been reported in this society as implicated in psychotic breakdown or episodes, as is true for psychedelics like LSD. However "Studies in India . . . and North Africa . . . show that cannabis psychoses occur in association with heavy use of potent forms of cannabis" (Blum 1967: 25). These are more probably hashish, which is much stronger in THC than most of the street marijuana available in America.

Medical Use of Cannabis

Surprisingly, so enthusiastic a supporter of "harmless" pot smoking as Goode does not mention positive uses of marijuana in medicine, for its analgesic and antibacterial qualities (see Mikuriya 1969), mentioned by LaBarre (1980, p.99) as already known to the sixteenth century French physician Rabelais, and only recently rediscovered in Western medicine.

Other Drug Use in Marijuana Users

"Many surveys have shown that the marijuana user is more likely than the non-user to try a wide range of hard, dangerous drugs such as heroin, cocaine and LSD" (Thio 1983: 336). This is simply to say that regular pot users are likely to be in, or connected to, subcultures favorable to a variety of drug use: unconventional, antinomian, hostile to law-enforcement, etc.

The single most important factor in getting started in smoking marijuana is having pot-smoking friends. Peer influence is clearly significant. Young people gravitate to others who are similar in important ways, such as attitudes toward drugs and the law. These attitudes are likely to lead to similarities in dealing with the law in other respects. Although probably the vast majority of recreational marijuana smokers are *generally* lawabiding persons, association with drug subcultures, easily overlapping from one type like pot to another like heroin, is apt to lead to relaxation of standards. Thence we find some involvement with criminal activities. Using easily leads to dealing and to other illegal activities.

Dangerousness in Addiction

A major feature of dangerousness lies in the *addicting* nature of certain drugs. Some drugs are definitely addicting, others not. Heroin and other opiates are. So are barbiturates, amphetamines, and alcohol. Marijuana and the psychedelics are not, and cocaine is technically not.

Nature of Addiction

Technically, the characteristics of addiction are these:
1) *Tolerance:* the user can take increasing doses of the drug, and then needs to do so, to get the same effect.
2) *Habituation: psychological* dependence on the drug: the user feels a need to have the drug, often in lieu of other satisfactions.
3) *Physical dependence:* the user physically needs the drug to avoid the withdrawal syndrome, i.e. severe negative physical symptoms of agonizing pain and terror. Withdrawal symptoms can include any or all of the following: delirium, insomnia, vomiting, convulsions, tremors, dizziness, sleeplessness, abdominal cramps, massive anxiety amounting to severe terror, in some cases cardiovascular pathology. These can vary with the type of drug, the dosage, and circumstances.
4) *Euphoria.* Some observers include an additional characteristic, that is, a euphoric state, an extreme, unrealistic experience of happiness and well-being. This feeling can be characterized negatively, as the absence of anxiety. It is questionable whether this euphoria should be included as universal in and intrinsic to addiction, since it is evident that for many addicts, the need to get a fix is overwhelmingly for the purpose of getting away from pain and anxiety, rather than for the positive, euphoric, "high" state. In any case, for the confirmed addict, the *only* time he is happy is when he is high.

This addiction does appear with certain drugs and not with others. There is a consensus that it does appear with alcohol, with the opiates (opium and derivatives morphine and heroin), with synthetic analgesics, and with barbiturates. Also with the amphetamines (Goode 1978: 243, and his sources). There is also consensus that it does *not* appear with marijuana, or with psychedelic drugs, or with cocaine (Spotts and Schontz 1980; Goode 1978). Spotts and Schontz, for example, from their own intensive study and a summary of related prior literature, conclude that cocaine produces a *psychological* dependency, but neither physical dependence, withdrawal syndrome, nor tolerance. When we say that a particular drug is addicting we have to qualify by saying: *but not invariably.*

Cases are reported where an individual uses heroin, for example, without becoming addicted. Some heroin users claim that they can take it or leave it, that they are *not* hooked. Such claims have to be investigated in each individual case, however. In drug users of all kinds, the probability of lying, or of self-deception is rather high.

Another problematic is that heavy users of one drug are also often users, in some cases heavy users, of other drugs as well. They use either at other times, or simultaneously. In some instances, the lack of availability of a preferred drug leads a user to substitute another drug. In addition, many users take two or more drugs simultaneously. In still other cases, a user is taking an assortment of drugs without knowing exactly what is being ingested. This leaves in a quandary any researcher who is trying to find out the effects of one particular drug.

Use of cannabis, as marijuana or as hashish, is the most common of the psychoactive drugs, and is almost invariably present in the background history of users of stronger, usually addicting drugs. It does not follow, however, that all or even most marijuana users go on to heroin or amphetamines or psychedelics. Some do but only on an occasional, usually experimental basis, not repeated after one or a few times.

Nearly every detailed case history of an addict or heavy user of stronger drugs, includes other drugs in current or prior use as well.

Thus it is sometimes arbitrary to consider a person as a "case" of heroin addiction, without qualification.

It is also likely that we cannot reasonably characterize the features of "all persons with addiction to x." That does not stop researchers from trying, and there is by now a vast literature on the characteristics, the sociology and the psychology of addicts, most studies dealing with heroin addiction. That addiction is extremely dangerous, there seems little doubt. Its life-threatening potential is there to see. It is persistent, and for the addict, almost totally consuming. Commonly referred to as a "monkey on your back", it is an enslavement extremely difficult to change. Usually psychotherapeutic methods of help to sufferers from other kinds of psychopathology, turn out to be of no avail with such persons. (See later section on psychological and psychoanalytic studies.) Such persons have been "hooked" on the drug.

Opiates

These are the drugs about which there is most consensus among popular writers and professional researchers. The universal view is that these drugs produce a horrible, undesirable condition known as addiction, and that these are destructive forces with no redeeming social significance. The natural versions derive from opium, rarely used in its pure natural state these days, processed to produce morphine, heroin, codeine and other derivatives. All of these produce the addiction syndrome: physical dependency, withdrawal syndrome (extreme negative physical reactions when the drug is withdrawn), psychological dependency, and tolerance (increasing doses needed to produce comparable effects). The user becomes "enslaved" to the drug, commonly referred to as "a monkey on his back." The synthetic versions are man-made chemical substances that have similar effects: meperidine (Demerol—the upper case indicates commercial names), hydromorphone (e.g. Dilaudid). oxycodone (e.g. Percodan) and methadone (e.g. Dolophine). Physiologically a central nervous system depressant, this kind of drug produces psychologically a high or euphoric state in which all cares and anxieties fall away, a state described as absence of pain. (Yochelson and Samenow disagree with this, in their characterization of the "rush," as a positive experience, not simply absence of negative feeling. See Yochelson/Samenow 1986: 169ff.) Besides relieving anxiety and tension, drugs like heroin diminish primary drive, such as hunger and sex, may produce drowsiness and apathy, impair concentration and reduce physical activity. It can also increse self-confidence and grandoise fantasies of wealth, power and omnipotence, as well as the illusion of greater creative capacity.

Heroin users who have been caught, convicted and incarcerated for other (usually property) criminal offenses, give the impression they have stolen to support their drug habit, leading to a prevalent conventional wisdom among social scientists that the drug addiction has preceded criminality. Yochelson/Samenow's and other studies indicate, however, that criminality has in most cases preceded drug use (see Yochelson/Samenow 1986: 59ff). Similarly, while the social science conventional wisdom that heroin addiction does not go along with or produce crimes of violence (see same, p.59), in fact users may become more violent during withdrawal, and are likely to be drawn into the criminal world where violence is inherent.

Sex

Although the prevailing opinion is that being high on heroin reduces or eliminates sexual interest, another kind of effect is reported: being able to maintain an erection for a very long period, without ejaculation or orgasm.

Other Depressants: Barbiturates

These sedative-hypnotics include familiar drugs available by medical prescription: pentobarbitol (Nembutal), secobarbital (Seconal). amobarbital (Amytal), combination of secobarbital and amobarbital (Tuinal), glutethimide (Doriden), chloral hydrate (Noctec), and methaqualone (Quaalude, Sopor.) These drugs, mostly producing physical dependence as well as psychological, produce drowsiness and sleep, used to reduce unwanted excessive environmental stimulation, and in some cases euphoria, tranquility and feeling of well-being. In some cases they produce effects like those of alcohol, talkativeness, loss of inhibitions, emotional volatility, faulty judgment; in some cases belligerency. Sometimes these are used along with heroin (to counter heroin withdrawal effect) or with amphetamines, combating the nervousness associated with amphetamine use. Secobarbital is reported to be associated with enhanced tendencies toward violence. One of these, methaqualone (Quaalude) was reported to be aphrodisiac, but this was challenged. Psychotic reactions as part of withdrawal have been reported.

Dependencies without Complete Addiction

While most researchers do not think drugs other than alcohol, barbiturates, amphetamines and the opiates are genuinely addicting, for many of the others there is clearly a danger of an extreme psychological dependency. Cocaine is a notable example. Others include the whole array of the psychedelics, and marijuana and hashish.

In some cases we are dealing with effects in a general life-style where it is not clear how much can be attributed to the drug use per se, or whether the drug use is an incidental concomitant of a general pattern of withdrawal from conventional pursuits and especially from any kind of active striving.

Certainly onlookers, including alarmed parents and friends who are not sympathizers of the drug use, see it as something clearly harmful to the young person's "health" most broadly considered. This opinion may be more particularly the case for the harder psychedelics, which were more prevalent in the 1960s, in the counterculture and elsewhere, and which seem to have declined in use since that time. (But some expert observers, e.g. Goode, claim that it has simply moved out of media attention.)

Psychedelic Drugs

These have earlier been called "psychotomimetic drugs" and "hallucinogenic drugs," both terms misleading. When such drugs were first synthesized, researchers thought they produced effects that "mimicked" psychosis, or that produced hallucinations, as in psychotic states. The designation as hallucination is not technically accurate, since the psychedelic drug user usually recognizes his visionary experience as imaginary, and does not, like a psychotic, take it as something real, "out there."

These are the drugs that in the 1960s became the most attended, the most controversial. Natural versions of these, peyote, psilocybin, mescaline, "magic mushrooms," had been in use for centuries in many civilizations (Masters and Houston 1966, LaBarre 1980, and their sources).

LSD

LSD (lysergic acid diethylamide 25) was first synthesized in 1939, and its psychedelic effects first recognized, accidentally, by Hofmann, in 1943. Known only to a few specialists for some years, it got attention from scholars, artists, and the like, with the publication of Aldous Huxley's *Doors of Perception* in 1954. Gradually interest in it spread in the intellectual community, becoming a matter of a *cause célèbre* with Timothy Leary and Richard Alpert at Harvard in the early 1960s. It was then picked up in force by the bohemian community.

This kind of drug produces a radically altered consciousness, including, in many cases, psychotic-like features (hence "psychotomimetic"): hallucinations, delusions, abnormal body sensations, time distortion (a short clock time can seem a very long time) and space distortion. It can include severe ego disturbances such as depersonalization, derealization, and deanimation. Many users claim deep mystical experiences, thought to be religious. The most serious of the earlier researchers, pre-mid-60s, like Masters and Houston (1966), claim that such experiences are rare, and available only to particularly mature, ego-integrated individuals, not to the mass of immature teenage hippies who became the main users later. Rather than getting really transcendant experience with such a drug, Sidney Cohen (1966) points out that with LSD we "get what we are . . . LSD springs the latch of disinhibition. What emerges depends on what was within and upon on all impinging influences from without." ". . . The hallucinogens are a fragment of the current predicament . . . an escape from frustrating existence for some . . . [while] others are sustained by the crystalline look at themselves and their world seen during that endless moment. And a few marvel at the vastness within" (Cohen 1966: 245).

Psychedelics and the "Counterculture"

In the 1960s "counterculture" of the hippies, these psychedelics were a prominent feature, embraced by the bohemian rebels for their "mind-expanding" qualities (see Chapter 7). "Good trips" were to take one to a "beyond within," to ranges of psychological experience beyond ordinary everyday consciousness, and, many believed, into a profound religious experience of mystical union with a supreme power or God.

"Tripping" transcended ordinary time experience, suspended ordinary categories of sensory experience, enabled synesthesia (hearing sights, smelling sounds, seeing smells) intensified enormously all ordinary sensations, such as the vision of a sunset, put totally into abeyance all ordinary everyday cares and worries, and inhibitions. However, with any of the same drugs, the subject may have a "bad trip," inducing overwhelming terror, and a state which certainly seems like at least a temporary psychosis, with extreme regression and de-differentiation. In some cases the subject may not come out of such a psychotic state. Or the subject may re-experience such bad tripping at a later time even without another dose of the drug, experiences called after-flashes.

The extreme regressions lead outsiders to the hippie life-style, especially the psychedelic subculture, to be very wary of the participants' use of these psychedelic drugs, as a potentially destructive force. The mature professionals involved in the earlier experiments with psychedelics in the late 1940s–1950s (see Masters and Houston 1966) were usually persons of a high and complexly differentiated ego development and psychological maturity, able to manage and derive enlightenment from such drugs. However, such maturity of reaction was generally not true of the young devotees of the hippie subculture and their later imitators. Some of these were exactly the "wrong" people to be trying LSD and other such drugs. As youngsters age twelve to nineteen, or at most early twenties the majority were automatically too immature. On top of that, *these* youngsters were likely to have very fragile ego structures to start with, given to poor reality testing and poverty of other crucial ego functions, all of which would further deteriorated with ingestion of psychedelic drugs. These were also likely to be young people, who because of their impulsiveness and other psychological difficulties, were already at odds with more conventional parents, relatives and peers, and therefore attracted to the "way-out" subculture of the hippies. They were extremely vulnerable to the lure of these "magical" chemicals. A further danger was that commonly the young person did not know precisely what drug was being ingested, since what was sold as LSD could be contaminated by any other ingredients, or other toxic drugs, like amphetamines.

Goode, like other sociologists who are sympathizers of drug subcultures, discounts any dangers in the psychedelic drugs. Some of these observers sound as though the actual psychotic breaks that have been well documented for the psychedelics, especially LSD, never really occurred, or dismiss them as an infinitesimally small minority of cases, and more explainable by ignorance and "hysteria" than by anything intrinsic to the drug experience. Needless to say, I strongly disagree.

Stimulants

These are drugs that stimulate and elevate central nervous system functions, make the user feel "up," more energetic, more capable. They include drugs from natural sources, like cocaine, from the leaves of the coca plant; caffeine; and many synthetic drugs of recent introduction, collectively called the amphetamines. The latter include amphetamine (Benzedrine), methamphetamine (Methedrine and Desoxyn), dextroamphetmaine (Dexedrine), phenmetrazine (Preludin), mephentermine (Wyamine), most of these in common medical use, by prescription, to combat depression, or to promote weight loss.

Amphetamines

A major feature, only more recently generally recognized, is that these are addicting drugs. They produce not only psychological dependence, but physical dependence, with pronounced withdrawal syndrome, tolerance, and psychological dependence, all of these qualitatively different in details from the addiction syndrome in opiates. In the "high" the user feels elation, euphoria, overconfidence, exhilaration; this is followed by a depression or "crash," which may be relieved only by another injection of the drug, producing a high-depression cycle. Use is strongly associated with violent criminal activities, since the drug releases aggressive impulses and promotes paranoid thinking and even delusions, increasing potential for violent acts. They are frequently combined with opiates like heroin, to produce "better" effects. Effects on sexuality are diverse, sometimes increasing, sometimes decreasing, sexual drive and competence, varying depending on prior personality predispositions of the user, as well as by dosage and setting. Some reports refer to marathon sexual activity with sustained erection and no orgasm.

Psychosis

Paranoid psychotic states induced by amphetamine use have been reported, lasting long beyond the period of actual drug use; along with "lively visual and auditory hallucinations, and paranoid delusions as an important feature." Such delusions may also lead to indiscriminate violence.

Cocaine

Derived from the coca plant, cocaine is a powerful stimulant that may produce psychological dependence, but, according to most authorities, not physical dependence, tolerance or withdrawal symptoms. It is one of the most expensive of drugs and on that account has acquired in recent years a certain chic. The cocaine "high" involves increased energy, clarity of mind and euphoria, and is very short-lasting (about half an hour), therefore requiring another dose, or by combination with heroin, a much longer-lasting euphoriant. The enhancement of energy gives cocaine a connection with crime: the user feels enhanced mental and physical energy, and the daring to commit a major crime if that is what he wants to do and may not otherwise have the nerve to do. The drug can also facilitate trends toward paranoia or violence if these are already present. But authorities claim it does not produce real aggression, violence or psychosis. Regarding sexuality, it is often reported to stimulate sexual interest, fantasy and activity, to work as an aphrodisiac. If the user so stimulated and energized believes this to be true, he can probably act accordingly, in the short run. Some researchers have claimed that cocaine sometimes produces a psychotic reaction consisting of paranoid ideation, megalomanic delusions and/or tactile hallucinations. However, others argue that such sensations are not really hallucinations, since the user does not believe these are real (condensed from discussion in Yochelson/Samenow, 1986: 63].

A recent development is the processing of cocaine into a more powerful drug: crack (called "rock" on the West Coast) said to be much stronger than ordinary cocaine, and decidedly dangerous, in some cases lethally so. (Note in 1986 two cases of famous athletes said to have died of the effects.)

Drug sympathizers (typically) discount such stories. In 1986, crack became a media sensation: available in rock-like pellets in a dose at a very low price (as little as $10) this brought in a much lower-income group of buyers. Crack is easily produced by mixing cocaine with baking soda and cooking in a test tube. The pellets are smoked in a pipe with an instantaneous and powerful effect, said to be so great that the user wants to do anything to get the next dose. This psychological craving is commonly reported as an "addiction," but there are no physical dependence, tolerance or withdrawal symptoms. So it is best to keep it defined, like cocaine generally, as "psychological dependency."

Polydrug Use

Most chronic users of any of the illicit drugs also use other drugs, often two or more simultaneously. Nearly all users of "harder" drugs, like heroin, also use—or have used—marijuana, commonly regarded as the gateway to the other drugs. Any of the following may be be combined by any particular user: alcohol, marijuana, hashish, barbiturates, amphetamines, LSD, mescaline, cocaine and heroin (that being the progression in pattern of use.) Almost any combination may be tried (Yochelson/Samenow 1986:85–87).

Extent and Demographics of Use

Thio (1983) estimates the following percentages of the American population have (at some time) used each of the following: marijuana 30%; cocaine 20%, PCP 15%, LSD 5%, heroin 1%. (p. 345, drawing on several major professional researchers.)

For nearly all of these the major population is young adults (16–25) and of those, predominantly male (though less so in more recent years, and less so for marijuana than for harder drugs.)

Alcohol

In this culture alcohol is perceived and reacted to differently from other psychoactive drugs considered here. In fact it is usually not dealt with as a "drug" at all, and the phrase "alcohol and other drugs" comes across as quite unfamiliar. Since the repeal of the "Prohibition Amendment," there has been no attempt at nationwide criminalization of alcohol in this society. Alcohol is thoroughly domesticated. Though its dangers, that is, the dangers of *addiction* to alcohol, have long been well recognized in the public at large, such addiction is commonly seen as an illness, and not a reason to criminalize the ordinary use, purchase and sale of this drug. "Ordinary" use refers to moderate social drinking, short of regularly becoming deeply intoxicated. The exact boundaries are not entirely clear, but seem to be well understood among peer groups. The focus of the law, in control, is upon untoward *consequences* of combining drinking alcoholic beverages with other activities, such as driving a motor vehicle and other "alcohol-related offenses," like violence when intoxicated.

Cultures can be classified according to prevailing attitudes toward drinking and toward drunkenness. The culture may be negative on both, making all drinking taboo, and regarding intoxication negatively. This would fit Islamic and Hindu cultures. Or it may be positive toward both, as in France and Ireland. Drinking may be regarded as permissible or even positively, but drunkenness as bad: American secular culture. Within this category, particular groups, e.g. particular ethnic groups, may regard drinking as permissible, but in a family context, while drunkenness is taboo; Italians are an example. Or drinking may be permissible, in a ritual context, and drunkenness taboo: Jews and Italians. A group may have (or have had) a traditional culture which is basically hostile to all alcohol use, but be in process of change through acculturation to a larger secular culture that is permissive to drinking at least. The traditional culture now cannot exert internal controls on drinking. This is true of people of many native American tribal ancestries who have been deracinated from tribal culture and also of many ethnic ancestries traditionally hostile to alcohol. American culture as a whole is a very mixed case, with many different versions of ambivalence and conflict coexisting. Briefly, during

Prohibition, the law tried to enforce nationally one particular cultural tradition (ascetic Protestantism). Once this law was repealed as unworkable, the country settled into a pattern of moderate regulation which has prevailed ever since. Advertising of hard liquor is prohibited on broadcast media, while allowed in print media, and social drinking is pervasively portrayed in a positive manner, in all media.

Thus, of the four types of cultural attitude toward the drug set out at the beginning of the chapter, alcohol fits best into category (2), permissive with some control. But that is for the country as a whole. In fact there is great variation in the population regarding appropriate cultural norms toward alcohol use, from strong moralistic condemnation of *any* drinking whatever, to total permissiveness. It varies by region of the country—South more abstentionist; by social class—the higher the class level, the more permissive; by religious affiliation—Protestants, especially fundamentalist versions, more abstentionist, Catholics more permissive, Jews selectively permissive; and by ethnic groups—Irish, Italians, and Jews more permissive, but in three different patterns. Prohibitionist sentiment was strongest among WASPs.

There is no consensus in the population, or among researchers, on definitions of basic categories, except for defining a complete abstainer. Otherwise, many different definitions are in use, of social drinking, acceptable drinking, problem drinking and alcoholism, with the result that different studies, using different basic definitions, are essentially incomparable.

For example, *who is an alcoholic?* Alcoholics Anonymous defines as alcoholic, *people who cannot control their drinking.* They cannot drink at all without becoming disruptive and getting into all kinds of trouble, with family, employers, the law. Also A.A. believes, "once an alcoholic, always an alcoholic." There is no such thing as a cured alcoholic or an ex-alcoholic; only a *recovered* alcoholic.

The A.A. view that alcoholics can never be cured is countered by a study, reported in Armour *et al.* (1976: 67, 70) that shows a high percentage of "former alcoholics" who have gone through some kind of treatment program, can drink moderately, at levels that customarily pose no threat to their health or safety. But evidently a different definition of "alcoholic" is being used in the two cases.

Other definitions of alcoholic include the following and anyone showing one or more of these symptoms qualifies:
1) withdrawal symptoms on being deprived of alcohol; 2) tolerance; 3) continued drinking in the face of strong penalties; or 4) major alcohol-related illness (National Council on Alcoholism 1972). All of these criteria are vulnerable to attack (Goode 1978: 287).

Yet another definition of alcoholic refers to ingestion of a certain definite quantity of ethanol per day: DeLint and Schmidt (1971) regard as alcoholic anyone who drinks at least 15 centiliters, about 5 oz., per day; the value of this kind of definition is that you can start from there, and then *investigate, empirically* what characteristics go with that level of consumption.

The same problems of definition arise with other categories, e.g. "the problem drinker." What amount of drinking, and what reaction the drinker himself and others around him, have to this drinking, can vary enormously from one individual and one situation to another.

There is a strong cultural component in the effects of alcohol. The Plains Indian drunk is quarrelsome, whereas the drunken Mohave falls into a sort of stupor. An alcoholic white American woman reacted differently to different kinds of alcohol: drinking champagne, she did her best to speak French and act like a stage version of a French lady's maid; drinking gin she acted like a British charwoman (Devereux 1980: 49–50). Irish Americans drinking a certain amount of alcohol are much more likely to get into trouble, e.g. brawling, than are Italian Americans. Jewish Americans have a relatively low percentage of total abstainers (8%) but also a relatively low percentage of heavy drinkers (8%) (Cahalan and Room 1974). Blacks have a high percentage of total abstainers (43%) and at the same time a high likelihood, if they drink, of getting into drinking-related trouble (31%).

Demographics and Numbers

Alcohol as an addictive drug has a very different profile from other addictive drugs. Whereas almost all regular users of heroin are likely to become addicted to it, with alcohol, probably less than 10% of regular users do (Trice 1966: 86). As of the mid-1960s, Trice reports an estimate of about 70 million regular drinkers, but only 3 to 5 million alcoholics. In 1978, however, Goode quotes a "commonly cited figure" for the total number of alcoholcs as 9 million (Goode, 1978: 286). (Obviously, different definitions of an alcoholic are involved.)

Whereas addiction to heroin is a phenomenon mainly of young males (teens to early 30s), alcoholism is much more a feature of middle and later years, and the disproportion of males to females, while still present, is much less than for other drugs and has been declining. Armour *et al.* (1976) report only 26% of males, compared to 44% of females, as total abstainers from alcohol.

Sociological Theories on Drugs and Alcohol: Retreatism

A category many sociologists have applied to drug use is *Retreatism.* This is one of the adaptations indicated by Robert Merton in his classic paper, "Social Structure and Anomie" (1937). Where reaching culturally approved goals in life is blocked, one kind of patterned response is to retreat, i.e. to give up the goals and also give up on legitimate means of achieving those goals. This response is coded minus-minus. Bohemianism is frequently cited as a prime example. Where heavy drug use is central to an individual's—or more importantly a group's—whole life pattern, the category of "retreatism" would seem to fit here too.

Cloward and Ohlin (1960) modify Merton's anomie theory specifically in reference to drug use; they point to juveniles who refrain from, or stop, delinquent activities, not because of internal (conscience) barriers to the use of illegitimate means, but because of lack of access to such means. They are thus, in Cloward/Ohlin's view, "double failures"—having failed in respect to legitimate pursuit of success, as well as illegitimate pursuit (crime), therefore turn to drugs.

Some sociologists however, protest this kind of image of drug users. They argue that heroin addicts, for example, far from living a passive life, are *actively* engaged in life pursuits like hustling, trying to sell stolen goods, chasing the drug seller, in short "*taking care of business.*" (Preble and Casey 1969).

Still, it seems strange not to consider such individuals as "retreatists" in Merton's terms, since they are certainly negative on using standard legitimate means to get what they seek and negative in *what* they are pursuing in relation to culturally prescribed goals, no matter how assiduously they exert themselves to pursue *their* goals. In fact, what conventional people in this society find so upsetting and objectionable about those really immersed in the drug world is that they have in effect "dropped out" of conventional society.

Of course not all drug users, even heavy habitual drug users, qualify as "dropouts" in this sense, and many of the younger ones are experimenting, trying it out, taking a psychosocial moratorium (Erikson). They will in time move on, to something more like conventional pursuits.

The Problem of Sociological Explanation

The patterns of drug use are too diverse for any one sociological formulation to fit them all. This is especially so for the predominant population using drugs, which is *young.* What fits some of them is perceived impossibility of getting basic satisfactions in life entirely through conventional means and in pursuit of conventional goals. For those blocked on means, this refers to a lower class population essentially. This is true for a major part of heroin addiction in our society. But heroin use has now spread into middle class circles, and other drugs are used at all class levels, many of these individuals being very far from deprived economically.

Anomie in the broader Durkheimian sense would seem to apply to a major part of the youth drug population—i.e. meaninglessness. Certain kinds of drug use may be not a solution but an escape.

The drug-using population in America has shifted substantially in the past century. In the early part of the twentieth century, opiate addiction was a phenomenon almost entirely of middle and upper class white females, of middle and later years, who had become addicted by being given morphine as a painkiller by physicians. Later, opiate addiction, now primarily in the form of heroin, shifted to a lower class, predominantly black and other non-white minorities, young, and male population. More recently, since the 1960s, it has spread to middle class youth, including whites, and especially college students. Marijuana use earlier in the century was predominantly black and jazz musician subculture. With the development of the beat bohemian subculture is spread to whites, and from the beats and their successors, the hippies, to college youth and then to increasingly younger contingents, of all races. Marijuana use in some but not all cases, led to use of other drugs, heroin, barbiturates, amphetamines, psychedelics and cocaine. These have appeared since the 1960s in youth of all class levels. Sociological background factors are responses to anomie in the sense of meaninglessness and normlessness, as well as to the perceived intolerable pressure of achievement orientation in the middle and upper class levels. Other factors are the blurring of class and race distinctions in American society generally, and a growing sense among many of the youth of the hypocrisy and illegitimacy of the formal institutions of the society, highlighted during the Vietnam War era.

Drug Use: Psychological Features

Sociological studies can delineate some of the conditions favorable to young people's developing an interest in psychoactive drugs. But they cannot tell us *which* youngsters "at risk" are likely to take on this interest, and which among them are likely to become seriously addicted. Occasionally it may be an accident of the details of the social situation. Other times it is likely to be a psychologically-predisposing factor, or lack of one. Claude Brown, writing *Manchild in the Promised Land* (1965) in his early adulthood recounts how a large proportion of the youngsters he grew up with in Harlem turned to heroin, and that he did not, only because when he was first offered some to try, he had a violent negative physical reaction which eliminated any desire to try it again. This he thinks was sheer luck.

Thus sociological knowledge of the setting could lead one to predict high percentages of the youth turning to drugs, and specifically to the dangerously addicting one, heroin. But it could not have predicted Brown's own idiosyncratic reaction, which had fateful positive consequences for him. For that we would need psychological knowledge of the particular personality.

Psychological Studies: Yochelson and Samenow Drug-Using Criminals

In their major work on criminals (reported in Chapter 2 above), Samuel Yochelson and Stanton Samenow (1976, 1977 and 1986) did a large-scale and intensive study of incarcerated criminals, the third volumes of which (1986) deals specifically with drug-using criminals. In Volumes One and Two, they presented their psychology of the criminal and a corresponding treatment plan. In the third volume, they treat specifically those criminals who were active and consistent drug users.

Not all criminals are drug users. And not all drug users are career criminals. The subjects of this study are those who are both. They are career criminals, repetitively and by choice carrying on criminal activities as their source of livelihood and essentially as a way of life—as distinguished from occasional or incidental offenders. The drug user part of this career-criminal population are people for whom drug use is not only occasional or recreational, but a constant and essential part of their life pattern. It commonly involves more than one drug, usually several, used seriatim or simultaneously, and these drugs usually include one or more that is definitely addicting like heroin or barbiturates.

The authors' major finding about the drug-using criminals is that they are not distinct psychologically or sociologically from the nondrug-using criminal population. They show the same patterns as the nondrug-using criminals. They are rebellious, unconventional, lying, deceitful, predatory and exploitative toward others. They deny responsibility and are determined not to change.

They are criminals first and primarily, and drug-users secondarily; they were criminals before they were users. Contrary to what is commonly stated, they did not turn to crime only after being hooked on drugs, in order to get money to support the habit. The pre-drug-use pattern of the criminal personality was like what has already been reported (see Chapter 2). This is a youngster constantly seeking excitement, engaging in forbidden activities, always trying to get away with whatever he could, conning and duping all the important people in his life, like parents and siblings. As long as they tolerate his deviant behavior, he is satisfied, and avails himself of the support and comforts of home life. When they do not tolerate, he rebels.

Lying and deceit become a way of life. He makes a secret life of his own, impenetrable by parents. He seeks out likeminded peers, rejecting "squares." School is irrelevant; there he covers up and avoids bringing trouble upon himself. He avoids, defers, defaults on all assigned tasks. He cons permissive teachers, etc. At school and later work, he makes minimal required effort and maximal exploitation for criminal purposes. Sexual conquests are pursued in the same exploitative and nonloving way, in any deviant or conventional forms. Here he has no concept of love, interdependence, mutuality. He cuts off both external deterrents (fear of being caught, etc.) and internal ones (conscience). Except to plan criminal scores, he cannot think long-term strategically. His violations of property, violence and sex expand as he gets older. He is confident he can get away with anything—noticing he is rarely apprehended and even more rarely punished.

Parents are kept as much in the dark as possible. They have their own needs to deny anything is really wrong with him. If his criminal acts are revealed, he becomes counter-aggressive. While he may go through motions of compliance to some therapeutic program "to keep them off his back," he is rarely sincere. Parents are at first shocked and disbelieving about his drug use and its extent and/or willing to be persuaded by a well-meaning but ill-informed therapist that it is "their fault." He was not enticed into drug use, as commonly thought, rather set out to find the drugs. That is easily done. If caught the user can claim he was corrupted by others, a claim authorities readily believe.

By the time of his first drug use he typically knows a great deal about the drugs, and is already streetwise. He denies all risks and dangers; others may get hooked, not he. Others may get caught dealing, not he. He relies on the whole roster of typical denials and justifications. His ties to responsible peers are minimal, and cut when any become informing threats. Drugs are taken in a social situation, in a well-developed drug subculture, and frequently associated with other criminal patterns. School administrators and employers are readily persuaded that the drug use is *their* fault, a gross misunderstanding of the drug users' needs and intents. Similarly in the military, drug use rules are commonly violated. Disciplinary enforcement is typically patchy, internally conflicted, ambivalent. Common lore tells of huge numbers of servicemen who "became drug users (or addicts) in combat service," e.g. in Vietnam. Again we find denial and self-obfuscation among the military authorities, and self-exculpation among users. Drug-using criminals give the same reasons for taking drugs, as nondrug-using criminals give for committing crimes. They claim to be beset by the intolerable burdens of life, whatever these may be in their particular case. It is always something external, it is asserted, that is causing them to deviate in their particular way. For the drug-user criminals, they claim the drugs are to blame for their criminal careers.

Every psychological feature found in the nondrug-using criminal is found, more exaggerated, in the drug-users. They are highly suggestible, fearful, limited in concept of injury to others. Compared even to other criminals, they have limited time perspective; their prejudgment in making decisions is more circumscribed; they are less trustworthy; have a more intense sense of their own uniqueness. Drugs facilitate lying and deceit. Users show massive resistance to any change, and are likely to believe change is impossible.

What is basically different about them (compared to nondrug-using criminals) is that drugs *enhance* the cutting off of fear, that is of both external deterrents—fear of getting caught—and of internal deterrents (force of conscience), so that "when I'm on drugs, I can do anything."

Many different drugs can be used for the same effect—opiates, depressants, stimulants, hallucinogenics—depending on characteristics of the individual, what he has heard or read, his own experiences.

Chein and Colleagues on Adolescent Drug users

Looking at a different population, in this case younger, and all users of heroin specifically, Isidor Chein *et al.* 1964, draw a detailed portrait of inner-city slum youth who become addicts or regular users. The personality part of the study indicates the following. Of the boys in this study, by far the predominant portion had ego-damaging experiences. The parents had a disturbed relationship with each other. The boy was overindulged or harshly frustrated. Parents had unrealistically low aspirations for the boy, or in a few instances, unrealistically high aspirations. The boys had superego-damaging experiences. Parent figures were cool or hostile. Parent-child relations were weak.

Parents were unclear and inconsistent in disciplinary policies. Masculine identification was poor, with fathers physically or emotionally absent; or present but cold and hostile toward the boy. The parents also did not encourage a future orientation or career aspirations for the son based on his abilities, even though other parents in the same slummy neighborhood did so. Parents themselves displayed pessimism and distrust toward authority figures such as teachers and police. Availability of drugs in the neighborhood was a condition, but not the cause of the addiction of these boys.

At the unconscious level, the shooting up works for the young man, are like the mother's breast. Such symbolism is probably not important in the *genesis* of the addiction. It can be important in its progression, as ever-larger portions of the psychic life are given over to this primitive level of gratification. Craving, dependence and tolerance enter the situation. Presence and degree of craving vary by individuals, by degree and kind of personal pathology, the need to reduce pain and anxiety, the need to avoid whatever distress, and probably also by constitutional differences among individuals. Craving in turn leads to dependence, that too varying individually, but strongest in individuals who become addicted. Youngsters with poor capacity to set and pursue long-range goals, are unable to take adequate consideration of the consequences of permitting the degree of dependence to build up. As dependence builds, abstinence syndrome becomes more likely and more painful, though not necessarily unbearable. Tolerance also builds up, on both physiological and psychological grounds. This forces either increasing dosage or resort to a free period, that is, a period of abstinence to enable returning to the beginning of the cycle again, at a lower dose.

Psychoanalytic Studies

Psychoanalysts have rarely treated addicted persons, at least not by any standard psychoanalytic method. Addicts are very poor candidates for that. Thus there is relatively little standard psychoanalytic clinical literature on this kind of person.

Psychoanalytic literature on drug addiction reveals a wide range of opinions, with no clearcut consensus. (See Yorcke 1970 for thorough short review of the literature to that time.) What can be said is that addiction to chemical substances, including alcohol, does *not* represent a single clinical syndrome, any more than does homosexuality. Rather, as Yorcke sums up the view of Savitt 1963: "addiction is a symptom-complex which occurs in a wide variety of psychiatric conditions . . . schizophrenia, depressive states, psychoneuroses, perversions, borderline states and character disorders. In all of these conditions the common addictive characteristic is passivity" (Yorcke 1970, 154).

Technically addiction involves tolerance, psychological habituation, and physical dependence with a definite withdrawal syndrome. The addict *has* to have the drug, whether alcohol, opiates or barbiturates. He is "enslaved" to the habit. There is a combination of physiological and psychological effects.

The addict case with strong manic-depressive psychotic features is not so easily distinguishable from other manic-depressives, aside from the addiction itself. Similarly if schizophrenic. Another exasperating feature (from the viewpoint of trying to make psychoanalytic distinctions) is that any psychodynamic characteristic present in any particular addict case, may be found also in psychologically similar but nonaddicted personalities. Examples are intense oral cravings or strong oral features in object relations. One is described as having strong anal-sadistic features in object relations. Another as having grave difficulties in expressing aggression. One has intense oedipal problems. Another strong counter-oedipal trends. And so on through a whole list of pathological characteristics that can be delineated in any particular case history.

What we can say all of these "cases" have in common is only the extreme craving for the drug that is of overpowering importance in the person's life, so much so that it takes precedence over all other interests.

Ralph Little and Manuel Pearson (1966) discuss the role of a pathological interdependency between two persons in the etiology and maintenance of a drug addiction. Unlike the subjects of many other studies, the patients here are all middle class or higher. Many of them are wives of medical doctors who out of their own unconscious sadistic needs got their wives addicted to barbiturates or other drugs they could prescribe for them, thus maintaining the pathological interdependency of the two individuals. The addicted person in such a relationship expressed hostility toward the addictor by maintaining all the various psychosomatic ailments that the drug is to relieve, and the hostile dependency on the addictor perpetuating the addiction, expressed, among other ways, by the complications accompanying the addiction.

The drugs involved were barbiturates, amphetamines, cocaine, and codeine.

This is am interesting study combining an interactional element with the unconscious psychodynamics of both of the individuals involved.

Psychoanalytic Work of Rado

Sandor Rado attempted a psychoanalytic formulation of the nature of drug addiction (1933). He noted in male addicts a lack of masculinization, because of absence or inadequacy of fathers, and continuing dependency on a mother figure and fixation at oral infantilism. The addict, in a state of "tense depression," finds relief in the opiate drug and with that a powerful feeling of elation. As that feeling recedes with the decline of the effect of the drug, infantile omnipotence has been shattered, and depression returns. Now it is intensified, requiring another dose of the drug. Increasing doses of the drug build up tolerance, till the sufferer is faced with a pharmacotoxic crisis, from which only three routes of exit are possible. First, suicide. Second, psychosis; or third, flight into a free interval. There the pains of withdrawal gratify masochistic wishes, and leave the sufferer free to start his drug-using cycle again at a low dose.

Glover

Edmund Glover (1932, 1939) provides another classical psychoanalytic view. Addiction is neither a neurosis nor a psychosis, though it shares some elements with each. It can have connections with many different developmental stages, mostly very early ones. Elements of compulsion underline neurotic features. Addictions may be of a depressive or a paranoid type. In the manic-depressive type, the elation phase is manic, the down period depressive. In paranoid types, the addict uses the drug to destroy an internal enemy. An addiction may also preserve its victim from becoming psychotic. Dangerous drugs are selected because of infantile projection of sadism, and the addict feels there is something bad inside him, evil parental spirits, bad body organs or simply anxiety and guilt, which can be mastered and defeated by ingesting the substance. The badness is thus literally internalized.

Problems with Psychoanalytic Formmulations

In the nature of the case, any of the formulations just given may fit some particular addicted individuals, but not others, and addiction or an addiction-like state may appear, as Savitt argues, in conjunction with any of several different pathologies, neurotic, psychotic, borderline, depressive, paranoid, etc. (see Yorcke).

Hendin on Student Drug Users

The psychoanalyst Herbert Hendin treated and studied college students in the early 70s (Hendin 1975).

Several of these were heavy users of drugs—amphetmines, marijuana, heroin, psychedelics, or several combined. The common element to all Hendin sees as these students' craving to "restructure their own emotions, not to be themselves, but to live as some 'other.' " (1975: 121). All these face "turmoil over performance, achievement and success, the increasing terror of become 'too' involved with anyone." They had repressed rage at their parents and all authority, defying them by their drug use and providing their own punishment. Drugs also provided them with "the illusion of pleasurable connection with other people."

Students turning to amphetamines as their preferred drug were predominantly women. By contrast, male students using drugs were predominantly "dropping out" and their drug of choice was more likely marijuana.

The amphetamine-using women students were busy complying with their parents' dictates to do well in school and college in order to pursue some prestigious career, and also to marry well. They felt alien to both of these demands and at the same time were unable to resist their parents' pressures. Amphetamines provided their "solution." Amphetamines enable them to function without regard to their real feelings. To get "too involved" with any other person means such a woman will destroy that person. Amphetamine users strongly resist recognizing what they feel toward themselves or other people. If they were to get in close touch with their feelings they would either destroy others with their rage or themselves be overwhelmed by their needs and appetites. Amphetamines supply them with the energy and the detachment to control their feelings and function efficiently in activities, which give no real satisfaction. The language of amphetamines—"speed" or "flying"—reflects how much these students seek a life where they are moving too quickly to think about what they do and how they feel. Preoccupation with success, performance and emotional control, traditionally a male style, now appears in women. These amphetamine users demonstrate that and also the traditional demands on females to live up to other people's expectations, minister to others' needs and sacrifice themselves.

The drug choice for young men, beset with conflicts over ambition, achievement and success, is clearly *marijuana,* which enables them to "drop out" out of the work ethic into a more passive, introspective style. Hendin notes that expressed alarm about marijuana use concerns the eroding of the work ethic. ("Amotivational syndrome," Hendin sees not as caused by marijuana use, but simply as incidental to a whole antiwork-ethic lifestyle.) These male student pot smokers have enormous inner conflicts about competition, which they feel will lead to murderous action against the rivals, ultimately the father. For some of them, to "care passionately—for a sport, a woman, a career—meant . . . to be willing to assault [or kill] anyone who challenged what he valued. To succeed inevitably meant to destroy." But losing meant unbearable humiliation. Marijuana is taken to subdue combativeness and anger, the feeling of life as war. In one case, marijuana use did not signalize a change in life values for the young man; rather it enabled him not to change at all. Marijuana was not the cause of the man's problems, but the tool to deal with them. His sense of life as war typically derived from his early relationship to his father. The outcomes would be either victory with the antagonist destroyed, or defeat, with himself cut to pieces. Typically he identified with his father's aggressiveness.

Mothers they felt to be half-interested at best and impossible to involve in their emotional lives. The intensity of their competitive rage is to be combatted by settling for something safer over which they feel no enthusiasm, or withdrawal as in one pot user's fantasy of going off alone into the Canadian wilderness. They say they take marijuana to "relieve the pressure and boredom of everyday life," or "to take the edge off [my] personality." Marijuana and involvement in the drug subculture, for many, dealing as well as using, gave them the illusion of defiance of paternal ideals or demands, while remaining locked in an ambivalent identification with the brutal father.

The *heroin users* display something else. There the mother seems to have been the primary pathogenic parent. Heroin is essentially a drug of despair. Demographically, these student users were different from the common profile; they did not come from disadvantaged slums. But these students had been intensely hurt very early and very deeply. Or the student identified with a parent hooked on alcohol, in one case the mother, in another the father. Or, he becomes more involved with a girlfriend, becomes terrified, and increases his heroin use to put distance between them. On heroin the young man could sexually "perform"—i.e. maintain an erection for hours, without ejaculation, a feat he regarded as giving his girlfriend great satisfaction, with no concern about intimacy. Heroin makes everything and everyone else unimportant. Anything important to him made him vulnerable to being hurt. Heroin numbs him from the pain of disappointment in his mother, at the same time keeping her involved in his life. On heroin he escapes from paralyzing confusion; everything becomes clear, and there are solutions to all problems. Or he is overtly and consciously hostile and manipulative toward his woman; he may help her to attempt suicide. Heroin may enable him to sustain a lifestyle of almost total passivity. Those more involved in the drug subculture, actively dealing as well as using, enjoy the illegality and its risks. Many of the heroin users are polydrug users, taking marijuana, barbiturates, other sedatives, such as quaalude or LSD, as well. Many have an obsessive concern with their women's infidelity, evidently not justified by the real behavior of the women. Becoming involved with a woman and losing her reawakens the pain of early relationship with the mother. Not letting the woman become too great a source of pleasure protects him from such pain. Heroin helps in such protection. The price is renouncing any hope of having experiences that would satisfy his needs. Heroin supports the illusion of invulnerability. Heroin was also frequently very destructive even for students who do not become addicted, but used it only once or twice. Heroin was the drug par excellence that connects a student to the outlaw world of the illicit drug culture, giving him a sense of solidarity with other such outlaws.

Psychedelic drugs, Hendin found, were sought out by students seeking to transcend the ordinary limits of their daily experience. Some alternate between random polydrug use and concentration on LSD and mescaline, which help achieve desired fragmentation. Or a user finds himself ordered about by a kind of supernatural power (the psychedelic drugs) much as he was ordered about by his domineering and unempathic mother. Some feel they are breaking the structure of their own personality with LSD, or seeking experience without emotion. The unpredictability of the psychedelic experience contributes to fragmentation. A ghoulish horror movie is enjoyed as preferable to real everyday experience. A male LSD user had, only when stoned, casual one-night stands with women. One sought contact with "ultimate knowledge" through LSD. One deals with real threats in the world, like young thugs robbing him, by blandness and denial of anger. Experience with his parents taught one that everyone will expect him to ignore his own feelings in favor of theirs. If he gives in to any enthusiasm, such as a girl, or his musical talent, he will be engulfed by it and be destroyed. In his science-fiction story, people live by draining life from others. For many students, LSD opened new worlds for them, but what was revealed "was mostly lousy"—nothing was as it appeared, relationships were all destructive. Psychedelic-induced fragmentation both liberated them from mundane existence and enslaved them (condensed from Hendin 1975, chs.5–8).

A difficulty with this kind of study is that each portrait of a particular drug user is believable, and the reconstruction of the personality dynamics and the user's early experiences with crucial figures like the parents is plausible. Still, one is not convinced that these configurations apply only to users of particular drugs, or even combinations of drugs, and would not also be found in many individuals of the same generation and circumstances, who are *not* drug users. That argument, in fact, is frequently hinted at in Hendin's account, whenever he discusses common problems faced by youth—at least more advantaged youth who appear at elite colleges, at that period in this society.

Alcoholism: Psychological Factors

There is no consensus in psychological, psychiatric and psychoanalytic studies, on the existence and features of an "alcoholic personality." However, we can delineate a number of characteristics that are *more likely* in alcoholics than in others, at least in the majority of cases (Catanzano 1967: 38ff). The personality portrait looks like this: Drinking is used to still anxieties in interpersonal situations. These anxieties do not disappear with a moderate amount of alcohol, but being deeply rooted, continue and get worse, resulting in more drinking. The alcoholic is emotionally immature, needing instantaneous gratification, or is impulsive in expression of feelings. This individual may be extremely dependent in an infantile way, and in the case of males, covers this by a domineering stance toward others, especially toward the women in his life.

He (males outnumber females) is constantly in conflict between such dependency and subservience and the need to be dominant and mighty, and is ambivalent toward all versions of authority. He has low frustration tolerance, often expressed by turning to drink. He is grandiose, sober as well as when drinking. He may in his cups boast about enormous achievements (usually imaginary) and later berate himself extravagantly for being an absolute nothing, itself a grandiose exaggeration. To be all that bad is no small accomplishment either.

Grandiosity may function for many defensive purposes, including defense against feelings of guilt as well as shame. Typically he has very low self-esteem, feels worthless, and drinks heavily, to try to assuage that feeling. When he comes out of the drinking bout, feels even worse about himself: "What a lousy and worthless crumb I am." In the course of becoming a more confirmed drinker, already isolated from others, he becomes even more so. Feelings of being worthless, of being unlovable and therefore unloved, tie in with grandiosity, as well as perfectionism and compulsiveness. The alcoholic must perfect himself, working compulsively to prove he is better than others, so that he will not feel so guilty and ashamed about his real failures in the world. Such compulsive perfectionism may alternate with his bouts of drinking, during which he does the opposite.

This is an extremely dependent, infantile, individual, and in the case of males, in a great deal of conflict about that dependency. He is supposed to be adult and able to stand on his own, but his real feelings are to expect that someone strong, powerful and loving (like a perfect parent) will always take care of him. Such feelings contradict the wish to be grown up and independent and able to care for others, making him perpetually angry, with others, or with himself, or both. Or he finds that his extreme and insatiable dependency needs are not met by the people close to him, like the wife or girl friend. Therefore he is in a state of almost constant anger at her. Such anger cannot be overtly expressed, so he drinks more. That makes matters worse. Typically he has a difficult time expressing his angry feelings, holding them in most of the time, and then suddenly exploding in verbal or physical violence.

The background usually contains a great deal of pathology in the family of origin. Mothers may be extremely negligent, because of their own conflicts about taking care of helpless others, or inconsistently indulgent and not allowing the child to develop or acquire age-appropriate autonomy. Or the mother has kept the child in an extreme state of dependency, by domineering control "for the good of the child." The pathological family background also commonly includes social deviancy of various kinds in the father, or the mother, or both, including in many cases criminal activities, and alcoholism or at least heavy drinking.

Psychology of the Stages of Alcoholism

Alcoholism as a disease progresses in certain standard patterns:

1) Pre-Alcoholic Phase: Meets everyday tensions by drinking.

1a) Heavier drinking, more often, to get the same effect.

2) Early Alcoholic Blackouts: brief amnesias, then become more frequent.

2a) Sneaking drinks; then preoccupied with alcohol, hiding bottles; then guilty avoidance of the subject. now a "heavy drinker," denying there is a problem, but he and his family know it is getting out of hand. Various avoidance mechanisms.

3) Addiction: has lost control; if he takes one drink, he feels *compelled* to take another and another. He has become *physically* dependent; he has horrendous withdrawal symptoms, tolerance, disastrous psychosocial effects.

4) Final phase: benders, sprees, descent to skid-row associations, severe medical complications, such as liver cirrhosis. The whole process is intensely self-destructive.

However, many drinkers do not follow this whole process, some drinking heavily but not becoming addicted, some going on to advanced stages only on weekends.

If dried out by a control-rehabilitation process like Alcoholics Anonymous, he may take on its ideology that "once an alcoholic, always an alcoholic," to which only total abstinence is the answer. (Note the A.A. view is contradicted by the experience of many heavy drinkers.)

Interactional Elements: Wives of Alcoholics

One interactional element is indicated in an interesting study by Thelma Whalen (1975) on "Wives of Alcoholics." Whalen found a limited number of types of women married to these alcoholic men. Without attempting any psychological analysis, she described "Punitive Polly," "Suffering Susan" and others.

"Punitive Polly" is a woman whose tie to her alcoholic husband is a punitive one. She punishes him in the variety of ways at her disposal, for his drinking and withdrawal from family responsibilities. She does not simply dissolve the marriage, however, but stays and continues to punish him. It is evident to the researcher, that at some level, she *needed* to be married to a man who would drink, and increasingly so, this gives her the justification for punishing him.

"Suffering Susan" is one of those women who need to suffer in marriage or close relationship. Her husband's increased drinking causes her suffering. While at the surface level she objects, complains, whines and nags, in effect she does nothing to stop his turn to alcoholism.

A third type is "Controlling Catherine." Her need is to dominate her man; that is basically, though not overtly, why she married him. Another type has a need to depreciate the mate.

In each case the husband's alcoholism makes him that much more suitable to fulfill the wife's needs. So while the conventional picture tells us how the man's descent into alcoholism is destructive of his marriage and his wife and children, this portrait underlines the ways in which the wife in effect colludes in this process.

While Whalen does not explicitly do this, we can give an interactive-psychological interpretation to her data. The husband who becomes alcoholic is an intensely dependent personality who needs a woman like a controlling dominating mother. Her controlling or punitive behavior assaults his self-esteem even further, therefore he needs to drink more. Or she may be playing "Suffering Susan" and his drinking is a way of punishing her, for whatever it is that she represents to him. Her suffering does not stop his behavior, rather in effect encourages it. They are caught in a pathological interdependency. The process is similar to that dealt with in Little and Pearson's study on dependency on other drugs (see above).

Psychological Study of Cocaine Users

One study of cocaine users is significant (Weiss, Mirin, Michael and Sollogub 1986). The researchers studied a group of 30 hospitalized serious cocaine abusers, nearly all white, voluntarily admitted to a drug treatment program in a private urban hospital. Two-thirds were males and the patients had high occupational status (executives, professionals, white-collar workers). They were compared with 124 hospitalized patients who were dependent upon opiates or central nervous system depressants. Nineteen of the these thirty (63%) cocaine cases met criteria for diagnosis other than substance abuse, and sixteen (53%) had affective disorder. They had a significantly higher rate of affective disorder than did the opiate and depressants abusers. The researchers also found a significantly higher rate of depressive disorder among first-degree relatives of the cocaine abusers when compared to the other group.

An important finding was that cocaine users were more likely to use more cocaine when already "up," either on a previous dose, or in a non-drug-induced euphoric period of a chronic bipolar depression. Also they did not typically take cocaine when feeling depressed in such a cyclic pattern. Cocaine made endogenously produced elevated mood states more intense and more long-lasting. Probably where such occurred a euphoric state made the patient more impulsive and more disinhibited, therefore more likely to use drugs out of recklessness and poor judgment.

The researchers identified three subtypes of heavy cocaine abusers in their sample: 1) patients with a history of major depression or attention deficit disorder, who may initially use cocaine as a form of self-medication; 2) patients with cyclothymic or bipolar disorder who use cocaine primarily when endogenously euphoric in order to intensify or prolong their pleasurable symptoms; and 3) patients whose major psychopathology is characterological, these being mainly borderline and narcissistic disorders.

A major difficulty with this research is that it does not reveal the source of the indicated depression. Is it pharmacological effects of the cocaine itself, considering they are all being studied *after* they have become heavy cocaine users? Or is it an effect of the "crash" after they cease using cocaine? Or is it adverse life experiences common in heavy drug users? Or—it would be important to know—does it derive from personality patterns pre-dating the cocaine use? We can note that these individuals started drug use somewhat later in life than users of other drugs. Also the presence of depressive symptoms in close relatives is suggestive, but was not pursued or speculated upon by these researchers. (Is there perhaps a genetic factor? Or an environmental-genetic one?) Those persons who have abused drugs from an early age may never have entered the age of risk for affective disorder in a drug-free state. Also heavy drug users are typically unreliable in recall of early-life-history features relevant for psychiatric history.

Summary on Pychological Aspects of Drugs

There are few firm generalizations we can make about the psychology of drug experiences. Few drug users limit themselves to one particular drug, and many will take almost anything that is available, often without knowing exactly what it is. The very riskiness about what is ingested even constitutes part of the appeal for some users, fitting into a pervasive antinomian approach to the world. Similarly getting into criminal activities, if only dealing in drugs, becomes almost a standard part of regular drug experience. Then there is a whole range of involvement in drug-taking activities, from rare occasional experimenter to constant habitual user. For those toward the higher end of that scale, a common thread is disaffiliation from conventional life of routinized hard work toward conventional goals. Drug taking may be a relief from the "pressures" of regular work, ambition, pursuit of "success," or felt as "earned" respite from that, if only on an occasional basis, then itself becoming a consuming central part of life. This may be the case with any of the serious drugs, from addicting narcotics like heroin, through barbiturates and amphetamines, through the most commonly used recreational drug, alcohol, and its near rival marijuana, into the exotic psychedelics, and the chic of cocaine and its variations.

Though strong devotees of one particular drug may scorn the others, most have at least tried them, and will again if their preferred drug is not available. Practically everyone who has gone beyond marijuana has tried at least several others.

As the individual preferences vary, so do the primary motivations of the users, within any one drug or group, and between drugs. For some it is momentary recreational pleasure, for some, surcease, for some oblivion, for some transcendant ecstasy, for some mystic experience of the ineffable, and in some cases, for the same individual something different at different times and circumstances. For depressive personalities, cocaine or amphetamines may be the preference, but they can be so for others too. "Insecure, dependent and immature" may fit the profile of many alcoholics, but would also apply to many users of pot and of heroin too. Passivity may be the most common psychological characteristic of users of many types of drugs, but that does not particularly differentiate them. At the same time many on the surface at least appear to be very activist adventurers, risking much at the frontiers of this poorly boundaried world. In many cases, for males particularly, the latter may be cover for deep-lying passivity, a counterphobic feature.

Drugs *may* be the medium for expression of deeply psychopathological trends. Deep involvement in them may certainly be the channel for deviance, at least from the trends of more constrictive elements of mainstream society, as well as conduit for strong *conformity* to widespread trends of the social world. At the same time, drug use *may* be associated with "good-enough-functioning," psychologically. By that we mean the person is not particularly neurotic, psychotic, or suffering from psychopathy, or borderline or narcissistic personality, and has psychological resilience sufficient for the occasion. Similarly he or she may not be particularly deviant from the ways of the world of her/his particular social milieu.

Chapter Summary and Conclusion

From time immemorial human beings have used various chemical substances, derived from plant life, or manufactured deliberately in laboratories, to accomplish a variety of purposes. These products are to relieve pain or discomfort, to feel an experience of transcendance, to keep awake through long arduous tasks, to go to sleep, to have more interesting dreams, to feel "high" rather than low, to experience religious revelation, to relieve boredom or fatigue from stultifying work, or simply to feel happy. Some of these were widely accepted, even revered, in particular societies. Our own modern society has made a number of these items and pursuits against the law, expressing cultural norms of particularly constricted and wishing to be authoritarian political controllers. Often these controls are imposed "for the good of the sufferers," to prevent or forestall personal pains and tragedies. In the process of criminalizing many drugs of questionable harmfulness to the partakers, as well as others clearly harmful, while large numbers of persons continue to, or start to, desire the drugs, huge markets have been created for these illicit goods. As long as the society has a market system of economy, suppliers of the demanded goods appear, and learn how to make huge fortunes in the illicit business. In the process they have a stake in keeping up with the demand, which is done by every means at their disposal, and with the more than willing collaboration of the buyers of the drugs. In effect, though no doubt without conscious deliberate intent, the law and the criminal syndicates collaborate in creating the expansion of the drug trade. Part of the effort of law enforcement consists of propaganda messages to the potential buyers, especially the most susceptible public, adolescents and young adults. These messages warn of the dangers of the drugs in terms that are frequently out of line with a reality discoverable by the young. That reality can be learned from their own experience or that of their peers. As a result the drug law enforcement agents have no credibility with the young, or with much of the public altogether. At the same time for all those seriously involved in drug activities, the drug law enforcement agents are almost automatically "the enemy." This attitude in turn reinforces whatever antinomianism already exists in the drug-using population, and extends to all "authorities." These include not only law enforcement, but also scientific researchers (perhaps exempting drug-sympathizing social scientists), and discredits even sober realistic study showing the very real dangers of addicting drugs such as heroin.

Thus by the very existence of puritanically-based and almost entirely unenforceable antidrug laws, a major part of the drug-using population are automatically "deviant" in reference at least to the laws on the books, and no doubt also in the minds of a large part of the conventional population. Attitudes vary by type of drug—heroin addicts most so, and social drinkers of alcoholic beverages least so—and are in a state of flux among different populations.

Then on the question of psychopathology, there is scarcely any agreement at all. Even people who became long-term psychotics evidently triggered by psychedelic drug experiences, were not so recognized by many surrounding observers (including prominently some sociological observers, e.g. Howard Becker). The psychopathological potential of long-term opiate addiction—as consequence, and, otherwise viewed, as precondition—is recognized by some observers and ignored or denied by others. None of the serious drug involvements—addiction to heroin, amphetamines, barbiturates, or intense psychological dependency on cocaine—is seen by psychopathology experts as itself any kind of clinical syndrome. But it is seen as probably, though not invariably, associated with some identifiable neurotic, psychotic or character disorder syndrome. Exasperatingly, not with any consistency, with any *particular* psychopathological pattern. Some but far from all, of the cocaine cases are associated with particular patterns of depressive disorder. Also, as noted, it is difficult to impossible to isolate patterns related to a particular drug, because users rarely concentrate on one drug to the exclusion of others. All we can say with any assurance is that various kinds of psychopathology may appear along with, or preceding, any instance of drug use, or the user may not be definable at all in terms of psychopathology.

To summarize, the drug user may be deviant or not, and suffering from psychopathology or not, and if yes on either, to any degree ranging from minimal to strong. And if there is both deviance and psychopathology in a particular drug-using person, they may or may not be connected.

REFERENCES

Addiction Research Foundation. 1983. *Cannabis: Health Risks.* Toronto: ARF Books

Anonymous. 1969. "The Effects of Marijuana on Consciousness." in Tart 1969, ch.22: 335–355

Armour, David J. *et al.* 1976. *Alcoholism and Treatment.* Santa Monica, CA: Rand

Becker, Howard S. 1963. *Outsiders.* New York: Free Press

Blum, Richard. 1967. *Narcotics and Drug Abuse.* Task Force Report, Presidential Commission on Law Enforcement and Administration of Justice

Blum, Richard *et al.* 1964. *Utopiates* New York: Atherton

Brown, Claude. 1965. *Manchild in the Promised Land.* New York: Macmillan

Bruin Humanist Forum, Issues Study Committee. 1969. "Marijuana (Cannabis) Fact Sheet." in Tart 1969, ch. 21: 325-334

Cahalan, Don, and Robin Room. 1974. *Problem Drinking among American Men.* New Brunswick, NJ: Rutgers Center of Alcohol Studies

Catanzano, Ronald J. 1967. "Psychiatric Aspects of Alcoholism." in: David J. Pittman, ed. *Alcoholism* New York: Harper and Row

Chein, Isidor *et al.* 1964. *The Road to H.* New York: Basic Books

Cloward, Richard and Lloyd Ohlin. 1960. *Deliquency and Opportunity.* New York: Free Press

Cohen, Sidney. 1966. *The Beyond Within.* New York: Atheneum

DeLint, Jan, and Wolfgang Schmidt. 1971. "Alcohol Use and Alcoholism." *Addictions.* 18:1–14

Devereux, George. 1980. *Basic Problems in Ethnopsychiatry.* Chicago: University of Chicago Press.

Fabing, H. D. 1956. "On Going Berserk: A Neurochemical Inquiry." *American Journal of Psychiatry* 113:409–415

Fenichel, O. 1945. *The Psychoanalytic Theory of Neurosis.* New York: Norton

Glover, E. 1932. "On the aetiology of drug addiction." *International Journal of Psychoanalysis.* 13: 2 298–328

__________. 1939. 2d ed. 1949. *Psycho-Analysis.* London: Staples

Goode, Erich. 1978. *Deviant Behavior.* Englewood Cliffs, NJ: Prentice-Hall

Grinspoon, Lester. 1971. *Marihuana Reconsidered.* Cambridge, MA: Harvard University Press

Hendin, Herbert. 1975. *The Age of Sensation.* New York: Norton

Huxley, Aldous. 1954. *The Doors of Perception.* New York: Harper

Inciardi, James. 1986. *The War on Drugs.* Palo Alto, CA: Mayfield

Katz, Solomon H., and Mary M. Voigt. 1986. "Bread and Beer: The Early Use of Cereals in the Human Diet." *Expedition.* (Journal of the Museum of Archaeology/Anthropology, University of Pennsylvania). 28:2:23–35

LaBarre, Weston. 1969. *The Peyote Cult.* 4th ed., Enlarged. New York: Schocken Books

__________. 1980. "Psychotropics." Chs. 2,3,4, in LaBarre *Culture in Context.* Durham, NC: Duke University Press

Little, Ralph B., and Manuel Pearson. 1966. "The Management of Pathologic Interdependency in Drug Addiction." *American Journal of Psychiatry.* 123:554–560

Mann, Peggy. 1980. "Marijuana: The Myth of Harmlessness Goes Up in Smoke." *Saturday Evening Post.* July/August, 1980.

Masters, R. E. L, and Jean Houston. 1966. *The Varieties of Psychedelic Experience.* New York: Holt, Rinehart, Winston

Merton, Robert K. 1937. "Social Structure and Anomie." *American Sociological Review.* 3: 672–682. Reprinted in Merton, *Social Theory and Social Structure.* 1949, 1957.

Mikuriya, T. H. 1969. "Marihuana in Medicine: Past, Present and Future." *California Medicine.* 110: 3–40

Mogar, Robert E. 1969. "Current Status and Future Trends in Psychedelic (LSD) Research." in Tart 1969, ch. 26: 381–397

Pittman, David J., ed. 1967. *Alcoholism.* New York: Harper and Row

Preble, Edward, and John J. Casey Jr. 1969. "Taking Care of Business—the Heroin User's Life on the Street." *International Journal of the Addictions.* 4.

Radford, Patricia *et al.* 1972. "Heroin Addiction: A Psychoanalytic Study." in *Psychoanalytic Study of the Child.* 27: 156–180

Rado, Sandor. 1933. "Psychoanalysis of Pharmacothymia." *Psychoanalytic Quarterly.* 2:1–23

Savitt, R. A. 1954. "Extramural psychoanalystic treatment of a case of neurotic addiction." *Jl. of the American Psychoanalytic Association* 2: 494–502

__________. 1963. "Psychoanalytic Studies on Addiction: Ego Structure in Narcotic Addiction." *Psychoanalytic Quarterly.* 32: 43-57

Spotts, James V., and Franklin C. Shontz. 1980. *Cocaine Users: a Representative Case Approach.* New York: Free Press

Stevens, William K. 1987. "Does Civilization Owe a Debt to Beer?" *The New York Times,* Mar. 24, 1987, p. C3

Tart, Charles T., ed. 1969. *Altered States of Consciousness.* New York: Wiley

Thio, Alex. 1983. *Deviant Behavior.* 2nd Edition. Boston: Houghton Mifflin

Trice, Harrison. 1966. *Alcoholism in America.* New York: McGraw-Hill

Wasson, R. Gordon. 1968. *Soma: Divine Mushroom of Immortality.* New York: Harcourt Brace World; The Hague: Mouton

Weiss, Roger D., Steven M. Mirin, Jacqueline L. Michael, and Ann C. Sollogub. 1986. "Psychopathology in Chronic Cocaine Abusers." *American Journal of Drug and Alcohol Abuse.* 12 (1 & 2):17–29

Whalen, Thelma. 1975. "Wives of Alcoholics." in William Rushing, ed. *Deviant Behavior and Social Process.* New York: Rand McNally: 311–317

Yochelson, Samuel, and Stanton Samenow. 1986. *The Criminal Personality: Vol. III: The Drug User.* Northvale, NJ: Jason Aronson

Yorcke, Clifford. 1970. "A Critical review of some psychoanalytic literature on drug addiction." *British Jl. of Medical Psychology* 43:141–159

Chapter 5
THE MENTALLY ILL*

> We are not total abstainers from reason, but use it with fanatical moderation.
>
> —Robert Lowie, 1929

As suggested in the Introduction, the mentally ill as deviants are disturbing to the general population. If seriously ill, i.e. psychotic, the way such a person perceives the world is off-base in reference to the rest of society; he may act in ways considered at the very least eccentric, violating ordinary rules of conduct or discourse. When conversing with you, he may look, not into your eyes, but rather at your ears or your chest or your feet. So in terms of that fourfold table (Deviants? Yes or No? Sick, Yes or No?) they would seem to fit readily into cell 1, deviant yes, and sick yes. So what is the problem? why are we discussing them at all under the concept of deviance? or of psychopathology? Well, believe it or not, many sociologists nowadays want to deny any psychopathology in these persons, or at least to regard this as a controversial matter. On the other side, there are psychoanalytically minded persons, this author for one, who would argue that many people not ordinarily considered deviant, may be psychologically ill, as in the case mentioned of the "well-adjusted" (socially functioning) accountant who is an obsessive-compulsive neurotic.

The transcultural psychiatrist Alexander Leighton conducted interviews with native healers in Nigeria. He had this encounter:

> On one occasion a healer said to me, through an interpreter: "This man came here three months ago, full of delusions and hallucinations; now he is free of them." I said, "What do these words 'hallucination' and 'delusion' mean? I don't understand." I asked the question thinking of course, of the problems of cultural relativity in a culture where practices such as witchcraft, which in the West would be considered delusional, are accepted. The native healer scratched his head and looked a bit puzzled at this question, and then he said, "Well, when this man came here he was standing right where you see him now and thought he was in Abeokuta (which is about

* Parts of this chapter are adapted from Endleman 1981, Part 5.

> thirty miles away), he thought I was his uncle and he thought God was speaking to him from the clouds. Now I don't know what you call that in the United States, but here we consider that these are hallucinations and delusions!" (Quoted by Townsend 1978: 66)

This story illustrates the viewpoint on psychological disorder known as clinical universalism, or the *trans*cultural, as distinguished from *cross*-cultural, perspective. Except for superficial variation in *content,* psychiatric disorders are fundamentally the same throughout the world. Cultural relativists, favoring cross-cultural comparisons and contrasts, emphasize differences from one culture to another, including the idea that psychological functioning can vary importantly from one culture to another. By contrast, the transculturalists, including this writer, emphasize the commonalities in psychic functioning, of all human beings, as discussed in Chapter 1 of this work (as well as my earlier writings—see Endleman 1981, part V especially). As Leighton had to learn from a native healer, if you see things that are not objectively there, and believe things that are readily falsifiable by ordinary observation, you are having hallucinations and delusions, and this will be so universally whatever the common cultural beliefs in different societies.

Sociological Approaches

One would think that on the topic of *mental* illness, which is about *psychological* ailments, sociologists would have relied heavily on psychological scholars and practitioners, and deferred to their judgments. Not always so. Recently, hardly so at all. In fact, since the 1960s, one major trend in the sociology of mental illness has been combating the viewpoints of psychological experts, especially psychiatrists and psychoanalysts. In some cases they deny these viewpoints entirely, to emphasize a conception that what is *pronounced* as "mental illness," is the outcome of a social process, and not intrinsically connected with the actual inner mental state of the individual so defined. Earlier, however, other sociological approaches appeared. In one of these, the sociologist *assumed,* for example, the basic capacity of psychological experts, specifically psychiatrists and by extension clinical psychologists and psychoanalysts of all kinds, to assess more or less accurately and reliably the psychological disturbance of afflicted individuals, and therefore correctly characterize them as ill. The sociologist could then proceed to take these characterizations and plot them in relationship to social and cultural variables. Thus there were a whole series of researches on the relationship of mental illness to social class, and, to a lesser degree, to other demographic variables like age, sex, race, ethnicity. There the sociologists accepted the psychiatric categories of psychosis, neurosis and whatever other subcategories of psychic ill were in current use, more or less ready made from the psychological experts. So we had a series of studies starting with Faris and Dunham (1939) on mental disorders in urban areas, and Hollingshead and Redlich (1958) on social class and mental illness. (Cf. on that topic, Dohrenwend and Dohrenwend 1969.) The sociologists also noted how differently people with evidently similar psychic ills were handled by health practitioners and/or hospitals, depending on class variables. Psychotics were found more commonly associated with the poor or lower class; neurotics with middle or upper class. The poor were more likely to be institutionalized in state hospitals; the well-to-do were given private outpatient treatment, or in more severe cases, were placed in private hospitals with more individualized professional care. Until recently, office treatment by a clinician, whether psychiatrist, psychologist, psychoanalyst, or other clinical practitioner, was almost entirely confined to well-to-do and middle income clients (see Richman 1985 for recent changes).

Other social scientists, wondering whether the identified mentally ill seen in hospitals or in private therapy might represent only the tip of the iceberg, devised ways of assessing the "mental health" of a whole (putatively) normal population. Srole *et al.* (1962) surveying a carefully chosen sample of the entire nonhospitalized population of a section of Manhattan in New York City, found that about 80% of them had "some degree of psychological impairment," and about 20% were impaired severely enough to require, urgently, intense psychiatric attention. Additional studies of this kind have been done in other parts of North America, e.g. Leighton 1959, and in other countries.

These prevalence studies run into all kinds of difficulties: how to get a sample large enough and carefully enough selected to be representative of the population in question, and how at the same time to get intensive enough data to enable characterizing the state of mental health or impairment of the persons involved. Typically extensive studies—i.e. using large and carefully constructed samples—have not been intensive enough to give what clinical practitioners would regard as an adequate picture of the psychological state of the individuals involved. A typical "instrument" of such a study consists of 22 question items (constructed by T. Langner and associates from much larger lists developed in earlier studies) which are intended and claimed to be a reliable "psychiatric screening" inventory. Items included are "are you usually generally very happy, rather happy, not so happy, rather unhappy, or very unhappy?" or "do you have headaches, (backaches, other aches and pains) very frequently, somewhat often, not so often, rarely, hardly ever at all? The composite score on such a list is claimed as highly correlated in preliminary studies with psychiatric clinical judgments based on intensive clinical interviews. Whether such studies are valid indicators of amount of mental illness is open to question. Most critics doubt that they are reliable from one place and context to another, i.e. that average scores in one place/time are really comparable with those in another. Similarly studies comparing different ethnic and racial groups by such methods, are subject to great questioning.

By contrast, studies of mental illness of particular individuals, or of patterns within the general phenomenon of psychopathology, conducted by clinicians, professionals devoted to the treatment and relief of persons with psychological ills, tend to be complexly *intensive,* but not very *extensive.* They are unlikely to include a large number of cases, or to sample a whole population. The latter, almost in the nature of the cases, is extremely rare in clinical reports. The clinicians, in turn, are apt to believe that only they are really qualified to render a judgment on whether a particular person is mentally ill at all, and if so, just what the diagnosis is.

But clinical specialists are also notorious for having very little consensus on the specific diagnosis of a person they all consider psychologically disturbed in *some* way or degree, only they cannot agree how much or how (Cf. Blum 1962, Ash 1949, other references in Kaplan 1972).

In addition, there are different kinds of clinical practitioner, psychoanalysts, psychiatrists, clinical psychologists, psychiatric social workers, and others. They may well disagree with each other on diagnosis and dynamics. They also may all be somewhat more tolerant of the ambiguity of such a situation than "hard-nosed scientists" such as experimental psychologists and some sociologists who aspire to be "hard scientists."

Common to all these studies, however, is a basic assumption that there is such an entity as psychological disturbance which may be called mental illness, even though the exact boundary may be unclear between persons who have it and those who don't. Agreement on that boundary may also not be very widespread, among various specialists. It is assumed also that there can be reasonable assurance among practitioners that properly qualified professionals *can* identify cases of the phenomenon with some agreement from peers. It is important to point this out, because some of the more recent work on the sociology of mental illness, as well as of certain psychiatrists, suggests we are in a kind of relativistic morass on this matter, one faction's "mental illness" being another's "normality" or "health."

Varities of Psychopathology and Relation to Deviance

As discussed earlier, the deviant (norm-violating) is not necessarily psychologically sick, and the psychologically sick is not necessarily deviant. These are analytically distinct categories.

Psychological malfunctioning has been classified in a variety of ways, and there is no complete consensus among professionals in the field. A handy classification for our purposes is that we distinguish "organic" from "functional" disorders. Organic disorders have a biological basis, malfunctioning or lesion in the brain or other part of the biological system, as in paresis, or consequences of venereal disease or other toxic physiological processes. If careful biomedical examination rules out an organic basis, then we hypothesize a "functional" basis, namely something in the *psychological* functioning of the individual.

Among the functional disorders, we distinguish two main categories, psychosis and neurosis. The psychoses are more serious ruptures from normal psychic functioning, evidenced symptomatically by such cognitive malfunctions as delusions, hallucinations; by extreme confusional states; extremes of primary process thinking; or extremes of affective state such as intense, and not environmentally explainable, depression, or mania, or more rarely, an alternation of both. Extreme "out-of-this-world" reactions may appear. Also possible is extreme and irrational suspiciousness, with or without delusions of grandeur or persecution or both, not amenable to reality testing.

A major feature of psychosis is to be "out of it", i.e. out of ordinary contact with ordinary "reality." (Of course there are enormous potential difficulties in defining such a "reality.") Holders of a transcultural viewpoint, including this author, consider that this kind of disorder, in its *dynamics,* not necessarily its contents, is a panhuman universal potentiality, and can and does appear in any culture in the world at any point in history.

Many of the less severe disorders are classifiable as *neuroses.* These are states of intense and irrational anxiety without, however, clearcut breaks from consensual reality perception and reality testing. They involve unresolved and persistent inner conflicts interfering with attainment of consciously pursued goals. They include irrational fears such as phobias; hysterical reactions; obsessive-compulsive ritualistic acts and observances. Here the person, unlike the psychotic, is still very much in the world and connecting with it, but constantly experiencing difficulties. These are not simply conflicts with persons or forces in the environment more or less realistically perceived. Rather they are conflicts stemming largely from within and not amenable to "realistic," "rational" and "commonsensical" advice and counseling.

There are now also recognized a variety of other disorders different from psychotic (not as severe or incapacitating) but also from neurotic:

e.g. "character disorders," alcoholic and other substance-abuse personality organization; narcissistic personality disorder; borderline syndrome; and psychopathic or antisocial personality syndrome.

Are these deviant?

General answer: some yes, some no. The psychotic are usually sociologically deviant as well; their "weird" and "crazy" way of perceiving and reacting to the world is seen as at least disturbing and unsettling to others, as violating normative expectations of how people are supposed to think and act in society, but this behavior is usually deviance different from law-violation as in delinquents and criminals, different from substance-abusers and sexual deviants (though the psychotic may be any one of those as well). Most criminals are not psychotic, but some are (see Chapter 2, and later in this chapter.) Neither are most homosexuals, but a few are, as discussed in Chapter 3. For other kinds of psychological disorder, not psychotic, the person may or may not be also sociologically deviant. His neurotic trends might lead him to act at odds with the law, such as "the criminal from a sense of guilt" (see Chapter 2). Some very neurotic homosexuals might repeatedly get into minor brushes with the law in a kind of masochistic quest for punishment (see chapter 3). Persons with character disorders might also be so impelled to get themselves into conflict with the law; while some others may not be sociologically deviant at all, as in the case of the obsessive-compulsive accountant or librarian where the psychological malfunctioning ties in with *conformity* with certain role demands.

By contrast the psychopathic (or sociopathic, or antisocial personality) is most likely to be socially deviant as well. He is drawn to behavior violating social norms, if only the mores, but often the laws.

Labeling Sociology

A radical challenge to ways of thinking about "mental illness" earlier shared by psychopathologists and sociologists of mental illness, started to appear in the 1960s, and came to be called the "labeling perspective," (or even, more pretentiously, the "labeling theory.") An example of a case evidently made to order for sociologists of this persuasion, is the situation of psychiatry in the Soviet Union in reference to dissidents against the regime.

Case 4: Soviet Psychiatry

In the Soviet Union at the present time, political dissidents against the regime face the prospect of being examined psychiatrically and being declared "psychiatrically sick," largely on the basis of their dissidence, and therefore incarcerated in a mental hospital (see Fireside 1979).

Western psychiatrists question this diagnosis (Reich 1983). This is an excellent case for examining the relationship between deviance and psychopathology, and the relevance for serious understanding, of making a distinction between the two. Clearly political dissidence is "deviance," i.e. going against the rules of the society, at least of the regime in power. What is problematical is the designation of these individuals not as traitors or enemies of the state (obviously possible) but as psychiatrically sick, a negative judgment from a very different arena of discourse. Objectors to this procedure argue that the designation as "psychiatrically sick" does not reflect an accurate appraisal of the dissident's psychological state, but rather indicates an act of political persecution. In one instance at least, Western psychiatrists found no evidence of psychiatric disorder in a person who had been hospitalized by the Soviet psychiatrists on such a diagnosis (Reich 1983). Without an independent psychological evaluation by professionals not beholden to a particular political regime, we cannot concur in the judgment of psychiatric illness. Part of the process of arriving at their diagnosis of "illness" in these cases, the Soviet psychiatrists say themselves, involves the following consideration. In the political system of the Soviet Union, any overt opposition to the regime in power, or to the Soviet "system" is so exceedingly dangerous to one's job, one's security, even one's life, that one would *have* to be "deranged" (in some sense, to some degree) to dare to do this. Dead heroes are survived by live cowards. The better part of rationality, of circumspection, thus of "sanity." would lead people not to dare to dissent, even with compelling, plausibly rational reasons, for doing so. Therefore the dissidents "*must* be crazy." Thus the very act of dissidence is taken as the indicator of the psychopathology.

What Walter Reich, an American psychiatrist, and his Western psychiatric colleagues found on investigation of these cases, was that the Soviet psychiatrists tended to be "sincere," and not simply craven toadies of an all-powerful political regime. In most cases they really *believed* their diagnoses, and believed they were based on competent professional practice (Reich 1983: 25).

Sociologists of deviance of the labeling persuasion, particularly those working in the area of the sociology of mental illness, are likely to find in this kind of case, an apt confirmation of their view that typically psychiatric diagnosis of illness represents the application of a system of control over certain kinds of deviants, those who become labeled as "mentally ill." They argue that particularly, persons who are troublesome to society or its powerful segments, on political or social grounds, are more likely than others psychologically similar, to be designated ("diagnosed") as mentally ill and treated accordingly. The designation ("labeling") and the consequent "treatment," incarceration in a mental hospital, are instruments of *social control.* In the view of that kind of sociologist, the case of the Soviet dissidents provides only the most extreme, obvious and blatant example of that process. Such sociologists are likely to argue that the Soviet dissidents' case demonstrates that it is impossible to have a universal, transcendant set of criteria for the assessment of "mental health" or "mental illness" that is not rooted in the particular culture and society and its political system, necessarily different from other cultures and other societies.

Without independent psychological evaluation by psychological professionals holding a *trans*cultural viewpoint such as that aimed at in psychoanalysis, it is not only impossible to demonstrate satisfactorily that persons such as the Soviet dissidents are "psychiatrically sick" as the Soviet experts claim. It is also not possible to know for certain that they are *not* sick. If the Western psychiatrists, who judged the dissidents they were able to examine as "not sick," were simply bowing to a different set of political assumptions and purposes, we would be left with dangling statements of the order, "The As say yes, the Bs say no." (A equals Soviet psychiatrists, yes equals psychiatrically ill; B equals Western psychiatrists; no means not psychiatrically ill.) We would be left in the same morass of relativism, with only the faith that "we" (Westerners) are "better people" than "they" (the Soviet leaders).

Most of the relativistic sociology of deviance, especially that of the labeling orientation, essentially leaves it at that, assuming the values they espouse in their distinctly non-value-neutral manner, freedom, autonomy, respect for individual rights, and the like, are superior to those of more totalitarian regimes.

Note also the political paranoia of the labeling sociologists, arguing that the Soviet cases are "really no different" from what goes on in the West. Here too, they claim, we use hospitalization as a technique of social control.[1] These supposedly worldly social scientists find it possible to ignore totally, the huge difference between a totalitarian political system, the Soviet Union and a Western democracy. Perhaps like so many other leftward leaning social scientists, especially those of the counterculture and "radicalism" of the 1960s and their latter-day descendants, they are incapable of such distinctions (see later chapters).

To return to the question of how to make an adequate psychological appraisal that is not enslaved to a particular political view, consider the following.

By contrast, a *psychoanalytic*-sociology of deviance approach here would argue that, theoretically at least, we *have* the tools for making a *trans*cultural evaluation of the mental health of the individuals involved, and they are the tools that psychoanalysis and allied clinical disciplines have developed over the years. If by that kind of examination we can demonstrate that the "psychopathology" of the dissidents is either non-existent or is greatly exaggerated by the Soviet psychiatrists, and that that exaggeration serves the power needs of the regime, then the psychoanalytically oriented sociology of deviance has in fact made a stronger case than is made by a culturally-relativistic one. By and large, the standards the Western psychiatrists used to arrive at their conclusions in the cases they examined, *are* those of a transcultural dynamic psychology, of the kind we are propounding in this work.

The More General Problem of the Sociology of Mental Illness

Typically, some of the Western sociologists of deviance, particularly those of the labeling persuasion, tend to take a case such as the Soviet psychiatry one, and over-extrapolate from it to *all* applications of psychiatric evaluation of mental illness. Some suggest there is no essential difference between the U.S.S.R. practice and what is commonly done in hospitalizing psychotics in our society. They argue that other individuals who may be no less disoriented or odd are not so handled; therefore those who *are* sent to hospitals are not sick, and should not in justice be so institutionalized. Only contingencies of their being noticed and labeled make the difference.

Basic elements of this approach go back to Edwin Lemert's work of 1951:

> . . . a psychotic disorder . . . is not in itself the reason for collective action to bring mentally disturbed patients under restraint. Rather it is the highly visible deviations of the psychotic person from the norms of his group.

At that point, the existence of psychotic disorder as an entity was still assumed. Not so later. Note Lemert was *not* saying there is no psychopathology here; rather that existence of psychopathology is a necessary but *not sufficient* condition for the person to be hospitalized. That distinction disappears in the later labeling work.

Contributions to the emerging labeling viewpoint came from the work of three otherwise different thinkers, Erving Goffman, Thomas Szasz and Ronald Laing (see Endleman 1981: 373-375). Goffman in *Asylums* (1961) gave a particular patient's-eye view of a mental hospital as mortifying, humiliating and depersonalizing its victims (patients). Szasz denounced the "myth of mental illness" (1960, 1961, 1981) perpetrated by psychiatry's "medical model." (The people called "patients" are suffering from "problems of living," not disease analogous to physical illness.) Laing (1967) presented people called schizophrenic as mainly victims, who in fact are responding appropriately to an insane society. (The latter two, because of coming out of prior psychoanalytic work and thus in effect exposing the goods on their erstwhile colleagues, especially delight sociologists of this persuasion.)

In the same period, we had the work of Howard S. Becker (1963, see Chapter 1) telling us that there is no such thing as behavior that is deviant *per se,* but only behavior that is *defined* as deviant (and by implication, might not be so defined in another group or society.) Then a major figure appeared, applying this labeling approach to the sociology of mental illness: Thomas Scheff (1966, 1975). Though in early work Scheff at one point claimed his purpose was *not* to reject psychiatric formulations *in toto,* but to forge an alternative model later to be integrated with the psychiatric (1966: 25–27), the main line of his work on this topic, and certainly of all his epigones, contradicts that. They reject almost totally any psychological formulations, and in more extreme versions, deny there is any such thing as mental illness (Cf. Szasz). Scheff rejected the "medical model" which he claimed mistakenly takes mental disorder to be an objectively real and definable entity, similar to a physical disease.[2] Scheff frequently refers to "the so-called mental illness" of schizophrenia, which he discusses as though it were an ideological invention.

According to Scheff, the medical model is not only inadequate, misleading and incorrect. It is insidious, threatening and persecutory:

> current definitions of insanity *mobilize society* to locate, segregate, and 'treat' schizophrenics and other persons who are "out of touch with reality" (Scheff 1975: 19—italics mine)

We get the impression of a sinister conspiracy to persecute helpless innocents who are in no important way different from anyone else. All these people have done is to commit "residual deviance," that is, violate shared but unnamed understandings. An example would be, in conversation, looking at your interloculator's ears, not his eyes. Such violations are not classifiable by categories such as theft, prostitution, or drunkenness. When onlookers "yet are certain an offense has been committed, they may resort to this residual category" (1975: 7). Once it was witchcraft, spirit possession or devil possession; today it is mental illness.

No doubt such interaction processes do go on. But Scheff and his followers take them for warrant for denying psychopathology and rejecting the whole idea of examining the person involved from an *intrapsychic* perspective. How did they "happen to be" violating such residual rules in the first place? Such a question points to *etiology*. But now looking for etiology is declared both irrelevant and worse, (because part of the "medical model") pernicious and persecutory.

The influence of Scheff's ideas on sociological discussion of mental illness has been substantial. Perrucci (1974) studying part of a particular mental hospital, refers to "the insane as casualties of the social order," (p. 10) and poses the debate "are the insane 'patients' or 'victims'?" (pp. 14ff) arguing the latter. Implication: if they are victims, they must not be sick. He sees the mental hospital as a "system of justification" of the victimization of the people called insane (pp. 30ff).

However he starts his book by sketching a history of the treatment of the "insane" or "mad" in different historical periods and societies. This presentation of course implies that there were indeed people in each of these societies sufficiently disturbed or eccentric as to be regarded as "out of their minds," or any other synonym. Are we to believe that all of those were also only victims of labeling and stigmatization, without reference to the reality of their state? Sociologists have variably referred to such behavior. Sometimes it is seen as "disturbed behavior," but without reference to possible intrapsychic factors producing that disturbance. Occasionally there is recognition that *something* is amiss, but then attention shifts to the labeling process. The "something amiss" can be "interpersonal difficulties" or "trouble getting along in social relations" or just "problems in living" (Szasz). These phrases point to a *sociological* situation, not an intrapsychic one. The view is often hedged: *maybe* the patient is in fact disturbed, but that is irrelevant to his being a victim. Often it is simply denied that the patients are sick. Views reflecting this labeling sociology approach to mental illness inform the discussion of mental illness found now in a number of major texts in the sociology of deviance, e.g. Goode 1978; Schur 1972, 1979; and partially in many others. Such scholars are intent on concentrating on an externally-connected, interpersonal, social interactional component in the process of assigning the label of mental illness (which may be true enough). Following from that, they then deny the existence of the intrapsychic dimension which is at the core of any mental illness, especially the serious ones clinicians call psychoses. We find a most remarkable denial of parts of readily observable reality operating in these writings. They imply (sometimes state) there is no such thing as mental illness, or psychopathology. If that were true, what do these sociologists make of any of the following:

-Kate is not psychologically capable of handling the simplest everyday tasks;

-Donald cannot distinguish between his fantasies and objective reality;

-William is convinced all around him people are spreading malicious rumors about him; there is no objective evidence that this is the case;
-Georgina simultaneously believes that her mother died last year (which she did) and that she is coming to visit Georgina tomorrow;
-Arthur is so withdrawn that he cannot bear even minimal emotional contact with any other human being;
-Peter is scared out of his wits by a situation that presents no objectively verifiable danger to him;
-Zinia is so overwhelmed with feelings of hopelessness and doom that she cannot put herself in even the simplest ways into the everyday stream of life;
-Marion sees enemies everywhere and cannot believe there exists any person in the world who has no hostile intent toward her;
-Patricia is convinced she is Joan of Arc; Flora that she is Mary Mother of God; while Quentin believes he is Napoleon Bonaparte; each ingeniously interprets immediate events to fit these beliefs;
-Carl hears voices (that no one else can hear) telling him he is chosen to save the world; while Vera sees the Virgin Mary coming to her, offering her solace;
-Fred has created and has conversations with a whole imaginary society in whose reality he firmly believes and can prove to you, but no one else can see or hear them or in any way confirm their objective existence.

To claim, as the labeling sociologists do, that the "psychopathology" of all of these individuals is entirely a matter of their being victimized by unfair negative labeling by established authorities, is not only a literally fantastic distortion of the reality of these persons' lives and situation, but also implicitly an anti-humane denial of the right any decent society would accord them to be treated appropriately in terms of their actual psychological state.

The labeling theorists on mental illness thus grossly mislead their readers on the nature of serious psychological disorder. Many less extreme forms of irrationality are widespread. They need to be examined with subtlety and discrimination. Making such distinctions is what the whole perplexing and exasperating work of diagnosis and therapy requires.

Of course as clinicians dealing with persons like Kate *et al.*, we make judgments, *from a transcultural vantage point* (see above). Szasz claims that the norms we (clinicians) use "must be stated in terms of *psychosocial, ethical* and *legal* concepts" (Szasz 1961: 115; his emphasis). I argue that here he is profoundly wrong. Clinical (transcultural) norms are *not* the ethical values of society. (Eric deceived Lester to win Jane, that's unethical, we may disapprove, but that's not sick.) The standards for judging sickness are not the same as the *mores* or the laws. Irrationality is not a culturally-relative standard. Denial of objective reality is such, regardless of whether it is statistically normal in that society to do so, or culturally normal there to accept a myth that expresses that denial. Belief that the earth is flat is objectively in error, no matter how widely believed. (For fuller development of this transcultural view, see Endleman 1981, part V, and LaBarre 1954 and many other writings.)

Critiques of the Labeling Sociology of Mental Illness

Not all sociologists of deviance, or of mental illness, have accepted Scheff and company's view. Walter Gove (1970a, 1970b) presented a trenchant criticism (1970A, 1970B) based on careful examination of available evidence from his own and others' studies of processes in mental hospitals. He summarizes his critique as follows:

> The evidence shows that a substantial majority of the persons who are hospitalized [do in fact] have a serious psychiatric disturbance. . . . Once prospective patients come into contact with [mental health] public officials, a substantial screening still occurs, presumably sorting out persons who are being railroaded or who are less disturbed. . . . [S]tudies reviewed, while in no way denying the existence of the processes outlined by [Scheff] do not bear out the allegation that hospitalization necessarily or typically leads to chronic mental disturbance. (Gove 1970a: 882; see also Scheff's response, 1975: 21–34)

We can note also critique by Fletcher and Reynolds, 1968. Sagarin (1975) summarizes his own and others' critiques of the labeling approach generally, and its application, specifically, to mental illness.[3]

Why the Appeal?

Considering the substantial flaws in this labeling theory sociology of mental illness, how do we account for its appeal to and acceptance by so many sociologists? We can suggest a number of factors:

A. Tendencies within sociology, and differences from psychoanalysis: 1) underdog ideology; 2) sociology's external emphasis, psychoanalysis' internal; 3) overgeneralization from mental hospital cases.

B. Inherent difficulties and ambiguities in the phenomena under consideration: 4) unevenness of application of psychiatric standards; real deprivation of hospital patients; 5) real difficulties in diagnosis, classification, understanding cases.

C. Anxiety reactions, evoked by B) and by intrapsychic thinking generally; manifested in 6) paranoid-persecutory fantasy; 7) totalistic theories, denying ambiguity; and 8) anxiety-based factors in reactions against psychogenic theories.

Tendencies within Sociology and Differences from Psychoanalysis

1) *Underdog ideology.*

Sociology attracts many people of maverick or rebel orientation to the world (Cf. Endleman 1981: 372). Sociologists are very susceptible to sympathies with underdogs of various kinds—racial and ethnic minorities, lower classes, proletariat versus bourgeoisie; outsiders of many kinds; sexual deviants (see Chapter 3)—the esoteric, and here, particularly deviants of all kinds. David Bordua commented on this orientation as follows, in 1967:

> Sociologists have traditionally . . . provide[d] a sympathetic link to various underdogs, but the details change from period to period. The deviant as underdog seems to be coming into his own. . . . [I]t now seems easy for this perspective to turn into a kind of witchhunt in reverse—witches now being the decision-makers rather than deviants.

In the sociology of mental illness since 1967, this is just what has happened. (Compare the biases in most sociological discussion of homosexuality, Chapter 3 above.)

The sociology of mental illness has been an especially fertile field for the cultivation of this underdog viewpoint. The alternative of identifying with the professionals who have to make these evaluations, namely psychiatrists or clinical psychologists, is not so psychologically available to sociologists, because they are usually excluded by lack of competence in the necessary psychological expertise. One way to make up for that shortcoming is to declare the clinical professionals' expertise irrelevant, or even, pernicious and anti-humane.

The sociology of deviance is made to order for this underdog viewpoint; its holders have value biases that are obvious. Correspondingly, they deprecate the majority, the conventional, and the supporters of traditional values. They are hostile toward the privileged, the powerful, the influence-wielders, and the possessors of expert knowledge other than the sociologists' own. The world can be cast into the roles of victims and oppressors—here the mentally ill and their keepers.

2) *Sociologists emphasize overt external behavior; psychoanalysts emphasize inner intrapsychic processes.*

To a large degree on this matter these two fields are talking past each other. Scheff *et al.* assume that what the psychiatrists label as "mental illness" is the odd *behavior* of the person. From a psychoanalytic viewpoint, this seems an attack on a straw man, for the psychoanalysts emphasize *internal* psychological states and processes, of which the overt behavior is only a symptom, and these inner states are almost totally ignored by the labeling theorists. This attitude is a pervasive and fundamental difference of perspective. Most sociology of deviance, or sociology generally, does focus on overt behavior and conduct, usually in relation to an *external* social situation. Psychoanalysts emphasize the internal, intrapsychic state, much of it unconscious (and having to be inferred) in relation to a total personality complex.

3) *Sociologists have over-generalized from mental hospital cases.*

These are cases diagnosed as psychotic. They are of course the more dramatic cases, with psychosis diagnoses being more consequential and often stigmatizing. But that leaves out the wider range of what clinicians consider pathologies: neuroses, character disorders, psychopathic states, narcissistic disorders, neurotic depressive states, etc. and the whole range of clinical practitioners attending to them, many of whom are at odds in their own way, with hospital psychiatry.

B. *Inherent Difficulties and Ambiguities in the Phenomena under Consideration*

4) *Unevenness of application of psychiatric standards.*

The situation confronted by sociologists studying mental illness, particularly the phenomenon of mental hospitalization, involves many realistic inherent difficulties. Not all persons who might conceivably be so classified do in fact get classified as "mentally ill" enough to require the drastic societal reaction of hospitalization. Epidemiological studies like those of Srole *et al.* (1962) indicate that probably 80% of a putatively normal nonhospitalized population, living in the community, have at least some degree of "psychological impairment," and 20% rather severe. Yet only an extremely small number of people, by comparison, do actually get considered for admission to mental hospitals. Thus a powerful selective factor appears to be present, and often it does not appear to be the degree and kind of psychological disorder the prospective patient has. Also a close look at the actual internal functioning of some psychiatric hospitals indicates conditions that seem not consistent with an intent of therapy and cure, and the real depersonalizing and dehumanizing processes that are there in actual cases have been documented, e.g. Goffman 1961.

Granted that that picture is exaggerated and skewed by the biases of observers—and Goffman certainly seems to be such a case—it is unlikely to be totally incorrect. Other sociological studies, in different settings, show institutional functioning often at odds with official goals. So the sociologist's suspicions are aroused.

Also, there seems to be a certain plausibility to the argument that "illness" in the term "mental illness" is misleading at the least, because it is hard to see the parallels with physical disease implied in the terminology. Many clinicians now eschew these aspects of the "medical model." Many find reason to question whether biological malfunctioning is actually involved.

There is however a problem here: much current research does point to biochemical/physiological factors in many functional disorders, especially in psychoses. Those arguing that there cannot possibly be any such biological connection are foreclosing the matter, probably on ideological grounds.[4]

5) *Inherent difficulties in diagnosis and classification with whatever method or system is used.*

This leads to the impression, so striking to sociologists new to this scene, that such evaluation is enormously unreliable and arbitrary. They therefore postulate factors unrelated to the psychological problems involved, as dictating the "diagnosis" that is made.

Commonly enough, some appraisal and classification needs to be made rather quickly, on the basis of limited information, usually about overt behavior, the meaning of which cannot possibly be fully understood by even astute clinicians in these circumstances. The professional tends to presume illness, since the individual under consideration has come or been brought to the clinical facility for some, often urgent, reason. Usually the professional has at the start only *behavior* which (in the psychological view) is seen as a *symptom* of the disturbance (or "illness") which then needs to be inferred from the symptom. A psychological professional would not consider one item of behavior alone as indicative, but would look for a total complex, and try to get as many indicators as possible. The *internal* psychological state of the person (the intrapsychic dynamics) can never be directly observed, but only inferred from the behavioral, e.g. verbal, fantasy, motor, manifestations. These are subject to *interpretation.* It is difficult to get a consensus, even among similarly trained professionals, about the inner meaning.

Experienced clinicians are fully aware of this difficulty. By contrast, the sociologists here seem to have utopian expectations. In the hospital admissions situation, the prospective patient must be quickly categorized, at least as "mentally ill enough to warrant admission" or not. That may not be difficult in extreme cases, e.g. a raving violent man convinced he is Attila the Hun; but the more common run of cases may be much more subtle and perplexing. Because diagnosis is difficult does not mean there is no such thing as severe inner disturbance, whether you want to call that "mental illness" or something else.

Errors in Identification of Cases

Problematics of identification of cases are inherent in the phenomenon. Errors may be made: (1) someone who is in fact sick may not be so identified; (2) someone not really sick may be identified as sick.

Which type of error is more likely? Intimates of the odd one want to deny as long as possible the presence of serious psychological disorder. We could therefore expect that type (1) errors would be far more frequent. But by their nature we won't hear about most of these cases unless something drastic happens, forcing the intimates to confront. Type (2) errors are probably, I think, statistically *rarer,* but when they do occur, they are likely to be dramatic, and arouse particular feelings of indignation from civil libertarians, sociologists of deviance, and others. It is usually more difficult to diagnose "normality" than "abnormality" (cf. Devereux 1980: 21). And clinicians are professionally slanted to be attuned to "pathology." Also, as Rosenhan notes (see later section), for the medical professional, "it is clearly more dangerous to misdiagnose illness than health. Better to err on the side of caution, to suspect illness even among the healthy" (Rosenhan 1973: 253).

Probably type (1) error is more often made by the lay public, specifically relatives and intimates of the disturbed. Yarrow *et al.* (1955) and Schwartz (1957) write about wives of psychiatric hospital patients, who typically resisted as long as possible, defining the husband's "strange" behavior—in some cases florid delusions and/or hallucinations—as evidence of "mental illness." Alongside this, type (2) errors may be more frequently made by health professionals.

Case 5: Sane in Insane Places

D. L. Rosenhan (1973), in a now famous piece of research, reports a particularly dramatic case of type (2) error: eight actually sane persons being kept in hospitals as "insane." This research is much cited by behavioral and social scientists with an axe to grind to discredit psychiatric practice and theorizing. It is rewarding to review it briefly here.

Rosenhan persuaded eight persons who were all basically nonpsychotic, to present themselves at a psychiatric hospital. Each claimed he was "hearing voices." The voices were saying "empty," "hollow," and "thud." Each was admitted to the hospital as a patient for observation. Each then in the hospital dropped the faked "hearing of voices," and "acted as sane as they really were." Hospital professionals in every case treated the "pseudopatient" as actually insane, discounting any "normal" behavior. Each pseudopatient had a hard time convincing the staff to release him on grounds of absence of sickness. Even then he was only labeled "in remission." Rosenhan writes, "Despite their public 'show' of sanity, the pseudopatients were never detected" (p. 252). (Some *patients,* however, suspected they were fake.) Rosenhan titles that section: "The normal are not detectably sane" (in the hospital, that is). The implication is that psychiatric professionals don't know what they are doing, in these hospitals, cannot differentiate seriously disturbed from normal, are likely unjustly to keep actually sane people incarcerated indefinitely, etc.—the full horror story that labeling theory sociologists love to retell.

But wait a minute! The "pseudopatients" did in fact present themselves as "hearing voices," clearly an auditory hallucination, commonly an indicator of serious disturbance, probably a psychotic episode, maybe a full-fledged case of schizophrenia. They did not later deny that they had ever heard such voices, or that they were hearing them just prior to admission. They only said later that they "no longer" heard the voices. What tentative diagnosis would Rosenhan have made if presented with such material, and without any indications that a hoax was being played? And what would he have the admitting psychiatrists do? Tell each of these pseudopatients, "Go home, what you're reporting is normal"? What reason might the admitting health professionals have for suspecting a deception of this kind? How many "well" people are clamoring for admission to psychiatric hospitals? So, from the clinicians' viewpoint, the reasonable working hypothesis—which is all an initial tentative diagnosis intends to be—is that there is some intrapsychic disturbance in this individual that is being manifested by the reported symptom. One could argue *ex post facto* that surely a really thorough clinical appraisal would have detected the fraud. Then all the study would be showing is that the clinical staff in such hospitals is not as thorough as all that. It can be argued that it is utopian to expect them to be. Even clinicians with the luxury of prolonged repeated intensive contact with the disturbed person, as in private practice, find it hard to assess the level and type of disturbance. (To the labeling theory ideologues who say at this juncture, "you're *assuming* disturbance!" the answer is, "of course, what else? why else did that person come here for help?")

Thus the Rosenhan research in its conclusions is tendentious in the extreme, evidently in the service of an ideological view. So are the implications drawn from it by the labeling sociologists. They like to cite this case to demonstrate that there is no such thing as mental illness. The psychiatrists are a bunch of quacks and incompetents, in thrall to wrong theories." (Granted this is an exaggeration of what is being said and written, but not much.)

Anxiety Reaction from Inherent Difficulties and from Intrapsychic Probing

In the nature of the case, thinking or theorizing focused on intrapsychic forces and emphasizing intrapsychic interpretation is bound to provoke anxiety in many others. Even the most seasoned analysand continues to show resistance to the deeper wellsprings within himself, i.e. the unconscious. How much more so the psychoanalytically inexperienced layman, including many sociologists? Psychological probing, especially at the depth level pursued by psychoanalysis, is disturbing, and likely to produce in many, intense negative reactions and aggressive fighting back. This is evidently part of what we see in the negative responses of many sociologists to psychoanalysis or to psychiatry. Following Freud's own thoughts on this matter, resistance to the whole idea of unconscious mental functioning is inevitable, given the fact that the "unconscious repressed" became so in the first place as a defense against intense anxiety. Accordingly, we could expect that psychoanalysis, in its most radically probing aspect, would never become fully acceptable in society, or, in this case, in most of the social sciences.[5]

Responses to such anxiety take a number of forms:

6) *Paranoid-persecutory fantasy.*

The underdog ideological view of the mentally ill as victims and the designating and "treating" officials and professionals as oppressors frequently is presented in a way that looks like a *paranoid-persecutory fantasy.* Scheff refers to people being labeled as having a "so-called mental illness such as schizophrenia." The oppressors are those carrying out these official functions of examining, labeling and coercively acting upon these helpless victims. The patients are incarcerated, stigmatized, humiliated, dehumanized, and deceived by lies that they are being "treated" to be "cured."

Here is another example: Sagarin, in a general text on deviance (1975) that is otherwise better balanced, writes:

> A youth who stole a chocolate bar is incarcerated in a mental institution for several decades and emerges after the better part of his life has been passed in a place supposedly reserved for the insane, the mentally unbalanced and the mentally incompetent. Yet he was never less than totally sane and competent; he was merely a man who, in his early youth, had stolen a chocolate bar. There are countless cases of this type. (Sagarin 1975: 181)

One expects here a footnote with *documentation* of this horrendous miscarriage of justice. There is none. Skeptics will deduce the author made it up. Incarcerated for decades in a mental hospital just for stealing a chocolate bar!

One can identify the probable psychic sources of such a fantasy.[6] Part of it is the actual situation confronted in dealing with the bizarre and the odd, and with the ambiguities and tensions of the labeling process itself. Many cases can plausibly be construed as cases of injustice. In the paranoid, the thinking is not usually totally delusional, and there is likely to be *some* basis in external reality for the paranoid's idea of hostility directed toward him. Here too we can find a mixture of plausibly "realistic" appraisals and hostile fantasy that is out of touch with external reality. That fantasy is very much connected with an internal reality, that of the scientists forming these theories. The extreme portraits of oppressors and victims as painted by Perrucci are bound to be exaggerations and simplifications. No real world is peopled this way.

The paranoid-persecutory mode also conduces to considering the *effects* or consequences of certain situations as the *motives* for the actions that lead to them. Perrucci's work is full of examples of this. He claims, for instance, that the hospital "espouses the noble goal of treatment and return of people to society, but in fact . . . functions . . . as a dumping ground for societal rejects" (Perrucci 1974: 31).[7]

Susceptibility to such fantasy is intrinsically connected at the sociocultural cognitive level with underdog ideology. At the intrapsychic level it is probably connected with anxiety generated by the stresses of that kind of research situation, and the strain imposed by the extreme ambiguity, and whatever idiosyncratic factors in the psychic history of the researcher. Countertransference distortion may also be at work (Cf. Devereux 1967). Perhaps it is the case that sociologists, as a type, have considerably lower tolerance for ambiguity than do psychoanalysts or clinical psychologists. (Such tolerance is an essential for clinical work.)

One response to anxiety-provoking ambiguity is to construct an extreme one-sided theory. Conspiracy theories have abounded in sociology, especially political sociology, and will probably continue. In deviance theory, less political-structural in orientation, the villains are the particular wielders of power in the mental health profession, especially the psychiatrists in the mental hospitals, who are the designated oppressors.

Allegations that innocent sane persons are being railroaded into mental hospitals are probably rarer now than in the past, but they still appear, and as such they feed this same kind of paranoid-persecutory fantasy.

7) *All-or-none theory.*

Another aspect of response to the situations of intolerable ambiguity faced in the mental illness field is the construction of a totalistic theory, of an all-or-none variety. Either psychological explanations are all, or sociological ones are all. Since the first are unacceptable, one must embrace the second whole-heartedly, in an all-or-nothing way. Such a theory must explain *everything.* Hence there is no such thing as mental illness. It is totally an oppressive construction imposed on hapless victims, who just happen to be a little odd. This dogmatism alleviates anxiety in the investigator. It rarely serves the interests of truth or understanding.

8) *Anxiety-based (non-rational) features in reactions against psychogenic theories.*

Psychogenic theories of deviance have had hard sledding among sociologists. (Cf. earlier chapters, in reference to crime, to sexual deviation, to drugs.) Particularly so for psychoanalytic theories. Nonpsychoanalysts find psychogenic theories about crime hard to accept, bizarre and incredible. Similarly for other kinds of deviance. It is hard to sort out how much of this antagonism comes from reasonable grounds: has the theory been over-generalized? For example, are *all* criminals explained by a particular psychoanalytic theory? Are the propositions difficult to test? Does this deal with only part of the picture, not all? How much, rather, comes from nonrational sources such as anxiety-based reactions? Some of the reactions of sociologists to psychoanalytic ideas about crime or other deviance sound in tone, very much like those of outsiders greeting Freud's early presentation of his ideas.

Some sociologists of deviance are ready to grant that psychological theories, or specifically psychoanalytic ones, may be useful in understanding the more bizarre and "senseless" cases of deviance, (e.g. a weird killing) but not the more ordinary everyday ones. Though a plausible position if they mean that *psychopathology* is to be presumed in the former case, but not in the latter; however such selective and partial use of psychoanalysis is intellectually unacceptable. If the theoretical principles are valid, they must be applicable to *all* types of of human behavior. The procedure might also be a method of destruction by partial incorporation.

Reprise: The Gap between Labeling Sociologists' and Psychoanalytic Views of Mental Illness

In many respects these two fields can be seen as talking past each other. Psychoanalytic approaches to mental illness or psychopathology are concerned with the *intrapsychic* process of how a person becomes psychologically disturbed, how that process continues, and how it is changed through therapy. The labeling sociologists are dealing with the *interaction process* of how others react to the manifestations of the psychic disturbance. One part may be the process of labeling the person as "mentally ill" and thereupon instituting some kind of "societal reaction" (e.g. hospitalization) and how that in turn may produce more deviant behavior ("secondary deviation"). They think they are explaining how mental illness comes about. Clearly they are not. What they are contributing is an analysis of the *social interaction* that goes on around and connecting it with the psychopathology of the disturbed individual. Contrary to their view, the identifiable psychopathology does exist. It is difficult to identify and classify clearly, and to understand, but psychoanalysis and allied clinical disciplines do have the tools for that understanding. Sociology does not. At least no sociology does that is not also informed by psychoanalysis or some other relevant and appropriate theory of the intrapsychic process.

The psychoanalytic conception of psychopathology does not rule out the interaction processes that the sociologists have been attending. Not at all. But all of these interactions also have their intrapsychic dimension. What is leading the other actors responding to the person showing bizarre behavior ("residual deviance") to react as they do, to carry out stigmatizing and measures of help and control? To repeat: theories such as Scheff's are not theories of mental illness, but theories of *social reaction* to mental illness, and of the social interaction between persons defined as mentally ill and the others in various roles around them. Such interaction analysis does not tell us what is going on internally in the "mentally ill" person, nor in any of the others. It is a typically sociological *external* view looking at the external overt behavior, and not at the underlying psychodynamics.

Gove in his critique of Scheff points out that the available evidence "suggests that a person's behavior determines the expectations of others to a much greater degree than the reverse." Devereux points to the strong element of "social negativism" in psychotics and neurotics (1940, reprinted in 1980). This social negativism is particularly evident in many mental hospital patients, as demonstrated in the following case, "Weapons of Insanity."

Case 6: Weapons of Insanity

In a study with this title, Ludwig and Farrelly (1967) challenge the by-then fashionable view of mental hospital patients, especially chronic schizophrenics, as "poor helpless unfortunate creatures made sick by family and society and kept sick by prolonged institutionalization," and its attendant treatment philosophy. Countering the "patient-as-victim" view, they point out the evidence of "staff-as-victim" and patient as aggressor. For example, the patient asserts "squatter's rights" in a hospital that has been, in effect, a model of an idealized childhood home in which all needs are supplied and no demands for social responsibility imposed. The patient takes an "all-or-nothing" attitude: he must be *guaranteed* all the rewards of status, power, love and material goods that are to come with discharge, otherwise he will not cooperate with specific measures of rehabilitation. He exerts a "tyranny of the weak," uncannily accurately using "social pushbuttons" of nuisance behavior evoking staff irritation; overt sexual behavior evoking outrage; aggressive-combative behavior evoking fear; stubborn withdrawal evoking frustration; and crazy-bizarre behavior evoking confusion and helplessness in the staff. The rules of the modern hospital forbid staff ever to display any of these reactions. Patients have "diplomatic immunity" for all kinds of deviant behavior, e.g. masturbating or defecating in public. These are clear-cut indicators of the "social negativism" of the mentally ill.

This is not to deny the existence of the many pains of incarceration endured by the hospitalized mental patients, nor the actual phenomena of stigmatization, mortification, depersonalization and the rest, that people like Goffman, Szasz, Scheff and others have pointed out. Rather, these elements, where present (and in many hospitals, they are little in evidence) are only part of the picture. And they do not explain the mental illness, or the continuation of mental illness, of the patients.

We can also note that sociologists of the Scheff persuasion would regard these "weapons of insanity" as demonstration of the deviants labeled mentally ill going at it, i.e. playing out the deviant role, with a vengeance: "I'm sick; this is how sick people behave; you can't hold me responsible." In that sense, there is some reality to the allegation that hospitalization may itself *keep* the patient sick. This may be the case at least under conditions where staff are required to follow the treatment philosophy Ludwig and Farrelly describe, that is, of total forbearance and lack of holding the patient responsible for his conduct. But there has to have been something amiss that got the patient into the hospital in the first place, and it is that usually very real psychopathology that the labeling sociologist tends to underplay or even deny exists.

Sociologists such as Scheff who want to erase the hospitals have confused two very different issues: one, is there such a thing as mental illness? and two, are mental hospitals *the* (or *a*) good way to deal with persons having these characteristics? One can recognize that something is seriously amiss with these individuals (whether one wants to call it mental illness or not) and still object on humanitarian or other grounds to their "treatment" in mental hospitals, or to the whole idea of such hospitals as a type of institution.

The insistence that deviance is entirely (or essentially) a social creation distorts the reality of interplay between intrapsychic and social mechanisms, and at its extreme, paints a false picture of human beings as entirely the pawns of social pressures and without an intrapsychic history and capacity for self-determination.

Kinds of Psychopathology in Relation to Culture and to Deviance

As discussed earlier, psychological malfunctioning can be classified in a number of ways. First we distinguish "organic," that is, biologically based, from "functional" disorders, that is psychological ones. Among functional disorders, we distinguish the extremely serious ones, the psychoses; and then the others, neuroses, character disorders, borderline conditions, narcissistic disorders, and psychopathic states. Earlier in this chapter we have discussed these as *individual* phenomena. Here we want to develop them further in relation to culture.

Any of these forms of psychopathology may appear in culturally stylized versions, or in more idiosyncratic versions. The idiosyncratic versions are those most familiar to clinicians in Western and Western-influenced societies.

Taking note of the dimension of cultural patterning, we can distinguish five main kinds of functional disorder:

1) Idiosyncratic neuroses, character disorders, and other disorders short of psychosis;
2) Idiosyncratic psychoses;
3) Ethnic psychoses;
4) Culturally stylized psychopathological variant;
5) Culturally stylized character disorder.

1) Idiosyncratic neuroses, Character Disorders and Other Nonpsychotic Disorders

Idiosyncratic disorders are less serious than psychoses, in that they do not involve a sharp break from the everyday reality that most people in the society recognize. Rather they involve irrationality derived from deep inner conflicts, that usually—except in the psychopathic states—may involve suffering and feeling different from supposedly "normal" persons. Unlike the culturally stylized character disorders, e.g. obsessive-compulsive character in certain occupations such as accountancy, in the idiosyncratic neuroses there is lack of cultural support for the symptoms, and an ego-alien quality. In some cases of these types, the individual may be unobtrusive, escaping attention, therefore not be subject to labeling or stigmatization as a deviant. This would be more likely in individuals with more schizoid trends, expressed by social withdrawal. Still, in most other cases, if the neurotic difficulty is expressed in particular interactive contexts, it is likely that the idiosyncratic neurotic will also be considered deviant. For example, if flowing from the neurotic trends, he is perceived as difficult or abrasive or disturbingly odd, he then gets labeled as "sick," clearly an epithet of deviance in this context. The defenses used to deal with these conflicts may not have strong cultural stylization. Hence there is great variation from one individual to another. The neurotic may have a sense of isolation and aloneness in relation to others in his society. To the extent that such a neurotic's difficulties and sufferings separate him from others, and do not evoke an answering call of empathy from them, his intrapsychic troubles are compounded by social alienation. Then the feeling that the surrounding social world is mainly hostile and alien tends to be confirmed by the actual reactions of others, in a vicious circle of interpersonal pathology compounding the intrapsychic pathology. The formulation of the modes of experiencing and expressing his intrapsychic conflicts may be statistically prevalent in the society, or in his specific social milieu, and at the same time not be culturally stylized. In fact, the individually suffering neurotic, particularly one whose anxieties keep him largely isolated from others, is likely to be quite unaware of how statistically prevalent his kinds of problems are. He may imagine or assume he is the only person in the world in this kind of psychic state, or at most one of a very small number. Thus a state of "pluralistic ignorance" may prevail—large numbers of individuals in the same kind of intrapsychic distress who are unaware of their commonality.

The reversal of this is found in situations such as a homosexual's "coming out," that is, the first time he recognizes himself as being "a homosexual," accompanied by recognition that there are thousands of others out there just like himself. This contrasts with his prior experience as an adolescent when he had assumed he was the only person in the world with these feelings and the attendant anxiety and guilt. The recognition of kinship and similarity with many others, who share the same deeper feelings and intimate responses, may so intensely relieve anxiety and dissolve alienation that the individual now, almost in a flash, consolidates his distinct social and psychic identity with a great rush of positive self-feeling. Then past and recent psychic distress is suddenly dissolved.

By contrast, the idiosyncratic neurotic, while he may be aware that there are many others who are impaired in some way, possibly similarly, he usually tends to feel they cannot be suffering in quite the same way as he. While homosexuals may constitute a "minority group" (see Chapter 3), it is unusual, though not unheard of, to refer to "neurotics as a minority group." They are not generally discriminated against on the basis of some commonly held and negatively valued characteristic. Correspondingly they do not have the positive supports of a minority group subculture.

Another idiosyncratic disorder not psychotic in dimension, is psychopathic personality, which is unlikely to involve neurotic suffering, and likely to involve deviance including law-violation (see chapter on crime above).

2) Idiosyncratic psychoses

Psychoses are more serious ruptures from normal psychic functioning. Symptoms may be delusions, hallucinations, extreme confusional states; extremes of primary process thinking; or extreme affective state like irrational depression (not explainable by environmental circumstances), or mania, or alternation of both. The psychotic may suffer extreme irrational suspiciousness, with or without delusions of grandeur or persecution (or both), unamenable to reality testing. A major feature is to be "out of it," that is, out of the ordinary everyday reality of the surrounding persons.

Such states may be idiosyncratic, i.e. peculiar to the particular individual, or culturally patterned in some ways, as in types 3) and 4) in the following section. Idiosyncratic psychotics are usually sociologically deviant. Their "weird" and "crazy" way of reacting to the world is disturbing and unsettling to others, as violating normative expectations of how people are expected to act in society. Usually their deviance is different from law-violation (criminality), from substance-abuse or sexual deviation, though the psychotic may be either of those as well. Most criminals are not psychotic, but some are (see Chapters 2 and 6). Neither are most homosexuals, but a few are (see Chapter 3).

The idiosyncratic psychoses originate in the idiosyncratic rather than the ethnic portion of the unconscious (see below). The traumata from which they stem are likely *not* to be statistically prevalent in that society, and there are usually not culturally provided defenses against them. In effect, the idiosyncratic psychotic is told: "Don't go crazy, but if you do, you're on your own, you have to invent your own way of expressing it." Therefore individualized psychotics are likely all to be very different from each other in detail, and not to fit neatly into types of whatever syndrome the clinician sees this individual as approximating. Hence the divergence of clinical opinion about each case, one of the factors leading the labeling sociologists—and many others—to be so skeptical about the competence of the clinicians doing the evaluating, as discussed above. Clinical specialists can disagree substantially about the appropriate diagnosis and therefore appropriate treatment for each patient, because each case may appear, in its combination of symptoms, to be essentially unique.

All the psychotics have in common severe impairment of ego-functions In some cases, they have never developed at all. Also, in a certain sense, paradoxically, they show a combination of extreme individuality and extreme de-individualization. The individuality leads to the clinician's sense that "no other case is exactly like this." The extreme de-individualization means that there is no coherent recognizable structure to this person. He or she is all in bits and pieces, scraps of many different potential personalities. This type of disorder is ego-dystonic, and statistically rare. Sufferers are also socially deviant. People around consider them "crazy."

3) Nonidiosyncratic psychoses: ethnic psychoses

The relativists try to assert that our conceptions of psychopathology in the West are ethnocentric. They claim that in other societies certain kinds of psychic disorder that we find in the West are entirely absent, e.g. schizophrenia. They also say that some other societies, especially some of the exotic tribal ones studied by anthropologists, have certain kinds of disorders that are entirely different from anything found in the West. Such disorders include running *amok* in Malaya, the *windigo* psychosis found in the Northern Algonquin tribes in North America. Those adducing these cases try to make the point that we cannot assume, as most psychoanalysts do, a universal psychology and potential for psychopathology.

George Devereux who has written most searchingly on this topic, contests that last inference very strongly (Devereux 1980, ch. 1, revised from 1956). Devereux gives us, instead, the bases for distinguishing five different kinds of psychopathology, all of them comprehensible by Western psychoanalytic psychology. The term ethnic psychosis comes from Devereux (1956, 1980, Chapter 1). It refers to severe forms of derangement, each of which is peculiar to the particular society and culture in which it appears. The disorder in each case is of a severity and quality to be characterized as a psychosis. That is, there is a fundamental break from ordinary reality, involving extreme impoverishment of the ego, severe dedifferentiation and de-individualization (Devereux 1980: 28ff).

The source of this kind of psychosis is in extreme idiosyncratic but *statistically prevalent* traumata in the early life experiences of the individual, for which there are no culturally stylized defenses provided, but which are culturally recognized as following a particular pattern. In effect, the culture provides certain forms of enactment of this disorder, for the individual to play the role of a person so afflicted. In effect, the person is being told: "Don't go crazy, but if you do, you do it in this particular way."

The exotic maladies just referred to—*amok* and *windigo,* or *imu,* and *latah* mentioned below, etc.—belong in this category. The responses to the traumata, and the experiencing of the traumata, originate in the individual or idiosyncratic portion of the unconscious (as distinguished from the "ethnic unconscious. "The latter refers to those aspects of unconscious functioning that derive from culturally standardized aspects of repression in the individual. Though recognized culturally, these disturbances are definitely ego-dystonic, and they are clearly socially deviant in the society in question. They are also statistically rare.

Though none of these exotic maladies corresponds exactly to psychotic disorders familiar in the West, such as the schizophrenias and psychotic depression, they are all comprehensible by dynamic concepts of Western psychoanalysis. *Latah* of Southeast Asia is understandable as like a hysterical psychosis. The "heartbreak syndrome" of the Mohave Indians (Devereux 1961) is like a classical mourning depression. The *imu* of the Ainu of Japan is a kind of hysteria. Other examples are the Malayan *running amok.* the "Crazy-Dog-wishes to die" syndrome in the Crow Indians; *susto* among Indians of the South American Andes. Blocked and frustrated women in certain parts of Puerto Rico suffer from *attaque,* a hysteria-like disorder that follows a clear cultural pattern (see Kathleen Wolf 1952; Endleman 1967: 82–126).

It is instructive to look at one of these ethnic disorders in more detail. "Crazy-Dog-Wishes-to-Die" occurs among the Crow Indians, under specified conditions. (Devereux 1980, ch.1; Lowie 1935). The Crazy Dog went into battle with an "insane" disregard for his safety and unparalleled physical bravery, very useful to the tribe and often suicidal. He was a recognized psychotic. One became a Crazy Dog only in response to certain kinds of intolerable frustration. Such may be his reaction if his ambition to become a chief is frustrated, but not if thwarted in love, or by another man claiming his wife. The Crazy Dog reacts totally negativistically: tell him to do one thing and he will do the opposite. This negativism extends only as far as culturally expected. For example, a Crazy Dog honored by a companion warrior for his brave exploits, by the companion's sending his wife to the Crazy Dog for the night, does cohabit with the other's wife, without needing a command, "do *not* cohabit with this woman." This psychotic episode is of controllable duration, and terminated according to a culture pattern. The Crazy Dog who did not die in battle before the leaves turned yellow was free to give up being a Crazy Dog. The Crazy Dog's negativism can be seen as a kind of reverse suggestibility, as a powerful defense against suggestibility, with parallels in many schizophrenics in our society.

4) Culturally Stylized Psychopathological Variant (Shamanistic Disorder)

The most notable example of this pathological type is the *shaman,* on whom there is a very substantial anthropological and ethnopsychiatric literature (see Devereux 1956, 1980; Ducey 1976, and references therein). Here again, Devereux' formulation is most instructive. The role is institutionalized; still, the person who becomes a shaman and practices as such is socially recognized within the tribe as a disturbed person who is essentially "crazy," but in a way that is culturally useful, perhaps even essential, to the tribe.

This person has been variously described as a "lightning conductor" of the troubles of the tribe, as the man or woman par excellence, who enables the members of the tribe to survive, psychologically, the strains and stresses that the technological culture of the tribe is unable to handle. This is the one who helps people to deal with the problems of existence and ultimate concerns, as distinguished from the more mundane problems of subsistence and practical protection from dangers in the material world and the interpersonal and intertribal world. This is the one who helps people deal with problems of the soul, as well as those of the body, though typically in tribal societies that dichotomy is not part of the familiar philosophical territory.

The shaman is distinctive from both the ethnic-psychotic and the idiosyncratic psychotic. His difficulties originate in traumatic experiences that concern the *ethnic unconscious,* that is, those aspects of repressed material that are common to people of the tribe or society, and unconscious defenses related to them that are partially those commonly shared and partially those that have a particular individualized quality that nevertheless resonates with unconscious needs of many other people of the society.

This may produce in non-shaman onlookers or audience participants feelings of "uncanny" recognition and appreciation that enable the shaman to function professionally. His kind of "craziness" is both stylized and in a certain sense institutionalized. He or she is regarded with a mixture of awe, fear, dread, anxiety and respect, as well as, often, with some skepticism which leads some hardy souls to question and challenge the shaman's supernatural imprimatur.

The origins are in culturally stylized (therefore cross-culturally variable) kinds of traumata which are, however, though recognizable, not statistically prevalent in the society. The responses to such traumata are also culturally stylized to some extent. There are culturally stylized and provided defenses here, but they do not typically lead to stabilization of the personality, rather, in the typical fashion of psychopathology, they lead to further difficulties and the necessity for further, secondary defenses, etc. in a vicious cycle manner. Or they may lead to periods of apparent stability, which is only a period of remission, since the underlying conflict has not been resolved, followed by other periods of craziness.

What distinguishes this kind of variant from the purely idiosyncratic psychotic, or neurotic for that matter, is that there is an institutionalized role into which one can be fitted. The criteria for entrance into this role include the sort of psychopathological disturbance the potential shaman experiences, which in tribal societies is typically interpreted in supernaturalistic terms. (Basically, supernatural equals the unconscious.) Compare the berdache in many tribal societies, (see Chapter 3) the qualifications for which are the revelations of a dream thought to be supernaturally visited upon the boy. In the case of the shaman, the concrete details of the symptoms, e.g. just how the individual "rants and raves" and with what imagery when he is "in one of his states," will be definitely patterned according to the culture. In addition, and just as important, the psychic *mechanisms* will be culturally patterned.

The psychic experiences of the shaman can be described as partly ego-syntonic, partly ego-dystonic. It can vary from one time to another. The very affective volatility of this kind of individual is itself a mark of the shaman type. This is clearly a socially deviant type, one that is institutionalized, culturally patterned, and socially structured. It is also statistically rare.

The formula here is: "If you go crazy, or act strangely, you may do so in this particular way; everyone will see you as crazy, but also treat you with awe, respect and fear." The message also says, "Once you have started in this direction, and shown the signs of this, you must go through with it; there is no turning back." The surrounding relatively normal people of the society thus typecast the shaman-deviant, and encourage him to melodramatic enactments of his "calling." Such encouragement resonates with his histrionic hysterical qualities.

Besides the dramatic example of the shaman, there are others that fit this category such as the berdache (discussed in Chapter 3) and in certain senses the "village idiot" of small rural communities in many parts of the world. The local eccentric or "wild man," again more typical of small communities, is in effect licensed to be oddball in his own particular way, and is typecast in that role and not allowed to act otherwise. (Erikson's cases of young people taking on a "negative identity"—Erikson 1959—are a similar, though usually more transitory, phenomenon.) Other examples would be the *guapo* (hyperaggressive and hypersexual rogue male) of certain Puerto Rican communities (Endleman 1967: 90–92, based on the work of Kathleen Wolf 1952) as well as the "clown-idiot" role of these same communities.

Statistical rarity is essential to these types. There must be relatively few of them in any one community.

5) Culturally Stylized Character Disorder

Rather than being rare, the culturally stylized character disorder may well be statistically prevalent in a particular society or subsociety. He is also different from the other three by not being considered deviant by the rest of the people in the society. In fact, the character trends he exhibits are presumed to be normal by others in that society, as well as himself. "Normal" in this case means conformist or adjusted to the prevailing expectations of that society.

Accordingly, the characteristics that would correspond to the symptoms of the neurotic are experienced as ego-syntonic, and do not arouse feelings of internal conflict or distress. The most obvious example would be, in our society, extremes of obsessive-compulsiveness displayed by minor bureaucrats, librarians, accountants, certain types of scholars, and people in many other occupations that require a high degree of time-discipline, orderliness, punctiliousness, scrupulous attention to large quantities of detail, and the like. Here reaction-formations against anal messiness are consolidated into an entire character style which is experienced positively and ego-syntonically, and serves, ordinarily, as a strong protection against anxiety.

Some might question whether this syndrome should really be considered a disorder, because unlike the obsessive-compulsive neurotic who is in agonies of conflict and internal distress, and whose rituals, while allaying anxiety, are still experienced as ego-alien, the compulsive *character type* experiences his orientation as ego-syntonic and gratifying, and feels comfortably conformist to the demands of his roles. Still the *rigidity* of this orientation would qualify it as a disorder.

At the extreme, we find individuals so mired in the petty details of the rules and regulations that have to be obeyed or enforced unconditionally in their work, that they are unable to adapt to even minor changes of situation, or handle any experience that departs in the slightest way from the pattern they expect to encounter. This hyperdevelopment of means-rationality may well subvert the larger goals of the organization or enterprise in which this work is enmeshed.

An obvious cost of such punctiliousness, for the individual caught up in this pattern, is the lack of spontaneity, isolation of affect, incapacity to "open up" emotionally, frequently enough also a lack of access to one's own feelings. These characteristics can hardly be regarded as indicative of optimal psychic functioning.

This is probably the most striking case of statistical normality (prevalence), combined with cultural normality in conformity to occupational and other cultural demands, along with transcultural abnormality in the form of character disorder. It must be noted however, that in this kind of case, it is a culturally stylized and supported character disorder, and such stylizations and support have implications for and effects upon the total balance and equilibrium of such a personality. They are therefore not to be dismissed as irrelevant to understanding the psychic processes involved.

Summary on Five Kinds of Psychopathology

Five kinds of psychopathology are related to culture patterns and to social processes of defining deviance and conformity. They differ in the *severity* of the disorder, in the *origins* of the pathology, in *ego-syntonicity,* in *cultural stylization* and also in their *relationship to deviance* and its attribution.

Severity varies, from psychoses, to pathological variant (possibly intermittently psychotic), to character disorders, compared to neuroses.

Origins of the pathology differ. They may come from the ethnic portion of the unconscious (as in shamans, and possibly also in the culturally stylized character disorders) or from the more idiosyncratic part of the unconscious, as in the three other types.

Ego-syntonicity varies: positive in the culturally stylized character disorders; mixed ego-syntonic and ego-alien in the shamanistic disorder; and largely ego-alien in the other three, the ethnic psychoses, the idiosyncratic psychoses and the idiosyncratic neuroses and character disorders.

Cultural stylization of the defensive process differs from one type to another. The shaman type (culturally stylized pathological variant) and the culturally stylized character disordered both have defensive systems that are essentially provided by the culture, and thus have validation from the surrounding social world, if only, in the case of the shaman, in an identity that is recognized as deviant. By contrast, in the other three cases, ethnic psychoses, idiosyncratic psychoses and idiosyncratic neuroses and character disorders, the individual has had, in effect, to improvise his own personal defensive systems, leaving him without important cultural supports.

In such individually improvised defensive systems, there is room of course, for the development of certain idiosyncratic creativity. Some observers have suggested that in every psychotic there is in effect a creative artist. There is a kernel of truth to this statement, but it needs important qualification. True, either the ethnic psychotic or the idiosyncratic psychotic has a kind of access to primary process thinking that the rest of us approximate only in our dreams. Also, some types of neurotics may have a kind of functioning that is more repressed in more "normal" persons. It is also true creative individuals need and use such access. What is missing in the more individualized psychopathological individual, that is present in the creative artist—*when* he is functioning and really doing creative work—is the measure of ego strength and creative mastery over the warring and dissident elements in the personality, and the capacity to transform these into creative products as works of the imagination.

Relationship to deviance and its attribution differs also, in the different types of psychopathology. The psychotic, whether ethnic or individualized, are all clearly regarded as deviant by others around—they talk crazy, act crazy, show all kinds of "social negativism," etc. associated with their psychopathology. The ethnic psychotic is deviant in a more culturally standardized way (every case is a classic "textbook" case) but deviant nonetheless. Because he is deviant in a standardized and therefore expectable way, there are also standardized ways others have available to respond to him. By contrast, the great idiosyncratic variety of individualized psychotic behavior and symptomatology makes such an individual's deviance more disturbing to onlookers and interacting persons. They don't know quite what to expect. Therefore their anxieties are greater than those of people dealing with the ethnically psychotic.

Many of the idiosyncratic neurotics and character-disordered are also likely to be considered deviant by the people around them. The extent and quality of such characterization can vary a good deal. That variation depends on the nature of the symptoms and the way these are socially defined. The *obtrusiveness* of the symptoms is likely to be positively correlated with the degree of deviance attributed to the individual, whereas it is likely to be *negatively* correlated with the malignancy of the pathological process (see Devereux 1956, 1980, ch. 1).

Persons with shamanic type disorders are considered deviant, but because the role is institutionalized, they are deviant in a somewhat acceptable way. (It is a "right way to do wrong things.") The reaction is not uniformly negative, but more ambivalent.

By contrast with all the others, those with culturally stylized character disorders are not considered deviant at all, at least not by those with whom they are connected in standardized interactive processes. The petty bureaucrat, ritualistically devoted to the letter of the rules, may be annoying, but he is "doing his job." Even here, however, there may be differences of degree. Some of the interacting role players may be more instrumentally—and less sacredly—oriented to the rules and regulations, and regard the over-punctilious as "deviant" in the sense of "overconforming."

To repeat: the deviant is not necessarily psychopathological and the psychopathological is not necessarily deviant. These are analytically distinct categories, and coalescing them into one and the same is a serious distortion of psychosocial reality.

Being considered deviant when one is not psychologically sick, may cause distress. One may then use defensive maneuvers that in turn may create some vicious-circle processes. But someone with a relatively strong ego-structure, and well-functioning conflict-free portions of the ego, is likely to be able to withstand the stresses of such deviance-attribution, if those attributes that others regard as deviant stem from healthy capacities for adaptation.

The joker then is the thorny question, adaptation to what? Clearly, if deviancy consists in failure or refusal to adapt to what is essentially a "sick society," then it is not difficult to attribute psychic health to such refusal, and to empathize with the "deviant's" difficulties as a matter of trouble with external relationships.

Such instances, however, are likely to be rare. More likely, nonconformity may be a complex mixture of both adaptive and regressive features, involving some kinds of psychopathological processes, alongside resources of psychic health.

Summary and Conclusion

Deviants are not necessarily (psychologically) sick, and people psychologically sick are not necessarily deviant.

We used to assume mental illness was the province of psychological disciplines, clinical psychology, psychiatry, psychoanalysis. Some sociologists are now saying: NOT NECESSARILY. Labeling theory sociologists have challenged the whole concept of mental illness, arguing that people usually hospitalized (clinicians would call psychotic) are not necessarily sick at all, but only people committing "residual deviance." A whole "labeling approach" to deviance has been applied especially to mental illness, under the influence particularly of Thomas Scheff, seeing mental hospital patients essentially as victims of negative labeling and stigmatization, as though the victims of some foul conspiracy. The villains here are the mental health professionals, mainly the hospital psychiatrists. Sociologists of this persuasion are likely to think what happens to Soviet dissidents who are declared mentally ill, is generally what is happening here too, to ordinary mental hospital patients. We thus get a peculiar paranoid-persecutory view of the world denying and distorting the psychic reality of persons suffering from psychological ailments, a viewpoint that has a large appeal to sociologists with an underdog identification and lacking in any expertise in the intricacies and ambiguities of intrapsychic disorder. People of this persuasion also accept with glee reports such as the Rosenhan research in which a number of psychology students faked being mentally ill and got themselves admitted to mental hospitals, and then had a hard time convincing staff that they were "really sane," a totally tendentious piece of research intending to prove that mental health professionals don't know what they are doing. Another study of the same period, however, by Ludwig and Farrelly, argues that patients ingeniously use "weapons of insanity" like the tyranny of the weak, provocative deviant behavior (to which staff is not supposed to respond) and similar devices to attain their ends. There we are presented with a picture that seriously challenges the notion of patients as poor helpless victims.

Next we considered five main kind of psychopathology, examined in relation to culture, to social interactions toward deviance, and to cultural and statistical conceptions of normality. In opposition to the cultural relativism prevailing in many approaches to the sociocultural and psychological sciences, we present *trans*cultural principles, applicable in all cultures and times, that enable sorting out in a sophisticated manner, these five different kinds of psychopathology.

The next chapter will continue the discussion of madmen, taking up implications in three different areas of public issues, namely deinstitutionalization, the insanity defense, and assassins mad and sane.

Notes

1. Many other American social scientists, particularly left-leaning ones, are also likely to take this view. For example, the Marxist political scientist Michael Parenti, in a letter to the *New York Review of Books* Mar. 9, 1978, claims that the U.S.A. is just as guilty as the U.S.S.R. of psychiatric repression, Soviet style. (Cited by Paul Hollander, 1981: *Political Pilgrims:* 69, 448)

2. True, Scheff is not entirely consistent on this point, and his work is more ambiguous, complex and convoluted than is suggested by selecting only his most dogmatic formulations, which at their extreme sound like the most paranoid elements in Goffman, Szasz and Laing. Also note in more recent years Scheff has moved in a direction much more sympathetic to psychoanalytic ideas, a direction his supporters in labeling theory sociology must find distressing or even traitorous. For our purposes, we concentrate on his labeling theory writing on the question of mental illness, since it was taken up so enthusiastically by a whole cadre of sociologists, particularly those embattled against that enemy, psychoanalysis. They in turn sound like the ideologically embattled gay-liberationist sociologists (see Chapter 3) with a similar animus against psychoanalysis.

3. Sagarin (1975: 129–142) summarizes his own and others' objections to the labeling approach generally. It is applicable to a limited range of deviance; it incorrectly generalizes from special cases; many of its propositions are unsupported or contradictred by empirical studies; its extreme relativism invites ethical nihilism; it turns away from etiology and rehabilitation; it neglects unofficial stigmatizing, and secret deviance. Specifically in reference to mental illness, labeling sociologists neglect or misidentify the screening procedures actually carried out on admitting potential

patients and incorrectly charges "patients" get sick through hospitalization.

4. Biologically based thinking in psychiatry and psychology has a long tradition that is still going strong, abetted in recent years by the intensified use of psychotropic drugs in treatment of psychiatric disorders. On biologically based psychiatry, see Brady *et al.* 1977, Snyder 1980, Usdin 1975. On psychopharmacology (which presupposes physiological malfunctions) see DiMascio and Shader 1970, Caffey *et al.* 1970 (and their bibliographies). For biologically oriented theory in personality see Sheldon 1942, Eysenck 1967. Biogenetic views on schizophrenia extend from the classic Kallman 1937 work, on to the present (Sperber and Jarvick 1976). For brain functioning in relation to violent offenders, see Goldman 1977 and his thorough bibliography, and Mednick and Christiansen 1977.

5. It is commonly stated that psychoanalysis found a real foothold in America. To the extent that that is true, it has been largely at the cost of great dilution of the originally radical Freudian view. (See Jacoby 1975, Endleman 1981, 1982b and their sources.) Classical psychoanalysis as therapy is very much on the decline, giving way to a host of more superficial therapies.

6. I realize that here I expose myself to a common complaint against psychoanalysts, that is, that if you don't agree with them, they tell you there is something psychologically wrong with you, that you're repressing or denying, rather than dealing with the substance of their criticism. Frequently psychoanalysts do seem to argue in a "heads-I-win-tails-you-lose" fashion. All I can say in answer here is that commonly apparently rational arguments do have a nonrational component and genesis, often *not instead of* a logical force, but rather *in addition to* it, and such cognitive complexities are part of what psychoanalysis has to explore.

7. Interestingly, the ideological animus here gets in the way of basic *sociological* analysis. By now every student of sociology should have learned about the "unintended consequences of purposive social action" (Merton 1936, with antecedents in Weber and others). Any good organizational analysis would have been attuned to this factor. Perrucci, so intent on seeing the functionaries of this hospital as oppressor villains, misses it entirely. Failure here is clearly related to ideological bias reflecting, in turn, a paranoid-persecutory fantasy.

REFERENCES

Ash, P. 1949. "The reliability of psychiatric diagnosis." *Journal of Abnormal and Social Psychology.* 44:272–276.

Becker, Howard S. 1963. *Outsiders: Studies in the Sociology of Deviance.* New York: Free Press

Blum, R. H. 1962. "Case Identification in Psychiatric Epidemiology: Methods and Problems." *Milbank Memorial Fund Quarterly.* 40:253–288.

Bordua, David. 1967. "Recent Trends: Deviant Behavior and Social Control." *Annals of the American Academy of Political and Social Science.* 369:149–163.

Brady, John Paul *et al.* eds. 1977. *Psychiatry: Areas of Promise and Advancement.* New York: Spectrum

Caffey, Eugene M. Jr. *et al.* 1970. "A Survey of Drug Treatment in Psychiatry." in DiMascio and Shader 1970: 343–384.

Devereux, George. 1940. "Social Negativism and Criminal Psychopathology." *Journal of Criminal Psychopathology.* 1:325–328. (Reprinted in Devereux 1980, ch.3)

__________. 1956. "Normal and Abnormal." in J. Casagrande, and T. Gladwin, eds. *Some Uses of Anthropology.* Washington, DC: Anthropological Society of Washington. Reprinted in much expanded version, in Devereux 1980, Chapter 1.

__________. 1961. *Mohave Ethnopsychiatry: The Psychic Disturbances of an Indian Tribe.* Washington, D.C.: Smithsonian Institution Press

__________. 1967. *From Anxiety to Method in the Behavioral Sciences.* The Hague and Paris: Mouton

__________. 1980. *Basic Problems of Ethnopsychiatry.* Chicago: University of Chicago Press

DiMascio, Alberto, and Richard Shader, eds. 1970. *Clinical Handbook of Psychopharmacology.* New York: Jason Aronson

Dohrenwend, Bruce, and Barbara Dohrenwend. 1969. *Social Status and Psychological Disorder.* New York: Wiley

Ducey, Charles. 1976. "The Life History and Creative Psychopathology of the Shaman: Ethnopsychoanalytic Perspectives." in W. Muensterberger, A. Esman, and L. B. Boyer, eds. *The Psychoanalytic Study of Society,* 7:173–230. New Haven and London: Yale University Press.

Endleman, Robert. 1967. *Personality and Social Life.* New York: Random House

__________. 1981. *Psyche and Society: Explorations in Psychoanalytic Sociology.* New York: Columbia University Press

__________. 1982a. "Commentary" (On Review of *Psyche and Society.*) *Jl. of Psychoanalytic Anthropology.* 5:349–352.

__________. 1982b. "Sociocultural Factors in Variations in Psychoanalytic Theory." Conference on WHAT IS PSYCHOANALYSIS? Psychoanalytic Society of the New York University Postdoctoral Program, Jan. 1982.

Erikson, Erik H. 1959. "Identity and the Life Cycle." *Psychological Issues.* 1. New York: International Universities Press

Eysenck, Hans J. 1967. *The Biological Basis of Personality.* Springfield, IL: Charles C. Thomas

Faris, R. E. L., and Warren Dunham. 1939. *Mental Disorders in Urban Areas.* Chicago: University of Chicago Press

Fireside, Harvey. 1979. *Soviet Psychoprisons.* New York: Norton

Fletcher, C. Richard, and Larry Reynolds. 1968. "Residual Deviance, Labeling and the Mentally Sick Role: A Critical Review of Concepts." *Sociological Focus.* 1:9–27.

Freeman, Richard B. and Brian Hall. 1986. *Report of the National Bureau of Economic Research: Permanent Homelessness in America?*

Goffman, Erving. 1961. *Asylums.* Garden City, N.Y.: Doubleday

Goldman, Harold. 1977. "The Limits of Clockwork: the Neurobiology of Violent Behavior." in J. Conrad and S. Dinitz eds. *In Fear of Each Other.* Lexington, MA: D. C. Heath. 43–76.(see especially bibliography)

Goode, Erich. 1978. *Deviant Behavior.* Englewood Cliffs, N.J.: Prentice-Hall

Gove, Walter. 1970. "Who is Hospitalized: a Critical Review of some Sociological Studies of Mental Illness." *Journal of Health and Social Behavior.* 11:294–303.

Hollingshead, A. B. and F. C. Redlich. 1958. *Social Class and Mental Illness.* New York: Wiley

Jacoby, Russell. 1975. *Social Amnesia: A Critique of Psychology from Adler to Laing.* Boston: Beacon

Kallman, F. 1938. *The Genetics of Schizophrenia.* New York: Augustin

Kaplan, Howard B. 1972. *The Sociology of Mental Illness.* New Haven, Ct.: College & University Press.

Laing, Ronald. 1967. *The Politics of Experience.* New York: Random House

Leighton, Alexander. 1959. *My Name is Legion.* New York: Basic Books

Lemert, Edwin. 1951. *Social Pathology.* New York: McGraw-Hill

Lowie, Robert H. 1929. *Are We Civilized? Human Culture in Perspective.* New York: Harcourt Brace.

__________. 1935. *The Crow Indians.* New York: Farrar and Rinehart.

Ludwig, Arnold and Frank Farrelly. 1967. "The Weapons of Insanity." *American Journal of Psychiatry* 21:737–749.

Mednick, S., and K. O. Christiansen, eds. 1977. *Bio-Social Bases of Criminal Behavior.* New York: Gardner

Merton, Robert K. 1936. "The Unanticipated Consequences of Purposive Social Action." *American Sociological Review.* 1:894–904.

Perrucci, Robert. 1974. *The Circle of Madness: On Being Insane and Institutionalized in America.* Englewood Cliffs, NJ: Prentice-Hall

Reich, Walter. 1983. "The World of Soviet Psychiatry." *The New York Times Sunday Magazine,* 1/30/83: 21ff.

Richman, Judith. 1985. "Social Class and Mental Illness Revisited: Sociological Perspectives on the Diffusion of Psychoanalytic Ideas." *Journal of Operational Psychiatry* 16:1–8

Rosenhan, D. L. "On Being Sane in Insane Places." *Science* 179: 250–258.

Sagarin, Edward. 1975. *Deviants and Deviance.* New York: Praeger

Scheff, Thomas. 1966. *Being Mentally Ill.* Chicago: Aldine

__________. ed. 1975. *Labeling Madness.* Englewood Cliffs, NJ: Prentice-Hall

Schur, Edwin. 1971. *Labeling Deviant Behavior.* New York: Harper and Row

__________. 1979. *Interpreting Deviance.* New York: Harper and Row

Schwartz, Charlotte. 1957. "Perspectives on Deviance: Wives' Definitions of their Husbands' Mental Illness." *Psychiatry.* 20:275–291.

Sheldon, W. H. and S. S. Stevens. 1942. *The Varieties of Temperament: A Psychology of Constitutional Differences.* New York: Harper and Row

Snyder, Solomon H. 1980. *Biological Aspects of Mental Disorder.* New York: Oxford

Sperber, Michael A., and L. Jarvick, eds. 1976. *Psychiatry and Genetics.* New York: Basic Books

Srole, Leo, Thomas Langner, *et al.* 1962. *Mental Health in the Metropolis.* New York: McGraw-Hill

Szasz, Thomas. 1961. *The Myth of Mental Illness.* New York: Paul Hoeber

__________. 1981. "Power and Psychiatry." *Society* 18: 16–18.

Townsend, John Marshall. 1978. *Cultural Conceptions and Mental Illness.* Chicago: University of Chicago Press

Usdin, Gene, ed. 1975. *Schizophrenia: Biological and Psychological Perspectives.* New York: Brunner, Mazel

Yarrow, Marion Radke *et al.* 1955. "The Psychological Meaning of Mental Illness in the Family." *Journal of Social Issues.* 11:12–24.

Wolf, Kathleen. 1952. "Growing Up and its Price in Three Puerto Rican Subcultures. *Psychiatry* 115:401–433.

CHAPTER 6
MENTAL ILLNESS AND PUBLIC ISSUES

Introduction

The outlines of a psychoanalytic sociology of mental illness that we have developed in the preceding chapter have bearing on a number of public issues. We shall deal with three of these in this chapter.

-De-institutionalization: removal of patients from the mental hospitals, and the attempt to close down the mental hospital system; have we in fact improved the lot of the mentally ill by getting them out of the "snakepits" and into the public? How is it that so many of them are now on the streets and part of the population of the homeless?

-Crime and the Insanity Plea: can some offenders, particularly in capital cases, claim that their legal responsibility is diminished or eliminated because they are psychologically pathological in some important way? Is it fair to them or to society to have such persons declared "not guilty by reason of insanity?"

-Assassins: Mad and Sane: are the men and women who kill (or try to kill) presidents and other important public figures, all in fact madmen and madwomen, as has commonly been presented in the public media?

De-Institutionalization

Combined with other forces, the views of the labeling sociologists and others of similar persuasion, have been influential in bringing about a major change in the lives of mental hospital patients, namely the massive de-institutionalization out of the mental hospitals that has been going on for about two decades. That process has ruined the lives of thousands of ex-patients now out of the hospitals and mostly without any alternative care, now on the streets of our large cities, and in many instances homeless and unable to maintain their basic subsistence. This is an ironic and tragic consequence of sentimental good intentions having combined with budgetary conservatism.

One of the effects, partly intended, of the peculiar view of mental hospital patients as helpless victims, has been the drive to get the patients out of the hospitals and in effect to abolish the whole mental hospital system. This is a political process—with other sources as well, of course. In the past couple of decades, hundreds of thousands of such patients have been "released" from the psychiatric hospitals. Where the state mental hospitals had at their zenith about a half million resident patients nationwide, the numbers declined to about 475,000 in 1965, to 193,000 in 1975; to 130,000 in 1980, and probably less today (Gralnick 1985; Appelbaum 1987).

Another statistic:

In 1955, in Illinois, there were 48,000 beds for mental patients in state hospitals, who spent an average of 10 years and 8 months there. In 1982, there were 10,000 beds in the state, half of them for the severely retarded, and the average stay for someone mentally ill was 22 days (Caplan 1984, p. 26).

Large numbers of those who have been discharged from the hospitals are now helpless and also homeless, on the streets. Estimates today are that 25–40% of the street homeless are mentally ill. These people are without any kind of psychiatric care, and often without even minimal material needs.

This process began in the 1950s by a convergence of "young Turk" psychiatrists, intent on remedying what they saw as the deplorable conditions of the "snake-pits" of large state hospitals. These psychiatrists had had experience during and just after World War II of alternative, often very effective, emergency treatment of the mentally ill, very different from the usual state hospital methods of that time. Then in 1952 came the discovery of Chlorpromazine, a tranquilizer that proved very effective in reducing or even eliminating many of the most disturbing symptoms of psychotics. Introduced in the United States in 1954 as Thorazine, it rapidly became standard in hospital treatment of psychotics. The drive to empty the mental hospitals was on.

It was accelerated as liberal-minded civil-libertarians pressed to carry out de-institutionalization in the name of compassionate caring for the mentally ill. It was to take them out of enforced incarceration. The reformers were also influenced by the iconoclastic psychiatrists Thomas Szasz, who was insisting that mental illness was a myth, and Ronald Laing, who romanticized schizophrenia as a "sane response to an insane world" (see Chapter 5). In turn, they found support in the new sociological studies such as Goffman's *Asylums* and others which contended that the deplorable mental state of patients was a product not of psychic disease, but of the oppressive forces of institutionalization itself. Other sociologists contributed to this viewpoint, as described in the preceding chapter, especially the labeling theory sociologists with their denial of the reality of deviance and specifically of mental illness. That viewpoint was eagerly accepted by many of the dissident psychiatrists and their civil-libertarian reformer allies. Add to that set of alliances, the drives of fiscal conservatives to save money for the states, and we got a peculiar coalition of a certain type of "liberal" with the fiscal conservatives that succeeded in making de-institutionalization a reality. This policy severely hurt the vast majority of mental hospital patients that it was intended to benefit. The process became, as Appelbaum indicates (1987) an ideological crusade, negligent of the real nature of the mentally ill and their needs, and negligent of the need to adopt and implement hard-thinking policies for alternative (and preferably better) care for the former mental hospital patients and their later counterparts.

This is a good example of unintended consequences of purposive social action, as well as of liberal humanely intended ideas resulting in the opposite effects when implemented.

The psychiatrist Alexander Gralnick, the medical director of a psychiatric hospital, makes a strong "Case against Deinstitutionalization" (1985). Modern psychiatric hospitals were developed in the nineteenth century to remedy the brutal and inhumane treatment of the mentally ill in almshouses and jails. Since the 1950s various forces set out to empty the mental hospitals, and now have largely "succeeded." With what results?

Gralnick asks, "Has community care lessened the incidence of mental illness and the numbers of mentally ill? Has it diminished the numbers of chronically ill in our midst? Has it significantly lessened the mistreatment and suffering of our sick in the community? Are our patients getting better treatment and is the future more promising for them? With little exception, the answer to [all] these questions is a resounding 'no.' " Fewer than 50% of discharged patients continue their medication, and only 25% continue in aftercare. Moving from a single state hospital system to multiple community programs destroys the ability to pinpoint the responsibility for care. The situation of the mentally ill in the community is no better, and often much worse than it was in the hospitals. Increasing numbers of the mentally sick are in our jails, in nursing homes, or at best, in seedy single-room-occupancy hotels. As many as 50% of the patients in nursing homes now are mentally ill. Many are homeless, wandering the streets, taking shelter in subways and tunnels. They compose an estimated 25% to 40% of the growing population of the homeless.

Other tolls are those on the legal system and on coerced family members. There is relative neglect of the acutely ill and consequent amassing of the chronically ill. Now, unless deemed harmful to oneself or others, a person cannot be hospitalized. Hospitalization, if available at all, is usually limited to 30 days, far too little for effective treatment. Neglect of treatment of acute episodes leads to long-term chronicity, with dire, even disastrous consequences. The hopes for a "community psychiatry" in which emotionally ill persons would be warmly welcomed into the community, provided necessary housing, appropriate care, and meaningful productive work—all this has proven to be a chimera. "Normal" people of the community do not welcome "mentally ill" into their midst, let alone provide them with any of those necessities. The mentally ill are as much contemned, feared and stigmatized as ever (how would we expect ordinary people of the community to change on these issues?) Additionally, now a general public feels these weird people have been dumped on *them* (why us? why here?) with none of the protection for either the sick or the others that used to be provided by the segregation of people in hospitals. States are unwilling to vote for the huge sums of money needed to provide adequate alternative care in the much-touted community-based small facilities, and the professional staff they would need. Ironically the whole process has not saved money, since large hospitals have not simply been closed, but rather have reduced censuses, with therefore greatly increased per-patient costs.

Most de-institutionalized mental patients do not become more autonomous and capable of organizing and conducting their lives simply by having the coercion of hospitalization removed. More than half in board-and-care arrangements do not wish to change anything in their lives (see Appelbaum 1987, Gralnick 1985, and Morrissey 1982).

Appelbaum, a professor of psychiatry and director of the Law and Psychiatry program at the University of Massachusetts Medical School, argues it is time to recognize the whole de-institutionalization policy as a tragic failure, and turn it around, by devising a rational program to give proper care to the mentally ill. This would comprise moderate expansion of the number of beds in state facilities for the severely ill who cannot take care of themselves, and who need the supportive protective structure of an institution. It would require good community-based facilities for those who *can* function outside an institution but need supportive care. A third desideratum would be greater authority of the state to detain and treat the severely mentally ill for their own benefit. This would be done, if necessary coercively, if they pose a threat to themselves and/or others (as many such psychotics clearly do) and in other cases even if they do not.

The relationship between de-institutionalization and homelessness is illustrated in the pathos and bizarre oddity of a case like that of "Billy Boggs." This woman is not one who was a patient in a mental hospital and had then been discharged, in the de-institutionalization drive. She was never in a hospital, but psychiatrists who examined her were of the opinion that she should have been. Probably in the age before de-institutionalization, she (or her counterpart) would have been. Here is her story.

Joyce Brown (aka Billie Boggs), encountered in 1987, had been living on the streets of New York for over a year. She had been hurling insults at passersby, burning money given to her, defecating on the streets, and doing other outrageous things. Project Help refused to try to get her hospitalized ("not an immediate danger to herself or others") but Mayor Koch applied a more flexible standard and had her coercively removed to Bellevue where she was diagnosed as a chronic schizophrenic. Doctors tried to medicate her; she refused. With the aid of New York Civil Liberties Union, she litigated her release, became a momentary celebrity, went on a lecture tour with her NYCLU mentors on behalf of "the homeless."

In a significant article, Thomas J. Main: "What we Know about the Homeless," *Commentary,* May 1988: 85:5: 26–36, deals with the question: Are most of the homeless mentally ill? Answer: No, but a significant proportion, about a quarter to a third are. Relevant studies he cites include Richard B. Freeman and Brian Hall (Harvard U.) "Report of the National Bureau of Economic Research: Permanent Homelessness in America?" 1986. They estimated the total [nationwide] number of homeless about 250,000–350,000, about one-tenth of figures used by various advocacy groups. These numbers are confirmed by several other studies by various researchers, using several different methods, in Chicago and several other cities. Of these about 25–35% are mentally ill, and though not directly the product of de-institutionalization, most of which occurred earlier, more than 90,000 of those on the streets today would have been in mental hospitals in the days before de-institutionalization. Almost all surveys show between a quarter and a third of the homeless are indeed mentally ill.

Of the homeless about 70–80% suffer from one disability or more. Rossi (study of Chicago on this point, 1980s) found 82% of his survey population had *at least one* of the following disabilities: poor or fair [physical] health; previous mental hospitalization; previous stay in a detoxification unit; clinically high scores on tests for depression or psychotic thinking; sentence(s) by a court. Other studies show similar figures. Thus the homeless are NOT "just like you and me," and most do have "something wrong with them" which contributes to their homelessness. Import of the article: homelessness is a much *smaller* problem [in numbers] than commonly presented. but also much more *intractable* than advocates understand, because of disabilities which require authorities to exert *authority* to deal with these people, e.g. refusing to allow Joyce Brown to live in the streets. The "advocates" of the homeless typically distort the situation by grossly exaggerating the numbers (by a factor of about ten) and by indulging in the typical mystifications asserting the "tyranny of enlightened minorities" (Cf. Endleman 1981, p. 353), in ways parallel to some of the strands that brought about the de-institutionalization in previous decades.

Crime and the Insanity Plea

Some years ago, George Devereux was called in as an expert consultant, as a combined psychoanalyst-and-anthropologist, in a murder case where the defendants, two Acoma Pueblo Indian half-brothers, had been accused, tried and convicted of murder. The prison psychiatrist could find no *culturally neutral* evidence of psychological disorder in these two men. The two men indicated belief in witchcraft, but the psychiatrist, being anthropologically knowledgeable, felt that for the Acoma Pueblo Indians, such belief was normal. Therefore he declared the men sane; they were sentenced to death for the crime. Still the psychiatrist felt troubled about the case, and called in Devereux. Devereux talked with each of the men separately. Each within ten minutes poured out to Devereux a flood of data about witchcraft, consistent with Acoma belief. But this outpouring was strange, for this reason: in field work this kind of material would be elicited from an informant only after much hard preliminary work. It was therefore totally out of line with "normal" Acoma behavior for a usually suspicious, distrustful Acoma to reveal such esoteric material to a total stranger on first meeting. Further inquiry led Devereux to conclude that the two men had ceased to *experience* these cultural beliefs as objective cultural material, and were now experiencing them in a delusional manner. Instead of dealing with a perceived threat of witchcraft in a culturally conformist Acoma manner, i.e. by asking the help of the ritual societies in charge of neutralizing witches, they had sought to take the law into their own hands, by killing the suspected witch. It was as though, Devereux points out, a brilliant but paranoid electronics engineer in our society, believing he was being persecuted by radar, designed and constructed a new improved radar device which in turn persecutes him; he uses existing cultural material efficiently, but at the same time delusionally.

In the Acoma Indians' case, Devereux continues: Having determined the *manner* in which they had distorted cultural reality, Devereux was able to elicit from them personal and idiosyncratic delusional material as well, variant from the Acoma culture pattern and revealing a full-blown paranoid schizophrenia in one of the brothers and a psychotically tinged psychopathy in the other (Devereux 1980, pp. 66–67). The psychiatrist argued these diagnoses on the appeal of their cases, and they were not sentenced to die but rather confined for psychiatric disorder. Devereux points out that while sometimes a cultural belief is mistaken for a psychotic delusion, here the psychotic delusion—i.e. the delusional *manner* of experiencing Pueblo cultural belief about witches—was almost mistaken for a belief.

The General Problem of the Insanity Defense

A basic principle of Anglo-American law is that someone who knowingly and intentionally commits an offense should be found guilty and appropriately punished, assuming that the accused was at the time of the offense of sound mind, basically rational, and in control of his will. The corollary, sustained for many centuries, is that if the accused was *not* of sound mind, was in some manner mentally incapacitated, then he is not—or not fully—responsible for the criminal act. The modern legal phrasing is that the individual is judged to be "insane." This is roughly—but only roughly—equivalent to the psychiatric concept of psychotic.

The aims of the criminal law in modern democratic societies are fourfold: protection of society by incapacitation of offenders, deterrence, rehabilitation and retribution. Imprisonment or execution keeps convicted offenders out of the way, thus protecting potential victims. (So would incarceration in another facility, such as a mental hospital.) Deterrence means not only stopping apprehended offenders from committing crimes again, but also persuading lawabiding citizens *not* to commit offenses they might be tempted to carry out. Rehabilitation means changing criminal offenders into lawabiding citizens who no longer commit crimes. And retribution—called by some authors "just punishment"—means getting even. Someone has done some harm, therefore some harm or pain should be inflicted on him. (Many of tender sensibilities feel this aim or motivation should play no part in formal law in a modern enlightened society, seeming to them to resemble the *lex talionis* of more archaic and more barbaric societies. Psychologically, however, it continues to be—and probably will always be—an important part of public reaction particularly to especially heinous crimes. Note how frequently fictional crime stories in the popular media end with the death of the killer in a shoot-out with the police or by accident or some manner other than formal legal execution, fulfilling an audience demand for immanent justice.

Where ordinary psychological competence in the offender is assumed, the normal processes of the criminal law fulfill these four demands. A person proved in a proper trial to be guilty beyond a reasonable doubt of a particular offense, is to be incapacitated by imprisonment. This is to deter him (and other potential offenders) from repeating this offense—

assuming he is "rational" and can "learn a lesson." He can be rehabilitated by appropriate retraining showing him the positive value of being law abiding and the negative of committing crimes. The public's demand for "justice" in the form of appropriate punishment, has been fulfilled.

What if the person under consideration is *not* normally rational? Can a person who is seriously psychologically impaired be considered a proper moral agent, responsible and accountable for his actions and their consequences?

This is where the "insanity plea" comes in.

There is a centuries-long background history for this concern in the law.

The M'Naghten Rule

Present-day controversies can be traced to 1843 in Great Britain, where in reaction against the acquittal on grounds of insanity of a defendant named M'Naghten, a committee of the common-law judges formulated a rule for the courts that became known, ironically, as the M'Naghten Rule. That rule states that an accused is to be found not guilty by reason of insanity if, "at the time of the committing of the act, the party accused was laboring under such a defect of reason from disease of the mind as not to know the nature and quality of the act he was doing, or if he did know it, that he did not know he was doing what was wrong" (Kaufman 1982). Great Britain continues to use this rule today. So do about twenty states of the United States.

From a present-day perspective of psychological knowledge the defects of this formulation are manifold. It concentrates entirely on *cognitive* features of the personality, and leaves out everything else. including ability to *control* one's actions. Many severely sick individuals *know* the difference between right and wrong, but cannot stop themselves from doing something wrong. Many courts tried to improve on the M'Naghten formulation, without throwing it out completely. One such "improvement" was to introduce the idea of an "irresistible impulse" driving the defendant. This was hardly adequate; focusing on spur-of-the-moment reactions, it left out entirely cases that involved long-term planning but nevertheless were based on serious delusional thinking. It also involved this dilemma: could not the defense argue that since the impulse was not resisted, it must have been "irresistible?"

The Durham Rule

In 1954, in *Durham v. United States* Judge David Bazelon of the United States Court of Appeals for the District of Columbia, set forth what came to be called the "Durham Rule." A defendant is not criminally responsible "if his unlawful act was the product of a mental disease or defect."

This had the merit of recognizing that a wide variety of diseases or defects may impair the mind and lead to unlawful acts, but its formulation was too general to give judges and juries adequate guidance.

American Law Institute Rule

In 1966 Judge Irving R. Kaufman gave an opinion in *United States v. Freeman* based on the American Law Institute: "a person is not responsible for criminal conduct if at the time of such conduct as a result of mental disease or defect he lacks substantial capacity either to appreciate the wrongfulness of his conduct or to conform his conduct to the requirements of law." With slight alterations, this formulation is now the law in a majority of the United States and Federal Circuits (Kaufman 1982).

This sets a standard, but that is only the beginning of the problems of the courts. Implementation in any particular case presents innumerable difficulties and dilemmas. This was evident in the trial of John Hinckley Jr. for his attempted assassination of President Reagan and wounding of several others. The jury's verdict in that case of "not guilty by reason of insanity" outraged a good portion of the American public. In American courts, the insanity defense is actually invoked in only an infinitesimally small number of cases—about one in a thousand, due to the obviously enormous expenses of hiring the necessary expert witnesses. However, the principle involved is important and significant. Is justice served if a clearly psychotic individual is sent to prison rather than to a psychiatric hospital, or an obviously normal individual sent to a mental hospital instead of a prison?

Can we reliably determine which is which? The spectacle of teams of psychiatrists on the opposing sides presenting bewilderingly conflicting testimony showing the defendant is seriously sick or showing that he is as normal as any average person in the population, as happens in all of these sensational trials, undermines public confidence in "expert" opinion about who is crazy and who is not. Thus in the Hinckley case, thousands of the lay public were convinced that Hinckley was just a confused and spoiled rich kid who deserved the fullest punishment of the law, while others were convinced he was really patently extremely crazy. If the psychiatrists, the supposed experts, could not agree, then why trust their opinions at all? Besides there is a built-in Catch-22 in these cases—anyone who commits such a crime *must* be crazy. If so, then all serious killers must be "not guilty by reason of insanity," or, alternatively, guilty regardless of their psychological state, meaning that the insanity defense itself must be worthless.

We need to sort out a number of distinguishable problems here.

1) *Is expert opinion worthwhile?* My answer is, of course it is. It is generally superior to lay opinion. But neither psychiatry nor any of the other disci-

plines dealing with the human psyche is an exact science, and probably never could be. Psychoanalytic understanding attunes us to the enormous ambiguity and contradictoriness of human behavior and thinking and feeling. Psychological knowledge must necessarily be approximate and of course, in its nature, it is subjective. (That is often held against it, by believers in "objective" science; an absurd charge. The most we can expect is some degree of concordance among the various subjectivities of different kinds of observers.) Still, if the law were asking us to distinguish which individuals are *very seriously* disturbed, i.e. psychotic, we can probably achieve a fair degree of consensus on that. For example, most clinicians would probably see John Hinckley as suffering from psychotic disorder. His belief that by killing the president he was going to win the girl he idolized from afar (Jodi Foster) and then move with her into the White House, is clearly delusional. Other cases may be more problematical, but it could be argued that any mental state short of psychosis should not be considered as qualifying for "insanity" in the legal sense used here.

2) *Where should the burden of proof be placed?*

Different jurisdictions answer this differently. In the federal court trying Hinckley, the rule was that the *prosecution* had to prove the accused sane, beyond a reasonable doubt. (Given that instruction, the jury *had* to conclude that Hinckley was *not* sane, even though they might disagree among themselves about how severely sick he was.)

In other jurisdictions, the burden of proof is on the *defense,* and in some cases, this has only to be "by a preponderance of evidence."

My own conclusion in the Hinckley case is that the jury was entirely correct, and that the result was definitely *not* a travesty of justice. Hinckley was psychotic; he was delusional. Other evidence indicated clearcut defects of ego functioning, including breaks from ordinary reality. He therefore belonged in a hospital, not a prison. Yes, he needed to be segregated from society, because his actions indicated a threat to the safety of others around him, not only of political figures. By our system of justice, he did not belong in a prison.

3) *What shall be counted as evidence of the "insanity?"* Many people feel when faced by a heinous crime, that the perpetrator *must* be crazy to do something like that. Here the offense itself is taken as the evidence for the psychological disorder. Carried to its logical extreme, it could be applied to all offenders. What the court needs, in the kinds of cases concerning us here, is *independent* evidence of the psychological disorder, other than the criminal act itself. This is what the psychiatrists or other mental health professionals have to provide.

4) *Who should make the determination of "insanity?"*

Here there are quandaries. A jury, necessarily of laymen, may have a very hard time understanding the professional technical testimony of psychiatrists and other experts. Many informed observers have advocated that the determination of the accused's psychological state be made a separate part of the proceeding, that the jury should be involved only in the determination of guilt or innocence. And similarly, psychiatrists should not be making moral judgments. However, advocates of the rights of the accused argue that the jury should be involved in arriving at any verdict such as guilty as charged, or not guilty by reason of insanity. They argue that this is a better protection of the defendant's rights than a determination by "experts." On this side too, are those who say that a jury of layment, in however humble occupations, are just as capable as anyone else of coming to a conclusion even on a complex issue like the insanity defense, as indicated in the Hinckley case where the jury was more rational about its decision than that outraged segment of the public.

By contrast, the jury in the case of Arthur Bremer, who tried to kill George Wallace, and almost succeeded, decided he was *not* insane within the meaning of the law, judging by evidence similar to that in the Hinckley case. See later discussion.

5) *Possible alternatives? "Guilty but Mentally Ill"?*

Various suggestions for changing the structure of such trials have been made, but they all involve difficulties. For example, there is the suggestion of another possible verdict, namely *guilty but mentally ill.* As of 1982, eight states had instituted this kind of approach. A jury coming in with this verdict is saying that the defendant is mentally ill, but this illness does not negate his ability to understand the unlawful nature of his conduct, or his ability to conform his conduct to the requirements of the law. The defendant is then sentenced as a criminal, but undergoes psychiatric evaluation, and, if found mentally ill, is placed in a psychiatric hospital. If at any time prior to expiration of his sentence, he is found to be no longer mentally ill, he is then transferred to prison to complete his term. Many of the jurors of the Hinckley trial said in post-trial interviews that if given that option, they would have voted for such a verdict. This option would seem to satisfy both demands, for justice in the sense that someone does not "get away with murder," and consideration of the psychological state of the offender. Kaufman however (1982) worries that it might increase, rather than decrease, jury confusion.

In the criminological literature, it is argued that in some, particularly capital cases, the defendant may try for an insanity defense, counting on getting off with a relatively short stay in a mental hospital as contrasted with a much longer term in prison. However, since mental hospital commitments are usually for indefinite periods while a prison sentence is always for a finite term, with definite conditions for parole, the former may not be a "better deal." Many sociologists, also, especially of the labeling persuasion, think of mental hospitals as even more depriving institutions than prisons. If the "guilty but mentally ill" provision is followed correctly, moreover, it could not be used to get a better deal for an offender. True, part of the public expressed outrage at the Hinckley verdict, arguing that he could be out of a hospital within a couple of years, being pronounced no longer mentally ill, and go out on the streets and commit other violent offenses. That could not happen under a "guilty but mentally ill" verdict, because under that system upon release from the hospital when "no longer mentally ill," he would still have to serve the rest of his sentence in prison.

Clarke in his book on American assassins (1982) does not deal with the "guilty-but-mentally-ill" possibility, but six of his cases might qualify (see below).

One of the publicly expressed antipsychiatry statements widely pronounced in cases like the Hinckley one, is that psychiatrists cannot reliably predict if and when a previously violent offender will repeat a violent act. This is quite true. No one in the mental health professions can make such a prediction. (See discussion of this point in Chapter 2.) No comforting answer exists. The alternative lines of action are 1) to keep all *potentially* violent offenders locked up for the rest of their lives; and 2) to take a chance and release prisoners who have served their term and mental hospital patients who *seem* to be recovered and give no evidence that they are presently dangerous. The latter procedure is more in line with the values of our legal system, that persons are to be dealt with in terms of what they have actually done, not of what they might do.

6) *What kinds of Cases?*

I would also suggest the following: reasonable application of the Kaufman rule would seem to fit only cases of *very serious* psychic disorder, i.e. psychoses (and not all of those at that), and should not include any of the myriad other psychological disorders, i.e. neuroses, character disorders, or, particularly, "psychopathic" or "sociopathic" personality. The psychopathic, for example, might attempt to claim "insanity," while understanding perfectly well the unlawfulness of his acts, and also being entirely capable of controlling his conduct, though he may well be trying to give the impression that he cannot. Psychopaths conning or trying to con psychiatrists or psychologists is a common phenomenon, as discussed earlier. Laymen outraged by a "not guilty by reason of insanity" verdict may be thinking of that kind of case.

Herostratic Acts

There are cases, probably rare, of individuals who kill or try to kill a major public figure, expecting fully to be caught, and expecting to become a famous figure in the history books by this act. (On the latter aspect, it works.) Here the offender clearly knows the wrongfulness of the act, and is clearly able to decide to carry it out (therefore able, conversely, to control his actions, and *not* commit the act). This kind of case would certainly *not* qualify for the insanity defense, though probably such a person is psychologically very disturbed. Ironically, *not* sentencing such a person to prison or execution would be profoundly disappointing and upsetting to the accused, and we could debate the justice of depriving him of that gratification. If a person is committing a spectacular crime from such motives, and as a mode of committing suicide, should the law deprive him of the suicidal result? Quite a number of the sixteen assassins studied by Clarke (see next section), seem to have such a Herostratic motive: Oswald, Byck, Fromme and Moore (all Clarke's Type II's); and Bremer and Guiteau [killer of President Garfield]. In the Guiteau case this is clearly part of a psychosis; in the Type II cases and one of the Type III [Bremer] part of serious psychological disturbance not of psychotic dimension.

Assassins: Mad and Sane

Clarke's Study

In Chapter 2 we mentioned the political scientist James W. Clarke's 1982 study of *American Assassins: The Darker Side of Politics,* which studied closely sixteen individuals who killed (or tried to kill) American presidents or other prominent political figures. Clarke's central purpose is to challenge the conception of presidential assassins as necessarily crazed killers, a "pathological theory of assassination" that he says has prevailed through the past century and a half, in American journalism, political studies, and psychiatry.

He found the sixteen individuals (including two women) could be classified into four psychological types, only one of which is clearly psychotic on psychiatric grounds. That type includes only three of the sixteen individuals. Two other types were psychologically disturbed, but definitely *not* psychotic. A fourth type, which comprises five individuals, could certainly be classified as sane and rational, and carrying out their assassination (or attempts) for a purely *political* purpose. There are two other assassins whom Clarke lists as unclassifiable—Carl Weiss, who, allegedly, killed Huey Long, and James Earl Ray, the killer of Martin Luther King Jr.

Since Clarke is not a psychiatrist, nor does he profess any psychoanalytic or other clinical credentials, it is worthwhile to examine the rationale he uses for his types and the inclusion of particular individuals in them. His typing amounts to a kind of rough-and-ready self-education in clinical evaluation, done by the author, and in effect a devising of his own version of the "insanity test."

In the 140 years from 1835 to 1975, sixteen individuals assassinated or tried to assassinate American presidents or other prominent political figures. (The presidents were Jackson, Lincoln, Garfield, McKinley, both Roosevelts, Truman, Kennedy, Nixon and Ford. The other leaders were Huey Long, Robert Kennedy, Martin Luther King Jr. and George Wallace. Clarke's research was completed before John Hinckley's attack on President Reagan.) Clarke carefully studied all the biographical information available on each of the assassins. He concludes that they do *not* support the "pathological theory of assassination" (the view that all assassins are madmen) that he says has prevailed in American journalism, political studies, and psychiatry. Some are, many are not.

He found that he could classify all but two of the assassins into four distinct types. Only one of these, Type IV, fits the picture of the psychotic killer, and only three assassins fit into this category: Richard Lawrence, who attacked Andrew Jackson; Charles Guiteau, who killed James Garfield; and John Schrank, who tried to kill Theodore Roosevelt. Clarke set up his own criteria for such psychosis: severe emotional distortion, severe cognitive distortion, presence of hallucinations and/or delusions, extremely distorted reality contact, social relations very isolated, and a primary motive that was irrational. From the data available on each of these, probably any clinician would agree that each of these men was clearly psychotic. Clarke accepts the notion that bad heredity is also a feature of psychosis, and finds indications of direct ancestors and collateral relatives who were known to be "insane" in each of these cases.

Richard Lawrence was convinced he was King Richard III of England and that he had large financial claims against the U.S. federal government. Jackson's opposition to the establishment of a national bank blocked his claims, so he had to kill Jackson. He was, Clarke opines, certainly what today would be called a paranoid schizophrenic.

Charles Guiteau, who killed President Garfield, also had obvious delusions of grandeur, very poor reality contact, and irrational motives. He also was convinced he was an instrument of God and had no clear conception of the social reality around him.

At the opposite end of the spectrum, category I, Clarke discerns those clearly not psychotic, but acting out of essentially political motives. Five killers fit in here: Booth (Lincoln), Czolgosz (McKinley), Collazo and Torresola (Truman) and Sirhan Sirhan (Robert Kennedy). These were obviously rational individuals in contact with reality, acting rationally in terms of their political premises, and without psychotic features. They had no delusions or hallucinations, no pronounced cognitive distortions, only mild emotional distortion, varied but not pathological social relationships. The political motives for the assassination [attempt] ranged from sectionalism (Booth), to class conflict (Czolgosz), to various kinds of nationalism. Sirhan acted from Arab nationalism and anti-Israeli hatred. Collazo and Torresola, shooting at President Truman, were acting for Puerto Rican independence. "Moreover the strong ethnic, class or sectional grievances involved were shared by millions of others." (Clarke, 262–3) The joker is that the "millions of others" did not try to kill the political target. What distinguishes those who did from those who did not is still mysterious. Clarke also qualifies about political motivation. For both Sirhan and Booth, this is accompanied by intense *personal* hatred of the targeted person.

Clarke's characterization of type IV as clearly psychotic is persuasive; as is his view of type I as definitely not psychotic, but a political killer.

The problems come with the other two categories, II and III. For both of these he sees the individual killers as disturbed but not psychotic, and as having motives that are either "personal/compensatory" (II) or "personal/provocation" (III). In reference to these two types, Clarke's admitted lack of expertise on psychiatric or psychoanalytic matters, shows up.

In Type II, Clarke classifies four killers: Lee Harvey Oswald [John Kennedy], Samuel Byck [aborted plan to suicide-bomb Nixon's White House], Lynette Fromme and Sara Jane Moore, (each separately tried to kill President Gerald Ford, 1975). None of these was psychotic, Clarke asserts. Though each had moderate emotional distortion and disturbed social relations, they are all lacking psychotic elements like cognitive distortion, hallucinations, delusions or poor reality contact. In each case, the subject approximates Lasswell's "political personality," i.e. someone who displaces essentially personal motives onto public/political objects. These are individuals "ruled by anxiety and emotion," with strong hostile feelings toward various social or political objects which may *sound* paranoid but in fact have some objective basis.

Type IIs are not devoid of ordinary feelings of love, empathy, remorse and guilt, but are rather overwhelmed by such feelings. "Beset with seemingly unmanageable problems in their personal lives, these subjects project and displace their personal frustrations onto paradoxically *less* threatening *public* targets." Oswald and Byck each did this. Each of the two women represents another version of anxiety-based motivation, neither of them psychotic, nor clearly political. Clarke's case is most problematic for regarding Oswald as belonging in this type and as an essentially political actor, and not as psychotic. Much of Clarke's discussion of the other political types could be applied to Oswald too. He clearly wanted to prove himself in the eyes of the Cuban leaders and President Kennedy was an obvious target for that purpose, and decidedly an "enemy" in light of Oswald's Marxist perspective, as much as McKinley was for Czolgosz. On the other side, the complexities of Oswald's disturbed personality, while evidently not qualifying him as "psychotic" in Clarke's view, would certainly have led psychoanalytically-minded clinicians into diagnostic battles about him, which would have happened if Oswald had survived and been brought to trial. Arguments similar to those in Hinckley's case later, in 1981, would have raged.

In the case of Lynette Fromme, it is evident that extreme emotional disturbance led her through her Charles Manson cult affiliation (she regarded Manson, literally, as the Savior) and on to her political terrorism in the attack on President Ford. Again, though not psychotic by Clarke's rather arbitrary standards, she is an extremely disturbed personality.

Type III is also problematic; here Clarke includes the pathetic Giuseppe Zangara who tried to kill Franklin D. Roosevelt in early 1933 and erroneously killed Chicago Mayor Anton Cermak instead. (Zangara was executed in the electric chair, refusing to claim insanity.) Clarke also includes Arthur Bremer, who shot George Wallace, permanently incapacitating him.

Clarke believes Zangara was not psychotic, because he did not show clear-cut cognitive distortion, had neither hallucinations nor delusions, and was ordinarily in touch with social reality. However, he seemed to me as a psychoanalyst, from the presented material, to be extremely disturbed and probably even psychotic. Clarke appears to have a simplified and overly cognitive conception of psychosis, which does not leave room for the kind of constricted empty life Zangara had.

Briefly, the boy Giuseppe had at the age of six been forcibly taken out of school by his father and put to work carrying bricks and tiles. He developed a stomach disorder, evidently never adequately treated, which lasted and plagued him the rest of his life. He hated his father for doing this to him, and also hated all government and authority, which he associated with the root of his stomach disorder. "The real cause of exploitation in the world and the incessant burning in his stomach were, he now believed, caused by political leaders" (p. 169). Zangara was then a young volunteer in the Italian army. He decided to kill King Victor Emmanuel III (of Italy) but never got the opportunity. Later, an immigrant to America, he found work as a bricklayer, and lived a spartan, frugal, and totally isolated life. He did some traveling, but evidently never socialized with anyone on these trips. He worked only as much as absolutely necessary, otherwise lived off savings. His money running out, in early 1933, and hearing Hoover being blamed for the depression, and with still no relief for his burning stomach, he decided he would get even with that no good capitalist Hoover. He bought a pistol, planned to travel from Miami to Washington to kill Hoover. Accidentally he learned that Franklin D. Roosevelt had been elected to the presidency, and would be visiting Miami the next day. He readily switched his target, positioned himself to get a shot at the president-elect in an open touring car, aimed to fire, but missed. He hit Chicago mayor Cermak instead, along with several bystanders. He was convicted for assault on the latter, then when Cermak died, tried for murder. He entered a remorseless guilty plea—saying he was only sorry he had not hit Roosevelt.

Clarke thinks that Zangara was not psychotic because he had no hallucinations or delusions, and seemed to have adequate grasp of social reality, but it is evident that the whole pattern of his life, from early childhood on, was far from normal, and far also from usual forms of neurosis. His constricted, isolated life seemed at best a buffer against a serious psychotic breakdown, so did his bizarre social-political beliefs (not developed enough to constitute anything like an ideology). He believed capitalists and/or government were responsible for exploitation and his bad stomach, which casts doubt on the proposition that he was in contact with social reality. Would he have qualified under some version of the insanity defense? Was his act a product of mental disease? I think yes. Did he understand the wrongfulness of his act? Probably yes in one sense. Was he able to control his conduct to make it conform to the rules of right and wrong? Again I think highly problematic. *My* impression is that this man was most severely disturbed, not too differently from many ambulatory schizophrenics we can encounter on our streets today.

Clarke's psychology does not begin to do justice to this personality.

Similarly for the other subject Clarke classifies as Type III, Arthur Bremer, who in May 1972 tried to kill George Wallace, then campaigning for the Democratic party nomination for the presidency. Clarke classifies Bremer as disturbed but not psychotic, but also not a political killer. He acknowledges "severe emotional distortion" but that term (reflecting Clarke's limited psychological acumen) barely begins to characterize this man. He is presented as "without emotions," whereas the evidence indicates the intense emotion of rage. To say that he was "emotionally dead" is also a distortion. Expectably, the clinicians called to evaluate his sanity, split; the defense psychiatrists/psychologists said he qualified as "insane" according to the law. The prosecution clinicians said he did not. Considering the legal principles, he could be seen as knowing exactly what he was doing when he stalked Nixon to kill him, then switched his target to Wallace and stalked him. Clarke concurs with the jury. Bremer was sane enough to know exactly what he was doing, plan carefully, understand the consequences of his action. He was rational within his premises. On the other hand, his decision that he had to do something "against society" that would attract maximum publicity, his hesitations about using Wallace as the target (not famous enough for international audiences), his feeling that this was the only action left to him, a combined homicide/suicide, all indicate extreme disturbance. Whether this is properly to be judged "psychotic" is left uncertain, and evidently, a strict cognitive application of the Kaufman principles would not justify a legal verdict of insanity.

Not surprisingly, the expert witnesses split evenly on whether the evidence produced, including Bremer's diary, indicates psychosis or not. Clarke comments, cynically, or at least skeptically, that the split was inevitable, the defense witnesses finding him psychotic, the prosecution not. Clarke does not raise the most pertinent question, that is, is the evidence such that the best qualified and most conscientious clinical experts might honestly disagree about the presence of psychosis. This case most obviously demonstrates the dilemmas of trying to apply even the best legal formula to the complexities of a real and difficult personality.

Critique of Clarke's Classifications

My overall judgment of this important book is that Clarke makes his case rather well for the extreme types, I (basically a *political* and non-psychotic motivation and personality) and type IV (clearly psychotic, and coverable under the legal formulation of insanity), but that he is much less persuasive in reference to all the six cases in types II and III, for which his simplified psychology is inadequate to the task. He is evidently out to "prove" his case that very few (three out of sixteen) of the assassins studied fit the picture of the psychotic killer.

We mentioned in the preceding section, on the insanity defense, the possibility that some of Clarke's "cases" might have merited a verdict of "guilty but mentally ill." The six for whom this might have been justifiable are Lee Harvey Oswald, (killer of John Kennedy); Lynette Fromme and Sara Jane Moore (both made assassination attempts on Gerald Ford); Giuseppe Zangara (killed Cermak when aiming at FDR); Arthur Bremer (attack on George Wallace) and Samuel Byck (Nixon). Though questionably psychotic, according to Clarke, all were, in my opinion, sufficiently disturbed to qualify as "mentally ill," and just as some members of the Hinckley jury said they would have rendered a verdict of "guilty but mentally ill," had it been an option, I find it probable that it may have been chosen (if available) by juries on these other six cases.

All of these type II and type III cases show once again how extremely difficult it is to arrive at a consensus on a clear formulation of what is going on in a disturbed but not obviously psychotic personality, in this case publicly important and problematical. These difficulties are not just a matter of the bias or personality of particular "experts," but in the nature of the case. This should be a very sobering realization.

Summary and Conclusion

We have looked at three public issues involving mental illness: de-institutionalization, the insanity defense, and assassins, mad and sane.

Part of the background basis of the de-institutionalization process, are notions about the mentally ill, especially the most severely ill, the psychotic, that portray them as innocent victims of a sort of conspiracy by the authorities of society and question the reality of mental illness. They were allied with fiscal conservatives who intended by the abolition of the mental hospitals to save the states huge sums of money, and civil-libertarian organizations imagining they were thus defending victims' rights. The alternative programs for care of the mentally ill that were supposed to be established to replace the old hospitals, did not materialize beyond a paltry token, and the formerly hospitalized were left much worse off than before, in seedy single room occupancy hotels, with unwilling relatives, in nursing homes, and in many cases, homeless on the streets of the cities.

This situation demonstrates the unintended consequences of purposive social action, in this case the benignly and "progressively" intended freeing of the hospital-incarcerated patient-victims, resulting in the greater degradation and dehumanization of homelessness. It is also an instance of deceptive mythology of the self-styled enlightened, overcoming the sense of competent professionals.

Another instance of a public issue regarding mental illness, is the persistently unresolved problem of the "insanity defense" of persons who have committed serious, even capital, crimes. The question in Anglo-American law is whether a person can be held accountable to the law for illegal acts, if he is not "of sound mind" and in full possession of his faculties. In other words, can one claim an "insanity defense," under what conditions? We have traced briefly the developments in British-American law from the nineteenth century M'Naghten Rule, to twentieth century American innovations in the form of the Durham Rule and later the Law Institute's Kaufman rule, and the continuing dilemmas of each of these. The most widely used formulation in the United States today is the Kaufman rule, which specifies that an accused is considered "not responsible for criminal conduct if at the time of commission of such conduct, as a result of mental disease or defect, he lacks substantial capacity either to appreciate the wrongfulness of his conduct or to conform his conduct to the requirements of the law." Implementing this formulation requires a trial with expert witnesses testifying on the psychological state of the defendant, frequently resulting in spectacular confrontations of opposing expert teams, one showing the defendant "insane", the other showing him sane.

In the process public confidence in the expertise of mental health professionals is eroded, and typical antipsychiatry feelings already prevalent in the lay population come to the fore. All the difficulties of clinical professionals in evaluating the health or sickness of the individual, and if sick, how much and in what way, come out in the open. The alternative of relying on lay opinion is much worse. That psychiatrists (or any other mental health professionals) cannot predict if and when a previously violent offender will commit another violent act, is disturbing to the public and to officers of the law. However, it is a fact of professional life for which there is no satisfactory answer. It leaves the legal system with the alternatives of keeping any *potential* repeat violent offenders locked up forever, or taking the chance of allowing release after expiration of a mandated prison term, or upon pronouncement of the mental hospital that the accused is no longer ill and dangerous (a hopeful guess). Our values and our legal system favor the latter, risky as it is.

In spite of the formidable ambiguities and unreliabilities involved, it *is* still possible to assert that one can arrive at some degree of consensus about the most severe mental illness, i.e. clear-cut psychosis. Professionals can also probably agree that lesser degrees and kinds of mental impairment, neurosis, character disorder and especially psychopathic personality, do not belong in this arena, because they are usually accompanied by an understanding of the moral nature of one's acts and strength of will to conform one's conduct to the law. A possible alternative verdict of "guilty but mentally ill" is being tried in a number of jurisdictions, and shows promise of solving some of the dilemmas of trials like Hinckley's, that is, satisfying the public demand for "justice" while at the same time, taking into appropriate consideration the psychological state of the offender.

Cases like Hinckley, and at least six of the sixteen cases Clarke analyzes in his study of American assassins, show the enormous complexity of many cases reaching the law where an insanity plea is possible, and the inherent difficulties even the most skilled and conscientious clinical specialists will have in assessing the ambiguities of a sick personality. Such difficulties will not simply disappear with growing psychological sophistication or with tinkering reformulations of the law. The psychology can give only an approximate picture, and the law only a general formulation.

These discussions fill out the picture not only of mental illness, the subject of these two chapters, but also of crime and delinquency (Chapter 2), both of them perennial problems of society and of the individual personality.

REFERENCES

Appelbaum, Paul S. 1987. "Crazy in the Streets." *Commentary.* 83:5:34–39

Caplan, Lincoln. 1984. *The Insanity Defense and the Trial of John W. Hinckley Jr.* Boston: David Goldine

Clarke, James W. 1982. *American Assassins: The Darker Side of Politics.* Princeton, NJ: Princeton University Press

Devereux, George. 1980. *Basic Problems of Ethnopsychiatry.* Chicago: University of Chicago Press

Gralnick, Alexander. 1985. "The Case against De-Institutionalization." *The American Journal of Social Psychiatry* V:7–11

Kaufman, Irving R. 1982. "The Insanity Plea on Trial." *The New York Times Sunday Magazine.* 8/8/82: 21ff.

Main, Thomas J. 1988. "What we know about the Homeless." *Commentary.* 85:5:26–31

Morrissey, Joseph. 1982. "De-institutionalizing the Mentally Ill: Process, Outcomes and New Directions." in W. R. Gove, ed. *Deviance and Mental Illness.* New York: Sage.

CHAPTER 7
BOHEMIANISM

Varieties of Bohemianism

In 1961 David Matza published a seminal essay, "Subterranean Traditions of Youth." In it he argued that at least since the early days of the Industrial Revolution, there have been a number of more or less organized protests against or departures from the social structure and culture of industrial capitalism. These departures take three main forms: delinquency and crime, bohemianism, and radicalism. Crime and delinquency are departures consisting of violations of the *laws* of the modern society, in pursuit of personal gain and profit. In Merton's terms (1936) these are "innovationist," accepting the goals the culture prescribes, but deviating on the means (see Chapter 2). Another major form of departure is radicalism (what Merton calls "rebellion"). This involves selectively accepting some of the goals and some of the means, but departing importantly on other goals and means. "Rebels" idealistically seek to fulfill certain of the "ideal patterns" of the culture, like "social justice," and try to overturn and radically transform the social structure to bring this about. The third major kind of "subterranean tradition" is bohemianism, a disaffected dropping out of the conventional system.

Matza's central point is that each of these kinds of protests or departures itself constitutes in some sense a "tradition" of its own. It carries on from one generation to another (in the case of the latter two, with some temporal breaks). And it embodies a set of norms of its own, involving the goals to be pursued in life, and the appropriate means for seeking them. These are not simply random protests of some individuals, but they follow a distinct cultural pattern with certain social structural accompaniments.

These patterns have a particular appeal to the youth of the population, as possible modes of rebelliousness against a conforming and conventional society and culture felt to be oppressive or impossible to adhere to.

The bohemian tradition has certain elements, distinguishing it from delinquency on one side and radicalism on the other. Unlike participants in delinquency and crime, bohemians do not *set out* to break the laws of the society in order to gain advantage or material goods not otherwise available to them. (However bohemians may *incidentally* violate some laws, not usually in the way criminals and delinquents do.) Unlike radicals, they are not actively trying to overthrow the existing social order in its political or economic aspects, to substitute a more just or more perfect society. Generally bohemians are unlikely to espouse or articulate any particular social or political theory or dogma, or to have a plan for any concerted social action. In fact activity, of almost any kind, is not sought. Rather than *doing,* the bohemians' life is concentrated on *being,* an approach activists are likely to regard as passive.

Bohemians are neither trying to acquire more (material things, wealth) from existing society, nor to transform it, but essentially, wish to *drop out* and seek to be left alone to pursue their own pleasures in their own way. The bohemian style of life is marked by romanticism, spontaneity, populism, dedicated voluntary poverty, and primitivism. It also includes a kind of medievalism, as against the bureaucratic "regimentation" of modern society. It seeks expressive authenticity, some kind of primitive communitarianism, or monasticism. Bohemians have a fascination with the outré and the forbidden. They pursue unconventional experience. A romantic interest in primitive societies and cultures is also an important component.

Some version of this orientation to the world has appeared and disappeared and reappeared a number of times in modern Western culture since its first [modern] incarnation in Paris in the 1830s (Graña 1964, Parry 1933). In the 1830s there came together in Paris, some young people of bourgeois family background, artistic interests and pretensions, and relatively high level of formal education but poor prospects of any satisfying employment. The likelihood of a minor government post in a bleak provincial town was unappetizing in the extreme. They invented a style of life emphasizing voluntary poverty, living in garrets and other such quarters alongside the genuinely (*in*voluntarily) poverty-stricken of the urban slums. They sought expressive freedom and freedom from bourgeois sexual constraints and the pursuit of ART. They got to be called "Bohemians," meaning Gypsies, who were thought to come from Bohemia, later part of Czechoslovakia. The name stuck and was immortalized in romantic literature and opera. From Paris the pattern spread to other European metropolises and later to America. The name "Bohemian" persisted through the 1920s; but was not used by the participants themselves in the later version that reappeared in the late 1950s and the 1960s. Then they became "the beats" (or "beatniks") and "the hippies." "Hippies" was originally a disdainful diminutive for "hip" but soon acquired a nonpejorative connotation. There is no consensus among scholars to explain the rise and fall of this phenomenon.

When it was at its peak in the 1960s in America as "the hippies," some observers, including some sociologists, thought it was to be a kind of permanent feature of our cultural landscape. The sociologist Fred Davis, in 1967, titled a paper "Why All of us May be Hippies some Day"—only to see this "counterculture" all but disappear in the 1970s. It has not of course *totally* disappeared, even now going into the 1990s. Many elements of it survive in what is left of rural or urban communes, in the variegated "alternative press," and the variety of cult- or sect-like movements drawing variously on Eastern traditions of one sort or another, that still dot the urban and rural landscapes. It is also possible that the whole phenomenon may see a new recrudescence, under new names and different physical and ideological garb, in the 1990s and into the early twenty-first century. (Thus one additional rationale for treating this apparently passé phenomenon here.)

Contemporaneous accounts of the hippies, or of the counterculture, if they attempt any explanation at all, variously refer to the problems facing the youth in modern society, or in America specifically. They refer to the strains of a competitive society, the Vietnam War, the "meaninglessness of life" in modern industrialized society. They allude to the emptiness of affluence, the alleged breakdown of the modern family, the decline and increasing meaninglessness of formal religion ("God is dead"), and any one or combination of the sundry ills of modern society. Any of these "explanations," since it is used to explain everything (from drugs, to crime, to suicide, to sexual experimentation, and all the rest) explains nothing, and there is no clear answer. For example, frequently allusion is made to the "ambiguity of adolescence" in modern society, which makes adaptation especially difficult, and therefore it is likely that adolescents will turn to strange and "way-out" modes like the counterculture. This is plausible, but the "ambiguous status of adolescence" is hardly a new phenomenon starting in the 1960s, nor disappearing in the period after that. It has been present through the whole modern period from at least the time of the Industrial Revolution.

Similarly, all the "explanations" for the rather rapid *dis*appearance of these phenomena in the 1970s, are similarly *ad-hoc* and equally plausible or implausible depending on the mind-set and assumptions of the reader or observer.

Bennett Berger pointed out (1967) that many of the elements of the "hippie" (read, more broadly, bohemian) mode have an ancient history in the Western tradition. Examples are the ideal of childhood innocence as having a moral superiority to sophisticated adult "wisdom," and the value of unconstrained self-expression.

There are other antecedents. Other periods of unrest and social and cultural chaos, showed some similar patterns of reaction. There was the decline of Rome after the third century A.D., with the rise of multiple heretical movements. There was the whole period described as the "later Middle Ages." In *The Pursuit of the Millenium* (1961) Norman Cohn describes millenarian sects that espoused complete sexual liberty and ceremonies that seem remarkably like the Western hippies of the 1960s.

Similarly in evident reaction against the rise of the Industrial Revolution and of the French Revolution and the Napoleonic effort to rationalize the culture of Europe, there arose the whole Romantic movement in Germany, England, France and Middle Europe, one specific manifestation of which was the bohemianism of the Parisian drop-outs.

These are precursors of modern bohemianism, or at least elements of it, sporadically in the history of the West all the way back at least to the Roman Empire decline. The specifically modern version can be dated from the Parisian garrets of the 1830s, and related to the emerging culture of the Industrial Revolution.

The participants in bohemianism came from definitely bourgeois or middle class backgrounds, not working or lower class. The same has been true of the later versions, which have definitely not had enthusiasts from working and lower classes. That bourgeois culture had these features: imposition of puritanical restraints; strong emphasis on discipline and *self*-restraint; emphasis on regimentation of time and place; asceticism; an instrumental approach to the world; and emphasis on work, particularly systematic work geared to long-range goals. The invention of the bohemian style of life served as an antithesis to all of these. It was to overthrow puritanical restraints, particularly in sexuality and other modes of personal expression. It was to replace an instrumental mode (doing things for a particular, especially material or pecuniary purpose) by an expressive mode—doing things for their expressive gratification. Adherence to the conventions of social and personal life is replaced by acceptance and pursuit of unconventional ways, as in personal styles of adornment, and unconventional ways of handling time and money. Obsessive concern with money and material possessions was to be replaced by a casual attitude toward these, and willingness to put up with poverty conditions for the sake of personal freedom and expressive authenticity. Rationality (on the rise as a cultural value in the development of modern science and associated technology) is to be denied. It is to be replaced by various versions of culturally-patterned irrationality—interest in the Kabbalah, in Tarot cards, in astrology, in witchcraft, in the occult, in various magical beliefs from many different cultural traditions. Spontaneity replaces regimentation; romanticism is to replace practical-mindedness.

We are to tolerate, indeed encourage eccentricity in personal behavior. Where conventional society emphasizes organized relationships based on role structures in business and the professions, bohemianism emphasizes a kind of direct community based on feeling of oneness and ideally, solidarity and love. In opposition to the hierarchies of the conventional world, the bohemian world emphasizes equality and recognition of common humanity. It also embodies some version of primitivism, fascination with exotic non-Western cultures and their modes.

Related to this is take-over of some patterns that had earlier appeared in or were limited to lower class subcultures, particularly in America, lower class blacks. For example, we find the spread of the use of drugs, starting with marijuana and heroin; and emulation of what middle class whites believed to be the freer sexuality of blacks, or specifically of black jazz musicians. This last was prominent in the white beatniks of the 1950s, who saw black jazz musicians as the ideal of the free, "stretched-out," unrepressed, expressive and sexually-uninhibited. In many respects middle class bohemian culture, and youth culture generally, embraced a diffusion of life patterns from lower to middle class.

Recent (1960s) American bohemianism included a fascination with "primitive" American Indian cultures, idealized as superior to the artificiality and rigidity of the culture of the modern society. This attraction was usually not accompanied by any real understanding or appreciation of the actual qualities of these cultures, or empathy for the feelings of real native Americans. For example, in some cases hippies in New Mexico carelessly fouled the upstream waters of streams essential for the life of particular downstream Amerindian tribes.

Role of Art

A major concern of earlier bohemias (but not of the 1960s hippies) was Art—its creation, particularly in unconventional forms, and its pursuit as a primary value in life, in opposition to the philistinism of the standard bourgeois society. Though there is little record of great new art actually being created in the bohemian garrets and studios, the intention (and often, pretension) was there. In a later incarnation, the beats of the 1950's, the denizens certainly liked to give the impression that each of these disheveled and oddly garbed rebels was in process of creating the new masterpiece of painting or writing, as earlier in the 1920s American expatriates in Paris included many writing the great novel of the twentieth century in the sidewalk cafes of the Left Bank or Montmartre. Significantly, even the pretension to such creativity, disappeared in the 1960s hippies. (One factor by then was the greatly lowered age of the participants, now dipping to as low as 12 years.)

Unconventional Life Styles

Another feature was the pursuit of unconventional, even outrageous experiences—particularly drugs. In the nineteenth century this could include opium. In the 1950s beats, alcohol was the main drug, followed by marijuana, while minorities used barbiturates, amphetamines, peyote and heroin, in that order. (Rigney and Smith 1961). By the 1960s, the hippies were deep into the harder psychedelics, LSD and the range of other psychedelics, natural and synthetic, as well as amphetamines, barbiturates, and by then as a prosaic "of course," marijuana. (Von Hoffman 1968; Yablonsky 1968; many other sources).

Drug use was not as prominent a part of earlier bohemias as it became for the 1960s hippies. One could argue that the pressure for rebellion against middle-class conformity had by then become so intense, and the price for outrageousness so inflated by the already permissive atmosphere of conventional middle class culture. The 1960s "flower children" were already the children of affluence, of materially comfortable (if emotionally uncaring and/or disrupted) homes, for whom further material prosperity held no lure. Again the difference from working or lower class youngsters was striking. *They* had no use for voluntary poverty or quest for transcendance, they wanted a better chance in the race. For the bohemians the quest was not for money or material abundance, but rather for *meaning.* To them the expensive and materially well stocked house in the suburbs, with the three or more cars per family, swimming pools, with father endlessly struggling for still more promotions up the corporate ladder, all that was meaningless. Why bother? Also any demands on themselves, to toe the line, go to college, finish college, get "out there in the real world, and get a decent job" had become onerous and meaningless. What was the point of it all?

The issue of *work* is important. The expectation that all men will work is central for the whole development of modern industrialism. By now it has become prevalent that this expectation extends to women, too, though there are still hold-outs adhering to the older tradition that a woman's task is to catch a good husband and be supported by him, while she tends to his household and the rearing of the children. A major feature of modern feminism is that women should have not only the same opportunities but also the same obligations as men, to participate in the paid labor force. Bohemians reject this emphasis on work. In a sense they recall an older *aristocratic* tradition, in which the ideal is not to have to work at all, in the usual sense, but to have the freedom (and resources) to pursue the activities that give meaning to life, which can include complex entertaining, demanding leisure pursuits, special crafts, horsemanship, fencing, and, significantly, art. Particularly, any kind of regimented work, is to be avoided.

The values here are similar to those of the artist. It is not that he does not work. In fact he probably works a lot harder than any employee. But he does so with autonomy, he sets the terms of his goals and his means, the times of his activity, not by dictate from any outside power.

For many bohemians, without any special talents of artistic or other kinds, the negative attitude toward work is simply that: I want to work as little as possible, I just want to enjoy life, to live and to love. (The solid burgher replies, so do I, but I'm willing to *earn* that, by working first—then I can enjoy leisure, because then I deserve it. The bohemian categorically rejects that kind of moral calculus.)

In bohemianism, there is a similar departure from conventional attitudes toward *time.* A frequently heard comment about the 1960s hippies was this: "You can tell a hippie on sight. A hippie never wears a watch." Living by the clock has become standard in modern society. Bohemians reject that, as they do any other aspects of what they see as regimentation of people's lives.

Time is the ongoing flow of life, not a mechanistic set of seconds, minutes and hours. Drug experience is also likely to take the individual out of the ordinary perception of time, making it feel as if it is passing much slower or much faster than ordinary time, and to be connected only to inner experiences rather than any external markers. Time is, or should be felt as, organic rather than mechanical. Time should not be a constraint on an individual. Hippies neither wear watches, nor make or keep appointments. This is a further feature about the bohemians that disturbs or outrages solid conventional people—the bohemians seem to epitomize a spirit of irresponsibility.

Another feature about time is the distinction between future-orientation and present-orientation. The pressures of modern industrial society are all toward valuing future orientation. The bohemians reject that idea, and emphasize the present. They are also not interested in the past, and typically have little or no historical sense. In the conventional culture, people are pushed constantly to think of present actions in terms of their probable results in future situations. This relates to the distinction between instrumental and expressive. In the conventional culture the emphasis is on doing things for a purpose (instrumental); here the emphasis is on doing things for their own sake (expressive).

One sociologist, Jesse R. Pitts, (1969) sees the counter-culture of the 1960s as in part a reaction against the pressures of the *meritocracy.* Meritocracy means a stratified occupational and social order based upon individual personal talents, merits and achievements, resulting necessarily in inequalities on those bases, rather than race or family background or any other ascribed features. The meritocracy of modern society, seen positively, involves "equality of opportunity", not equality of results. It also poses a threat to all those who, though starting out with family advantages, e.g. solid middle class status of achieving parents, have neither the talents nor the personal characteristics to "make it" at the level expected of them. An existing bohemian subculture provides them with a world into which to "drop out."

Drugs

The role of drugs is also important. Although present in earlier bohemias, by the time of the hippies, they had become paramount. The line between conventional culture and deviant subculture had by then become extremely thin and difficult to draw. Use of some kind of chemical substances to alter moods and provide variant psychological experiences, had of course existed for centuries (see Chapter 4). By the 1960s such use had become widespread. Alcohol had long since become culturally domesticated, and fitted into a variety of conventional patterns, but other substances, marijuana and the psychedelics, were spreading rapidly. These had a different set of "mind-altering effects" (see Chapter 4) and a different set of attached meanings in the views of conventional people. These were appealing especially to any kind of rebellious youth, and were experienced as dangerously threatening by conventionals. Even more so LSD and other hard psychedelics. "They're fucking with the *mind!*" a liquor-imbibing police officer exclaimed.

Outrageousness intensifies the appeal. Add the thrills involved in the illegality and the dangers in procuring the drugs. Add too the uncertainty about what you are buying and ingesting, and there is a powerful appeal.

Here the subculture of bohemianism connects with and overlaps with that of crime and delinquency. Hippies scrabbling to provide a basic living for themselves also find a ready recourse in the drug trade, as using easily shades over into dealing.

Drug use was certainly not exclusive to the bohemians, but there it was more common and more definitive of their outcast identity.

Fluidity of the Bohemian Population

The population involved in the bohemian subculture is inherently fluid and unstable. People drift in and out of it. People intensely opposed to any kind of organized society can easily find ways not to be traceable in the labyrinthine networks of such outcasts and self-exiled. Apparent innocents learn the skills of conning and living by their wits, joining forces in various ways with the demi-mondes of petty and not-so-petty crime, bound in a solidarity whose main ingredient is a fierce hatred of the common enemy, the cops. Here also we find alliances and solidarity with another subterranean group, the political radicals, which have an ebb and flow of their own. In the 1960s the young radicals had many affinities and contacts with hippies, though the more deadly serious radicals, the revolutionaries, regarded the hippies with disdain if not hostility, much as Lenin derided "bourgeois-romantic adventurers and sentimentalists" who wanted to join his revolutionary movement (see next chapter). Hippie males wore long hair and unkempt beards, were disheveled and slovenly, antagonistic to the whole bourgeois cult of neatness and cleanliness. Hippie women were also likely to be disheveled, and dressed in any manner except what was conventionally fashionable. Where fashion decreed miniskirts, they wore dresses down to their ankles. Seriously radical males wore their hair short-clipped, and dressed in clean neat workingmen's clothes. They were also much more restrained about drug use.

Boundaries

The problem of boundaries pervades any discussion of the bohemians, who was in, who was not, never clearly settled. Also unclear were what life-style activities were definitive as distinguished from those overlapping with other groups, even conventionals. "At what age do you stop being a hippie and start being just a bum?" asked an aging (getting toward 30) denizen. And always there was the problem of the invasion of bohemian haunts and ways by outsiders who were would-be insiders ("phonies") and by outright tourists from the conventionals. You could become a hippie for a weekend, then return to your sober conventional life. There was borrowing or theft of bohemian styles and artifacts as a piece of fad or fashion among the respectables. For examples, in the 1950s, a "beatnik look" in clothing for women. Longer hair for men became generally acceptable in the whole young and youthful population, leading to hair-styling salons for men becoming a lucrative business. We saw a wholesale loosening up of gender distinctions in personal decoration and grooming, wearing of jewelry and multiply-colored and exotically patterned clothing by men. The problem for the bohemians became how to keep themselves distinctive from the general population.

Because of fluidity of boundaries and lack of organizational structure of bohemian groups as communities, it is difficult to sustain bohemian patterns with the same people over any length of time. This is especially so considering bohemians' aversion to anything like conventional roles and rules. Conventionals took over many bohemian patterns as styles and fashions. Bohemians overlap with petty criminals on many fronts; and with political radicals on many others. Groups appeared that combined elements of all three, e.g., Jonestown, and the Manson cult. Many people could graduate from the bohemian pattern and become solid respectable people pursuing conventional careers, with much greater ease than moving from criminal or even radical careers and identities.

Sexual Mores

Sexual mores were a central issue. These were of course changing in the general population in the 1960s. The hippies could be said to be at the forefront of these changes. By the late 1970s, only a minority of the population at large still regarded it as wrong to have premarital sexual intercourse. (A poll by *The New York Times*/CBS News in 1979, found that 55% of those polled "think premarital sex is not wrong", as compared with only 21% giving that response in a Gallup poll in 1969, at the time of the "Woodstock Nation" gathering of half a million youngsters at Bethel, N.Y.—see Reinhold 1979). And the bohemians went further than the population at large, allowing, in fact encouraging, not only nonmarital "straight sex", i.e. heterosexual genital contact, but every imaginable variation involving sex of partner, number of simultaneous partners, and body parts involved. "If it feels good, do it," became a basic maxim. The body is a temple of pleasure. Nothing is to be denied. Infantile polymorphous perversity prevails. (Regression was the common psychological mode.) If premarital heterosexual intercourse in the usual way was becoming acceptable for the conventional population at large, the hip have to go much further. Sexual self-restraint and puritanism became the refuge of religious fundamentalists and reactionaries.

The hippies were in effect at the extreme edge or the forefront of the so-called "sexual revolution" of the 1960s and 1970s. As the psychoanalyst Otto Kernberg comments regarding that phenomenon:

> From a historical perspective, repeated cultural oscillations can be observed between "puritanical" periods in which love relations become deeroticized and eroticism goes underground, and "libertine" periods in which free sensual sexuality deteriorates into emotionally degraded group sex. In my view, such oscillations reflect the long-term equilibrium between the dynamics of the social need for destroying, protecting, and controlling the couple, and the couple's aspirations to break out of conventional restrictions of sexual morality, a freedom that, *in extremes,* becomes self-destructive.
>
> From this viewpoint, the so-called sexual revolution of the 1960s and 1970s, would reflect one more swing of the pendulum within conventional morality, and indicate no real change in the deeper dynamics of the relationship of the couple and the social group.... (Kernberg, 1988, pp. 80–81, in a volume of papers on *Passionate Attachments* Gaylin and Person, eds. 1988.)

A corollary of Kernberg's point about prevailing conventions generally, that applies to the "hippie" type bohemians of the 1960s, is that *their* "sexual freedom," involving descent into infantile polymorphous perverse sexuality, commonly as a *group* phenomenon, frequently became for the hippies a new enslavement now into an alternate conventionality, the conventionality of the self-proclaimed liberated, rather than the genuine autonomy of a mature sexual couple maintaining its privacy, autonomy, and secret passionate involvement against any environment.

Also, hippies upset *gender* roles and conduct, insisting in effect upon erasing the distinctions between "masculine" and "feminine" conduct and standards. This de-differentiation has however been somewhat asymmetrical: it seems to be more a matter of de-masculinizing the males. Males are permitted to wear long hair and clothing of fabrics, colors and designs heretofore considered "feminine" and other elements of "feminine" adornment. These were not only permitted, but often required. More than that, the male is now allowed, even expected, to conduct himself in a manner considered "soft," "passive" and "unassertive," in effect to become, in self-presentation, the opposite of the violent "macho" male. True, the same hippie ethic allows women to be assertive and aggressive (thus, by more conventional standards, more "masculine") but this is less emphasized, and in communes the women are likely to take on traditional feminine roles—sewing, cooking, cleaning.

Associated "Institutions"

In July 1967, the poet Allen Ginsberg, a leading "beat" poet of the 1950s, claimed that "the new generation, variously called hippies, flower children, love generation, now generation . . . have a whole set of subcultural institutions of their own. For social workers, there are the diggers; for politicians, the provos; for police Hell's Angels and other bikers; religion consisted of an amalgam of Tibetan, Egyptian, Hindu, Zen and astrological speculation, all facing in a deliberately mystical direction, drugs and sexual rituals serving as sacraments. For charismatic leaders, there were Leary, Kesey and others. Language was reinvented, as was music." (quoted with obvious approval by Gioscia 1969, reprinted 1973.) This was a typical bit of romanticizing of the hippie phenomenon, common to many sociocultural observers of the period, with the usual pretentiousness, lack of clarity about boundaries, and gaping admiration of mindlessness (Leary, Kesey) and potentiality for totalitarian direction (Hell's Angels and bikers as police).

The groping toward some kind of communality, as in the efforts at communes, is worth some specific consideration.

Communes

One can immediately demur here and insist that discussion of "communes" belongs in the chapter on radicalism rather than in this one on bohemianism, since communes seem to be proposing and trying to live out, actively, an alternative to the prevailing socio-economic-political order of society. No doubt in the period of the 1960s-1970s, the hippies and the radicals had much in common, particularly in their negativism toward the prevailing political order. Still in terms of ideal-types, where the radicals wanted to overturn the existing politico-economic establishments, the hippies or counterculturalists wanted merely to *drop out* of conventional society. In organizing communes, they simply wanted to do something different on their own, preferably away from the mainstreams of existing society. Whereas the radical outlook was "we'll fight you and overthrow your corrupt political order . . ." the hippie one was "leave us alone, we just want to do our own thing; if enough establishment people are inspired by our example, maybe the whole existing system will just collapse anyway." That last idea was central in the thesis of a writer presenting himself as a serious social scientist, namely Charles Reich, in *The Greening of America* (1970) whose work had quite a vogue among hippie-sympathizing social scientists at the time. Many others in turn proposed various combinations of these two viewpoints. Many radicals, as already noted, embraced something like hippie life-ways (despised by the hard-core Leninists of the movement) and many hippie-like individuals joined in large public demonstrations organized by radicals, like anti-war rallies. Many radicals smoked pot. It was almost emblematic of anti-establishment style. Some tried harder drugs, but not seriously or for long if they were still radicals. But disillusioned radicals, despairing of the possibility of the radical movement bringing about the desired "revolution," turned to a hippie-like quietism.

Still, many of the communes of the '60s and '70s came out of the hippie rather than the radical movement, and therefore need to be discussed here. Their usual fragility and failure were evidently derivative from the more unviable aspects of the hippie way.

A continuous and reasonably patterned community life would seem to be inherently contradictory to the basically anarchic, "do-my-own-thing" outlook of the hippie type bohemians of the 1960s and shortly after. Yet large numbers of the counterculturalists did try to develop "communes" in which similarly-minded rebels could live together, "close to nature," and in what they conceived as a kind of primitive freedom. They seemed unaware that there was any inherent conflict between communalism, which in its nature would seem to require *some* restraint upon individuals, and the anarchistic individualism of the hippie outlook. That outlook is hardly a "creed." Such a term would distort the nature of hippie beliefs, which resist any clear cognitive organization, and extol feeling over thinking, and "letting it all hang out." Hippies wanted to be "loose," not "uptight."

Still, numbers of the hippies did try to live in a communal manner, and in the late 1960s and early 1970s, many "communes" were started. Usually in a particular case the impetus came from some strong-minded central figure who had acquired some wilderness land, or simply took possession of it, and was *de facto* the leader of the group. However, formal acknowledgment of any leadership would be anathema to the free spirits who flocked to live together in such arrangements. Primitivism was evident, in the makeshift dwellings, lack of sanitary facilities, and casual and unorganized pursuit of food-quest, co-existing with parasitism on usually despised formal government.

In some cases, many members subsisted on welfare, or it was even the main source of economic support of the whole commune (see Berger *et al.* 1974). Hippies found no contradiction (or tolerated the contradiction) with their much vaunted "independence" and hatred of formal political authority. (One could hardly expect logic from people who despised serious thinking in any case.) Or in some instances one member had financial backing from wealthy family.

Occasionally an individual more central in decision making would glimpse the need for some cohesion-building set of beliefs, preferably religious, (or equivalent). For example:

> Bill Wheeler of Wheeler Ranch and Lou Gottlieb [of Morningstar] are now [1971] attempting to create a new religious view that will give a sense of unity and purpose to the communal movement. The "Morningstar Faith" . . . has as its purpose "the living of a primitive life in harmony with revealed Divine Law," [which] seems to be an amalgam of Buddhist, Yoga, Druid and pantheist beliefs . . . (Roberts 1971, p.50)

The contrived nature of such "religion," not growing out of the real needs and experiences of the members, should have boded ill for the endurance of these communes, as proved correct.

Turnover in communes like Morningstar was enormous, and the lifespan of any of the dozens of communal experiments was very short. Rosabeth Moss Kanter, a serious sympathetic student of the "movement" observed in 1970, presciently enough: "The prospects for most of today's anarchistic communes are dim; they lack the commitment-building practices of the successful communities of the Nineteenth Century." (Kanter 1970:78; see for the latter, Kephart 1976. See also Kanter's larger work, 1972.) Or, Kanter might have added, the practices of a genuine and successful twentieth century commune movement, the Israeli kibbutz, which has survived since 1909, and is now into a fourth generation. There a central feature is commitment to a distinct and definite ideology, that of democratic-socialist Zionism, which is for the members the functional equivalent of a religion. All members commit themselves to subordinate self-interest and self-seeking to the discipline of the community as a whole, something almost utterly lacking in the hippie approach to the world. (See among the many writings on kibbutz, Endleman 1967, 1981, and sources.) Few of the new communalists had any knowledge at all of the Israeli kibbutz. This ignorance should not be surprising in this poorly-informed and anti-intellectual group. Those who knew anything about the kibbutz rejected it entirely as a possible model, seeing it as "rigid," "too structured," and as "irrelevant to our needs." Perhaps the major objection (unstated) was that it works! Many of the slightly later radicals would reject it out of hand because it was Jewish, and Zionist and they (the radicals) were sympathetic to the Palestinians.

How hippies could organize themselves into commune life at all was quite remarkable. The turnover was always great. Hedgepeth, one of the saner social scientists looking at the commune scene (1970) noted that people who drop out of straight society tend to drop out of communes when the going gets rough. Utopian expectations are bound to be disappointed or smashed when confronted with the reality of a group of people living together on a day-to-day basis. This would be especially so if they are isolated from outside society—one can't just pick up a phone and reach a favorite and understanding aunt, and probably would not want to try to reach the parents who have been rejected.

The value of absolute individual freedom would preclude the adoption of any rules about personal behavior like sexual conduct. How does a sexual utopia deal with conflicts among individuals for the availability of particular sexual partners? How does work get done if all resist the idea of *any* kind of division of labor, with particular persons having responsibility for particular tasks? (The communalists' typical answer was "someone will want to do it.") Babies are conceived and born; who takes care of them? Or adults bring infants or children with them. Who takes care of them? Again, a typical answer is: "there'll always be someone around who'll be interested."

Not surprisingly many observers found rampant infant and child neglect, while parents and other adults were strung out on drugs or otherwise "doing their own thing." (Some of these children turned up a few years later in child therapists' offices, with serious psychological disturbances, as did their mothers who by then were drop-outs from the hippie movement.)

Berger *et al.* (1974) noted the inherent conflict on child-rearing on the communes, between the ideal of complete freedom of the *child* to "do his own thing" and thus become the desired completely autonomous personality, and the desire of the communards to raise a new generation faithful to *their* communal way. Inability or unwillingness to impose discipline on the children easily shaded over into neglect and indifference to real dangers, e.g. allowing a 16-month-old baby to smoke his father's pipe, for fear of oppressing the child.

Some sociologists sympathetic to the hippie movement (as ever, romanticizing "underdogs") could perceive these conditions and still maintain a positive stance, for example, Bennett Berger *et al.* 1974; Ron Roberts 1971; Roy Ald 1971; William Hedgepeth 1970. Faith in the possibility of utopia seems to spring eternal in certain observers.

There was no assured economic base, or any plan for how to achieve one by the much-acclaimed self-sufficiency (growing their own food) or how not to be dependent on hand-outs from welfare or rich relatives, or occasionally sympathetic neighboring farmers. Planning of course requires some rationality (inherently despised by the hippie outlook) and some future-orientation, also condemned.

Not surprisingly most of these ventures failed. What is surprising is that any of them lasted even the short time they did. (One estimate was an average longevity of two years—probably an overestimate.)

Hippies trying to live in a commune seem wilfully to ignore anything that human beings have ever learned about the basics of social or political organization, e.g. the necessity of *some* division of labor, of *some* kind of coordination, with someone or group in a role with that function, and some kind of transcendant shared belief, preferably religious or functionally equivalent. It is part of the same mentality that informs the sense the commune members have that everything they do has to be invented from scratch. There is no past, or if there is one, nothing to be learned from it, and no precedents for our conditions in the experience of other communal groups. We are unique and distinct, and born fresh at the beginning of time, an idea compatible with the mushy-headed mysticism pervasive in the counterculture. The implied solipsism is also of a piece with the infantilism and narcissism of many of the participants.

Leadership

Lack of leadership was an inherent problem on communes. Ragingly opposed to having *any* kind of authority imposed on them, the communards had to deny even the existence of leadership (where it did exist) and refuse to think out or plan for its presence and any principles under which it was supposed to be fairly administered. In many instances, *de facto* the person responsible for getting, buying, or simply seizing the land, became by that token a kind of leader. In other cases, where a typical anarchy prevailed, leadership fell perforce to the most psychopathic members (Yablonsky 1968). These were usually male; though if asked about it, hippies would say females and males are equal, in practice, wherever there was the usual inequality in political power, males held sway, as much so, or even more, than in conventional society. Also *de facto,* females gravitated to the more traditionally feminine tasks; they "discovered the joys of sewing, cooking, cleaning," and the like. This despite the fact that the same women rejected the "chains of traditional feminine roles in suburbia." These are far from havens of women's liberation.

Is there a Bohemian Personality?

There is certainly a bohemian *style,* demonstrated by the hippies and their predecessors. But can we say there is a distinct bohemian *personality* type, or set of psychological characteristics? Since many of the typical characteristics of the hippie population were elements shared with middle and upper class youths generally in any modern Western society—a background of relative affluence, "permissive" childrearing, extreme ambiguity of the status of the adolescent stage of life—were there typical psychological characteristics more likely to make a particular youngster a hippie, than others?

Such a question is difficult to answer, precisely because of the lack of distinct boundaries that mark off clearly enough who is a hippie and who is not. So any answer has to be tentative.

Efforts by some psychologists and psychoanalysts to delineate a type are problematical. Nathan Adler (1968) wrote of an "antinomian personality." But interestingly, his paper is more sociocultural and historical than psychological. The psychological elements are these: the antinomian is given to diffusion of boundaries. Paradoxically, "theirs is a rage for order," that is, the self-assertive quest for the excessive and extravagant, constitutes a kind of effort at binding and anchoring that is lost in the usual conventional life that has lost all meaning for the rebels. "Pantheistic cosmic expansion, erotic moment, manipulations of immediacy—all are attempts to bind the self and to reinstate its boundaries" (p.331).

Antinomianism means rejection of the norms (of conventional society, i.e. while embracing those of the counterculture). It means being against standard figures of authority, especially the police, or any political authorities. Alongside this the subject is ready to immerse himself in a dissident cult which promises self-realization in some mystical manner. Such readiness reveals a potential for an intense authoritarian submission of totalitiarian potential—this is Endleman, not Adler speaking—as evidenced at its extreme in the Manson cult, Jonestown, and the fictional world of the movie *Tommy.*

How about other attempts to delineate the psychology of the hippie?

Harry Brickman, a psychiatrist, views the psychedelic "hip scene" as manifesting a "return to the death instinct" (1968). Brickman sees this scene as particularly attractive to young people who are intensely in need of a "psychosocial moratorium" (Erikson 1950) in this crucial period of adolescence, a period of relief from pressures of responsibilities and demands, especially felt in middle and upper class youngsters (the working and lower class presumably simply cannot afford such psychological luxuries). The psychedelic drugs are of special appeal to such youngsters. Regression to infantile states of consciousness seems to be part of that appeal. The ultimate regression would be return to the womb, and the "mystical" appeal appears to be of that order: immersing oneself totally in a supportive and boundaryless environment.

Psychology of Psychedelics

In the 1960s "counterculture" of the hippies, a prominent feature was the spread of natural and symnthetic psychedelic drugs: psylocybin, peyote, mescaline, and especially the synthetic LSD and various further synthetic developments. These drugs were embraced by the bohemian rebels for their "mind-expanding" qualities. "Good trips" were to take one to a "beyond within," to ranges of psychological experience beyond ordinary everyday consciousness, and many believed, into a profound religious experience of mystical union with a supreme power or God. Tripping took one out of and beyond ordinary time experience, suspended ordinary categories of sensory experience, enabled synesthesia (hearing colors, smelling sounds, seeing smells, etc.), intensified enormously all ordinary sensations, e.g. the vision of a sunset, put totally into abeyance all ordinary everyday cares and worries, and inhibitions. However, with any of the same drugs, the subject may have a "bad trip," inducing overwhelming terror, and a state which psychiatrists would regard as at least a temporary psychosis, i.e. extreme regression and de-differentiation. In some cases the subject may not come out of such a psychotic state. Or the subject may re-experience the bad tripping experience at a later time even without another dose of the drug—experiences called after-flashes.

Sympathetic observers (e.g. Brickman 1968, *op. cit.*) emphasize these qualities of the psychology of the psychedelic experience: its transcendental experience, often euphoric, an experience of the universe as beautiful and harmonious; and secondly a profoumd experience of ego dissolution *and re-integration* [my emphasis—RE], often perceived as death followed by rebirth. Other psychological accounts agree on the question of ego-*dissolution,* but are not unanimous in seeing a process of reintegration occurring as well. If the ego-dissolution is profound, therefore involving extreme regression, it is likely to produce the "bad trip" experience, and sometimes, a not easily reversible psychotic episode. For a viewpoint similar to Brickman's in its positive view of psychedelics, but without illusions about their dangers, especially for young, immature and poorly formed individuals, see Masters and Houston 1966.

The extreme regressions lead outsiders to the hippie, especially the psychedelic subculture, to be wary of the participants' use of these psychedelic drugs, as an actually or potentially destructive force. On one hand the mature professionals involved in the earlier experiments with psychedelics in the late 1940s-1950s—see Masters and Houston 1966—were usually persons of a high and complexly differentiated ego development and psychological maturity, able to manage and derive enlightenment from such drugs. On the other, this was, and is, generally not true of the young devotees of the hippie subculture and their later imitators. Some of these, in fact, were exactly the wrong people to be trying LSD and other such drugs. As young people age 12–19 or at most early 20s, most were automatically too immature, and on top of that, were likely to have very fragile ego structures to start with, given to poor reality testing and poverty of other crucial ego functions, all of which would be further deteriorated by ingestion of psychedelic drugs. These were also likely to be young people, who because of their impulsiveness and other psychological difficulties, were already at odds with more conventional parents, relatives and peers. They were thus attracted to the "way-out" subculture of the hippies, and therefore also extremely vulnerable to the lure of these "magical" chemicals.

A further danger was that commonly the young person did not know precisely what drug was being ingested, and what dosage, since what was sold as LSD could be contaminated by any other ingredients, or other toxic drugs, like amphetamines. That danger in turn, rather than frighten the potential user away from the drug, in many cases increased the allure—the dangerous, the forbidden, in effect the Russian-roulette element in the situation. "We're all going to die sometime, so what's the difference?"

The psychoanalyst Herbert Hendin (1975) writing about early 1970s college students, including a number heavily involved with various drugs, wrote of the psychedelic drug users: "[here] both the desire to feel alive and to go beyond feeling were common" (p. 202). "Students who habitually used psychedelic drugs proved to be out of touch with much that is crucial in their emotional lives . . . [they seemed] cut off from their inner feelings . . ." One user felt (when under the influence of the drug) as though he was breaking out of his own personality. . . . LSD arouses the anxiety that he is cracking the structure of his personality beyond repair . . ." (p. 206). "The unpredictable quality of the psychedlic trip contributes to the sense of fragmentation it produces . . . [These subjects] strive for meaninglessness as a protection against what they see as the pain that will inevitably hit them if they become emotionally involved with anyone or anything. . . ." (p.217).

Varieties of Hippie Personalities

It is unrealistic to expect to delineate a single personality type as fitting bohemians generally, or specifically the hippies of the 1960s. Too many different kinds of people drifted in and out of the many hippie "scenes." That very variety and fluidity was a central feature, and for many of the participants, the very attractive part, of the phenomenon. Still for purposes of discussion, one can describe some of the main variations. One distinguishing feature is age: "older hippies" meaning over 21 or so, in age as of the time of entry into the hippie scene, as distinguished from the younger ones, in their largely unformed and therefore probably psychologically deficient in ego resources, also undergoing the usual stressful transitions of adolescence in this society. They are also therefore extremely vulnerable to the allures of the exotic, anarchic and in many ways chaotic world of the counterculture.

It is also more likely that one could find in the former, the older, some degree of ego structure, some capacity for reality testing, and capacity for self-direction less likely in the younger participants.

A Sketch of Types

Starting with this distinction of age, we can attempt to sketch some main types of personalities on the hippie scene. We need to make the caveat that these "types" appear not only in this bohemian subculture, and thus are not entirely distinctive of hippiedom. Nor do they exhaust the kinds of persons appearing in that vaguely boundaried scene. Nor are these full-scale personality portraits, any more than Adler's or Brickman's are.

They can be summarized as follows:

1) Young, immature, fragile-ego, infantile, dependent; not psychotic but very vulnerable;
2) Usually older than 1). More intact in ego structure, thus relatively healthier, and relatively less vulnerable to psychotic disintegration;
3) Passive-aggressive personalities, various ages;
4) Psychopaths;

5) Psychotic, usually schizophrenic; probably already were so before arriving on the hippie scene, or at least incipiently so; and more overtly so after psychedelic drug experiences.

1) Infantile, dependent, fragile ego

These are more likely to be in their teens rather than older, at the time of entry to the hippie scene. Many of these, more girls than boys probably, were the "flower children" with their endearingly and poignantly childlike innocence of manner, who worked a beguiling influence on "straight" people who encountered them. They could, that is, until, in some instances the latter, a middle-aged couple of tourists, looked more closely and saw this was their own 13-year-old Mary Ellen!

Many social scientists and other cultural observers, were so beguiled, as shown in their uncritically-admiring writings, that they had little or no awareness of the depths of psycho- and sociopathology covered by that innocent facade.

Ego capacities here are very rudimentary: reality-testing, capacity to delay gratification, capacity to discriminate friend from exploiter, capacity to maintain a coherent and constant sense of self. Object relations are likely to be rudimentary and infantile. Similarly superego development is at least as poor, if not worse. Rejection of nearly all standards of middle class morality is not simply on principle, but built on a need for immediate gratification; or a need to define the self primarily in terms of opposition to something conventional and approved. Here it is more likely rebellion is associated not with ego strengths, but with weaknesses, which can be summarized as a kind of anarchic dependency. This dependency has not been satisfied in relations with familial authority, who represented either arbitrary power-wielding, or, more likely, chaotic neglect, inconsistency and lack of emotional response to the youngster. This lack was linked to the parents' pursuing their own lives, or divorced, or themselves chaotic in various psychopathologies. Such parents are felt to be mindlessly uncaring and the opposite of the loving the youngster craves and needs.

The fragile ego structure of such youngsters made them the absolutely worst candidates for the potentially transcendant features of the psychedelic experience, and also the most likely candidates to be lured into the psychedelic world. Drugs, probably particularly psychedelic drugs, provide the most acutely pointed medium of rebellion and defiance against the conventional parents. At the same time, they are the means for psychological escape into a state of consciousness where the ordinary concerns of everyday life recede from awareness and importance. Even trips that are not really good trips, but not entirely bad ones, can be savored for the felt-to-be-healing effect. The other people involved in such experiences, can be regarded as co-travelers on a road that is distinctive, exotic, and "out of this world."

The very dangers of the drug experience and the pursuit of the illicit substances are themselves appealing. They are the antithesis to the former life of conventional safeties and dullness. The quest of such danger, even the danger of self-obliteration, is appealing. The sense of community with the other voyagers in this illicit territory—however illusory the "community." The "community" is probably illusory because it is problematic how much genuine "loving" is available, among these similarly-starved and fragile and psychologically poorly put together comrades. The contact with the criminal underworld necessitated by the drug trade, also makes these vulnerable youngsters easy prey for exploitation by hard and often psychopathic criminals, as demonstrated in the rapid deterioration of the Haight-Ashbury supposed paradise of freedom into a hellhole of criminality and exploitation soon after the great summer of 1967 with its influx of hundreds of thousands of joy-questing youngsters from all over the continent. (There is no full accounting of how many youngsters simply disappeared, or were finally discovered dead, in that kind of scene.)

The infantile-dependent, while rejecting totally any traditional authority—parents, teachers, police, religious leaders—were nevertheless easy prey for newly appearing ad-hoc "authorities" of the hippie scene. These were the self-proclaimed gurus and the like, to whom such fragile youngsters were willing to give mindless and near-total allegiance and obedience. Here ego-capacities of discrimination were further deteriorated by psychedelic and other drugs. Such gurus were able to exercise a Svengali-like control over these youngsters, particularly the females. The appallingly extreme case was the Manson family.

2) Relatively more ego-intact

Some were psychologically well enough to band together in mutually supportive groups. Some of these in turn were able to take in and provide sustenance, security, and a semblance of "loving" for others who were more fragile and unlikely to be able to survive on their own in the hippie jungle. These others were also unable or unwilling to return to homes of conventional families. Various communes did get started, in spite of the inherent obstacles (see above). In more fortunate communes, leadership might devolve on some of these relatively healthier individuals. These were people (interestingly more likely men) with more intact reality testing and greater capacity to resist the disintegrating effects of psychedelic drugs. They were better able to help more fragile neophytes through that experience. Many of these males were sufficiently capable of being aware of, utilizing and developing, the "feminine," more nurturant aspects of themselves, a capacity associated with their disaffiliation from conventional society and culture with its cult of the macho emotionally inexpressive male. While able to help a succession of younger, more fragile, usually female neophytes in the hippie, especially the psychedelic, experience, these same men were also apt to have extreme difficulties in forming and maintaining stable and lasting object ties. In that respect, the hippie world, with its ephemeral and constantly shifting population, is made to order to people like this.

3) Passive—Aggressive

A good example of this kind of personality in the hippie context is reported in the Berger *et al.* account of child-rearing on hippie communes (1974). A young father lets his 16-month old infant son smoke the father's pipe, and will not try to take it away from the infant. His attitude is that the child should be "free to do his own thing." It does not seem to occur to him that this permissiveness gone wild is likely to be injurious to the child. This parent, like many hippie parents, rationalizes about making the child "free to do his own thing" as a cover for his aggression toward the child.

4) Psychopaths

Some of the people in the hippie world fit the type of the psychopathic personality (see Chapter 2 and Chapter 5). They are totally amoral, exploitative, likely to take over control at times when the relations of others are in a state of chaos and anarchy. Some of these will probably gravitate to, or just take over, leadership positions in a commune where anarchy prevails (see above). They are also likely to take advantage of the drug dependency of, particularly, type 1)s and type 3)s

5) Psychotic

Some of the hippies go into psychotic episodes as the result of LSD or other psychedelic drug "trips." Some of these may be already psychotic or close to it, even before the psychedelic usage. The chaotic and disorganized scene in Haight-Ashbury or the East Village serves, among other functions, as a hiding place for seriously disturbed individuals. They are simply not so noticeable in this environment where "anything goes" and all surface behavior is at least odd and eccentric by conventional standards. The fragility and regressiveness of youngsters of type 1) may in certain cases, be sufficiently extreme that the individual may be classifiable as an ambulatory schizophrenic. Delusional states may to the surrounding people be indistinguishable from common drug effects. Paranoia is so prevalent in the hippie population as not to be noticeable, or to be considered even deviant, let alone as possibly indicative of a serious psychological disorder. In some cases only extreme "bad trip" reactions may get the individual to professional attention that would force the recognition of a serious psychotic state. The most fragile of the type 1) infantile dependent individuals are generally in greatest danger when experimenting with hard psychedelic drugs, and many of these may have gone over the edge of psychosis well before it is recognized in an extreme bad trip reaction. As discussed before, some of these do not recover. Defenders of the hippie tripping may say that the bad trip is apt to have such dire consequences only when there is intrusion of conventional psychiatry into the situation, and a youngster then being treated in a conventional mental hospital is likely only to exacerbate the situation. They may say that his "paranoia" in that situation is only a rational and expectable reaction to the "oppression" imposed by conventional psychiatrists and conventional mental hospitals. Defenders of this position (usually anti-psychoanalytic social scientists like Howard Becker) are usually the same people who claim there is no such thing as mental illness—(see Chapter 5).

The Passing of 1960s Hippie Bohemianism

Though clearly, as already discussed, hippiedom has not *totally* disappeared and leaves various legacies to the present day, the hippie phenomenon as a widespread "movement" has largely disappeared. Rather it petered out and became more invisible, by about the mid-1970s. The explanation for its demise is not entirely clear.

As many earlier observers pointed out (Matza 1961, Parry 1933) one dilemma of bohemianism is that many of its elements—most readily surface ones that can be taken over into fashion—are subject to borrowing and absorption by mainstream society, a kind of "destruction by partial incorporation." This has certainly happened to many of the features of the hippies or their communes. Sexual mores have been altered in Western populations as a whole, not only because of the hippies, but in the same direction, so that sexual liberation of unmarried individuals is practically an accepted fact of life in modern communities. More "hang-loose" styles of clothing, hair, personal decoration, and the like, became widespread. Men did not have to be hippies to wear long hair, to wear all kinds of jewelry, or to wear exotic clothing. Interest in Eastern religious ideas, appeared in many parts of society, other than the counterculture. Mysticism has had its vogue in many quarters, including its influence in serious psychology and psychotherapy. Psychotherapy generally has expanded into many different modalities far from traditional varieties, many of these influenced by or derived from the counterculture of the 1960s in any of its protean versions. Various groups within conventional society are pursuing countercultural interests or forms of organization. These include dietary enthusiasms—especially vegetarianism and the cult of "organic foods," backed up by what purports to be scientific evidence. They embrace a variety of health-oriented activities, with the word "natural" prominent in their hype. Also here are a variety of "save-the-environment" programs again with something purporting to be scientific backing. Then there is the recrudescence of many forms of magic, many of them never having disappeared, but having for decades, even centuries, been eclipsed from respectability by their antiscientific and antirationalist slant. Here we find cults of witchcraft, (or at least belief in it), and of the occult. Then there is the enormous popularity of astrology, with thousands of otherwise apparently sane modern people believing in it and following astrological charts and the like, and giving a lucrative practice to astrological advisers. Though most of these beliefs and practices long predated the modern hippies and counterculture of the 1960s, they seemed to get an enormous boost by those movements of that period, as many erstwhile hippies and their sympathizers moved into adulthood in the 1970s and 1980s. The prevalence and popularity of such beliefs and practices should lead us to question how deeply the culture of modern rationality has really penetrated into the mass of the population. A glance at the advertisements in such a publication as *The Village Voice* would surely indicate how much nonrational and antirational elements pervade the culture of today. And there is the phenomenon of an entire range of the "alternative press" with a great variety of publications all sharing some countercultural slant.

However, as "movement" it went into decline.

Perhaps a phenomenon like the hippies and counterculture of the 1960s is likely in any case to spend itself, having little institutional support, and no clarity of structure—unlike, for example, the Israeli kibbutz or sects like the Hutterites—and having elements that are easily subject to borrowing or stealing by mainstream society. Also, many of the participants do not face insuperable difficulties returning to a version of conventional society, or finding a marginal niche within it, like opening up a hippie-type craft shop.

Academics or cultural observers who romanticized, even glorified, the hippies while they were in ascendancy, can find other topics later and expect their hippie enthusiasms to be forgotten.

Summary and Conclusion

Bohemianism has been for centuries a potential alternate life pattern for large numbers of disaffected or questing young people in society. It has appeared and disappeared and then reappeared, under various guises, a number of times in modern history, and is likely to reappear as a large-scale phenomenon in the later part of the twentieth or the early twenty-first century. Though some elements of it are as old as civilization, the modern form emerges in the wake of, and in opposition to, the Industrial Revolution of about two centuries ago. It represents neither criminality (with breaking the laws at the center of life activities) nor radicalism, i.e. an attempt to overturn the existing socio-economic-political order and replace it by a more just and humane one, more responsive to real human needs. The bohemians by contrast with both of those, want simply to *drop out* of existing society and culture and live life by their own precepts. They reject the whole modern culture of rationality, time orientation, work discipline, "linear thinking," asceticism, and body rejection. They extol raw feeling as opposed to thinking, infantile polymorphousness as opposed to narrow sexual channelling, freedom in all possible senses as opposite to discipline, restraint and order, and particulary embracing the outré experiences to be derived from ingestion of chemical substances. In each period of recrudescence of a renamed bohemia, whole populations of people, mostly young, gathered in centers of the "movement," and defiantly pursued a lifestyle in opposition to their elders and to conventionality in general. They became "the People Our Parents Warned Us Against" (Von Hoffman 1968). The boundaries of that population were extremely fluid, and people could "drop in" and usually also "drop out" of the subculture with ease. Some organized into communes, inherently contradictory to the total freedom of "doing your own thing" that was central to the bohemian way. The movement attracted a variety of personality types, including, prominently, young people of very fragile ego structure, not well matured and very vulnerable, some of whom may have already been essentially schizophrenic before joining the bohemians. Others became so with bad experiences of psychedelic drugs, and neither was easily identifiable within a population of anarchic counterconventional people dedicated to being so. Some of the protagonists had reasonably mature and healthy egos (probably a minority), were helpful to others less healthy, and offered a modicum of rational leadership. Still others were passive-aggressive personalities, likely to aggress against others by indirection and negligence, and some outright psychopaths, very dangerous to others. Efforts to organize "communes" were largely short-lived and failed, because of inherent contradictions between prevailing anarchistic feeling and action and the basic needs for cooperation, commitment and at least rudimentary discipline upon self-seeking pursuit.

REFERENCES

Adler, Nathan. 1968. "The Antinomian Personality: The Hippie Character Type." *Psychiatry.* 31:325–338.

Ald, Roy. 1971. *The Youth Communes.* New York: Tower

Berger, Bennett. 1967. "Hippie Morality—More Old than New." *Trans-Action* 5:19–24.

Berger, Bennett, and eight co-authors. 1974. "Child-Rearing Practices of the Communal Family." in Scott McNall, ed. *The Sociological Perspective.* 3d ed. Boston: Little, Brown, 521–534.

Braden, William. 1970. *The Age of Aquarius.* Chicago: Quadrangle Books.

Brickman, Harry R. 1968. "The Psychedelic 'Hip Scene': Return of the Death Instinct." *American Journal of Psychiatry.* 125: 766–772.

Cohn, Norman. 1961. *The Pursuit of the Millenium.* New York: Harper.

Davis, Fred. 1967. "Why All of us may be Hippies Some Day." *Trans-Action.* 5:10–18.

Endleman, Robert. 1967. "The Israeli Kibbutz: Social Structure and Personality," in Endleman, *Personality and Social Life,* New York: Random House, pp. 127–177.

———. 1981. "Gender Differences on the Israeli Kibbutz." In Endleman, *Psyche and Society.* New York: Columbia University Press, 159–170.

Erikson, Erik. 1950. *Childhood and Society.* New York: Norton

Gioscia, Victor. 1969. "Groovin' on Time: Fragments of a Sociology of the Psychedelic Experience." Hicks/Fink, eds. *Psychedelic Drugs.* New York: Grune & Stratton. Reprinted in Harry Silverstein, ed. *The Sociology of Youth: Evolution and Revolution.* New York: Macmillan, 1973, 454–465.

Graña, César. 1964. *Bohemian versus Bourgeois.* New York: Basic Books. Later edition, 1967. *Modernity and its Discontents.* New York: Harper. 1967.

Hedgepeth, William. 1970. *The Alternative.* New York: Macmillan.

Hendin, Herbert. 1975. *The Age of Sensation.* New York: Norton.

Kanter, Rosabeth Moss. 1970. "Communes." *Psychology Today* 4, no.2.

———. 1972. *Commitment and Community: Communes and Utopias in Sociological Perspective.* Cambridge, MA: Harvard University Press.

Kephart, William. 1976. *Extraordinary Groups: The Sociology of Unconventional Life-Styles.* New York: St. Martin's.

Kernberg, Otto. 1988. "Between Conventionality and Aggression: The Boundaries of Passion." in W. Gaylin and E. Person, eds. 1988. *Passionate Attachments: Thinking About Love.* New York: Free Press. 63–83.

Masters, R. E. L., and Jean Houston. 1966 *Varieties of the Psychedelic Experience* New York: Holt, Rinehart, Winston.

Matza, David. 1961. "Subterranean Traditions of Youth." *Annals of the American Academy of Political and Social Science.* 338:102–118.

Parry, Albert. 1933. *Garrets and Pretenders: A History of Bohemianism in America.* New York: Covici-Friede.

Pitts, Jesse R. 1969. "The Hippies as Contrameritocracy." *Dissent.* July-August. 326–337.

Reich, Charles. 1970. *The Greening of America* New York: Random House.

Reinhold, Robert. 1979. "Changes Wrought by 60s Youth Linger in American Life." *The New York Times,* Aug. 12, 1979, pp.1, 38.

Rigney, Francis, and L. Douglas Smith. 1961. *The Real Bohemia.* New York: Basic Books.

Roberts, Ron E. 1971. *The New Communes: Coming Together in America.* Englewood Cliffs, NJ: Prentice-Hall.

Silverstein, Harry, ed. 1973. *The Sociology of Youth: Evolution and Revolution.* New York: Macmillan.

Simmons, J. P. and Barry Winograd. 1966. *It's Happening.* Santa Barbara, CA: Marc-Laird.

Von Hoffman, Nicholas. 1968. *We Are the People Our Parents Warned Us Against.* Chicago: Quadrangle.

Yablonsky, Lewis. 1968. *The Hippie Trip.* New York: Pegasus.

Zablocki, B. D. 1980. *Alienation and Charisma: A Study of Contemporary American Communes.* New York: Free Press.

Zicklin, Gilbert. 1983. *Countercultural Communes: A Sociological Perspective.* Westport, CT: Greenwood Press.

CHAPTER 8

RADICALS[1]

Introduction

Once upon a time of great turmoil, people came together sharing their outrage over the evils and corruption of the world. Together they read the works of a prophet of a century before, discoursed upon them and added their own commentaries. Rejecting the venal luxuries of the exalted, these elect, seeing the true light, embraced a life of poverty. The present age must be coming to an end, so they dedicated themselves to ending it, thus ushering in the coming Last Age in which the pure would be united in brotherly communion and the present rulers chastised, punished, and, if necessary, eliminated. The teachings spread. Multitudes were fired with the new faith. Established powers pronounced against the dangerous new teachings, and persecuted the heretics. The believers in turn, heightened their fury against the authorities and sharpened their determination for apocalyptic change. They must actively bring about the New Order.

From their ranks a leader emerged, firm, pure, dedicated to poverty, frenzied with fixity of purpose and the total determination to act. He gathered an armed band of the faithful, and, against overwhelming odds, battled the armies of the entrenched authorities. The band's losses and privations were matched by its unwavering faith in victory and the coming of the Millenium. Alas, they were defeated, their leader killed. But the faith survived. New militants of purity rallied to the martyr's holy cause and continued the struggle.

In the same period, other groups pursued their own visions of the Perfect Order with equal zeal. One such espoused Absolute Liberty; once enlightened, a person was mystically one with God, nay, identical with God, and could therefore commit no evil. All liberties were thus sanctified: adultery, promiscuity, seizing of property ("God created all things in common") even violence and killing. Communal ceremonies in ritual nakedness signified the primal innocence of man before the Fall. Mystically qualified spiritual libertines pursued full gratification of all the senses: in erotic play; in eating sumptuously (preferably at others' expense); in dressing in costumes eccentrically combining luxury and poverty, They caused total confusion in status distinctions within the surrounding society. These heretics too had to be persecuted as threats to the Established Order. Many were executed, dying secure in their faith.

Still others were seeking Millenium or Apocalypse in their own ways, often combining the ascetic poverty of the first with the mystical eroticism of the second. Commonly such people came from families of wealth and honor, in the first case renouncing the comforts of that origin, in the second its respectability, to pursue the purity of their millenial vision. The common element in these visions was the fantasy of an ideal state in which differences in rank and wealth are abolished, and mankind returns to a golden age of communal egalitarianism.

Vaguely familiar? Student radicals and hippies of the 1960s? Not exactly. These descriptions (from Norman Cohn's *The Pursuit of the Millenium* [1961]) refer to the Joachites, a Franciscan Spiritual group of the thirteenth century, and to the Brethren of the Free Spirit, of the fourteenth—two among the many millenial movements springing up all over Europe in the later Middle Ages. Can these analogies be useful today? Consider:

The Joachites protested and challenged the power and luxury of the medieval Church and the Pope—the major political, ideological and military powers of the time—in the name of their transcendental vision of purity, a Last Age they must help create. Centrally a religious movement, they also carried on political, economic and at times military activities—e.g. Fra Dolcino's ill-fated battle against the Papal armies in 1300.

In the 1960s, student "revolutionaries" challenged the power of the spiritual authorities of their day—the universities—condemning their connections with the political, economic and military elites in the name of the secular Millenium, "The Revolution." These zealots too came from families of wealth and turned their backs on these comforts for ascetic purity.

Contemporaneously, each movement had its obverse: the mystical anarchism of the Spiritual Libertines then, and the exuberant antinomianism and eroticism of the "cultural revolution" of the 1960s—in each case interfusing in complex ways with the puritanism of the radicals.

True, the lexicon of either type of dissent in the 1960s was no longer Judeo-Christian chiliastic, but the spirit was much the same. An overwhelming fact about the great student rebellions in Western universities in the 1960s—one obscured by the *political* polemics aroused—was the quality resembling religious enthusiasm (a transcendental passion) within the trappings of secular political rhetoric and action.

Scattered throughout the literature on social movements are parallel treatments of religious and political movements. Cohn (1961) sees the millenialists as forerunners of modern secular totalitarianism. Paul Goodman (1970) sees various currents of youth unrest and dissent as a "New Reformation." My own outlook is strongly influenced by Benjamin Nelson's "The Future of Illusions" (1954—see Endleman 1970b, 1973).

Pursuing the analogy between the 1960s student radicals and the thirteenth century Joachites: the Church is now the University. Controversies rage within and around it—what is it really to be: a retreat for sacred comtemplation? a sanctuary of sacred lore handed down by tradition from the past? a system of power in itself? a link (and what kind of link) to the mundane authorities, and to the armed might of the state? How are its riches acquired, how are they used, how are they justified, in whose interests are they used?

The heretical sect arises, announces its intent to transform the Church and overturn its powers; it engages in outrageous and provocative actions. In the 1960s: enter the New Left, coalescing around the SDS (Students for a Democratic Society). This is a new-left radical group rejecting the old-fashioned Marxism of the "Old Left," the now aging remnants of the miniscule left-wing parties of the 1930s and 1940s—Communists, Socialists, Trotskyites—for a new formulation of left-wing radical dissent.

But the sect is not alone, nor united within itself. Protracted internecine battles ensue, with ever more subtle and sophistical argument and counterargument and struggles for power among the warring factions.

Students for a Democratic Society (SDS) History

The SDS had a brief and tumultuous history, well reflected in the collection of documents on the student rebellions, assembled by Wallerstein and Starr (1971). Reading through these documents, of manifestos and position papers, is a dizzyimg experience. One finds onself immersed in the sealed universe of passionately warring religious sects, an analogy perceived by some of the participants themselves. Progressive intensification of this kind of factional or sectarian infighting goes along with a progressive movement into an increasingly apocalyptic stance. By 1968 this was already being articulated not only among the inner circle of the elite, but to a wider constituency of supporters, as in the case of the Columbia University strikers of May. There John Jacobs openly advocated terroristic tactics (Wallerstein/Starr, II:213). By August 1968, one SDS spokesman, Les Coleman, was openly announcing that the aim is not to change the universities, but to shut them down. By 1969, SDS split wide open into warring camps, never to be reunited, and one of these, Weathermen, embarked on a program of terroristic violence. This was a direction accurately predicted by Lewis Feuer in his transhistorical study of student rebellions that have occurred since the early nineteenth century, *The Conflict of Generations* (1969). That work was strongly disliked by the supporters of the student rebels, evidently because of Feuer's refusal to romanticize the then current, or any of the earlier revolts.

Was that apocalyptic direction an isolated aberrent development within the New Left, or intrinsic? Feuer argued the latter view. The diversity of SDS views indicated by the record (see especially Wallerstein/Starr) suggests something more like the former.

Looked at in the political dimension of the movement, it seems that by that time (1968–69) the New Left had only two *active* directions to take: either reformism, left-liberal forging of instrumental alliances "within the system," hoping for steady incremental gains, or apocalyptic terrorism (Weathermen). Where the religious impulse, as discerned, is strong, the reformist option is unlikely to be attractive. Then the alternatives to apocalyptic terrorism are most likely to be quietist withdrawal, or attachment to the other main current of contemporary religious expression in secular guise, i.e. hippiedom or the "cultural revolution," divorced from specific political program or strategies. These latter appeared to have become, by the early 1970s, the dominant mood on the campuses among students who were earlier "radicalized" by the 1960s revolts, or who would have been potential radicals had they arrived on campus two or three years earlier. Within a few years after that, i.e. by the mid-1970s, both the radical and the hippie forms of dissent seem to have largely disappeared from the campuses. Then faculty who had been excited by the 1960s revolts, were bewailing the turn to conservatism or narrow egocentric careerism among the college youth.

The basic dilemmas of any extreme social movement attempting major transformatiosns of society (whether manifestly religious or political in guise) are the twin dangers of repression and co-optation. If the movement is too extreme and cannot develop a broad base of support, it is vulnerable to suppression by the forces of the legal order. If it moderates its aims or at least its public rhetoric, gaining a broader support from sympathizers sharing its values if not all its strategies and tactics, it runs the opposite risk of being absorbed ("co-opted") into more moderate change movements already operating in the society (Cf. Mauss 1971).

The student radical movement in the late 1960s agonized over these dangers, and opposing factions disputed bitterly about both of them. Co-optation of change agents and ideas into the established structure, as occurred when universities acceded to "student power" demands, both robbed the radicals of ostensible issues/grievances and enlisted them in "reform" activities "within the system" and outside the radical movement.

Students who went along with that were denounced for "selling out."

Faced with the prospect of that kind of Purgatory, the radicals had to escalate the extremism of their rhetoric, if not of actual action. That in turn would alienate them further from the potential support of more moderate sympathizers, and also invited suppression by the authorities. Members who were more integrated psychologically (those whose "idealism" stemmed from relative ego strength and relatively more mature superego—cf. Liebert 1971) are susceptible to shrewd co-optation by the authorities. In some cases they may try to convince themselves that this is not "full co-optation," that they are really working for radical change, but from "within the system." For example, you could go to law school to become a "movement lawyer." As this continues, the movement, having become yet more extreme in its frenzy to defend against the dangerous infection of such heresy, is likely to retain only the most extreme personality types, the apocalyptic nihilists whose "idealism" is based on a far more primitive and infantile superego (see below). Here their political activity, moving rapidly toward destructive and self-destructive terrorism, brings out into the open the massive infantile rage. Here there are analogies to one type of political assassin discussed by Clarke (see Chapter 6) who approximated the "political personality" of Lasswell, where personal private pathologies are worked out on a public stage where it is easier to aggress against a major political figure than against the original instigators of the rage.

Essentially the same types are described by Liebert as the "nihilists," by Hendin (1971) as the "revolutionaries" and by Feuer as those central in the later destructive and suicidal stage of the student movements. All of these are a very different breed from the attractively portrayed, relatively healthy "Young Radicals" of Keniston's admiring—and probably romanticizing—study (1968). See also Endleman 1981:357–367, and Endleman 1970a, for psychological portrayals of main types. See also later in this chapter for summary.

Feuer's depiction is no doubt accurate for *some* student radicals; his error is in generalizing them all; what he describes is one type, whom I would call the apocalyptic nihilists, exemplified best by the Weathermen. Remnants of these are still around as of the time of this writing, 1988. We find them engaged in shoot-outs with the police, acting like a gang of ordinary violent criminals holding up Brink's armored trucks for the money, only in this case the money is for "the revolution." Keniston's 1967 "radicals" would be, by the standards of the later more violent phase of the student revolts, simply "reformists," albeit still to the left of left-liberals.

The apocalyptic vein is also reflected by the adoption by some New Leftists of Marcuse's concept of "repressive tolerance," with the important corollary that the good radical must *refuse* to give tolerance or accord civic liberties such as free speech to his political enemies, e.g. "fascists," warmongers, militaristic imperialists, or anyone, student or faculty, supportive of these evildoers.

In intense internecine factional struggles, the same injunction is applied to one's enemies within the movement (Mark Rudd at Columbia, later a Weatherman.) This is the dogmatism of religious fanaticism. It is not the political language of conflict, but the religious one of heresy.

These pronouncements, evidently reflecting sentiments in at least the leadership of the New Left, are not frequently articulated publicly, and seldom if ever to a mixed audience including left-liberal allies. They bring out into the open the elitism and authoritarian, even totalitarian, potential that the New Left's critics have frequently discerned in it, especially those speaking from a democratic-socialist viewpoint, e.g. Irving Howe. Apologists and sympathizers of the New Left tended to gloss over such tendencies as incidental extravagances of rhetoric, explaining them as understandable in an embattled dissident minority. The critics, in contrast, tend to regard such elements as intrinsic to the movement. (See Feuer for the strongest statement of that view.)

Perhaps both are only partly correct. Any social movement will attract a variety of personality and social types, but a limited few of these will tend to stamp the movement, as it moves into coalescence, with the symbolisms reflecting their particular personality predispositions. The elitist-authoritarian element, with its absolutistic moral arrogance, is *one* important aspect of the movement—salient at certain junctures of its history—but not the whole.

The main personality types of the movement will be discussed later in the chapter.

Who Were the Participants?

In contrast with the bohemians of the '60s, the hippies, who were difficult to characterize precisely (aside from coming from middle or higher class backgrounds), the radicals were extensively studied during the 1960s, so that a good deal is known about them. First, as university students, they were several years older than the younger hippies; and as university students, in some cases graduate students, better educated than most of the bohemians.

Not all university students of the 1960s, of course, participated actively in the student rebellions. The main data drawn on here are from North America. Lipset 1971 draws on material from Western Europe as well. Ellul 1968 refers to France. Feuer 1969 refers to many countries, both modern industrial and others. The Western European sources indicate essentially the same patterns as for North America.

Various studies indicated which students were involved:

The students who were most susceptible to participation tended to be academically brighter students from upper-middle to upper-class backgrounds, with fathers who were more frequently in the professions, and mothers who had careers, often in some humanitarian service field, and with both parents more educated than average (Braungart 1969, Flacks 1967, Keniston 1967, 1968, Lipset 1968, Somers 1965, Watts and Whittaker 1966). The parents of student activists were typically liberal, left-liberal, or radical in their political orientation. The parents of activists were also likely to be permissive and egalitarian in their child-rearing styles, anti-authoritarian, respecting the child's autonomy and encouraging his individualism and the development of a questioning attitude toward the world.

Activist students were more likely than their colleagues to be enrolled in particular noncareer-oriented studies that are largely concentrated in the humanities and the "softer" social sciences (Auger *et al.* 1969, Braungart 1969, Flacks 1967, Keniston 1968, Somers 1965; and from France: Ellul 1968). The proportion of females among the activists varied from about one-third to one-half, depending on the level of participation, with fewer females being involved at the extreme levels or in leadership positions (Auger *et al.* 1969; Braungart 1969; Watts and Whittaker 1966; and deductions from Avorn *et al.* 1969; Rader 1969, Lipset and Wolin 1965; and much other literature on the New Left).[2]

What emerges is a portrait of a highly verbal, articulate, and sensitive minority of noncareerist "vanguard youth" from advantaged, socially aware, cosmopolitan backgrounds, largely deracinated from traditional Judeo-Christian religion, and products of, and participants in, the more "advanced" cultural trends of a sophisticated advanced-industrial world. For them, traditional religion had essentially decayed or was already dead. Judeo-Christian myths had been eroded by the rationalism of a scientific-technical-industrial civilization. These students also showed an ambivalent relationship to the official secular mythologies of their nation-state. They combined adherence to its universalistic ideals with great distrust of its specific institutional arrangements and the particular personnel in power. They were highly sensitive to the obvious gaps between official ideals and actual social conditions, especially on the issues of freedom and equality.

They were suspicious toward all forms of authority. Their parents had displayed at least verbal concern with the issues of freedom, equality and social justice, and encouraged their offspring to take a critical stance toward authority in general. These youngsters also tended to gravitate to these culturally more cosmopolitan universities that emphasize openness and relativism. A consequence is that they feel lack of fixity or certainty about anything, and a general quality of shapelessness to their lives. This is a more exaggerated version of the general difficulty of sub-adult status which is endemic in this society.

Background History of the Student Revolt

There is a background history to the radical revolts of university students going back at least two centuries in America, and in some respects much farther back in Europe (see Feuer 1969; Lipset 1971). Like the bohemian phenomenon, with which it is sometimes associated, as it was in the 1960s, it comes and goes in periodicities that do not seem to have any definite pattern, especially at the time it is "in." When it comes into full flower, it always seems a surprise to cultural, historical or (in modern times) sociological observers. Just before the 1960s explosions, in 1960, a major sociological theorist, Daniel Bell, was proclaiming "An End of Ideology," i.e. an end of the period in which leftist ideological enthusiasms derived from some version of Marxism animated sustained radical revolt, in theoretical thinking and even more so in praxis, against the political economy of capitalism. Bell was reflecting the 1950s conditions, in which youth, including university youth, had no overt political movement at all, and seemed to assume that condition would continue indefinitely. At the same time, in a paper published in 1961, David Matza ("Subterranean Traditions of Youth"—see preceding chapter) referred to radicalism as one of these traditions, and the latest example he could find of it in America were various campus revolts occurring in the 1930s. Nothing foreshadowing the student radicalism about to burst on the campuses only a few years later. Only a reference to the appearance and disappearance of political radicalism. Not only Bell and Matza, but most sociologists and cultural observers were caught by surprise with the radical developments of the 1960s.

In 1961 there was a small young element in YPSL (Young People's Socialist League). YPSL was an "old left" socialist and anti-Stalinist remnant of the 1930s and 1940s, mostly by that time at least middle-aged (a wag called them the MAPSLs). The group of youngsters, in their 20s at most, proclaimed themselves independent of the Old Left seniors. They disaffiliated themselves from the old, "outdated" factional fights of the Left, essentially of Socialists versus Communists. They called for a new leftist front with emphasis on youth, ideological flexibility and "participatory democracy," which was to replace the alleged hierarchical and thinking rigidities of the old left factions (see Students for a Democratic Society, *Port Huron Statement* 1964).

This became the nucleus for the New Left, with its major campus organization the Students for a Democratic Society (SDS) dedicated to a democratic leftist politics to join the fight against racism within America and the war trends of the establishment power, particularly the Vietnam War.

On major elite campuses—Berkeley, later Columbia, Cornell, Harvard and then many others, and spreading to many universities of lesser renown—they organized protests that escalated significantly in intensity and scope from one to the next. They had a variety of ostensible grievances, constantly expanding from one to the next. They had many different ostensible ideological rationales, starting with the "free speech" issue at Berkeley 1964–65. That one was about freedom to use "obscene" language in public demonstrations—an "issue" which became quaint in its innocence only a few years later. It escalated to charges that the university, especially in its research branches, was collaborating with the destructiveness and immorality of the "military-industrial complex" of a government insanely heading toward nuclear war. Then there were the perceived immorality and illegitimacy of the Vietnam War, the collaboration of the universities with the military draft, and in addition sundry local nefarious deeds. For example, at Columbia, it was the planning of a gymnasium to be shared with the adjacent black community, but in such a way as to underscore the subordination of that community. Thus the university was seen as collaborating in the "racism" of the society in general, and its national and local governments in particular.

The confrontation of the established powers, of the university, of the community, of the society at large, was carried out by a dedicated band of activists, skillfully rallying masses of troops of sympathetic students at large. At the peak of a particular demonstration like the occupation by the dissident students of most of the buildings on the Columbia campus, perhaps half of the student population rallied in support of the demonstration. The authorities initially refused the students' "outrageous demands." The standoff was prolonged enough to make the whole process a major incident, worthy of huge media attention.

These confrontations came, within a few years, to have a distinct pattern of their own.[3] They can be called the "Stages of the Great Ritual Drama":

1) *The Great Moral Issue* occurs: the university invites a "war-mongering" chemical company to recruit new young scientists on the campus; or a fiery radical popular instructor is fired; this produces Initial Protest, with some mild acts of civil disobedience by some of the protesters, followed by "disciplining of the culprits," etc. Then occurs:

2) *The Incident:* some misguided or ill-timed reaction by the administration, such as excessively punishing the alleged culprits, polarizing further the protesting students and the administration, with onlookers being pushed to take sides. Thus we have:
3) *Confrontation:* In response, the activists organize a massive confrontation: seizing a building; taking university administrators hostage. Civil disobedience escalates to major illegal acts. The Confrontation becomes a Point of No Return. It gains momentum and numbers of supporters and troops. Occupiers of buildings swell in numbers and enthusiasm.
4) *Carnival:* The élan of "liberation" of buildings generates an atmosphere of *Carnival* in a great exaltation of generational solidarity. Becoming a Group, they celebrate the abrogation of conventional constraint and traditional taboos.
5) *Escalation:* The authorities hesitate and vacillate, torn by conflicting feelings and advice. The Confrontation becomes more stiffly spined. Demands expand from two, to five, to ten or more. New dissatisfactions are discovered and voiced. The protesters demand total Amnesty for all the participants. The conflict expands and escalates. More buildings are occupied. The ordinary life of the university is ground to a halt. The media enter and make the occupation a major public ritual.

The protesters are cast in the role of "heroes" along with some sympathetic faculty. On the other side the administration and a few of the faculty oppose the occupation, and become the "villains" of the spectacle. Most of the faculty remain ambivalent, sympathetic to the protesting students' demands and claims, admiring their vitality and ostensible "courage," but disapproving the "excesses" to which the ritual drama has been building. The Moral Community of the protesters is ignited by the initial Carnival, and sustained, enlarged and deepened by the escalation and the extraordinary common experience. They have had days of occupation, meetings, cooperation, the suspension of everyday life, the emotional charge of collective taboo-violation and the communal confrontation with physical danger. The excitement reaches its apotheosis in the actual arrival of the police and their violence. If the police do not initially or spontaneously act in that violent manner, they can be easily provoked to do so, by the protesters' resistance and outrageous language and behavior.
6) *The Bust:* The Bust, awaited for days and nights of thrilling and terror-filled anticipation, becomes Reality. Many feel they would not have missed it for the world. (A student who found himself outside the campus at the moment the Bust began, tried to move heaven and earth to get back in—see Dotson Rader 1969.)

The police more than fulfill the demonstrators' expectations in their violence against rebels and bystanders alike. All the while, the remaining "liberators" scream, shout and chant, great choruses of ritual incantations against the cops—just the sacred-taboo obscenities most likely to spur the irrational fury of the foe.

Calculational errors by administration forcing hasty revisions of police procedure, and the breakdown of disciplinary control over the police, unleash the irrational fury of the cops. They now fulfill their role in the fantasied climax now become reality.

7) *Aftermath: Horror: "Radicalization."* Physically defeated, the radicals emerge as moral victors. Horror engulfs the campus and much of the onlooking world (the Bust is of course a major Media Event.) Martyrdom wins hundreds of converts to the radicals' faith: "They were right: this *is* a brutal fascistic police-state." "No more straddling fences; indifference means collusion. We must fight the system." A general strike is called, with vast support from this newly enlarged community of the faithful plus thousands of erstwhile neutrals who have by now been "radicalized." If it is late in the old ritual calendar (April or May), the whole institution may be in effect shut down for the rest of the year.

8) *Interlude:* Later, moderates, not radicals, undertake "reforms" of the university. It is a slow, tortuous and unexciting process. Outcomes of complex compromises and conciliations, the reforms are undramatic and not far-reaching. The radicals cast about for new "issues" to start the ritual cycle over again. The calendar works against renewal. Students disperse. Participants find it hard to revive the exaltation of the occupation itself. The world is grey again. Rituals of renewal are needed. The emergent elect of the movement hope to provide them, and try. Some of the innovations made during a particular enactment, become incorporated into later enactments—"what we learned from Berkeley (or Columbia, etc.)"—and conversely other actors in the drama, specifically administration in the villain role, learn not to repeat tactical disasters. For example, they learn to *avoid* bringing in the cops. Case in point: in 1969, a year after the Columbia turmoil, the University of Chicago administrators, quietly waited out the protesters , thus depriving the "heroes" of the moral victory of a kind of martyrdom at the hands of raiding police.

Associated Mythology

Viewed in the context of a religious system, the foregoing depicts the basic outlines of a several-times-repeated *ritual drama.* Ritual is accompanied by an associated set of *myths* or a *mythology.* Social scientists, mostly anthropologists, have disputed endlessly about which has priority, myth or ritual. Does ritual develop to express the mythology, or does ritual precede, and mythology follow, to explain or rationalize the ritual? Or do they interact in complex ways? I avoid that whole controversy here, as beyond my present scope. Suffice it to say there is an "associated mythology."

The mythology comes in the guise of secular socio-political thought, with multitudinous roots in earlier social-political theory and praxis.

Constituent elements of both the ritual and the mythology have complex antecedents in the sociocultural history of the West, However, to the participants in this movement, they have the quality of something new bursting upon the world. A similar lack of historical perspective we noted in the contemporaneous phenomenon of hippies and their communes. But here considering the higher educational level of the student rebels, and their supposed immersion in a world of rational pursuit of truth, one might have expected more historical awareness. In vain. Evidently the common denominator is simply *youth.* If they typically believe they have invented sex, why not also radicalism?

The basic elements of the mythology of this movement run roughly as follows:

Man is by nature good, with an inherent potential for beneficence, communality, and cooperation with his fellow man. Alas, however, he has become malformed and alienated by a corrupt society over which certain evil forces hold tenacious sway. These forces do so by brute power (through porcine agents, and an array of powerful magical, destructive devices) and through intricate manipulation. The rulers of this society are vastly rich and determined to maintain their wealth and power. They enslave the powerless, and manipulatively co-opt their lackeys by providing them with a modest level of comfort and the illusion of prestige. By terror and military might they exert an imperialistic control over the poorer peoples of the world, both inside and outside their borders, and they ruthlessly suppress any efforts of the powerless to rise up and liberate themselves.

Within, the powerless are kept in a state of perpetual misery, as an ever-ready resource for the senseless production machine, and for the armies sent to fight overseas wars of suppression. The less destitute are kept enslaved by manipulation, tranquilized by useless gadgets, contrivances, and entertainments, routinized into mindless bureaucratic discipline, and brainwashed into illusions of freedom. The rulers keep their monopoly of power by their control over the military, the technological instruments of destruction (instant Doomsday at their fingertips) and over the ostensible, supposedly popularly elected "government" of the country.

Most important, the rulers control the priests of the society, the putative wise men inhabiting comfortable retreats called universities. These priests, deceiving people into believing they are defenders of freedom and independent spirit, are in fact agents of the same evil ruling powers. These priests provide their crafts for the techno-magics of the rulers to brainwash the innocent with their theological justifications of the existing order. They train the cadres of future technicians and lackeys of the ruling powers, while they ruthlessly suppress any of their junior confreres who support real freedom for the young. The monastic or priestly order should be free, as it claims to be. It should be the vanguard of liberation. Among the masses of trainees under its tutelege are to be found eccentrics and malcontents who see through (or can learn to see through) the lies of the system—young people—who by some circumstance have not been thoroughly brainwashed. They, along with their allies from the younger priests and mandarins, must and can bring together the masses of potential allies, drawn, inevitably, primarily from among the young. For only the young have not as yet throughly sold out to the ruling powers, and in them beats loudest the throb of man's innate potential for good and for liberation. The monasteries ("universities")—microcosms of the whole society—must and will be the vanguard of the liberation, which will begin with the overthrow of the corrupt power structure within the monasteries themselves and then spread to the entire society. The day of liberation is at hand![4]

Significance of the Mythology

It is evident that this mythology can work to counter the malaise of the concerned and activist students. It provides a measure of certainty and meaningfulness to a world that otherwise abounds in confusions and contradictions. It does so in an acceptable, manifestly secular form, without reference to discredited or decayed transcendental allusions. It appeals to idealism, rather than to crass material self-interest. At the same time it promises egoistic gratifications in the notion of student power, meaning radical student power. It provides a sweeping "understanding" of the past and the agonizing present, and promises a redemptive future. It counters the shapelessness of the late-adolescent and student roles by elevating youth, (and specifically this kind of youth) to a central and redemptive role as the vanguard of a new, liberated society. It also presents an extreme simplification of the *dramatis personae* of the world into sharply etched heroes, villains and fools (dupes) focusing the intense moralism of late adolescence and youth.

The mythology crystallizes a version of the third kind of "subterranean tradition of youth" (Matza 1961; see previous chapter). The main elements are apocalyptic vision, populism, activist evangelism, and the transformation of the mundane into the extraordinary by unconventional politics. Apocalyptic vision suffuses the whole radical movement: not simply minor or piecemeal change or reform, but a total transformation of the world, in this case, civil society, is what is sought.

This becomes the extreme and violent stream of the student rebellions of the 1960s, leaving behind the masses of moderate supporters and moving into terroristic violence, on the assumption that nothing less will produce the "root-and-source" change needed. Hence not just radicalism, but revolutionary change. (See later discussion of the "apocalyptic" as one of the main personality types.) This kind of vision appeals to the romanticism of youth. It also enables a uniting of dedicated idealism and cold cynicism. We are cynical toward present holders of power and will not be deceived by them. We are idealistic about the future we will create. (Matza, drawing on K. Davis on parent-youth conflict 1940, notes this combination of idealism and cynicism as characteristic of youth.)

Populism is another major feature of radicalism. It is abundantly evident in New Left mythology. Though the self-appointed leaders of this "revolution" are students, in effect middle class people and intellectuals (of a sort) to boot, the mainstay of the revolt are supposed to be "the people," particularly the downtrodden, the poor and oppressed. This became rather strained in actual New Left practice, where, e.g. "downtrodden" blacks were rather less than beguiled about the prospect of being led to "freedom, etc." by this group of posturing, self-satisfied spoiled-brat white youths from wealthy families and attending elite colleges.

Activist evangelism was of course a central feature. The student leaders were out to convert as large a following as possible to their cause, and in huge demonstrations like building-occupations, had a field day of proselytizing for their cause. Evangelism presupposes absolute conviction of the moral righteousness of your cause, and this the radical student leaders certainly conveyed with more than a modicum of success during the high-enthusiasm stages of the ritual.

Unconventional politics was certainly a feature, and a major part of the appeal. Doing things out of the ordinary is good, outrageous if necessary. Outrageous would be all the better in fact, as long as not extreme enough to bring down the most violent sanctions. Then you get the *frisson* of danger and excitement, the opposite of tedious routine. In the Confrontation stage of the ritual drama, students have room to invent all kinds of new forms of unconventionality (e.g. sexually desegregating the toilets in university buildings).

Psychological Functions of the Ritual

There are three main elements here: the sacralization of aggression;

the significance of sacred-taboo language; and the emergence of communality.

Sacralization of Aggression

To the student "heroes" of the drama, a major function, and hence appeal, of the ritual of revolt, is to provide acceptable avenues of release for aggression derived from the varied frustrations and deprivations that contribute to the generalized malaise. With nondeliberate ingenuity, the ritual releases this aggression in such a way as to give it sanctity and righteousness. With the intense moralism of the righteous cause, the student heroes become immune to any sense of moral dilemma about their contribution to the violent denouement of the drama. The whole struggle is portrayed in terms of blackest Evil and whitest Purity, in the familiar Manichean pattern of religious fanaticism. Clearly moral dilemmas are involved in the decision facing the administration, of whether or when to call in the police, and in any attempt to assign relative weights of moral responsibility between student provocateurs and administrative decision makers. For the student participants and especially their leaders, no such dilemmas are even recognized. The extreme position is: we are right; therefore calling the police is entirely their responsibility. The resulting actual horrors and brutalities of the police bust "confirm" this view, because it is "they" and not "we" who are manifestly guilty of violence.

New Left mythology until late 1969 insisted on the nonviolent purity of its student heroes. (Later one faction of SDS renounced that view, and escalated *student* violence.) In that context, and until that time, aggression had to be expressed in other than overtly violent ways. When expressed in response to violence from other students, it could be excused on the basis of "unavoidable provocation" by others, but still treated with some ambiguity, neither condemned nor approved. Thus it maintains the myth of New Left nonviolence. Verbal aggression, however, abounds. This is not considered as "violence" by the rebel heroes. Nor is the major coercive use of force, which is the central action of the rebels. That consists of seizure of buildings, hostages, files, or the calculatedly outrageous stances toward the authorities. This kind of aggression is moralized and sacralized by a rationale deriving from the mythology. This is the "only way to force the oppressors to change things, since all standard channels for dissent have proved to be fruitless." Or, the occupation of buildings is not wrong, because "the campus belongs to the students in the first place—this is *our* university."

Still, a major direction of the students' aggression is against themselves, through the indirect method of maneuvering the authorities into "having no choice" but to call in the police. Here we find a parallel to the method of directing aggression against oneself through the agency of outside forces, found in such phenomena as the Mohave Indian "witch" who in effect, commits suicide by progressively provoking his fellow-tribemen to kill him (Devereux 1961). In the student rebellion case, it may rarely go to the point of getting students killed (it finally did at Kent State and Jackson State in 1970), but the dynamics are similar, and no doubt the more extreme "radicals" welcome such martyrs.

The provocation of police brutality is a deliberate conscious tactic (and in that sense rational-instrumental) on the part of the more dedicated true believers among radical leaders. "We'll force them to reveal their fascistic brutality and oppressiveness." This does not preclude, even for these leaders, that provocation has nonrational unconscious roots as well. For the followers, the provocation of the police is rarely a deliberate conscious tactic, but appears as a regrettable consequence of the choices the antagonists make. Here to be provocative probably feeds unconscious masochistic needs. How do we know? One may look at the emotional intensity concentrated on the anticipation of the "bust." Psychodynamically, the bust appears as the high point, the climax toward which the whole ritual drama is directed. If it were not, the more moderate elements among the building-occupiers would be better able to counteract the apocalyptic direction in which the intransigence of the "leadership" is clearly pointed. Instead, basically, the followers passively accept that direction. One may therefore presume that it meets some unconscious needs. In turn, the fulfillment of what must be basically a masochistic fantasy, by the actual brutality of the police, releases the verbal aggression of outraged invective, and intensified moral righteousness in the ritual participants, now cast as innocent victims. The mythology is vindicated: "we have felt that brutality of the 'system' on our own heads and bodies."

Collective excitement of mass activity enables the individuals here to carry out activities of provocative, aggressive and outrageous content and style that most would find themselves incapable of doing as separate individuals. But it is not only the collective sanction but the *moralizing* and *sacralizing* of these aggression releases that make them possible. That the means employed are coercive and infringe upon the rights of others with an equal claim as "members of the university community" is brushed aside in the waves of moral righteousness and indignation at the opposition.

The ritual thus provides a focus and a complex channeling of aggression, and a moral and sacred mystique for its expression.

Sacred-Taboo Language

The language of ritual is stylized, dramatically hyperbolic, arcane, full of sacred-taboo words and expressions. This is also true of the language of confrontation ritual, which is also replete with the sacred-taboo, in the form of what conventional society calls obscenities. "Bullshit!" "Motherfucker!" become sacramental invocations, which depend for their effect not so much on denotative meaning, as on their conotative and contextual aura. In the Comfrontation, the use of these words becomes a defiant badge of rebellion, used for shock effect on the older generation, and especially the genteel academics. Much of this speech is clearly aggressive in intent. (Cf. Mark Rudd's speech to the Columbia faculty—see Avorn *et al.* 1969, p.140.)

Although at the manifest level, the obscenities are used connotatively and metaphorically, one can look at their denotations to find the latent content of the ritual of confrontation. "Motherfucker" points to the obsession with the oedipal situation. And "faggots, cocksuckers and asslickers," e.g. shouted at the police, reflect the struggle with the demons of failed masculinity. In effect, the rebels are saying, not we, but they (cops, administrators, the enemy) are guilty of oedipal and homosexual crimes. The ritualized chanting of these obscene epithets at the police is precisely the kind of provocation—much more than any physical resistance—that drives the police to irrational fury, vented as brutality upon the rebels. "Sticks and stones can break our bones, but names can never hurt us," runs the children's rhyme, but deep down the rebels know this is false. Raised in families valuing verbal facility and the substitution of words for physical violence, they intuitively know the magical emotive power of language, and are here using it to the hilt, not all consciously, of course. The projection of oedipal and homosexual guilt upon the enemy—especially the cops—suggests some of the deeper resonances of the rebellion. (See Endleman 1970b, for further development.)

The Development of Community

A major function of ritual is to create bonds of communal solidarity by collectively shared symbolic action. This is clearly evident in the campus rebellion. Communal experience of ordeal marks the experience as consensual ritual and provides the setting for cognitively structuring the whole event along the "correct" rhetorical lines, i.e. in terms of the mythology. The communal element is salient enough to be consciously recognized as the high point of the whole experience by great numbers of the participants. Avorn and his (Columbia University newspaper) *Spectator* associates devote a whole chapter to the emergent life-style of the "communes" within the "liberated" buildings of Columbia, entitling it (without evidence of intended irony) "The Liberated Life." (Avorn *et al.* 1969, chapter 6):

> Personal liberation . . . here was founded on a common existential credential—all risked . . . by joining the protest; a common tactic—confrontation; a common enemy—the administration; and a common set of immediate goals . . . [students were] united by participatory democracy . . . Students were eager to create their own life-designs . . . Communal cohesiveness in the student-controlled buildings began [early in the events]. (Avorn, pp. 117, 118, 119)

Here communal solidarity developed out of collective violation of taboo; note also the special élan of the students in appropriating the university president's office (heretofore off-limits), invading his personal files, rationalized as a political act to uncover evidence of "secret collusive deals" with other "branches of the power structure," but here clearly suggesting tabooed oedipal voyeurism.

The life-style developed in the occupied buildings was a mixture of carnival spirit, busy coommittees, marathon ideological and tactical bull-sessions, and expressive and sexual liberation. Sexual segregation of toilets was abolished and privacy almost totally abandoned. Restrictions and compartmentalizations of ordinary middle class life were joyously overthrown. Many of the students were convinced that *this* was "the revolution."[5]

Specifically ritual elements were recognized by the student-journalists documenting the Columbia events (Avorn *et al.* 1969, pp. 129–130) including guerrilla-theater victimizing the university president, and much theatrical spontaneous ritual. The rituals of the student rebellion worked to develop or intensify solidarity among the student rebels. Running its full course, it could include as many as half the students of a campus, into a great (but momentary) wave of generational solidarity. Erstwhile moderates were "radicalized", fence-sitters moved to the left (at least somewhat). All of these shifts were temporary, it is true, but were felt as though a permanent "liberation" change by the participants. Not to at least sympathize with and identify with one's age-peers who have been subjected to such brutal oppression comes to be felt as a kind of generational treachery. Thus for the moment at least, the ritual functions to promote horizontal integration among large numbers of previously fragmented or isolated individuals or groups. This reduced the "alienation" of privatized and encapsulated lives, while at the same time increasing collective "alienation" from legitimate authorities and structures.

It may at the same time momentarily promote some degree of vertical integration, i.e. integration between the generations, to the extent that the bust brings portions of the faculty into sympathy with the rebels, or promotes guilt-laden efforts on their part to be more responsive to the students' needs and demands in the future. However, any resulting alliances between (part of) the faculty and the rebel students against the common enemy, the discredited administration, are likely to be fragile because of discrepancies of "commitment" to the ongoing university, and of generational perspective. The position of the faculty is particularly difficult and perplexing in these events, and merits detailed examination. See Endleman 1970b, Chapter XIII, "The Agony of the Faculty." Rather the major integrative force exerted is horizontal, i.e. *intra*-generational.

There are built-in difficulties, however, for this kind of ritual development as an emergent device for dealing with the manifold "religious" needs of the young. The drama is excessively dependent upon progressive escalation of the level of conflict in successive enactments. Such escalation then runs the risk of losing a portion of the converts as its irrationalist penchant toward violence by the students themselves and the suicidal potential of provoking armed agents of authority become increasingly manifest. The continuity of the ritual is also threatened by the transiency of any specific cohort of student participants: many of this year's "leaders" graduate, drop out, or are expelled: then what?

Relation of the Ritual to the Underlying Malaise

The psychological grounding of any religious movement is a commonly experienced *malaise* [6] among large numbers of similarly situated individuals, in this case university students in modern Western industrialized nations. The ritual of student rebellion described here expresses and partially (but only momentarily) answers much of the malaise of its student protagonists.

In place of the shapelessness or negative quality of the student status, the ritual places the students in a central and apparently decisive position in the ambiguous cultural complex known as the university.

It works a symbolic status transformation of the students involved, providing them not with "instant adulthood" but with the illusion of instant power and centrality on a national, even international stage. In this respect, as in the importance of shared ordeal as a condition for the communality, it shows some analogies to initiation ceremonies, especially those for males, found in tribal societies.[7]

Against the limbo state of delay and the apparently indefinitely prolonged "preparation for real life," the ritual of rebellion dramatically asserts the primacy of NOW! Against the passivity of the imbiber of learning, it provides ACTION that is designed to have an actual impact on the conditions of one's life, and of the surrounding world. Against the split of intellectuality from "actual participation in the real life of the world," it asserts a fusion of "theory" and "praxis" in the way the ritual enacts and provokes a confirmation of the mythology. Against isolation and interpersonal fragmentation, the ritual provides a highly emotionalized communality of sacralized taboo-violation, collective danger, and moralized collective aggression against a visible and identifiable enemy. For many a participant, for the first time in his life, he feels really alive. The ritual also provides a sacralized release for a variety of rages and discontents and achieves all these results in the guise of a rational secular action that gives the illusion of doing something concrete to combat the injustices and oppressions of the world.

It is an essential condition of this ritual that it be the creation of the young themselves. The same conditions that foster the development of a broader complex of youth culture, with assured subsistence and comfort, ample leisure, and freedom from "adult responsibilities," also facilitate the development, by a portion of these youths, of their rituals and ceremonials. Old faiths and practices decayed and the older generation discredited for "the mess they have made of the world" or "their failure to effectuate the ideals they profess," the young feel they must take things into their own hands. What could be more fitting for the sophisticated children of the television age than to stage their rituals as exciting morality drama before an audience of millions? Their skill in utilizing the mass media is undeniable; at last they are being *taken seriously,* not only coercing the older-generation antagonists into playing roles assigned to them by the young, but compelling the attention of a vast audience "out there in the real world."

Still, as enactment of fantasy, this is ritual. The "revolution" brought into being in the "communes" of "liberated" buildings is an illusion. The mythological "oppression" of students must be provoked into reality by the ritual of rebellion itself. The moral absolutism of the central protagonists obfuscates the complex realities of the actual world in which they live. The "power" attained by the rebels during the ritual revolt—a huge university ground to a halt—proves to be temporary and illusory. The objective impact on the larger "power structure" of the society is either negligible or is in a direction opposite to the announced intentions of the rebel leaders. Thus a frenzied need is generated to renew the ritual in intensified and escalated forms.

The secular guise and the lack of clear transcendental reference points vitiate the beliefs and practices as mythology and ritual. At the same time the irrationalist and illusionary elements vitiate the instrumental politics that the rebellion pretends to be.

Demise of the Student Rebellions

The whole process had a momentum of its own, but one with built-in limits on how far it can be escalated from one campus event to the next. The leadership of the rebels faced the dilemma of further escalation inviting repression, or moving in a more moderate, more compromising direction. In the latter they would allow themselves to be co-opted into the "establishment," as did those who worked with administrations for "reform" of the universities. The more extreme radicals had by this point (end of 1969) abandoned even the facade of nonviolence that had been a hallmark of their political mythology. In some cases, they also abandoned the facade that the universities were the locale for starting the revolution. "We're not out to reform the university, but to close it down," had been an understood agenda for some of the inner circle elite. It now become more manifest, and for some, the logical conclusion was to abandon the universities as scenes for radical revolt, and move violently into terrorism directly at the targets in the military-industrial-governmental complex. Hence Weathermen, and other offshoots, that persisted well on into the 1980s, as minute terroristic cells, already well divorced from university issues. These had of course become overtly Leninist, in their dedication to constitute themselves a vanguard elite, with contempt for their erstwhile comrades at the college barricades, and willingness to devote themselves totally to the "cause", even to the point of sacrifice of life.

By 1970, we saw the confrontation at Kent State, where *white* student protesters were killed for the first time. (Blacks had been killed at the partially separate black student uprisings before that point, but those events were not at the center of attention). The protesters now discovered that real martyrdom did *not* result in a predicted general nationwide student uprising, but rather in the whole student revolt movement essentially subsiding and soon disappearing.

Various pragmatic political causes were attributed for that demise—the economic recession, the winding down of the Vietnam War (an ostensible issue in the uprisings), a changing "climate." These all sound in retrospect very much like other *ad hoc* explanations presented, contemporaneously, by public commentators both for the rise and the later decline of each such movement. Each interpretation was plausible but not very convincing.

Viewed as a *ritual,* i.e. a religious event, rather than as a political one, the student revolts, and their decline, can be understood as groping efforts of the participants toward some kind of ritual revival, and its failure: it was an *aborted* ritual. As rites of intensification, they exhausted their potential. They depended too heavily on novelty, which cannot be sustained for long, on the illusion of spontaneity (which too has its limits) and the inherent dynamic of escalation, to be able to persist for long.

They were further vitiated as ritual by the secular guise of their associated mythologies, which, however momentarily attractive as reassuring articles of faith, nevertheless invite debunking and de-mystification. This would be done especially by bright and somewhat educated participants much of whose education has been devoted to learning skeptically to tear apart presented doctrines. The illusions of communal brotherhood in the "communes" of the collective building-occupants, cannot be sustained beyond the time of collectively-shared crisis-ecstasy. Afterward, rather than being magically transformed, the world is grey again.

Where many of the male participants experienced the confrontation at the time as a kind of ceremonial initiation into manhood, they then emerged into a world that gave no consensual validation to any such transformation. Thus the campus revolt failed as a puberty rite. It was also impossible for these rites of intensification to be converted into rites of order, again because of the necessity in them for the appearance of spontaneity and their heavy reliance on momentary collective ecstasy.

As political events they also lost their viability, when the New Left became aware of the dilemmas facing them as campus organizations, the dangers of both repression and co-optation, hence of the usefulness of tactical dramas like a campus revolt. Police brutality might momentarily "radicalize" some previously fence-sitting students, but many more of the less-than-radically-committed were scared away. That left the "movement" in the hands of increasingly desperate "inner-core" people of distinctly apocalyptic persuasion, who in turn alienated moderate supporters, with the vehemence of their invective and by now openly embraced violence.

Student Activist Personality Types

Portrayals of the student radicals of the 1960s in the professional literature of sociologists, psychologists and psychoanalysts, tended to be split into those largely admiring of the personality qualities of the rebels, and those largely skeptical of their "admirable" qualities, or hostile to what the observer saw as the authoritarian, even totalitarian trend of these protesters. The vast majority of those portrayed contemporaneously with the events, were in the first category. They included the then famous accounts by Keniston (1968), Flacks (1967), most of Liebert (1971). In the second category were the works of Feuer (1969), and Endleman (1970a, 1970b). (Liebert on "nihilists" recognizes "negative" elements.) It is evident in retrospect that what was seen and how it was analyzed, depended heavily on the political biases of the observer, those in the first category much closer to the positions of the New Left, and in the second, critical of them. It is also evident now in retrospect, that parts of each portrayal probably did fit *some* of the participants in the student rebellions, and that there were distinct types. These types were different, not only in how they reacted and performed in the student rebellion, but also in underlying personality dynamics.

There was no single student dissenter personality type. At the extreme we can say there were as many different personalities involved as students participating. But a few of these emerge as the most important, and as long as we recognize we are dealing with *types,* not specific actual personalities, we can delineate a few main categories.

For purposes of simplification we indicate three main types, quite distinct from one another:

1) the Apocalyptic Nihilist
2) the Proto-Commissar, and
3) the Humanistic Worker.

The Apocalyptic Nihilist

These are the extreme personality types depicted by Hendin as "the revolutionaries" (distinct from merely "radical") and by Liebert as the "nihilists" (Hendin 1971, 1975, Liebert 1971). They are also those at the center at the most destructive suicidal stage of the rebellion, in Feuer's (1969) portrayal. These were the most extreme, and the most likely to escalate the struggle into violent all-out attacks on "the system." With the demise of the campus rebellions, these die-hards gravitated to the more extreme off-campus movements moving toward terrorism, e.g. Weathermen, the terroristic offshoot of the once merely "radical" SDS. These are the types more given to irrational and nonrational extremes.

The Apocalyptic is a man (or woman) by demons possessed. The dynamics are likely to be somewhat different in the males than the females, and they are more studied and described. I shall deal with the males first. For the Apocalyptic the "Revolution" fills his whole being. He has a consuming drive to spectacular heroic action of catastrophic proportions; he is headed toward the Apocalypse of the final revolutionary confrontation. His whole life is stripped of irrelevancies or distractions. Women, enthralled by the violence they see in him, come unbidden to his bed. He uses them as objects and despises their motivation. Otherwise he has no feeling for them. Consumed with ideals for the good of "all humanity," he has no empathy, no human warmth, for particular human beings. They are to be manipulated for The Cause, in which he has absolute conviction. Underneath that hard surface, he is lonely and terrified of deep commitment to any particular human being. His demands upon the Enemy, and also upon comrades in the struggle, are totalistic and uncompromising.

He is enraged by any hint of "deals" or "negotiated settlements," that his weaker comrades might try, or seem, to make with the Enemy.

Nothing short of complete capitulation will be acceptable. Refusing that, the Enemy will unleash violence, and the Revolution is advanced. Of course there will be bloodshed. Terrorism will be the necessary next stage. Earlier the universities had some relevance in this struggle. By the early 1970s, they have become irrelevant, and the Revolution moves into the streets and into society at large. Bloodshed will be a necessity. The Revolutionary must be prepared at all times to sacrifice anything for the Cause, including one's life. One expects that many of one's comrades will be killed, perhaps even oneself. The Apocalyptic's visions are full of blood, violence, death. Intense emotional connectedness is experienced only in relation to such apocalyptic fantasies, or anything coming close to their realization, e.g. a particularly violent police bust of a campus building occupation.

In terms of social categories, the Apocalyptic accepts unquestioningly his being part of a vanguard elite (necessary to make the Revolution) but accepts too the strategic value of a pretense of egalitarianism in the Movement as a device for bringing in supporting troops from the masses of the student body. He concentrates on the Struggle itself. He pays little—if any—attention to drawing blueprints for the future better society (that is, presumably, to be brought about by the overthrow of the existing one). He has a feeling he will not live to see that day. A future that could be a real world with a working social organization and culture is in fact, at deep levels, not conceivable to him. His image of his own destruction in the apocalyptic final struggle is something that could well be a self-fulfilling prophecy. His own self-destructive drives could well bring this about, if the "reactionaries" do not do it for him.

The demons by which this revolutionary is consumed are his own unconscious rage, or the unconscious underpinnings of what is now a conscious rage, i.e. a rage at the emotional abandonment he has experienced by parents who have never actually emotionally responded to him as a real human being.

Liebert (1971, p. 170) describes the students at the hypothetical "nihilistic" pole of possible campus activist personality types, as "offering no programs for constructive change. He focuses his planning on violence and disruption as ends in themselves, and as sources of pleasure if achieved. He uses people as pawns in political struggle, obsessed with the problems of politics . . . to the exclusion of other relationships, interests and pleasures; and totally masking dreams of what might be with rage at what is, and denying anything positive [in surrounding reality] to maintain an essentially paranoid view."

Typically students of this kind have family backgrounds which fit neither of the two widely held notions about the radicals. In one of these, the radicals were the spoiled kids of affluent parents who were overpermissive and never required the child to develop self-control or self-discipline. The Apocalyptics do not fit. In the other, they were the rational libertarian children of rational libertarian and warmly humanistic parents. They do not fit that one either.

Studies such as Hendin's of these "revolutionaries" (1971) indicates that typically the parents were materially providing but emotionally extremely unresponsive to the child. Meanwhile they maintained the facade of pleasant cooperative family life and an illusionary conception of the child in question which bore little relationship to what the child was actually like, and particularly, made no connection with the child's emotional needs. Materially sated, they were emotionally starved, and developed defenses of non-involvement or of brittle irony against this devastating experience of abandonment. That feeling could never be acknowledged since the reality of its having happened was never recognized, let alone confronted, by the parents themselves. These were not really "permissive" parents. They were negligent and essentially uncaring. Neglect is rationalized as "letting the child go his own way." As a result, showing feelings at all, or even being able to get closely in touch with them, becomes extremely taboo. One such student said, "If you show your feelings, you get your legs cut off" (Hendin 1971, p. 24).

In many cases, in the families in which these students grew up, political discussions were the nearest thing to a personal exchange that took place within the family. Hendin sees this as connected with these students' use of politics to express feelings that are personal (p. 20).

Liebert found a similar trend in students who were more "nihilistic."

Outside authorities—more broadly, "the system"—become the displaced targets of that inner rage aroused by the parents' emotional nonexistence. By early adulthood, and caught up fortuitously in the "right historical moment" of the student rebellions, the student can then declare his specific parents "irrelevant," a fitting revenge for their having treated him as irrelevant up to that time.

Participation in a political action that the actors can declare as not only meaningful but fateful for the whole society gives the Apocalyptic's life a focus, and, for once, a crux of emotional meaning. He also acquires a pseudo-*Gemeinschaft* of the comrades in the struggle—though he has some inkling of how shallow that "community" is likely to be, as the Movement constantly generates factional battles and "heresies" in its ever-more-paranoid enactment of persecutory and avengimg fantasy.

In the process, more reasonable, more rational, less hatred-consumed, more politically moderate erstwhile supporters (more like the Humanistic Worker type) find themselves ever more dissatisfied and repelled by the increasingly evident violence, totalitarianism and self-destructiveness of the Apocalyptic and depart from the struggle to rechannel their political protest into more reformist measures essentially "within the system." The latter have thus cast themselves, in the revolutionaries' eyes, as having "sold out" and become part of the Enemy.

This is the stage at which, as discussed earlier, the Movement faced the twin dangers of repression and co-optation. Why did the Movement at that point become so dominated by the Revolutionaries (largely Apocalyptic types, with some Proto-Commissars)? Essentially because these, in contrast to the more humanistic types, were more single-mindedly determined, had a greater stake in extreme confrontation and polarization, were more cynical and manipulative toward the comrades (whom they really regarded as dupes in any case) and more attuned to using preemptive methods to maintain their own power, within the Movement. The departure of the more moderate, of the psychologically more flexible and healthier, left the movement in the hands of these most extreme types. Their penchant for violence and suicidalism in turn alienated still more potential supporters, ensuring that the struggle as campus struggle, would go into demise, and that the more dedicated activists would shift to off-campus terrorism.

As co-optation takes off more of the moderates, the leadership becomes ever more desperate, and falls more into the hands of the Apocalyptics. As the campus rebellions subside, for all of the various reasons we have discussed, these Apocalyptics move into terroristic activity, in which surviving members are still to be found into the 1980s, in various terrorist groups of many different ideological hues.

The Apocalyptic could of course be a she. Some of the most ferocious of the student revolutionaries have been women, as have been many of the more recent terrorists. The dynamics of the women student revolutionaries whom Hendin studied (1971, 1975) have shown a similar family situation as the male counterparts, with materially supportive but emotionally uncaring parents, leaving the child with massive unrecognized and unexpressed rage, now displaced onto the outside political world. Perhaps women gravitating into the extremes of this movement are even more ferocious and violence-prone than the men, on the model of the overconforming marginal person needing more desperately to prove her purity, (Some of these later, reacting against the male chauvinism of the radicals—"hey, we need a chick to type this up"—turned to radical versions of the feminist movement.) One side-comment: many of the young men on the barricades were intimidated into acts of greater courage than they might have otherwise—"some ferocious chick turned up and made us all feel we had no balls."

The Proto-Commissar

The second type is the *Proto-Commissar.* His guiding drive is Power. His *modus vivendi* is the concentrated direction of his high intelligence and drive upon the strategies and tactics of the revolutionary task. Consciously, for him, the fomenting and direction of campus disruption is an instrumental strategy in the radicalization of potential troops. The "bust" is a necessary instrument in this cause. There must be no negotiated settlement, for that would slow down and subvert the process of polarization and radicalization. The manifest issues and demands of the campus confrontation are necessary pretexts. Their being met is no goal, except as such momentary victory demonstrates the impotence of the authorities and the power of the radical movement as a step toward the next stage. Strategically, it may be necessary to destroy the universities rather than to get concessions from them, depending on instrumental calculations of comparative short-range and long-range gains and losses. There is ostensibly rational controversy within the Movement on these points. Some see winning on current issues as counterproductive—it involves too much risk of co-optation of wavering radicals into cooperation with the university establishment. Others see it as increasing the opportunities of boring from within.

Essentially, the Proto-Commissar is driven to destroy the power of the existing authorities, so that the Movement, with himself in a crucial role, will take over that power, in the Liberation brought by the Revolution. He and the small group of cohorts around him will direct the new society. His parricidal rage against all authorities is aimed at supplanting them in power. A facade of democracy will be necessary to bring the masses to the correct side, but the masses must be taught what is good for them. That, of course, is part of the task of the vanguard elite. He has seen enough of the vapidity, unreliability and sentimentality of student followers to know that neither they nor the broad masses are capable of *directing* the making of the Revolution (though they may be necessary to carry it out.) No more are they capable of running the future liberated society. They have neither the intelligence nor the single-mindedness of purpose and dedication. That is to be found only in the vanguard elite. Only they are capable of the sacrifice, devotion and discipline needed for the struggle, which will be long and bloody. Unlike the Apocalyptic, he does not especially relish the bloodiness, and will therefore not consciously throw himself into needless dangerous heroics. He regards his comrades, such as the Apocalyptic types, who do so, as dangerous, not alone to themselves, but also to the Movement. That could be needlessly set back by terroristic adventurism. Terrorism is acceptable, however, if rationally strategic for a given short-run or long-run political goal. People who have moral constraints against using it where practically necessary, he regards as sentimental, a prime defect of the bourgeoisie.

This apparently rational machiavellianism is, however, not without its irrational adjuncts. One of these is the cultivation of paranoid suspiciousness. All who are not allies are automatically enemiess—at least potentially. They must therefore be watched closely, especially all comrades in the struggle. Infiltration by enemy spies and agents of all kinds—from the police, the FBI, the CIA, university authorities, competing self-styled radical groups, ostensibly friendly faculty—is an ever-present danger of reality. As organization gets tighter in the escalation of the revolutionary struggles, this wariness becomes ever more necessary, and increases accordingly. Ultimately, there is no one he can thoroughly trust. The slightest trace of doctrinal impurity in any of his comrades must be carefully observed and scrutinized. On the campus everyone he comes in contact with must be appraised for probable loyalties both now and in the next stage of revolutionary ferment, especially all left-liberal or seemingly radical faculty. All clear-cut enemies must be noted and marked for appropriate retribution "after the revolution." All those having ambiguous loyalties must be scrutinized to determine their future fate in the new order.

In this setting, it is hard to determine where realistic appraisals end and paranoid fantasy takes over. The whole atmosphere of suspicion conduces to self-fulfilling prophecies. His own aggressive drives are discovered by projection in anyone and everyone in the world around him. That this *discovery* often corresponds some objectively verifiable reality in the world outside, does not negate the fact of intrapsychic origins of the need to make such "discoveries." His parricidal rage finds the reciprocation (and justification) in the hostilities the authorities direct against him and his comrades. These in turn are gratifying, for they confirm his intellectual picture of the world and also validate his importance as a danger to the established order. He also harbors, below consciousness, a heavy reservoir of guilt. This is shown in the combination of expectation of harsh punishment from the authorities and the obsessive repetitive assertion of his own moral purity. (If he were so convinced of this purity, why the necessity to reassert it constantly?) The whole process of purification of himself (by concentrated dedication to the Cause, to the exclusion of all other interests) and of the whole revolutionary vanguard, is also probably testimony to the underlying guilt.

Paranoid suspiciousness is also connected, in the males, with underlying anxieties about the adequacy of their own masculinity. The oedipal picture in the background here, as attested by many psychosocial familial studies of the student radicals (Keniston, Flacks and others) does not show a classical authoritarian father against whom the sons rebel in the mythical Totem and Taboo manner. Rather more likely, the father has been (perceived as) a relatively ineffectual figure, whose major sin has been failure to buffer between the son and the competent and sometimes overwhelming mother. She might not have been quite the CBI mother of the childhood of many male homosexuals (see Bieber 1962, discussed in Chapter 3) but she has tendencies in that direction, mitigated by the greater likelihood of career work in the labor force. The effect is of parents fairly egalitarian in relation to each other, and particularly a lack of patriarchal power in the father. While this situation produces something of the modern "enlightened" family supposedly fostering the child's independence, it also leaves the son without either a clear-cut powerful father against whom to rebel, and also measure himself, but also lack of any clear-cut model of masculine identification. In 1970a I argued as an "oedipal element" in student rebellions, a need felt by males to *construct* powerful, hostile, even sometimes violent authorities for their adversaries—if necessary bringing them into being by the students' own provocations—as an emotionally necessary process of testing their own manhood, and denying their own anxieties about their weakness on this score. That the sacred-taboo language of obscenity prominent in the 1960s campus revolts included, quite significantly, reference to homosexual acts, suggest the effort to exorcise, magically, those demons of failed masculinity. Also significantly, this reflected throwing back on the enemy, the cops, precisely those outrageous insults of homosexual attribution that the police made against the male students. (The relationship between paranoia and unconscious homosexual feelings was long ago presented by Freud in the Schreber case—see Freud 1911—and though needing later qualification, is still a staple of psychoanalytic interpretation.)

The sectarian fractionating that develops as the Movement intensifies indicates the casting off of negative fragments of the self. The bitterest hatreds are directed at ideological factions closest to one's own, that have split off over a minute doctrinal point. The narcissism of small differences comes into play here. The "impure" faction epitomizes hated, split off, unrecognized parts of oneself. (Parallels abound in overtly religious sects.) At this point the movement consumes itself in fratricidal wars, as though in repentance over the (fantasied) killing of the father. The struggles within the New Left by the end of the 1960s showed this process. (See the collection of documents from the SDS of that period, in Wallerstein and Starr 1971.) Thus part of Feuer's (1969) picture of irrational destructiveness seems to fit this type of radical as well: the elitist amorality, cynical manipulation of others (disguised as "liberation"), destructiveness (in the guise of rational strategy) and great intensity of (probably oedipal) guilt and parricidal rage.

The Humanistic Worker

This third type could be seen as fitting rather more closely the image of the student radicals portrayed by admirers like Keniston. The main drive of these was not for apocalypse, or for power, but rather for expressive freedom. They were more likely (than the other two) to have similarities to the bohemians (the hippies) and many ties with them. (In the major split in SDS in 1969, one group looked and acted much more like hippies—long hair on males, unconventional clothes, more drug use, and the like—while males of the other were more likely to have shorter hair, wear more conventional workingmen's clothes, be negative toward drugs, and to follow a much more disciplined personal style. They saw themselves as the true radicals (or even revolutionaries) while the others were self-indulgent bohemians playing at revolution. The radicals also, basically correctly, saw the more hang-loose types as more susceptible to co-optation by moderate elements in the university. I am hypothesizing also that the "radicals" or "revolutionaries" were more likely Proto-Commissars or Apocalyptics in personality type, the "hippies" more Humanistic.

The Humanistic Workers were youngsters at war with authority, too, but in a manner different from the other two types. As confrontations intensified, the Humanist could see the other two types as being just as likely as the establishment authorities, to push *him* (the Humanist) around and to be, "when push comes to shove," even more ruthless than the established authorities.

The Humanistic wants to be able to pursue—now!—whatever interests him at the moment and, given the freedom to do so, will pursue it with passionate intensity, a hallmark of youth. He is impulsive, moody, frequently beset with anxiety. Life is full of contingency—a source of anxiety at times, but also of expressive exuberance. He is infuriated by routinization and bureaucratic rules that are (to him) irrational and unnecessary restrictions on people's freedom. He hungers for simple straightforward answers to the dilemmas of life, and is infuriated by professors who emphasize the complexity and many-sidedness of the world. He has a passion for what he thinks is social justice. People are being oppressed; that should be stopped. The nation is fighting an immoral and unjust war; that should be stopped. Professors and administrators oppress students, that should be stopped. He is impatient to do something, sick of endless ratiocination. He is likely to be a "red-diaper baby," that is to have grown up in a family of liberal to radical parents stressing a high degree of freedom and "democracy" in the family. His "idealism" is not so much a reaction against overtly authoritarian parents as it is an attempt to extend into the wider world the ideals of his parents, often with the feeling that the parents themselves have fallen short of practical realization of these ideals. His idealism does not extend, however, to the fanaticism of the apocalyptic or the power games of the Proto-Commissar. He is thus willing to work hard where his pragmatic sense leads him to believe in the viability of a particular action, but he pulls back when encountering the authoritarianism and irrational destructiveness displayed by leaders of the movement who approximate either of the two other types.

This type is most easily co-opted into idealistically-tinged meliorist activity "within the system." When he participates in a major confrontation, such as occupying a campus building, he finds himself in a confusion of feelings. He is scared of the cops, but then a ferocious female comrade, an SDS hardliner, "makes him feel he has no balls," so he stays. Besides he can't let his "comrades" down. He feels vaguely guilty much of the time, not sure whether because he has acted, or because he has not.

The more aggressive women in the group make him uneasy. The ferocity of the "revolutionaries" makes him anxious. If the confrontation reaches the climax sought after by the more revolutionary, i.e. a police bust against the rebels, the Humanistic is momentarily convinced by this event that the whole "system" is indeed brutal, rotten, oppressive, and the rest. But that conviction does not last long as the rebellion fizzles out and the movement fractionates into fratricidal wars.

"Oedipal" Elements in the Humanistic Rebels

Much of my 1970a paper on "Oedipal Elements in Student Rebellions," applies to the Humanistic type. (That paper as a whole does not make the distinction I later made among the Apocalyptic, Proto-Commissar and Humanistic types.) Typically there is a childhood oedipal situation consisting of relatively egalitarian parents with mother probably stronger than the father. That father is far from a brutally authoritarian patriarch, so far in fact that the son *needs* to construct a kind of fantasied father or father-surrogate who is harsh, threatening and punitive. Thus the son who joins the radical rebels is able to find in the confrontation, in administrators who take a "hard" line against the rebels, and eventually in the police, in the terrifying "bust." The real father who was idealistic and weak in the son's eyes—never really *acts* on his left-liberal political views—reappears in the guise of the typical left-liberal faculty. Such faculty may agree (partially) with some of the political diagnosis put forth by the rebels, but hesitate to join them in action, particularly borderline-criminal action. Or they outright condemn the rebels' sometimes illegal coercive tactics. Such liberal faculty especially are likely to be the butt of radical contempt and rage, more so than that minority of the faculty who are overtly "conservative" or "reactionary" and unambiguously hostile to the radicals.

Critics who faulted Feuer for his interpretation of the rebellions as a "generational revolt," pointing to the factually permissive and egalitarian parents, especially fathers, of the 1960s rebels, have missed the point. The students nevertheless continue to have oedipal antagonisms, and if the real fathers are not themselves punitive castrating agents to the rebel sons, some of the administrators take that role, as well as some of the faculty, while others of the faculty attract the rebels' contempt for being like their real fathers, i.e. "liberal' but weak and ineffectual.

The ego functions of the Humanistic are apt to be more realistic than those of either the Apocalyptic or the Proto-Commissar; they are less internally driven by unconscious rage to push the antagonists into fulfillments of bloody fantasy. Their superego functions are also less likely to be based on very primitive superego elements, as in the case of the Apocalyptics, or to have the psychopathic tinge of the Proto-Commissars, with its penchant for cynical manipulation of others, including supposed comrades. Greater involvement in other aspects of life, especially the expressive ones from the counterculture, demotes the rank of the revolutionary struggle from first place, to something far from the exclusive central concern. Also the Humanistic is likely to experience ambivalence toward liberal faculty who can be personally supportive (as contrasted with the bullying proto-commissarish "comrades") and possibly guiding toward less radical meliorist activities on behalf of the "social justice" the radical protest is supposedly seeking. Thus students of this psychological persuasion are more likely to be co-opted into more "within-the-system" activities. When the campus rebellions subside, they will tend to move into more standard versions of left-liberal activities, in politics, the professions and academic life. In later years, many are found among the faculty in the humanities and the softer social sciences.[8]

Aftermath of the Student Rebellions of the 1960s

In a paper on "Afterthoughts and Prospects" (Endleman 1972), written in mid-1971, I said that "the big campus revolts of the sixties are over . . . [and] the New Left in near total disarray . . . Flacks has pronounced it already dead . . ." [though many observers saw it continuing in terrorist groups like Weathermen.] Further I wrote,

> Though many of us [faculty] seriously wondered about this during the convulsions of the late 1960s, the universities will probably survive [but

> continue to] be transformed by the forces already at work and the newer ones unleashed by the recent upheavals . . . [the latter including] irrationalist tendencies derived from both radical and hippie forms of dissent and the effect of both co-optation and repression on the radicals of the '60s—more radicals and ex-radicals on the faculties, especially in the humanities and the social sciences, with influences on curricula and pedagogical styles . . . also a more "pacified" and quietistic student population. The voice-of-doom predictions of wholesale departure of serious scholars from the universities in the wake of persistent disruptions appear now to have been unfounded. (1972, p.8)

Nearly all of this has come to pass. True, departures were not "wholesale"—outside the hard sciences too few academics have available alternative employments—but I was reminded (in response to my article) that there were some, and they were a serious indictment of universities which submitted too much to radical students' demands. Moreover, where faculty did not physically leave the university, many went—in response to such disruptions—into a kind of internal exile, restricting their participation in university affairs to an absolute minimum, thus seriously weakening the university as a community of scholars.

Reforms made in line with radical student demands in many cases also weakened the university as a center of scholarship, or even destroyed that quality. Wherever "democratization" went on to include student voices, undergraduate education largely ceased to exist as a center of scholarship, and serious work had to be done almost exclusively in the graduate schools. For a period, "expressive freedom" dictated a whole segment of the curriculum making a mockery of any kind of scholarly work, and this still continues in many institutions claiming to be universities. Apparently at an opposite pole of intentions but partaking of many similar principles, the university as a supermarket for training in salable skills in the workplace—by the 1980s, the dominant conception—has proceeded apace. And where faculty include ever-increasing proportions of alumni of the 1960s revolts, the politicization of study in the social sciences and the humanities has gone extremely far, with the "disinterested pursuit of truth" or anything like a "value-neutral social science" become quaint relics of the past. The proliferation of a range of offshoots of the 60s religious-like movements, either radical or bohemian, continues—from weird sects combining elements of all three traditions, criminal, bohemian and radical (e.g. Jonestown, or in another vein, the Manson family), continues through the 1980s and shows no sign of disappearing.

A revealing recent incident (1988) shows survivals of both radical and hippie elements, is the "Platzkrieg" at the Berlin Wall: (Coulson 1988).

POSTCARD* WEST BERLIN

PLATZKRIEG

ON JULY 1 West Berlin police set off the first mass flight into the arms of totalitarianism in the history of that divided city.

What sparked more than 100 West Berliners to climb over the wall to the Communist East was a dispute over the fate of the Lené Dreieck, 40,000 square meters of mud and shrubs directly bordering the wall in the one-time center of pre-war Berlin. In the 1920s this area near the Potsdamer Platz was one of the most frenzied parts of Berlin, with packed cafés that housed much of the literary community in winters when coal was short. Nearby was the bunker where Hitler took his life on April 30, 1945. Technically a part of the Soviet sector, the razed, overgrown area was one of the many chunks of land that the masons of East Berlin didn't manage to wrap in when the wall went up on August 13, 1961. Like left-over pieces of a jigsaw puzzle, the bits lay unclaimed and unused until a land barter deal earlier this year between East and West.

The land was not scheduled to change hands officially until July 1. But before West Berlin's city fathers could even dust off their plans for a superhighway on the site, a motley group of West Berlin ecologists and anarchists "occupied" the Lené Dreieck. Declaring the area to be a "liberated zone," dreamy-eyed hippies, ragged punks, and assorted others with time on their hands erected a small village of tents and huts. The West Berlin police were forbidden by law from entering East German territory. The East German border guards, after a few hails over the wall, decided to let the settlers remain. And so the village grew, the citizens of no man's land bathed naked in the sun, and the tourist hordes that came daily to peer over the wall were treated to a new attraction.

If there is anything the West Berlin police don't like, it's the thought of an area beyond the reach of the law. During the early 1980s, efforts by the police to dislodge illegal squatters from their homes led to week-long riots. Since then the police have vigorously maintained the "Berlin Line," clearing any occupied buildings or streets without hesitation, using whatever force is required. Last year the city created special squads for just that task, picked out for their physical size and fierceness and armed with four-foot-long clubs. Caught up in the heat of the chase during a demonstration last May, they cudgeled anyone within club's reach, including journalists and some of their own officers. Now the riot troops posted around the encampment were forced to look on helplessly as their arch enemies, the "*Chaoten*" (chaotic), painted "Cop-Free Zone" and "anarchy is possible" on the wall and hurled curses, spit, and occasional beer bottles in their direction.

BUT THE ecologist-anarchist front was experiencing its own inner angst, having split into two factions known as "Müslies" (after an indigestible mixture of grain and corn they liked to eat with milk for breakfast) and "Mollies" (after the Molotov cocktails they liked to heave at policemen). The Müslies sport long hair, beards, heavy wool clothing, and Birkenstock sandals, and like to count the species of plant life in abandoned lots and quote pantheistic poetry. The Mollies prefer proto-military boots and pants, shaved and dyed patterns of hair on their skulls, and black leather jackets with stenciled slogans like "Eat-Fuck-Kill." While the Müslies wanted to negotiate a settlement with the authorities and win popular support, the Mollies took to wearing face masks at all hours of the day to prevent identification, carried wooden clubs over their shoulders, and stockpiled projectiles for the eventual confrontation. When the Müslies questioned their commitment to ecological issues, they replied, "The world is going to hell no matter what we do, at least we want to have some action!" Factional strife threatened to destroy the fragile alliance until someone arrived at a novel alternative: Rather than fight or surrender, why not jump the wall?

A brilliant inspiration that begged a few technical questions. People who cross the wall from East to West tend to get shot or blown up. Would the border guards from the East be any friendlier to those coming from West to East? And once you get in, can you get back out? The GDR soldiers peering down at the village plenum offered no clues.

As the Prussian dusk faded to darkness on the night of June 29, the even of the formal *Anschluss,* the curious and sympathetic had swollen the crowd at the Dreieck to over a thousand. The whole-grain families with their barefoot, shaggy-haired children had largely disappeared. Their leather-jacketed comrades appeared to have invested the gains of a day's panhandling in cases of beer, firing their courage for the coming battle, and listing precariously as they moved through the crowd. An atypically eloquent demonstrator mounted a propaganda offensive with a megaphone, demanding immediate negotiations and comparing the special riot division to the SA and the SS. After about half an hour of harangue the police bullhorn finally crackled: "Please report your bullshit in another direction."

At midnight the mob fell silent. Every ear strained for the sound of approaching sirens. When the Valkyries failed to descend, the crowd found other means to release their combative energies. A bonfire filled the square with flickering light. To the beat of drums and a trash container of galvanized steel struck with bricks and metal rods, bodies broke into dance. Ares had vanished and Dionysus had descended.

IT WAS, needless to say, merely a strategic delay on the police's part. At 5 a.m., after allowing most of the crowd to stagger home or sink into dreams of anarchistic utopia, and with the necessary *Dämmerung* to enable photographic records of any who attempted to resist, 800 green-clad policemen in full riot gear descended on the sleepy village. The remaining demonstrators groggily retreated to the nine-foot strip of land at the edge of the wall that still belonged to East Germany. The police advanced without the slightest resistance. Defeat seemed inevitable.

Suddenly a woman perched on the coping of the wall turned from speaking with a border guard and announced, "It's fine. They say that we can all come over." Within a few minutes 180 demonstrators had scaled up makeshift ladders and upturned sections of police fencing and clambered into the waiting East German military wagons on the other side of the wall. Those who sought "temporary asylum" were treated to a large breakfast of sandwiches and tea, politely asked if they would like to take up permanent residence in the socialist system (an offer that no one accepted), and then allowed to filter back into the West in small groups at various border crossings.

The outcome seemed to please all concerned. Christian Democrat Senator Kewenig could fluff his feathers in front of a captured hoard of bottles and slingshot ammunition and reproach the East Germans for neglecting their responsibilities as "decent businessmen" to turn over a clean parcel of land. The Communist Party broadsheet *Neues Deutschland* managed to publish a heartrending account of the flight without once mentioning the wall itself. Of the breakfast scene the correspondent wrote, "One had a warm feeling in the stomach. Even when one knew that the village of huts would soon be ripped down. But one had won new friends. And new comrades . . ." The West German police union urged the *Chaoten* to remain in the East. Even the demonstrators seemed satisfied. They returned as heroes, having dealt the "police state" (West Berlin) a monumental black eye and proved that it is possible, at least this once, to visit East Berlin for the day without the customary currency exchange.

CROCKER COULSON

THE NEW REPUBLIC
SEPTEMBER 12 & 19, 1988

The quest for religiously tinged utopia, whatever the cost in totalitarianism, springs eternal.

Notes

1. This chapter is adapted from earlier writings; see References, Endleman.

2. The various studies differ widely in their criteria for inclusion as *activist,* and many do not clearly distinguish between committed leader and strong supporters and peripheral followers, or between a revolutionary and a reform orientation. Some refer only to "big events" such as Columbia 1968, whereas others refer to a variety of universities. Therefore all of these generalizations are necessarily rough and approximate, presenting a composite picture where different studies are basically in agreement, at least in direction, if not in precise proportions.

3. This schematic picture is based on personal observations, plus the documentary evidence available on the major campus rebellions of the 1960s. The best documented are the Berkeley disruptions of 1964–65, and the Columbia crisis of 1968. Major sources for Berkeley are: Draper 1965; Feuer 1969, Ch. 9; and Lipset and Wolin 1965. For Columbia see: Avorn *et al.* 1969; Cox Commission Report 1968; and the participant-observer memoirs of Kunen 1969 and Rader 1969. On the Harvard 1969 confrontations, see Kelman 1970. In addition, news journals and general intellectual journals all carried voluminous (and variably reliable) coverage and commentary on the campus disorders, which I make no attempt to cite systematically here.

4. Distilled from representative statements of New Left positions. Cf. Long 1969; Luce 1966; SDS 1964; the subjects of Keniston 1968; the many New Left position papers reprinted in Wallerstein and Starr 1971; see also the dissection of the illusions and absence of reality testing in the Harvard New Left's beliefs in 1968–69, in Kelman 1970, where what Kelman calls the "dreamworld" (which I refer to as the "mythology") is documented in detail.

5. The acceptance of such illusions by bright students ordinarily committed to standards of rationality is an indication of the religio-expressive quality of the experience, sufficiently strong that even the *Spectator* journalists, whose book generally shows a remarkable degree of objectivity, are partially taken in by the illusions (see Avorn *et al.* 1969).

6. "Malaise": I use this deliberately vague word here, since no more precise term, e.g. frustration, deprivation, apathy, adequately conveys the range of feelings and vaguely apprehended reactions to the world that pervades the atmosphere to which I am referring. The specific psychodynamic constellations may be highly variable from one individual to another, as may the phenomenology of the experience. *Malaise* expresses the common denominator of all of these, a feeling that "the world is out of whack."

7. This aspect is developed in Endleman 1970b, Chapter XI. Cf. Endleman 1967, Chapter 4, for a general discussion of such ceremonies and their manifold meanings; cf. also Bettelheim 1954; Whiting *et al.* 1958; Young 1965.

8. This present chapter has dealt little with the cross-cultural and cross-national evidence; see Lipset 1968 and 1971, and Feuer 1969. Such evidence shows that in other countries, other times, student groups have had a far more significant impact on political events in the nation at large, than they ever did in America; evidence since 1970 indicates that they still do to a considerable extent in Third World countries. I am also knowingly ignoring another whole set of phenomena about students and politics, namely the *right*-wing groups and movements, which co-existed with the left in the United States in the 1960s (though in much smaller numbers, and never as flamboyantly) and counterparts of which still exist today.

REFERENCES

Auger, Camilla, Allen Barton and Raymond Maurice. 1969. "The Nature of the Student Movement and Radical Proposals for Change at Columbia University." Paper presented at Meetings of the American Sociological Association.

Avorn, J. *et al.* 1969. *Up Against the Ivy Wall.* New York: Atheneum.

Bell, Daniel. 1960. *The End of Ideology.* New York: Free Press.

Bettelheim, Bruno. 1954. *Symbolic Wounds: Puberty Rites and the Envious Male.* New York: Free Press.

Braden, William. 1970. *The Age of Aquarius.* Chicago: Quadrangle.

Braungart, Richard G. 1969. "Family Status, Socialization and Student Politics: A Multivariate Analysis." Paper presented at meetings of the American Sociological Association, San Francisco, September. (See also Ph.D. Thesis of same title, Pennsylvania State University 1969.)

Cohn, Norman. 1961. *The Pursuit of the Millenium.* New York: Harper.

Coulson, Crocker. 1988. "Platzkrieg." *The New Republic.* 9/12: 11–12, 14.

Cox Commission. 1968. *Crisis at Columbia.* New York: Random House (Vintage).

Davis, Kingsley. 1940. "The Sociology of Parent-Youth Conflict." *American Sociological Review.* 5:523–525.

Devereux, George. 1961. *Mohave Ethnopsychiatry: Psychic Disturbances of an Indian Tribe.* Washington, DC: Smithsonian Institution Press.

Draper, Hal. 1965. *Berkeley: The New Student Revolt.* New York: Grove.

Ellul, Jacques. 1968. "The Psychology of a Rebellion—May-June 1968." (re Paris-Nanterre) *Interplay* 2:5: 23–27.

Endleman, Robert. 1967. *Personality and Social Life.* New York: Random House.

———. 1970a. "Oedipal Elements in Student Rebellions." *Psychoanalytic Review.* 57:442–471.

———. 1970b. *The Ritual of Student Rebellion.* (book length ms., unpublished).

———. 1972. "The Student Revolt: Afterthoughts and Prospects." (Review Essay) *Contemporary Sociology* 1:3–9.

———. 1973. "Student Rebellion as Ritual." in Harry Silverstein, ed. *The Sociology of Youth: Evolution and Revolution.* New York: Macmillan.

__________. 1974. Review of Lipset, REBELLION IN THE UNIVERSITY. *Contemporary Sociology.* 3:18–20.

__________. 1981. *Psyche and Society.* New York: Columbia. pp. 357–367: "1960s Rebellions: Complexities of a Case."

Feuer, Lewis. 1969. *The Conflict of Generatiions.* New York: Basic Books.

Flacks, Richard. 1967. "The Liberated Generation: Explorations of the Roots of Student Protest." *Journal of Social Issues.* 23:3:52–75.

__________. 1971. "The New Left and American Politics after Ten Years." *Journal of Social Issues.* 27:21–34.

Freud, Sigmund. 1911. "Psychoanalytic Notes on an Autobiographical Account of a Case of Paranoia (dementia paranoides)." [The Schreber case.] *Standard Edition.* 12. (1958).

__________. 1913. *Totem and Taboo. S. E.* 13:1–164 (1955).

__________. 1916. "Some Character Types Met with in Psycho-Analytic Work: III: Criminals from a Sense of Guilt." *S. E. 14:332–337. (1957).*

Goodman, Paul. 1970. *The New Reformation.* New York: Random House.

Heist, P. 1966. "The dynamics of Student Discontent and Protest." Paper presented to meetings of the American Psychological Association, New York.

Hendin, Herbert. 1971. "A Psychoanalyst Looks at Student Revolutionaries." *The New York Times Magazine* Jan. 17, 1971.

__________. 1975. *The Age of Sensation.* New York: Norton, Ch. 12, "Student Revolutionaries, Then and Now."

Kelman, Steven. 1970. *Push Comes to Shove.* Boston: Houghton Mifflin.

Keniston, Kenneth. 1968. *Young Radicals* New York: Harcourt Brace World.

Kunen, James S. 1969. *The Strawberry Statement.* New York: Random House.

Liebert, Robert. 1971. *Radical and Militant Youth: A Psychoanalytic Inquiry.* New York: Praeger.

Lipset, Seymour M. 1968. "Students and Politics in Comparative Perspective." *Daedalus: Journal of the American Academy of Arts and Sciences.* (Winter 1968) (Also reprinted in Silverstein 1973).

__________. 1971. *Rebellion in the University.* Boston: Little, Brown.

Lipset, Seymour M. and S. Wolin, eds. 1965. *The Berkeley Student Revolt: Facts and Interpretations.* Garden City, NY: Doubleday (Anchor).

Long, Patricia, ed. 1969. *The New Left: A Collection of Essays.* Boston: Porter Sargent.

Luce, Phillip A. 1966. *The New Left.* New York: David McKay.

Matza, David. 1961. "Subterranean Traditions of Youth." *Annals of the American Academy of Political and Social Science.* 338:102–118.

Mauss, Armand. 1971. "On Being Strangled by the Stars and Stripes." *Journal of Social Issues.* 27:183–202.

Nelson, Benjamin. 1954. "The Future of Illusions." *Psychoanalysis* (later called *Psychoanalytic Review*) 2:33: 16–37. Variously reprinted.

The Public Interest (journal). 1968. Vol. 13, fall. Entire issue: The Universities.

Rader, Dotson. 1969. *I Ain't Marchin' Anymore* New York: David McKay.

Somers, Robert H. 1965. "Mainsprings of the Rebellion: A Survey of Berkeley Students in November 1964." in Lipset and Wolin 1965: 530–558.

Students for a Democratic Society. 1964. *The Port Huron Statement.* New York: S.D.S.

Wallerstein, Immanuel, and Paul Starr, eds. 1971. *The University Crisis Reader.* 2 volumes. New York: Random House.

Watts, W., and D. Witaker. 1966. "Free Speech Advocates at Berkeley." *Journal of Applied Behavioral Science* 2:41–62.

Whiting, John W. M. *et al.* "The Function of Male Initiation Ceremonies at Puberty." in

E. Maccoby, T. Newcomb and E. Hartley, eds. *Readings in Social Psychology.* New York: Holt, Rinehart, Winston.

Young, Frank. 1965. *Initiation Ceremonies.* Indianapolis: Bobbs-Merrill.

CHAPTER 9
SUMMARY AND CONCLUSION

We have looked at criminals of various kinds, madmen and others psychologically disturbed, and various kinds of oddballs—drug users, sexual deviants, bohemians and radicals. Are all those who deviate from the norms of society psychologically sick? No, but some are. Are all those who are psychologically sick, deviant from the norms of society? No, but some are.

Those who believe that all deviants are sick, or that all sick are deviant, are wrong. So are those who believe deviants are *not* sick—as many sociologists like to proclaim. And so are those who believe that most people who are usually considered sick, are not sick, or that mental illness does not exist—again, as some sociologists claim.

The reality is much more complex. Some deviants *are* psychologically disturbed, and we can demonstrate how. Others are not, or at least not more so than most nondeviants. Some sick people do not appear as deviant at all, but are nonetheless demonstrably psychologically disturbed. Other sick people, most of those severely sick, are also deviant as well.

Illusion and Self-Delusion

A major theme that runs through all of these chapters, is the enormous role of illusion and self-delusion in the lives and ways of deviants: crooks—law-breakers of all varieties—provide themselves with all kinds of "techniques of neutralization," i.e. self-justifications that they themselves believe. They are not only using these as self-exculpating excuses. Many observers, including some professional social scientists, are conned by these thought-patterns, elaborating them into theories of how the disenfranchised and dispossessed *have* to turn to criminal pursuits—ignoring well known information about all those poor people who do not commit crimes, and all those rich ones who do. Drug users, whether or not also criminals on property, violence and sex, provide every variety of self-exculpating reason to see themselves, and to get others to see them, as victims—deprived, and endlessly "hassled" by the vicissitudes of life, either from the pains of poverty or the boredom and meaninglessness of middle class life. Sexual deviants, when organized into a civil-rights protest movement, develop a whole mythology about how they are oppressed, how they are as normal as anyone else, how their foes are suffering from a newly discovered psychopathology ("homophobia"), etc. etc. subjecting themselves to, and believing in, a collective illusion about the world (see Endleman 1981, ch. 14).

Purveyors of such illusions are forever discovering new underdog minorities of the opppressed, and promulgating an illusionary view of the world to defend and vaunt the claims of their favorite oppressed minority group.

The mentally ill are themselves seen by such ideologues as not really sick, as improperly oppressed by incarceration in hospitals, and on and on, in a world-view that utterly distorts the realities of their lives. That distortion has had results such as de-institutionalization casting thousands of these people into a helpless homeless condition on the streets. Bohemians of various stripes, in recent decades called beatniks or hippies, devise an illusionary view of the world demonizing ordinary lawabiding and mores-conforming folk as villainous oppressors, immersing themselves in drug subcultures—especially psychedelics—and maintaining an illusionary world of utopian escape. These in turn have a host of social-scientific and psychological admirers willing to buy in to the same illusions. And the political radicals, sporadically having a boom of popularity and a certain prestige, as in the 1960s, developing and disseminating their own brands of mitigating and reactive mythologies, sufficiently strong to persuade their own devotees and admirers of the villainous oppressive nature and intentions of all those who do not agree with them. They are matched by crowds of Western intellectuals, otherwise highly intelligent and well informed, who persisted, or started anew, to support, travel to and propagandize for "socialist" regimes in other parts of the world which they perceive as liberators. They ignore the fact that those regimes are totalitarian dictatorships stamping out all basic human rights (see Hollander 1981). The capacity for such illusion and self-delusion seems to be bottomless and ever-renewable, belying the alleged capacity of even well-informed, well-educated intellectuals, to "learn from history" even the recent history of the world of their own lifetimes. The "pursuit of the millenium" or utopia, or the perfect society, seems to be an ever-beguiling enticement to numbers of thinkers and fantasists, undeterred by any supposed increases in rational understanding of the world achieved in recent centuries (Cf. Nelson 1954). Their view is unclouded by actual exposure to the realities of those societies, or if exposed, any understanding of what was around them in these totalitarian systems they are so ready to romanticize as the hope of the world.

The world of criminality reveals multifaceted social elements, some of which come from the most economically and politically disadvantaged portion of the population, the lower or underclass, but not all of those, rather that segment psychologically most disposed. The latter turn out, on inspection, to have been at war with regulated society from their earliest years, chronically opposed in multifarious ways, and determined to take a predatory approach to gaining whatever satisfaction they seek. Though in some, probably a minority of cases, psychological illness—neurotic, psychotic or character disorder—may be involved, more commonly the chronic perpetrators are psychologically more or less intact, amoral and psychopathic, adept at using the techniques of neutralization to short-circuit any real working of conscience.

Special problems are presented in the judicial systems of democratic countries, by the question of the insanity defense.

Homosexuality

Then on the subject of sexual deviations, we are plunged into the sociopolitical turmoil of "liberation movements" and their opposition in the conventional population being characterized as reactionaries for maintaining traditional conceptions of homosexuality as deviant and wrong. Significantly in these battles, the purveyors of the new "conventional wisdom" which dictates that educated enlightened people must regard homosexual object choice as simply a casual variation of no moral or clinical significance, and practitioners of this orientation as simply part of a desirable variety in the population, of no important difference from the majority or putatively "normal" population. This is now "enlightened" opinion.

Cross-cultural studies indicate a range of incidence of and evaluative positions toward, homosexuality, in societies around the world. The one firm generalization is that in *no* society is *exclusive* homosexuality unambiguously approved as an option. Several societies have stage-transitional homosexuality common or even universal for males, typically expected to be followed by heterosexual dominance, marriage and procreation. Several have a segregated and tolerated, sometimes even sanctified, role for a small minority of incumbents, e.g. the "berdache," which involves gender-crossing, sometimes for males only, sometimes for males and females, and rarely, for females only. However, this role is clearly demarcated from the expectations and conduct of the vast majority of "normals" in the society. Also, many societies allow occasional or variational homosexuality within a bisexual, and predominantly heterosexual life pattern. But none put this variation on a par with predominant heterosexuality. These points need to be made, to contradict the now prevalent mythologies of the "gay-liberation movement."

Psychologically, there is still lively controversy. While most sophisticated clinicians of a psychoanalytic orientation, will not suggest that homosexuality is a distinct clinical psychopathological entity, psychoanalysts find it usually if not invariably associated with a variety of psychopathological conditions, where the development of homosexual orientation—especially if exclusive—is a major associated feature. The kind of psychopathology varies a great deal within the range of the diagnostic compendium, but is typically associated with severe psychosexual-developmental distortions. Not all Western clinicians share this view, and some are sufficiently influenced by sociologists and social psychologists, to argue that evident distress derives from the stigma prevalently attached to homosexuality in this society.

Despite the spread of "gay-liberation" viewpoints as a kind of enlightened conventional wisdom in this society today, in reality, much of the population still regards sexual deviants of this kind as "abnormal" regardless of the new enlightened outlook.

Of particular moment is the question of clinical normality: crudely, is homosexuality psychologically sick? In the early 1970s the political homosexual movement persuaded (pressured) the American Psychiatric Association to remove homosexuality from their influential handbook of psychological disorders (the *Diagnostic and Statistical Manual*) thus giving a sort of official stamp of approval to homosexuality from at least one prestigious segment of the mental health professional community. (Psychoanalysts, though not all, still however, maintain, that clinical psychopathology *is* involved in the development of homosexuality.) This can still be an issue of great emotional salience, since many of even the most sophisticated still find it difficult to differentiate a negative *clinical* judgment—of psychopathology—from any of the other negative judgments on homosexuality prevalent in society at large: that it is "unnatural," immoral, against religious precepts, that it is (or should be) against the law; that practitioners should be limited in their civil liberties and civil rights, discriminated against in employment, housing and the like. Many clinicians will therefore be hesitant to come out in the open with assessments of psychopathology in reference to homosexuality, for fear of being taken as endorsers of "reactionary" sociopolitical attitudes toward homosexuals. Many find it hard to separate clinical judgment—of pathology—from a moral social judgment which grants to homosexuals the same rights to live their lives as they choose, as anyone else.

The current AIDS crisis has brought into the open a great deal of anti-homosexual feeling. This attitude includes blaming the homosexuals for the epidemic, and regarding them as having brought divine retribution upon themselves and others for their sinful behavior. It involves, commonly, putting all homosexuals into a pariah status. These opinions certainly call into question the extent to which the society has moved to an accepting "live-and-let-live" position toward homosexuality. Looking at the psychodynamics of responses to homosexuality, one would have to expect that any further advances toward "liberalization" would be self-limiting, considering that male homosexuality at least (the case is different for female) is in its nature sufficiently threatening to the "normal" population, especially to the males, susceptible to strong castration anxiety, as to preclude casual acceptance counted as desirable by the new "conventional wisdom" of the "liberated." Add to this, anger on the part of these more conventional people, at being considered bigots and reactionaries, and we have the ingredients for a substantial "backlash."

Prostitution

On another major form of sexual deviation, prostitution, here we have a form of sexual conduct clearly deviant according to the norms of the society—or any society, for that matter, by definition. (That is, if it is only casual nonmarital sex without pecuniary exchange, then it is not prostitution; the former is common in many societies, and in many not considered particularly deviant.) Prostitution is sufficiently ubiquitous in more advanced societies (beyond an agricultural base) to have been considered, erroneously, the "oldest profession," and nearly always deviant even if tolerated as a "necessary evil."

Sociologists like Kingsley Davis distinguished the question of why the institution of prostitution exists, from the essentially psychological question of why a particular woman became a member of this profession. The relevant studies indicate that it is not poverty alone that leads individuals into this profession, since many poor women do not become prostitutes, and many not poor do. Rather the psychological characteristics that are relevant are low self-esteem, a history of family abuse, of mothers' multiple marriages and relationships, seduction by stepfathers and other male relatives, early experience of being rewarded for sexual favors. Some develop a dual orientation, one to the prostitution profession, the other to maintaining a cover of respectability, supporting children or a husband or other relatives; some identifying with the criminal and demi-monde world; still others alienated from both. Many of the more affluent prostitutes acquire tastes for conventional status symbols of wealth, prestige cars, furs, clothing, night club life, etc., these luxuries filling an otherwise empty life. Despair and suicide are common.

Drugs

On use of drugs we have a complex picture. Use of chemical substances to relieve stress and distress, to elevate mood, to facilitate either sleep or wakefulness, is so endemic in this society, that it is not difficult for defenders of "illicit" drugs to argue that these practices are simply part of the mainstream. Use of various chemical substances for their psychoactive effects has appeared across the board among human societies ranging from primitive to modern technological conditions, with a great variety of definitions in terms of deviance or conformity. The patterns of deviance in modern Western societies derive heavily from the patterns of the law, which in effect along with the criminal syndicates, keep a range of drug-taking illicit in the eyes of the law, thus creating cadres of criminals and other "deviants." These cadres are in large measure self-perpetuating and self-expanding, as puritanical mores interact with a widespread antinomianism of the young. Participants seek through chemical release, transcendance, ecstasy, oblivion, in patterns frequently (but not always) displaying various kinds of psychopathology. There is no one consistent pattern, of choice of drugs, or of use, or of association with other deviance (e.g. how much involvement with other forms of crime), or of association with psychopathology. Are the drug users deviant? Yes, commonly, but by definitions created by the formal institutions, and in the minds of the most normatively constricted of the population. Are they psychopathological? In some cases clearly yes, in others no, and in still others not clearly one or the other. If both deviant and psychopathological, these two are not inevitably connected.

Mental Illness

On mental illness we find a paradoxical picture that this obvious psychological problem is declared by (some) sociologists as properly in the sociological domain. Those declared mentally ill are, in this view, victims of a conspiracy of the mental health profession and the law, to have them "labeled" in a pariah manner for what is in reality "residual deviance." "Mental illness" in this view, is itself a myth and delusion of the professionals and their powerful allies. Commitment to a mental hospital in a Western country is seen as equivalent to the railroading of political dissidents into mental hospitals in the Soviet Union and other totalitarian communist countries. Clinicians are thus faced with the reality of the genuinely psychotic, with all their very real pains and sufferings, totally mischaracterized, much to the disadvantage of those who are in fact sick. Now with de-institutionalizion, partly as a result of labeling sociologists' views, the formerly hospitalized are on the streets without alternative treatment and often helpless and homeless to boot.

The relationship of mental illness to deviance is complex, and we can distinguish five types of psychopathology, in relation to normative structures: ethnic psychoses, idiosyncratic psychoses, culturally stylized psychopathological variant, culturally stylized character disorder, idiosyncratic neuroses and character disorders. The insanity defense and the "mad" status of presidential assassins are recurrent issues.

Bohemianism

Bohemianism is a major form of deviation from conventional social structure and culture, which has had a certain vogue at various, unevenly spaced, periods in modern history. Its participants reject the pursuit of wealth, power, ambition, worldly goods, and the like. And they reject use of the standard means of hard work, discipline, organized life, and rational means in general. They oppose conventionality in life style, in approaches to time and space, in personal relations, in sex and family relations, styles of adormment, and self-expression. In terms of the main features of modern Western industrialized culture, followers of the bohemian life style are oppositional in a passive manner. They are passive as opposed to active; exotic-chaotic rather than disciplined. They favor the nonrational and irrational over the rational. They feel time as experience, immersion, duration, rather than mechanized or calculated processes. They are attracted to mysticism rather than asceticism. They favor exploration of depths, including by psychedelic drugs, rather than domination by mechanized time-bound and external-reality-bound experience.

The most recent versions of bohemianism have been the beat phenomenon of the 1950s, and more widespread, the hippies of the 1960s, (alternatively called the "counterculture,") both exerting a great fascination on much of the middle class, including susceptible social scientists.

Psychologically, the main participants in the counterculture were of five varieties: 1) young, immature, fragile-ego, infantile-dependent; 2) at least slightly older, with more intact ego, relatively healthier and less vulnerable; 3) passive-aggressive personalities; 4) psychopaths; 5) psychotic, in some cases with triggering by psychedelic drugs.

Here again we find the element of collective illusions particularly strong. The whole movement is suffused with inchoate longings for instant community, for universal "love," to be had for the mere expression of the wish. We find a naive faith in satisfactions to be derived from indiscriminate eroticism, and failure to recognize human aggression as a basic force in social life. The susceptibility of people holding such illusions, especially when strung out on psychoactive drugs, leads easily to victimization by criminal psychopathic elements. Such people are also susceptible to totalitarian forms of organization, effectuated in reality in such groups as the Manson Family and the Jonestown cult, both heirs to the hippiedom and the radicalism of the 1960s.

Radicalism

Alongside bohemianism, radicalism is the other major stream of modern noncriminal protest. Here the participants don't want to drop out of organized society, or to violate its rules for egoistic satisfactions as in delinquency, but rather hope to transform society and culture to make them conform to their idea of social justice. Many of the same people were attracted to these forms as to the hippie way, sometimes maintaining both in an uneasy blend. The common thread is antinomianism toward the existing order, and similar collective illusions. This kind of collective deviance, too, has a considerable ancestry is its different elements, in Western history. It is unstably periodic in outbreak, each time seeming to be an unpredictable and unprecedented outburst, only in a few years virtually to disappear as surprisingly as it arose. Then it is quiescent for some time (at least two to three decades) only to reappear as suddenly and "unexpectedly" in other guises. High-mindedness and idealism easily move into self-righteousness and intolerance of disagreement, as more totalitarian elements take over the movement. This movement, even more than bohemianism, enlists passionate partisanship among the social scientists and psychologists observing the phenomenon, the majority developing quickly a "liberal" conventional wisdom supporting the rebels and seeing in them not only political but psychological mental-health virtues, defying the realities.

Again, a variety of psychological types appear, in psychosocial terms distinguishable as Apocalyptic, Proto-Commissar and Humanistic Worker types. Persons of the first two types are more likely to be psychologically disturbed, turning an intense inner rage deriving from materially comfortable but emotionally depriving childhoods, against outside objects in the sociopolitical world. They are then likely to move to the extremes of terroristic violence and a long-term underground. The third type, Humanistic Workers, are psychologically more variable, but apt to be better ego-integrated and with less primitive superegos, and therefore less amenable in the uprisings to totalitarian solutions. They are more likely to settle for melioristic activity "within the system," and with the demise of the radical movement, opportunistically find arenas for expression in reform politics, various reformist movements, e.g. the ecology movement, and significantly, in academe, where by now (late 1980s) they constitute a significant portion of the middle-rank academics, at least in the social sciences.

Persistence of Deviance

All of these phenomena—crime and delinquency, drug use, sexual deviations, mental illness, bohemianism and radicalism—are persistent elements of modern society and culture, variously combining social deviance (being at war with one or another feature of conventional society) and psychological disorder, in no one simple pattern. Some versions—bohemianism and radicalism—have a periodicity that makes them seem at certain periods (like the present, the late 1980s) very much out of date, but they reappear at a later time, then seeming "obviously" to reflect strains and "pathologies" of the society and culture of that time, and particularly the special difficulties for the young growing up in that time and place.

Throughout participation in and discussion of any of these forms of deviance, or combinations of two or more of them, a range of *mythologies,* appears, reactive and mitigating, in many cases espoused by the very social scientists who claim to be studying the phenomena. Such mythologies (cf. Endleman 1981, Chapters 10 and 14 in reference to the feminist and gay liberation movements) provide a belief system that is riddled with illusions about the real world. These may be reactive, that is, opposed to beliefs and ideologies prevailing in the conventional population. Or they may be mitigating, that is trying to mitigate the frustrations and malaises of particular populations (e.g. slogans like "gay is good.") Examples are beliefs propounded by many prostitutes that it is only *they* who are honest about life, in contrast to the hypocrisies of conventional people who subject the prostitutes to stigmatization. Wherever there is a well-developed deviant subculture of any of the varieties discussed, the participants are likely to develop or accept such mythologies, reacting against the negative conventional view of these deviants, and/or mitigating the difficulties of living in this way. Again, it is the task of the social scientist to recognize the illusionary elements in such belief systems and not get enticed into unthinking acceptance of such mythologies as proven truths about the world. Many social scientists in any of these fields signally fail such a test.

Connections among Types of Deviance

Taking up separately the topics of this work—crime and delinquency, sexual deviations, drugs, mental illness bohemianism and radicalism—we could miss or underplay the *connections* among two or more of them. The presence or absence of some kind and degree of mental illness, we have raised as an important issue in reference to each of the other forms of deviation. Are adult crooks and juvenile delinquents psychologically "off" in important ways? Are drug abusers? Are sexual Deviants? Are bohemians (recently, hippies) or radicals? In all cases we find that some of each are so, and some are not. And for those who are, we can specify how so and the possible origins of the disturbance.

Such conclusions are contradictory to common presentations on all of these topics in many sociological and other social scientific writings. They also fly in the face of the prevalent anti-psychological, particularly anti-psychoanalytic, trend in the social sciences.

On crime and delinquency, we find that, even when a great deal of ordinary street crime and drug-associated crime is committed by persons low on the socio-economic scale, in fact there is a psychological selective process as to *which* individuals from such environmental backrounds, do move on to heavy involvement with delinquency and later adult crime. (Most of the lower class population do not.)

Many of the later career criminals, those who continue in criminal behavior as their main life activity and main source of sustenance, show up quite early in life with patterns that are distinctive and not merely responsive to a depriving environment. They are headstrong, impulsive, bent upon egoistic satisfactions, manipulative, after the main chance, given to deception and selfdeception, and to"techniques of neutralization" of counteractive forces of guilt or conscience. The more talented of them by adulthood latch onto prevailing conceptions of "being out for number one," and "let's get away with what we can," giving their own version of the business world's priority of greed. Those heavily involved in hard drugs, commonly claim that it was only the pursuit of drugs that led them into property and violent crimes, whereas the studies actually show that those convicted of serious crimes who are also heavy drug users, did not get hooked on drugs first, but rather were already heavily engaged in crime *before* they started on drugs. They can be quite adept at parroting a conventional wisdom that the drugs cause the crime, for by proclaiming this they provide themselves with a convenient rationalization and self-exculpation.

It seems to many sociologists that these lawbreakers are a kind of victim and product of social forces beyond their control. Interestingly enough this victim picture is presented mainly about criminals who come out of the slums and deprived neighborhoods, and is rarely applied to "white collar criminals," people of middle and even upper class positions who violate business laws by securities frauds and the like. Again a basic truth is that not everyone in the slums commits such offenses, regardless of the temptations—again, an invitation to apply some kind of psychological analysis.

On the relation of drugs and crime, there are these logical possibilities:

noncriminal nondrug-users; criminals who *are* drug users; criminals who are not drug users; drug users who are not criminals (i.e. do not commit offenses other than those immediately involved in securing the drugs, such as holding, passing). The problem is that it is difficult for a user of illicit drugs, other than an occasional recreational pot smoker, *not* to get involved in illegal activities of the drug world, starting with simple dealing to get his own supply. Those *heavily* involved in the drug world are already connected with the culture that includes criminality, generally, as well as drugs.

A similar connection is the case for a great many, perhaps most, prostitutes. Of those, only a few maintain a life-style that is barely connected with other phases of the criminal world. In fact, one of the satisfactions a woman may get from life as a prostitute is to thus become disaffiliated from what to her is the drab boring world of conventional law abiding people. Again, the studies show that it is rarely poverty *per se* that leads a girl into prostitution, because many similarly poor do not turn that way, and many not poor, do.

Drug use connects also with psychopathology in a variety of ways, rather than in one simple correlation. Hendin's studies of elite college student drug users showed several pathogenic family backgrounds, somewhat different from one kind of drug preference, such as heroin, to another, such as amphetamines. This is so alongside the fact that the prevailing subcultures of college students in that period—early 1970s—were favorable to drug use, at least experimentation. In this atmosphere only certain psychologically preselected individuals responded by serious drug use. Again, this activity is going on in a culture that is saturated with positive messages toward all manner of chemical substances, only some of which are declared illicit. However that generalization does not answer the psychological questions of who is particularly disposed, and what specific psychological functions the drugs perform for them. Similar questions are raised about the most commonly used recreational psychoactive drug, namely alcohol, which for adults in most places is legally available and leads to abusive and later addictive use for a few, along particular psychological lines.

Drug use has had a particular place in the bohemian subcultures of recent times, the beatniks of the 1950s strong on marijuana and the hippies of the following decade on psychedelics, in each case the drug use fitting into a pervasively antinomian stance toward the world. Drug use attracted, among a variety of personality types, especially those most vulnerable to destructive effects of powerful psychoactive drugs. This led in many instances to at least temporary psychosis, in some of those to long-term psychotic impairment. Another feature was that the subculture also brought them in contact with criminal worlds, at the very least as victims of exploiters, in other cases as collaborators in that outcast world.

The hippies were also related to and overlapped with the student radicals of the 1960s. But at critical junctures, like the major factional split within SDS in 1969, the divergence of the two kinds of antinomian became clear. The hippies, or more hippie-like protesters, wanted to "hang loose," enjoy sex and drugs, and in effect drop out. The radicals wanted to discipline and harden themselves and their comrades for the struggle, rejecting "bourgeois" softness and sentiment, and use drugs only sparingly. *Their* task was to change the world.

In both of these phenomena, certain psychopathologies appeared in some of the individuals involved. In the radicals, two of the three main types, the Apocalyptic and the Proto-Commissar, diverged importantly from the admiring and romanticizing portrait of the student radicals presented by many social scientists and psychologists. The Apocalyptic showed an all-consuming destructive and suicidal rage, with deep pathogenic roots. The Proto-Commissars displayed a concentration on power and control over the world that rejected human contact, and was also pathological in origin. Only the third type, the Humanistic Worker, approximated the kind of ego-integration, absence of primitiveness of superego, and humane flexibility, clinicians would expect in a less pathological personality, and even these shared, in less extreme form, some of the elements of the first two.

Relating the radicals to criminals: the radicals clearly carried on para legal acts of civil disobedience which they did not themselves define as criminal, but rather as political acts. These they justified by the allegedly superior morality of their cause. In the Apocalyptics and the Proto-Commissars, these could escalate to extremely destructive (and sometimes self-destructive) levels, like blowing up a university's computer center or parts of a library. Later, in the terrorist direction taken by hard-line groups like Weathermen, they took to activities such as bank robbery, holding up armored bank vans for money for the Revolution, and shootouts with the police, like any violent career criminals. These groups were clearly at war with society and the state. If caught, convicted and imprisoned, they and their sympathizers then claim they are "political prisoners," a claim accepted by many uncritical social scientists.

Some social scientists of this kind go further and claim that all prisoners, or in one version, all prisoners of color, are really political prisoners, making America no different from totalitarian countries of the Right or the Left—more mythologies of "enlightened" minorities.

Another offshoot of both the radicals and the hippies has been the proliferation, since the '60s and continuing today, of cult-like groups, extreme examples of which are the Manson "Family" and the Jonestown cult. These combine elements of all three "subterranean traditions," criminality, bohemianism and political radicalism. In one case a flower-child-like devotee of the Manson family, namely Lynnette Fromme, turned up among the would-be assassins of major political figures. With her .45 caliber automatic, she threatened President Ford, and was convicted for attempted assassination. Clarke (1982) does not believe she was psychotic, but the evidence indicates extreme psychological disturbance. He does not see her, either, as a would-be assassin acting primarily out of political motives. No one suggested an insanity defense, though clearly it would have been as feasible for her as for Hinckley a few years later.

Need for a Combined Approach

On all of these topics, careful consideration of a range of studies and theoretical discussion, indicates that we really need a combination of social scientific and psychological (by my preference, psychoanalytic) modes and approaches. Consideration of the "deviant" status of any activities needs social scientific analysis of the prevailing mores and laws of an existing society, and consideration of psychopathology requires psychological expertise, for which psychoanalysis is in my view the best available. In other words, we need for all these topics a psychoanalytic social science. This is the attempt of this work.

REFERENCES

Clarke, James W. 1982. *American Assassins: The Darker Side of Politics.* Princeton, NJ: Princeton University Press.

Endleman, Robert. 1981. *Psyche and Society.* New York: Columbia University Press. Especially Chapters 10, 14, on reactive and mitigating mythologies.

Hollander, Paul. 1981. *Political Pilgrims.* New York: Oxford University Press.

Nelson, Benjamin. 1954. "The Future of Illusions." *Psychoanalysis,* vol.2, no.4, 16–37. (Journal later called *Psychoanalytic Review.*)

BIBLIOGRAPHY

Addiction Research Foundation. 1983. *Cannabis: Health Risks.* Toronto: ARF Books

Adler, Nathan. 1968. "The Antinomian Personality: The Hippie Character Type." *Psychiatry.* 31:325–338.

Ald, Roy. 1971. *The Youth Communes.* New York: Tower.

Alexander, Franz, and Hugo Staub. 1931. *The Criminal, the Judge and the Public.* London: Allen and Unwin.

Anonymous. 1969. "The Effects of Marijuana on Consciousness." in Tart 1969, ch. 22:335–355.

Appelbaum, Paul S. 1987. "Crazy in the Streets." *Commentary.* 83:5:34–39.

Armour, David J. *et al.* 1976. *Alcoholism and Treatment.* Santa Monica, CA: Rand.

Ash, P. 1949. "The reliability of psychiatric diagnosis." *Journal of Abnormal and Social Psychology.* 44:272–276.

Auger, Camilla, Allen Barton and Raymond Maurice. 1969. "The Nature of the Student Movement and Radical Proposals for Change at Columbia University." Paper presented at Meetings of the American Sociological Association.

Avorn, J. *et al.* 1969. *Up Against the Ivy Wall.* New York: Atheneum.

Becker, Howard S. 1963. *Outsiders.* New York: Free Press.

Bell, Alan P., and Martin Weinberg. 1978. *Homosexualities: A Study of Diversity among Men and Women.* New York: Simon and Schuster.

Bell, Alan P., and Sue Kiefer Hammersmith. 1981. *Sexual Preference: Its Development in Men and Women.* Bloomington, IN: Indiana University Press; an Official Publication of the Alfred C. Kinsey Institute for Sex Research. 2 vols.

Bell, Daniel. 1960. *The End of Ideology.* New York: Free Press.

Berger, Bennett. 1967. "Hippie Morality—More Old than New." *Trans-Action* 5:19–24.

Berger, Bennett, and eight co-authors: 1974. "Child-Rearing Practices of the Communal Family." in Scott McNall, ed. *The Sociological Perspective* Third Edition. Boston: Little, Brown, 521–534.

Bergler, Edmund. 1948. *The Battle of the Conscience.* Washington, DC: Washington Institute of Medicine.

Bergler, Edmund. 1956. *Homosexuality: Disease or Way of Life?* New York: Hill and Wang.

Bettelheim, Bruno. 1954. *Symbolic Wounds: Puberty Rites and the Envious Male.* New York: Free Press.

Bieber, Irving *et al.* 1962. *Homosexuality: A Psychoanalytic Study.* New York: Basic Books.

Blum, Richard. 1967. *Narcotics and Drug Abuse.* Task Force Report, Presidential Commission on Law Enforcement and Administration of Justice.

Blum, Richard *et al.* 1964. *Utopiates* New York: Atherton.

Blum, R. H. 1962. "Case Identification in Psychiatric Epidemiology: Methods and Problems." *Milbank Memorial Fund Quarterly.* 40:253–288.

Bordua, David. 1967. "Recent Trends: Deviant Behavior and Social Control." *Annals of the American Academy of Political and Social Science.* 369:149–163.

Braden, William. 1970. *The Age of Aquarius.* Chicago: Quadrangle Books.

Brady, John Paul *et al.*, eds. 1977. *Psychiatry: Areas of Promise and Advancement.* New York: Spectrum

Braungart, Richard G. 1969. "Family Status, Socialization and Student Politics: A Multivariate Analysis." Paper presented at meetings of the American Sociological Association, San

Francisco, September. (See also Ph.D. Thesis of same title, Pennsylvania State University 1969.)

Brickman, Harry R. 1968. "The Psychedelic 'Hip Scene': Return of the Death Instinct." *American Journal of Psychiatry.* 125: 766-772.

Broude, G. J., and S. Greene. 1876. "Cross-Cultural Codes on Twenty Sexual Attitudes and Practices." *Ethnology* 15:409ff.

Brown, Claude. 1965. *Manchild in the Promised Land.* New York: Macmillan.

Bruin Humanist Forum, Issues Study Committee. 1969. "Marijuana (Cannabis) Fact Sheet." in Tart 1969, ch. 21: 325–334.

Caffey, Eugene M. Jr. *et al.* 1970. "A Survey of Drug Treatment in Psychiatry." in DiMascio and Shader 1970: 343–385.

Cahalan, Don, and Robin Room. 1974. *Problem Drinking among American Men.* New Brunswick, NJ: Rutgers Center of Alcohol Studies.

Caplan, Lincoln. 1984. *The Insanity Defense and the Trial of John W. Hinckley, Jr.* Boston: David Goldine.

Catanzano, Ronald J. 1967. "Psychiatric Aspects of Alcoholism." in: David J. Pittman, ed. *Alcoholism.* New York: Harper and Row

Chambliss, William J., and Robert B. Seidman. 1971. *Law, Order and Power.* Reading, MA: Addison-Wesley.

Chein, Isidor *et al.* 1964. *The Road to H.* New York: Basic Books.

Chodorow, Nancy. 1978. *The Reproduction of Mothering.* Berkeley: University of California Press.

Clarke, James W. 1982. *American Assassins: the Darker Side of Politics.* Princeton, NJ: Princeton University Press.

Cleckley, Hervey. 1950. *The Mask of Sanity.* St. Louis: Mosby.

Clinard, Marshall. 1963. *The Sociology of Deviant Behavior* Rev. Ed. New York: Holt, Rinehart, Winston.

Cloward, Richard, and L. Ohlin. 1961. *Delinquency and Opportunity.* New York: Free Press.

Cohen, Albert K. 1955. *Delinquent Boys.* New York: Free Press.

Cohen, Robert K., and James Short Jr. 1958. "Research In Delinquent Subcultures." *Journal of Social Issues.* 14:20-37.

Cohen, Sidney. 1966. *The Beyond Within.* New York: Atheneum.

Cohn, Norman. 1961. *The Pursuit of the Millenium.* New York: Harper.

Conrad, John P., and Simon Dinitz, eds. 1977. *In Fear of Each Other: Studies of Dangerousness in America.* Lexington, MA: Lexington Books (D. C. Heath)

Cory, Donald Webster. 1951. *The Homosexual in America.* New York: Greenberg.

Coulson, Crocker. 1988. "Platzkrieg." *The New Republic.* 9/12–19:11–12, 14.

Cox Commission. 1968. *Crisis at Columbia.* New York: Random House (Vintage).

Davis, Fred. 1967. "Why All of us may be Hippies Some Day." *TransAction.* 5:10–18.

Davis, Kingsley. 1937. "The Sociology of Prostitution." *American Sociological Review.* 2:744–755.

———. 1940. "The Sociology of Parent-Youth Conflict." *American Sociological Review.* 5:523–525.

DeLint, Jan, and Wolfgang Schmidt. 1971. "Alcohol Use and Alcoholism." *Addictions.* 18:1–14.

Devereux, George. 1939. "Mohave Culture and Personality." *Character and Personality.* 8: 91–109.

———. 1940. "Social Negativism and Criminal Psychopathology." *Journal of Criminal Psychopathology.* 1:325–338. (Reprinted in Devereux 1980, chapter 3.)

———. 1950. "Heterosexual Behavior of the Mohave Indians." in G. Róheim, ed. *Psychoanalysis and the Social Sciences.* 2:85–108.

_________. 1951. "Neurotic Crime vs. Criminal Behavior." *Psychiatric Quarterly.* 25:73–80. (Reprinted in Devereux 1980, Chapter 7.)

_________. 1956. "Normal and Abnormal." in J. Casagrande and T. Gladwin, eds. *Some Uses of Anthropology.* Reprinted in much expanded version, in Devereux 1980, Chapter 1.

_________. 1961. *Mohave Ethnopsychiatry: The Psychic Disturbances of an Indian Tribe.* Washington, D.C.: Smithsonian Institution Press.

_________. 1967. *From Anxiety to Method in the Behavioral Sciences.* The Hague and Paris: Mouton.

_________. 1980. *Basic Problems of Ethnopsychiatry.* Chicago and London: University of Chicago Press.

DiMascio, Alberto and Richard Shader, eds. 1970. *Clinical Handbook of Psychopharmacology.* New York: Jason Aronson.

Dinitz, Simon. 1977. "Chronically Antisocial Offenders." in Conrad and Dinitz, 1977, pp. 21–42.

Dohrenwend, Bruce, and Barbara Dohrenwend. 1969. *Social Status and Psychological Disorder.* New York: Wiley.

Draper, Hal. 1965. *Berkeley: The New Student Revolt.* New York: Grove.

Ducey, Charles. 1976. "The Life History and Creative Psychopathology of the Shaman: Ethnopsychoanalytic Perspectives." in W. Muensterberger, A. Esman and L. B. Boyer, eds. *The Psychoanalytic Study of Society,* 7:173–230. New Haven and London: Yale University Press.

Durkheim, Emile. 1895. *Rules of the Sociological Method.* (English trnsln. New York: Free Press 1950.)

_________. 1897. *Suicide.* (English trnsln. New York: Free Press 1951.)

Eisenbud, Ruth-Jean. 1969. "Female Homosexuality: A Sweet Enfranchisement." in G. Goldman, and D. Milman, eds. *Modern Woman.* Springfield, IL: C. C. Thomas, 247–268.

_________. 1982. "Early and Later Determinants of Lesbian Object Choice." *Psychoanalytic Review.* 69:1:85–109.

Ellul, Jacques. 1968. "The Psychology of a Rebellion—May-June 1968." (re Paris-Nanterre) *Interplay* 2:5:23–27.

Endleman, Robert. 1967. *Personality and Social Life.* New York: Random House.

_________. 1967a. "Play Elements in Delinquency." in Endleman, *Personality and Social Life.* New York: Random House. pp. 421–440.

_________. 1967b. "The Israeli Kibbutz: Social Structure and Personality," in Endleman, *Personality and Social Life.* New York: Random House, pp. 127–177.

_________. 1970a. "Oedipal Elements in Student Rebellions." *Psychoanalytic Review.* 57:442–471.

_________. 1970b. *The Ritual of Student Rebellion.* (book length ms., unpublished).

_________. 1972. "The Student Revolt: Afterthoughts and Prospects." (Review Essay) *Contemporary Sociology* 1:3–9.

_________. 1973. "Student Rebellion as Ritual." in Harry Silverstein, ed. *The Sociology of Youth: Evolution and Revolution.* New York: Macmillan.

_________. 1974. Review of Lipset, REBELLION IN THE UNIVERSITY. *Contemporary Sociology.* 3:18–20.

_________. 1981. *Psyche and Society: Explorations in Psychoanalytic Sociology.* New York: Columbia University Press.

_________. 1981a. Homosexuality. in *Psyche and Society,* Part 4: Chs. 11–14.

_________. 1981b. "1960's Rebellions: Complexities of a Case." in *Psyche and Society,* pp. 357–367.

_________. 1981c. "Mitigating and Reactive Mythologies." in *Psyche and Society.* Chs. 10,14.

———. 1981d. "Gender Differences on the Israeli Kibbutz." In *Psyche and Society,* pp. 159–170.

———. 1982a. "Commentary" (On Review of *Psyche and Society.*) *Jl. of Psychoanalytic Anthropology.* 5:349–352.

———. 1982b. "Sociocultural Factors in Variations in Psychoanalytic Theory." Conference on WHAT IS PSYCHOANALYSIS? Psychoanalytic Society of the New York University Postdoctoral Program. Jan. 1982.

———. 1983. Review of Conrad & Dinitz, IN FEAR OF EACH OTHER. *Journal of Psychohistory.* 10:539–542.

———. 1984. "New Light on Deviance and Psychopathology?: The Case of Homosexualities and Sexual Preference" *Journal of Psychoanalytic Anthropology.* 7:75–100.

———. 1986. "Overview: Homosexuality in Tribal Societies." *Transcultural Psychiatric Research Review.* 23:187–218.

———. 1988. "Psychoanalytic Sociology and the Sociology of Deviance." in J. Rabow *et al. Advances in Psychoanalytic Sociology.* Malabar, FL: Krieger.

Erikson, Erik H. 1950. *Childhood and Society.* New York: Norton.

———. 1959. "Identity and the Life Cycle." *Psychological Issues.* No.1.

Erikson, Kai. 1960. *Wayward Puritans: A Study in the Sociology of Deviance.* New York: Wiley.

———. 1962. "Notes on the Sociology of Deviance." *Social Problems.* 9: 307–314.

Eysenck, Hans J. 1967. *The Biological Basis of Personality.* Springfield, IL: Charles C. Thomas.

Fabing, H. D. 1956. "On Going Berserk: A Neurochemical Inquiry." *American Journal of Psychiatry* 113:409–415.

Faris, R. E. L., and Warren Dunham. 1939. *Mental Disorders in Urban Areas.* Chicago: University of Chicago Press.

Fenichel, O. 1945. *The Psychoanalytic Theory of Neurosis.* New York: Norton.

Feuer, Lewis. 1969. *The Conflict of Generatiions.* New York: Basic Books.

Fireside, Harvey. 1979. *Soviet Psychoprisons.* New York: Norton.

Flacks, Richard. 1967. "The Liberated Generation: Explorations of the Roots of Student Protest." *Journal of Social Issues.* 23:3:52–75.

———. 1971. "The New Left and American Politics after Ten Years." *Journal of Social Issues.* 27:21–34.

Fletcher, C. Richard, and Larry Reynolds. 1968. "Residual Deviance, Labeling and the Mentally Sick Role: A Critical Review of Concepts." *Sociological Focus.* 1:9–27.

Ford, Clellan, and Frank Beach. 1951. *Patterns of Sexual Behavior.* New York: Harper.

Freeman, Richard B., and Brian Hall. 1986. *Report of the National Bureau of Economic Research: Permanent Homelessness in America?.*

Freud, Sigmund. 1905. "Three Essays on a Theory of Sexuality." *Standard Edition.* Vol. 7, 1953. London: Hogarth.

———. 1910. "A Special Type of Object Choice by Men." *Standard Edition* 11: London: Hogarth, 1957: 163–177.

———. 1911. "Psychoanalytic Notes on an Autobiographical Account of a Case of Paranoia (dementia paranoides)." [The Schreber case.] *Standard Edition.* 12. (1958).

———. 1912. "The Universal Tendency toward Debasement in the Sphere of Love." *Standard Edition* 11: London: Hogarth, 1957: 177–191.

———. 1913. *Totem and Taboo.* in *Standard Edition:* 13, 1955: 1–164.

———. 1916. "Some Character Types Met with in PsychoAnalytic Work: III: Criminals from a Sense of Guilt." *S. E.* 14:332–337. (1957).

Fumento, Michael A. 1987. "AIDS: Are Heterosexuals at Risk?" *Commentary.* 84:5:21–27.

Gagnon, John, and William Simon, eds. 1967. *Sexual Deviance.* New York: Harper.

Gallop Poll. 12/12/85.

Gioscia, Victor. 1969. "Groovin' on Time: Fragments of a Sociology of the Psychedelic Experience." Hicks/Fink eds. *Psychedelic Drugs.* New York: Grune & Stratton. Reprinted in Harry Silverstein, ed. *The Sociology of Youth: Evolution and Revolution.* New York: Macmillan, 1973, 454–465.

Glover, E. 1932. "On the aetiology of drug addiction." *International Journal of Psychoanalysis.* 13:2 298–328.

__________. 1939. 2d, ed. 1949 *Psycho-Analysis.* London: Staples.

__________. 1945. *The Psychopathology of Prostitution* London: Institute for the Scientific Treatment of Delinquency

Goffman, Erving. 1961. *Asylums.* Garden City, N.Y.: Doubleday.

Goldman, Harold. 1977. "The Limits of Clockwork: the Neurobiology of Violent Behavior." in J. Conrad and S. Dinitz, eds. *In Fear of Each Other.* Lexington, MA: D. C. Heath. 43–76. (See especially bibliography)

Goldman, Marion S. 1988. "Prostitution, Economic Exchange and the Unconscious." in Jerome Rabow *et al. Advances in Psychoanalytic Sociology,* Malabar, FL: Krieger. 197–209.

Goode, Erich. 1978. *Deviant Behavior: An Interactionist Approach.* Englewood Cliffs, N.J.: Prentice-Hall.

Goodman, Paul. 1970. *The New Reformation.* New York: Random House.

Gove, Walter. 1970. "Who is Hospitalized: a Critical Review of some Sociological Studies of Mental Illness." *Journal of Health and Social Behavior.* 11:294–303.

__________, ed. 1975. *The Labeling of Deviance: Evaluating a Perspective.* New York: Wiley (Sage).

Gralnick, Alexander. 1985. "The Case against Deinstitutionalization." *The American Journal of Social Psychiatry.* V:7-11.

Graña, César. 1964. *Bohemian versus Bourgeois.* New York: Basic Books. Later edition, 1967. *Modernity and its Discontents.* New York: Harper. 1967.

Greenwald, Harold. 1958. *The Call Girl.* New York: Ballantine. (Later edition under the title *The Elegant Prostitute.* New York: Walker, 1970).

Gregor, Thomas. 1985. *Anxious Pleasures The Sexual Lives of an Amazonian People.* Chicago: University of Chicago Press.

Grinspoon, Lester. 1971. *Marihuana Reconsidered.* Cambridge, MA: Harvard University Press.

Hacker, Helen Mayer. 1971. "Homosexuals: Deviant or Minority Group?" in E. Sagarin, ed. *The Other Minorities.* Waltham, MA: Ginn: 63–92.

Hatterer, Lawrence. 1971. *Changing Homosexuality in the Male.* New York: Dell.

Hedgepeth, William. 1970. *The Alternative* New York: Macmillian.

Heist, P. 1966. "The Dynamics of Student Discontent and Protest." Paper presented to meetings of the American Psychological Association, New York.

Hendin, Herbert. 1971. "A Psychoanalyst Looks at Student Revolutionaries." *New York Times Magazine* Jan. 17, 1971.

__________. 1975. *The Age of Sensation.* New York: Norton.

__________. 1975a. "Student Revolutionaries, Then and Now." Ch. 12, in Hendin, *The Age of Sensation.*

Henican, Ellis. 1987. "AIDS Carrier Who Sold Blood Charged with Attempted Murder." *Newsday.* 6/30/87. p.5.

Herdt, Gilbert. 1981. *Guardians of the Flutes.* New York: McGraw-Hill.

__________, ed. 1982. *Rituals of Manhood: Male Initiation in Papua New Guinea.* Berkeley, CA: University of California Press.

__________, ed. 1984. *Ritualized Homosexuality in Melanesia.* Berkeley, CA: University of California Press.

Hirschi, Travis. 1969. *Causes of Delinquency.* Berkeley: University of California Press.

Hite, C. 1974a. "APA Rules Homosexuality not necessarily a Disorder." *Psychiatric News* 9:1.

———. 1974b. "Members Uphold DSM-II Change." *Psychiatric News* 9:9.

Hoffman, Martin. 1968. *The Gay World* New York: Basic Books.

Hollander, Paul. 1981. *Political Pilgrims.* New York: Oxford University Press.

Hollander, Xaviera. 1972. *The Happy Hooker* New York: Dell.

Hollingshead, A. B., and F. C. Redlich. 1958. *Social Class and Mental Illness.* New York: Wiley.

Hooker, Evelyn. 1957. "The Adjustment of the Male Overt Homosexual." *Journal of Projective Techniques.* 21:18–31.

———. 1967. "The Homosexual Community." in Gagnon and Simon, eds. 1967: 167–184.

Huxley, Aldous. 1954. *The Doors of Perception.* New York: Harper.

Inciardi, James. 1986. *The War on Drugs.* Palo Alto, CA: Mayfield.

Jackman, Norman R., Richard O'Toole, and Gilbert Geis. 1963. "The Self-Image of the Prostitute." *Sociological Quarterly.* 4:150–156.

Jacoby, Russell. 1975. *Social Amnesia: A Critique of Psychology from Adler to Laing.* Boston: Beacon.

Johnson, Adelaide M. 1949. "Sanctions for Superego Lacunae of Adolescents." In Kurt Eissler, ed. *Searchlights on Delinquency.* New York: International Universities Press.

Kallman, F. 1938. *The Genetics of Schizophrenia.* New York: Augustin.

Kanter, Rosabeth Moss. 1970. "Communes." *Psychology Today* 4, no.2.

———. 1972. *Commitment and Community: Communes and Utopias in Sociological Perspective.* Cambridge, MA: Harvard University Press.

Kaplan, Howard B. 1972. *The Sociology of Mental Illness.* New Haven, Ct.: College & University Press.

Karlen, Arno. 1971. *Sexuality and Homosexuality.* New York: Norton.

Katz, Solomon H., and Mary M. Voigt. 1986. "Bread and Beer: The Early Use of Cereals in the Human Diet." *Expedition.* (Journal of the Museum of Archaeology/Anthropology, University of Pennsylvania). 28:2:23–35.

Kaufman, Irving R. 1982. "The Insanity Plea on Trial." *The New York Times Sunday Magazine.* 8/8/82: 21ff.

Keesing, Roger. 1982. "Introduction." G. Herdt, ed. *Rituals of Manhood.* Berkeley, CA: University of California Press. 1–43.

Kelman, Steven. 1970. *Push Comes to Shove.* Boston: Houghton Mifflin.

Kendell, R. E. 1983. "DSM-III: A Major Advance in Psychiatric Nosology." In: R. L. Spitzer *et al. International Perspectives on DSM-III.* Washington: American Psychiatric Press.

Keniston, Kenneth. 1968. *Young Radicals* New York: Harcourt Brace World.

Kephart, William. 1976. *Extraordinary Groups: The Sociology of Unconventional Life-Styles.* New York: St. Martin's.

Kernberg, Otto. 1988. "Between Conventionality and Aggression: The Boundaries of Passion." in W. Gaylin and E. Person, eds. 1988. *Passionate Attachments: Thinking About Love.* New York: Free Press. 63–83.

Kinsey, Alfred, W. B. Pomeroy, and Clyde Martin. 1948. *Sexual Behavior in the Human Male.* Philadelphia: Saunders.

———. 1953. *Sexual Behavior in the Human Female.* Philadelphia: Saunders.

Kitsuse, J. I. 1962. "Societal Reaction to Deviant Behavior: Problems of Theory and Method." *Social Problems.* 9:247–256.

Knauft, Bruce M. 1985. *Good Company and Violence: Sorcery and Social Action in a Lowland New Guinea Society.* Berkeley, CA: University of California Press.

———. 1987. "Homosexuality in Melanesia: Review Essay." *Journal of Psychoanalytic Anthropology* 10:2:155–191.

Kroeber, Alfred L. 1948. *Anthropology.* New York: Harcourt Brace.

Kunen, James S. 1969. *The Strawberry Statement.* New York: Random House.

LaBarre, Weston. 1969. *The Peyote Cult.* Fourth Edition, Enlarged. New York: Schocken Books.

_________ (under pseudonym Urson Cawqua). 1982. "Two Etymons and a Query: Gay, Fairies, Camping." *Maledicta* 6:224–230.

_________. 1980. "Psychotropics." Chs. 2,3,4, in LaBarre, *Culture in Context.* Durham, NC: Duke University Press.

Laing, Ronald. 1967. *The Politics of Experience.* New York: Random House.

Langness, L. L. 1967. "Sexual Antagonism in the New Guinea Highlands: a Bena-Bena Example. *Oceania* 37:161–177.

Leighton, Alexander. 1959. *My Name is Legion.* New York: Basic Books.

Lemert, Edwin. 1951. *Social Pathology.* New York: McGraw-Hill.

Levine, Martin. 1988. "Restructuring Gay Eroticism: Changing Patterns of Sexuality among Clones." Paper presented at meetings of the American Sociological Association. Atlanta. August.

Leznoff, Maurice, and William Wesley. 1956. "The Homosexual Community." *Social Problems* 3:257–263.

Liebert, Robert. 1971. *Radical and Militant Youth: A Psychoanalytic Inquiry.* New York: Praeger.

Liebow, Elliot. *Tally's Corner.* 1965. Boston: Little Brown.

Lindner, Robert M. 1944. *Rebel Without a Cause: the Hypnoanalysis of a Criminal Psychopath.* New York: Grove Press.

Lipset, Seymour M. 1968. "Students and Politics in Comparative Perspective." *Daedalus: Journal of the American Academy of Arts and Sciences.* (Winter 1968) (Also reprinted in Silverstein 1973).

_________. 1971. *Rebellion in the University.* Boston: Little, Brown.

Lipset, Seymour M., and S. Wolin, eds. 1965. *The Berkeley Student Revolt: Facts and Interpretations.* Garden City, NY: Doubleday (Anchor).

Little, Ralph B., and Manuel Pearson. 1966. "The Management of Pathologic Interdependency in Drug Addiction." *American Journal of Psychiatry.* 123:554–560.

Long, Patricia, ed. 1969. *The New Left: A Collection of Essays.* Boston: Porter Sargent.

Lowie, Robert H. 1929. *Are We Civilized? Human Culture in Perspective.* New York: Harcourt Brace.

_________. 1935. *The Crow Indians.* New York: Farrar and Rinehart.

Luce, Phillip A. 1966. *The New Left.* New York: David McKay.

Ludwig, Arnold, and Frank Farrelly. 1967. "The Weapons of Insanity." *American Journal of Psychiatry* 21:737–749.

McCaghy, Charles *et al.*, eds. 1968. *In Their Own Behalf: Voices from the Margin.* New York: Appleton Century Crofts.

McCord, William, and Joan McCord. 1964. *The Psychopath: An Essay on the Criminal Mind.* Princeton: Van Nostrand.

Main, Thomas J. 1988. "What We Know about the Homeless." *Commentary.* 85:5:26–31.

Mann, Peggy. 1980. "Marijuana: The Myth of Harmlessness Goes Up in Smoke." *Saturday Evening Post.* July/August 1980.

Marmor, Judd, ed. 1965. *Sexual Inversion.* New York: Basic Books.

Marshall, Donald S. 1971. "Sexual Behavior on Mangaia (Polynesia)." in: D. S. Marshall, and R. Suggs, eds. *Human Sexual Behavior: Variations in the Ethnographic Spectrum.* New York: Basic Books.

Masters, R. E. L., and Jean Houston. 1966. *The Varieties of Psychedelic Experience.* New York: Holt, Rinehart, Winston.

Matza, David. 1961. "Subterranean Traditions of Youth." *Annals of the American Academy of Political and Social Science.* 338:102-118..

Mauss, Armand. 1971. "On Being Strangled by the Stars and Stripes." *Journal of Social Issues.* 27:183–202.

Mednick, S., and K. O. Christiansen, eds. 1977. *Bio-Social Bases of Criminal Behavior.* New York: Gardner Press.

Merton, Robert K. 1936. "The Unanticipated Consequences of Purposive Social Action." *American Sociological Review.* 1:894–904.

———. 1937. "Social Structure and Anomie." *American Sociological Review.* 3:672–682. Reprinted in Merton, *Social Theory and Social Structure.* 1949, 1957.

———. 1949. "Manifest and Latent Functions." in Merton, *Social Theory and Social Structure.* New York: Free Press: 21–82.

Mikuriya, T. H. 1969. "Marihuana in Medicine: Past, Present and Future." *California Medicine,* 110:3–40.

Miller, Walter. 1958. "Lower Class Culture as a Generating Milieu for Gang Delinquency." *Journal of Social Issues.* 14:3:5–19.

Mills, C. Wright. 1943. "The Professional Ideology of Social Pathologists." *American Journal of Sociology.* 49:165–180.

Mitchell, Stephen A. 1978. "Psychodynamics, Homosexuality and the Question of Pathology." *Psychiatry* 41: 254–263.

Mogar, Robert E. 1969. "Current Status and Future Trends in Psychedelic (LSD) Research." in Tart 1969, Ch. 26:381–397.

Morrissey, Joseph. 1982. "De-institutionalizing the Mentally Ill: Process, Outcomes and New Directions." in W. R. Gove, ed. *Deviance and Mental Illness.* New York: Sage.

Nelson, Benjamin. 1950. *The Idea of Usury.* Princeton, NJ: Princeton University Press.

———. 1954. "The Future of Illusions." *Psychoanalysis* (later called *Psychoanalytic Review*) 2:33:16–37. Variously reprinted.

Ovesey, Lionel. 1969. *Homosexuality and Pseudohomosexuality.* New York: Science House.

Ovesey, Lionel, and Ethel Person. 1973. "Gender Identity and Sexual Psychopathology in Men: A Psychodynamic Analysis of Homosexuality, Transsexualism and Transvestism." *Journal of the American Academy of Psychoanalysis.* 1:53–72.

Parin, Paul, Fritz Morgenthaler, and Goldy Parin-Matthèy. 1963. *Die Weissen Denken Zuviel: Psychoanalytische Untersuchungen in Westafrika (Dogon)* (The Whites Think Too Much: Psychoanalytic Investigations in West Africa [Dogon].) Zürich: Atlantis; Munich: Kindler. (French Edition: *Les Blancs Pensent Trop.* Paris: Payot. 1966.)

Parry, Albert. 1933. *Garrets and Pretenders: A History of Bohemianism in America.* New York: Covici-Friede.

Paul, Robert A. 1982. Review of R. Endleman, PSYCHE AND SOCIETY. *Journal of Psychoanalytic Anthropology.* 5:333–336

Perrucci, Robert. 1974. *Circle of Madness: On Being Insane and Institutionalized in America.* Englewood Cliffs, NJ: Prentice-Hall.

Pfohl, Stephen. 1977. "A Psychiatric Assessment of Dangerousness: Practical Problems and Political Implications." in Conrad and Dinitz, 1977: 77–102.

Pittman, David J., ed. 1967. *Alcoholism.* New York: Harper and Row.

Pitts, Jesse. 1969. "The Hippies as Contrameritocracy." *Dissent.* July-August. 326–337.

Preble, Edward, and John J. Casey Jr. 1969. "Taking Care of Business—the Heroin User's Life on the Street." *International Journal of the Addictions.* 4.

The Public Interest (journal). 1968. Vol. 13, fall. Entire issue: The Universities.

Quinney, Richard. 1970. *The Social Reality of Crime.* Boston: Little, Brown.

Rader, Dotson. 1969. *I Ain't Marchin' Anymore* New York: David McKay.

Radford, Patricia *et al.* 1972. "Heroin Addiction: A Psychoanalytic Study." in *Psychoanalytic Study of the Child.* 27:156–180.

Rado, Sandor. 1933. "Psychoanalysis of Pharmacothymia." *Psychoanalytic Quarterly.* 2:1–23.

Reckless, Walter. 1933. *Vice in Chicago.* University of Chicago Press. Reprinted Montclair, NJ: Patterson-Smith, 1969.

__________. 1962. "A Non-Causal Explanation: Containment Theory." *Excerpta Criminologica.* 1:131–134.

__________. 1973. *The Crime Problem.* 5th ed. New York: Appleton-Century-Crofts.

Reckless, Walter, S. Dinitz, and E. Murray. 1956. "Self-Concept as an Insulator against Delinquency." *American Sociological Review.* 21: 744–746.

Redl, Fritz. 1945. "The Psychology of Gang Formation and the Treatment of Juvenile Delinquents." *The Psychoanalystic Study of the Child.* 1:367–376.

Redl, Fritz, and D. Wineman. 1951. *Children Who Hate.* New York: Free Press.

__________. 1953. *Controls from Within.* New York: Free Press.

Reich, Charles. 1970. *The Greening of America* New York: Random House.

Reich, Walter. 1983. "The World of Soviet Psychiatry." *The New York Times Sunday Magazine,* 1/30/83: 21ff.

Reinhold, Robert. 1979. "Changes Wrought by 60's Youth Linger in American Life." *The New York Times,* Aug.12, 1979, pp. 1, 38.

Richman, Judith. 1985. "Social Class and Mental Illness Revisited: Sociological Perspectives on the Diffusion of Psychoanalysis." *Journal of Operational Psychiatry.* 16:1–8.

Rigney, Francis and L. Douglas Smith. 1961. *The Real Bohemia.* New York: Basic Books

Roberts, Ron E. 1971. *The New Communes: Coming Together in America.* Englewood Cliffs, NJ: Prentice-Hall.

Róheim, Géza. 1950. *Psychoanalysis and Anthropology.* New York: International Universities Press.

Rosenhan, D. L. "On Being Sane in Insane Places." *Science* 179:250–258.

Sagarin, Edward. 1975. *Deviants and Deviance.* New York: Praeger.

Savitt, R. A. 1954. "Extramural psychoanalytic treatment of a case of neurotic addiction." *Jl. of the American Psychoanalytic Association* 2:494–502.

__________. 1963. "Psychoanalytic Studies on Addiction: Ego Structure in Narcotic Addiction." *Psychoanalytic Quarterly.* 32:43–57.

Scarpitti, Frank R., Ellen Murray, Simon Dinitz, and Walter Reckless. 1960. "The 'Good Boy' in a High Delinquency Area: Four Years Later." *American Sociological Review.* 25:555–558.

Schafer, Roy. 1974. "Problems in Freud's Psychology of Women." *Journal of the American Psychoanalytic Association.* 22:459–485.

Scheff, Thomas. 1966. *Being Mentally Ill.* Chicago: Aldine.

__________. 1975. *Labeling Madness.* Englewood Cliffs, NJ: Prentice-Hall.

Schofield, Michael. 1965. *Sociological Aspects of Homosexuality: A Comparative Study of Three Types of Homosexual.* Boston: Little Brown.

Schur, Edwin. 1971. *Labeling Deviant Behavior.* New York: Harper and Row.

__________. 1979. *Interpreting Deviance.* New York: Harper and Row.

Schwartz, Charlotte. 1957. "Perspectives on Deviance: Wives' Definitions of their Husbands' Mental Illness." *Psychiatry* 20:275–291.

Sellin, Thorsten. 1938. *Culture Conflict and Crime.* Social Science Research Council. Bull. 41.

Shapiro, David. 1965. "Impulsive Styles: Variants." in Shapiro. *Neurotic Styles.* New York: Basic Books. 157–168.

Sheldon, W. H. and S. S. Stevens. 1942. *The Varieties of Temperament.* New York: Harper and Row.

Silverstein, Harry, ed. 1973. *The Sociology of Youth: Evolution and Revolution.* New York: Macmillan.

Simmons, J. P. and Barry Winograd. 1966. *It's Happening.* Santa Barbara, CA: Marc-Laird.

Simon, William, and John Gagnon. 1967. "Homosexuality: the Formulation of a Sociological Perspective." *Journal of Health and Social Behavior.* 8:177–185.

Snyder, Solomon. 1980. *Biological Aspects of Mental Disorder.* NY: Oxford.

Socarides, Charles. 1978. *Homosexuality.* New York: Jason Aronson.

Somers, Robert. 1965. "Mainspringsof the Rebellion: A Survey of Berkeley Students, November 1964." in Lipset and Wolin 1965: 530–558.

Sperber, Michael A., and L. Jarvick, eds. 1976. *Psychiatry and Genetics.* New York: Basic Books.

Spitzer, Stephen. 1975. "Toward a Marxian Theory of Deviance." *Social Problems.* 22: 641–651.

Spotts, James V., and Franklin C. Shontz. 1980. *Cocaine Users: a Representative Case Approach.* New York: Free Press.

Srole, Leo, Thomas Langner *et al.* 1962. *Mental Health in the Metropolis.* New York: McGraw-Hill.

Stevens, William K. 1987. "Does Civilization Owe a Debt to Beer?" *The New York Times,* Mar. 24, 1987, p. C3.

Steward, Julian. 1945. "The Changing American Indian." in R. Linton, ed. *The Science of Man in the World Crisis.* New York: Columbia University Press. 282–305.

Stoller, Robert. 1975. *Perversion: The Erotic Form of Hatred.* New York: Random House.

Stoller, Robert, and Gilbert Herdt. 1985a. "Theories of Origins of Male Homosexuality: A Cross-Cultural Look." in Stoller, *Observing the Erotic Imagination.* New Haven: Yale University Press. pp. 104–134.

__________. 1985b. "The Development of Masculinity: A Cross-Cultural Contribution." in Stoller, *Presentations of Gender.* New Haven: Yale University Press. pp. 181–199.

__________. 1985c. "Theories of Origins of Male Homosexuality: A Cross-Cultural Look." *Archives of General Psychiatry.* 42: 399–404.

Students for a Democratic Society. 1964. *The Port Huron Statement.* New York: S.D.S.

Sutherland, Edwin. 1937. *The Professional Thief.* Chicago: University of Chicago Press.

__________. 1949. *White Collar Crime.* New York: Holt, Rinehart, Winston.

Sykes, Gresham, and David Matza. 1957. "Techniques of Neutralization: A Theory of Delinquency." *American Sociological Review* 22:664–670.

Symons, Donald. 1979. *The Evolution of Human Sexuality.* New York: Oxford University Press.

Szasz, Thomas. 1961. *The Myth of Mental Illness.* New York: Paul Hoeber.

__________. 1981. "Power and Psychiatry." *Society* 18:16–18.

Tart, Charles T., ed. 1969. *Altered States of Consciousness.* New York: Wiley.

Thio, Alex. 1983. *Deviant Behavior.* 2d Ed. Boston: Houghton Mifflin.

Thompson, Clara. 1949. "Changing Conceptions of Homosexuality in Psychoanalysis." in Patrick Mullahy, ed. *A Study of Interpersonal Relations* New York: Hermitage Press. 211–222.

Thrasher, Fredric. 1927. *The Gang.* Chicago: University of Chicago Press.

TIME Magazine. March 1983.

Townsend, John Marshall. 1978. *Cultural Conceptions and Mental Illness.* Chicago: University of Chicago Press.

Trice, Harrison. 1966. *Alcoholism in America.* New York: McGraw-Hill.

Tripp, C. A. 1975. *The Homosexual Matrix* New York: McGraw-Hill.

Turk, Austin T. 1969. *Criminality and Legal Order.* Chicago: Rand McNally.

Usdin, Gene, ed. 1975. *Schizophrenia: Biological and Psychological Perspectives.* New York: Brunner, Mazel.

Van Baal, J. 1966. *Dema.* The Hague: Martinus Nijoff.

Van Dine, Stephan, Simon Dinitz, and John Conrad. 1977. "The Incapacitation of the Dangerous Offender: A Statistical Experiment." in Conrad and Dinitz, 1977: 103–118.

Vanggard, Thorkil. 1972. *Phallos: A Symbol and its History in the Male World.* New York: International Universities Press.

Vold, George B. 1958. *Theoretical Criminology.* New York: Oxford University Press.

Von Hoffman, Nicholas. 1968. *We Are the People Our Parents Warned Us Against.* Chicago: Quadrangle.

Wallerstein, Immanuel, and Paul Starr, eds. 1971. *The University Crisis Reader.* 2 volumes. New York: Random House.

Wasson, R. Gordon. 1968. *Soma: Divine Mushroom of Immortality.* New York: Harcourt Brace World; The Hague: Mouton.

Watts, W., and D. Witaker. 1966. "Free Speech Advocates at Berkeley." *Journal of Applied Behavioral Science* 2: 41–62.

Weinberg, George. 1972. *Society and the Healthy Homosexual.* New York: St. Martin's.

Weinberg, Martin, and Colin Williams. 1975. *Male Homosexuals: Their Problems and Adaptations.* New York: Oxford.

Weiss, Roger D., Steven M. Mirin, Jacqueline L. Michael, and Ann C. Sollogub. 1986. "Psychopathology in Chronic Cocaine Abusers." *American Journal of Drug and Alcohol Abuse.* 12 (1 & 2): 17-29.

Wertham, Fredric. 1950. *Dark Legend.* New York: Doubleday.

Whalen, Thelma. 1975. "Wives of Alcoholics." in William Rushing, ed. *Deviant Behavior and Social Process.* New York: Rand McNally: 311–317.

Whitehead, Harriet. 1981. "The Bow and the Burden Strap: A New Look at Institutionalized Homosexuality in Native North America." in S. Ortner and H. Whitehead, eds. *Sexual Meanings: The Cultural Construction of Gender and Sexuality.* Cambridge: Cambridge University Press.

Whiting, John W. M. *et al.* "The Function of Male Initiation Ceremonies at Puberty." in E. Maccoby, T. Newcomb, and E. Hartley, eds. *Readings in Social Psychology.* New York: Holt, Rinehart, Winston.

Wideman, George. 1974. "Homosexuality: a Survey." *Journal of the American Psychoanalytic Association.* 22:651–696.

Williams, Walter L. 1986. *The Spirit and the Flesh* (The Berdache in American Indian Cultures). Boston: Beacon Press.

Wilson, James Q. 1975. *Thinking About Crime.* New York: Basic Books.

Wilson, James Q., and Richard Herrnstein. 1985. *Crime and Human Nature.* New York: Simon and Schuster.

Winick, Charles, and Paul Kinsie. 1971. *The Lively Commerce.* Chicago: Quadrangle Press.

Wolf, Kathleen. 1952. "Growing Up and its Price in Three Puerto Rican Subcultures. *Psychiatry* 115:401–433.

Yablonsky, Lewis. 1962. *The Violent Gang.* New York: Macmillan.

__________. 1968. *The Hippie Trip.* New York: Pegasus.

Yarrow, Marion Radke *et al.* 1955. "The Psychological Meaning of Mental Illness in the Family." *Journal of Social Issues.* 11:12–24.

Yochelson, Samuel, and Stanton Samenow. 1976. *The Criminal Personality: Vol.I. A Profile for Change.* New York: Jason Aronson.

__________. 1977. *The Criminal Personality: Vol.II. The Change Process.* New York: Jason Aronson.

__________. 1986. *The Criminal Personality: Vol.III: The Drug User.* Northvale, N.J.: Jason Aronson.

Yorcke, Clifford. 1970. "A Critical review of some psychoanalytic literature on drug addiction." *British Jl. of Medical Psychology* 43:141–159.

Young, Frank. 1965. *Initiation Ceremonies.* Indianapolis: Bobbs-Merrill.

Zablocki, B. D. 1980. *Alienation and Charisma: A Study of Contemporary American Communes.* New York: Free Press.

Zicklin, Gilbert. 1983. *Countercultural Communes: A Sociological Perspective.* Westport, CT: Greenwood Press.

NAME INDEX

(omitting their appearance in chapter references and general bibliography—see Bibliography for that) Parentheses () after a page number refers to multiple-author items, with name of first author mentioned in the bibliography item: e.g. Murray..7 (Reckless) means Murray is one of the *et al.* after Reckless, see end of chapter References, or Bibliography for full listing, at Reckless.

SUBJECT INDEX